TRANSLINGUAL PEDAGOGICAL PERSPECTIVES

TRANSLINGUAL PEDAGOGICAL PERSPECTIVES

Engaging Domestic and International Students in the Composition Classroom

EDITED BY
JULIA KIERNAN
ALANNA FROST
SUZANNE BLUM MALLEY

UTAH STATE UNIVERSITY PRESS
Logan

© 2021 by University Press of Colorado

Published by Utah State University Press
An imprint of University Press of Colorado
245 Century Circle, Suite 202
Louisville, Colorado 80027

All rights reserved

 The University Press of Colorado is a proud member of the Association of University Presses.

The University Press of Colorado is a cooperative publishing enterprise supported, in part, by Adams State University, Colorado State University, Fort Lewis College, Metropolitan State University of Denver, Regis University, University of Colorado, University of Northern Colorado, University of Wyoming, Utah State University, and Western Colorado University.

ISBN: 978-1-64642-111-4 (paperback)
ISBN: 978-1-64642-112-1 (ebook)
https://doi.org/10.7330/9781646421121

Library of Congress Cataloging-in-Publication Data

Names: Kiernan, Julia, 1980– editor. | Frost, Alanna, 1969– editor. | Blum-Malley, Suzanne, 1966– editor.
Title: Translingual pedagogical perspectives : engaging domestic and international students in the composition classroom / Julia E. Kiernan, Alanna Frost, Suzanne Blum Malley.
Description: Logan : Utah State University Press, [2020] | Includes bibliographical references and index.
Identifiers: LCCN 2021015262 (print) | LCCN 2021015263 (ebook) | ISBN 9781646421114 (paperback) | ISBN 9781646421121 (ebook)
Subjects: LCSH: English language—Rhetoric—Study and teaching (Higher) | English language—Study and teaching (Higher)—Foreign speakers. | Academic writing—Study and teaching (Higher)—Social aspects. | Multilingualism. | Translanguaging (Linguistics)
Classification: LCC PE1404 .T764 2020 (print) | LCC PE1404 (ebook) | DDC 428.0071/1—dc23
LC record available at https://lccn.loc.gov/2021015262
LC ebook record available at https://lccn.loc.gov/2021015263

Cover illustration: mural © Icy and Sot, https://icyandsot.com; photograph by Tawny Saez

CONTENTS

Foreword
Ellen Cushman   vii

Introduction
Alanna Frost, Julia Kiernan, and Suzanne Blum Malley   3

PART I: ENACTING TRANSLINGUAL PEDAGOGIES IN FIRST-YEAR COMPOSITION

1. Addressing Monolingual Dispositions with Translingual Pedagogy
   Ghanashyam Sharma   17

2. Criteria-Mapping Activities and the Transformation of Student-Teacher Relations in the Composition Classroom
   Daniel V. Bommarito and Emily Cooney   39

3. Unity in Diversity: Practicing Translingualism in First-Year Writing Courses
   Ming Fang and Tania Cepero Lopez   59

4. Keepin' It Real: Developing Authentic Translingual Experiences for Multilingual Students
   Norah Fahim, Bonnie Vidrine-Isbell, and Dan Zhu   92

5. An Integrative Translingual Pedagogy of Affirmation and Resource Sharing
   Gregg Fields   125

6. "Hay un tiempo y un lugar para todo": Literacy Autobiographies and the Cultivation of Translingual Rhetorical Sensibilities
   Esther Milu and Mathew Gomes   149

PART II: ENACTING TRANSLINGUAL PEDAGOGIES IN INTERDISCIPLINARY SPACES

7. Writing on the Wall: Teaching Translingualism through Linguistic Landscapes
   Mark Brantner   173

8. Following Labors of Recontextualization: Toward a Pedagogy of Translingual Mapping
   Brice Nordquist   191

9. Writing-Theory Cartoon: Toward a Translingual and Multimodal Pedagogy
   Xiqiao Wang   212

10. Translingualism as Pedagogical Methodology for Preservice Teachers and Peer Writing Consultants in Training
    Naomi Silver   236

11. A Framework for Linguistically Inclusive Course Design
    Julia Kiernan   263

    Afterword
    Thomas Lavalle   284

    Index   293
    About the Authors   303

FOREWORD

Ellen Cushman

The focus on trans-actions, that include translating, transforming, and transfer, could begin to unveil the ways that colonial matrices of power are built on intersecting, mutually sustaining nodes of everyday logics of practice that form disciplines and universities.
—Ellen Cushman (2016)

Over the last decade, translanguaging has become an important innovation that seeks to decenter English-only assumptions. Translingual language practices, a theory of language originally developed in the area of applied linguistics by Sinfree Makoni and Alastair Pennycook (2007), critiques the very category systems used to describe languages as discrete, well bounded, rule governed, and conventional. Makoni and Pennycook critique the linguistic imperialism implicit in understanding languages as a constellation of speech forms—as disciplinary constructs—that are constructed into languages. Makoni and Pennycook argue instead for languaging acts as indications of global citizenship through which individuals strategically deploy a range of styles, codes, and media to express themselves. This understanding of language and languaging has captured the imagination of scholars across disciplines because it frees scholars and teachers from rigid conceptions of language as a collection of rule-governed practices used to demonstrate fluency in a target language, which is, more often than not, English. Rather, the goal is to understand languages as having permeable borders across which speakers, readers, and writers move fluidly using a variety of codes, registers, and media to express themselves. The essential questions then become, How would we teach writing in ways that reflect our students' everyday language uses? How do we best draw upon and help student writers persevere in learning to move across linguistic borders?

It is precisely these questions that Suresh Canagarajah (2013), Ana Maria Wetzl (2013), and Ofelia García and Li Wei (2014) have since taken up in the area of applied linguistics as it relates to writing and education classrooms. And these are precisely the questions taken up in this important collection. *Translingual Pedagogical Perspectives* offers much-needed extension of scholarship on the teaching of English and writing classrooms that centers on translanguaging curricular and pedagogical innovation. The book achieves its significant contribution to the scholarship through an introduction that carefully places the work of translanguaging classrooms alongside scholarship on translanguaging perspectives on language and language use. By drawing upon interdisciplinary scholarship from areas that include bilingual education, applied linguistics, second language writing, and rhetoric and composition, the authors of this chapter illustrate several ways writing teachers can begin to challenge monolingual ideologies by innovating translingual approaches within the writing classroom. Julia Kiernan, Alanna Frost, and Suzanne Blum Malley open the collection with the acknowledgment that translingual orientations are reflected and deeply ingrained in everyday linguistic realities, and as such, these orientations form an integral component of the writing process (introduction). They lay the foundation for the collection of chapters that all seek to question and illustrate how students experience "translingual pedagogies and educational experiences" in an ongoing effort to make apparent to students their experiences and expectations related to language and communication. The chapters illustrate how each author-as-instructor draws upon the linguistic and cultural capacities of students in writing classrooms, and, in doing so, helps students begin to understand how signification creates convention from frequently used forms that then enable and constrain particular kinds of historically patterned uses. This book has engaged me with the demonstrations of curricular and pedagogical innovations that must surround the ways we think about what gets taught and how in the writing classroom. In doing so it has helped to unlock and illustrate the decolonial potentials of translanguaging, particularly as these take up and illustrate the "trans-actions" necessary for writers to move fluidly across language borders as they translate, transform, and transfer (Cushman 2016) language practices.

Each chapter does this by offering demonstrations of translingual pedagogy and curriculum as these unfold in classrooms and writing centers. A number of chapters focus on the ways languaging unfolds in the material world and popular culture. Sonja Wang offers an assignment that includes a "writing-theory cartoon exercise" that allows students to begin to understand transnational language and learning experiences (chapter 9). Through an assignment that asks students to analyze linguistic cityscapes, Mark Brantner proposes one way to develop students' language abilities as they engage the writing on the walls of their cityscapes in Singapore (chapter 7). Brice Nordquist offers a reinterpretation of linguistic mobility that accounts for not just circulations of writing, but also people, practices, materials, ideas, and resources (chapter 8). Each of these chapters provides the important link between multimodality and language sometimes missing in discussions of each topic individually or in isolation. Three chapters focus on the ways students write with us and through multiple languages that have been made possible by translingual innovations to the curriculum. Esther Milu and Mathew Gomes focus on the literacy autobiography, Daniel Bommarito and Emily Cooney explore an application of Bob Broad's (2003) concept of dynamic criteria mapping, and Julia Kiernan offers a framework for linguistically inclusive course design. The book also offers arguments for translingual writing practice in the first-year writing classroom (Fang and Lopez) and in the training of writing center consultants (Silver). Taken together, the chapters provide an array of sites and types of innovation that take their cue from translingual approaches to writing research.

The contributions of this book can be understood in the broadest terms of research in the teaching of English that reaches across scholarship that concerns itself with multimedia, pedagogy, writing centers, and first-year writing. While expansive, the illustrations offered in each chapter provide the details needed to expel the bedeviling critique of translingual approaches: How to teach from a complex theory of language? And the chapters do so while remaining mindful of those critiques and offering ways the particular practices unfolding in these classrooms complicate these critiques.

When I was asked to write this foreword, I understood the importance of this work because it begins to illustrate the ways students' own conceptions of language can be linked to the establishment of conventional uses, therefore revealing the ways the topic of linguistic ideology and power can be drawn upon in classrooms. What is most valuable about this book is that it begins to provide ways instructors and students can together challenge monolinguistic assumptions in the classroom. It offers not just criticism of monolinguistic assumptions but also ways to intervene at the level of classroom discourse in those assumptions, representations, and conceptualizations. And it does so while facilitating students' abilities to extend their everyday literary activities. *Translingual Pedagogical Perspectives* facilitates for those who take it most seriously the ability to help students become aware and move beyond the ways language is thought about in everyday life and particularly in the writing classroom.

REFERENCES

Broad, Bob. 2003. *What We Really Value: Beyond Rubrics in Teaching and Assessing Writing.* Logan: Utah State University Press.

Canagarajah, A. Suresh. 2013. "Negotiating Translingual Literacy: An Enactment." *Research in the Teaching of English* 48 (1): 40–67.

Cushman, Ellen. 2016. "Translingual and Decolonial Approaches to Meaning Making." *College English* 78 (3): 234–42.

García, Ofelia, and Li Wei. 2014. "Translanguaging and Education." In *Translanguaging: Language, Bilingualism and Education*, edited by Ofelia García and Li Wei, 63–77. London: Palgrave Macmillan.

Makoni, Sinfree, and Alastair Pennycook. 2005. "Disinventing and Reconstituting Languages." *Critical Inquiry in Language Studies: An International Journal* 2 (3): 137–56.

Wetzl, Ana Maria. 2013. "World Englishes in the Mainstream Composition Course: Undergraduate Students Respond to WE Writing." *Research in the Teaching of English* 48 (2): 204–27.

TRANSLINGUAL PEDAGOGICAL PERSPECTIVES

INTRODUCTION

Alanna Frost, Julia Kiernan, and Suzanne Blum Malley

As Claire Kramsch (2018) has argued in "Trans-Spatial Utopias," "Translanguaging reveals the deep relations that have always been there between codes, modes, and modalities but have been occulted by the artificial borders set up by nation-states, disciplines, professions, and linguists" (109). The exploration of those relations and their borders has, indeed, "captured [the] imagination" (Wei 2018, 9) of scholars in a wide range of fields connected to human communication. The construct of translanguaging, investigated by linguists, educators, and writing studies scholars,[1] describes the negotiations of and between language users who seek communicative clarity by drawing on a repertoire of semiotic resources. Such practices have long been evident in everyday communication, such as when people negotiate business contracts, share stories with friends, order food, shop, or text their mums. Since the early 1990s, sociolinguists and applied linguists studying language use in such exchanges have often presented their research as a direct challenge to the hegemony of English-language standards and a monolinguistic ideal. In such critiques, translanguaging troubles named language systems (e.g., Standard Written English as a dynamic and unfixed version of English) and historic separatist theories of language use (e.g., code meshing, code mixing, and multilanguaging) and challenges the theory that languages are discrete systems at all. Such systems create "artificial borders," as Kramsch (2018, 108) describes, and they prescribe a socially constructed, fixed set of codes that do not reflect the reality of usage. A trans perspective on languaging, in contrast, posits that "users treat all available codes as repertoire in their everyday communication, and not separated according to label" (Canagarajah 2013, 6), implying fluid and evolving repertoires of semiotic resources users continually draw from to make meaning.

This collection addresses the *lure* (Matsuda 2014) of translanguaging for writing studies scholars in relation to college-level, English-medium composition classes in the United States. As a discipline, rhetoric and composition has long wrestled with the complicity inherent in the promotion of institutional and public narratives of the existence of a standard English. Many reflections on the merits of the concept of translanguaging in the writing classroom begin by noting that the history of disciplinary attention to students' language use began in 1974 with the publication of the "Students' Right to Their Own Language" by the Conferences on College on Composition and Communication (Gilyard 2016; Horner et al. 2011). The political language statement, crafted by writing studies scholars concerned with the role of the institution in both homogenizing and denigrating the dialects of diverse US students, remains relevant in contemporary translanguaging scholarship. For example, its premise is noted by Jerry Lee and Christopher Jenks (2017), who assert that "assumptions surrounding standardness, correctness, and legitimacy of a particular variety of English are not inherent to the language itself but sustained through the work of institutional agents such as public education" (320). Politically and theoretically, then, there is widespread acknowledgment in writing studies that our collective adoption of translanguaging in the writing classroom supports the modification of our standard charge, which has historically been to instruct and measure English-writing performance. Notably and problematically, that performance is assessed against the "bankrupt" concept that there is one English against which to measure (Horner et al. 2011, 305). This conundrum leaves rhetoric and composition scholars at an important moment as we collectively evolve our theory and explore ways to open our praxis to greater awareness of the affordances of a translingual disposition.

We remain mindful that the affordances of translanguaging are intertwined with tenets of existing critical pedagogies. Importantly, contributors to this collection describe classroom practice and assignments framed by the construct of translanguaging as practice. Translanguaging itself, according to Li Wei (2018), "is using one's idiolect, that is one's linguistic repertoire, without regard for socially and politically defined language names and labels" (11). Importantly, this collection does not promote an investigation of translingual practices as evidenced in student writing with visible use of labeled idiolects, for example. Rather, the focus of the collection is on showcasing the ways translanguaging is used as a construct that undergirds continual and socially flexible language practice. It offers classroom practices and assignments that facilitate students' understanding of an essential, possibly intangible, facet of translanguaging theory, which, as Wei asserts "is not conceived as an object or linguistic structural phenomenon to describe and analyse but a practice and a process. It takes us beyond linguistic systems and speakers to a linguistics of participation" (7).

As editors of this collection, we have actively sought to counter the use of translanguaging as a catchall for language diversity, and we have worked to productively demonstrate our awareness that the term has been criticized fairly as a "popular neologism" (Wei 2018). Scholars working in second language writing have thoughtfully critiqued the uncritical adoption of translanguaging (Atkinson et al. 2015; Wei 2018; Matsuda 2014) and as Thomas Lavalle asserts in the afterword of this collection, translingualism as a threshold concept presents definitional "difficulties." Heeding such critiques, we adopt an emerging, writing studies epistemological lens for translanguaging as *disposition*, which Bruce Horner, Min-Zhan Lu, Jacqueline Jones Royster, and John Trimbur (2011) describe as "openness and inquiry that people take toward language and language differences" (311). The writing studies translingual disposition toward language and languaging has evolved to include calls for reexamining writing research using a translingual lens (Gilyard 2016; Trimbur 2016), creating awareness that "in translingual writing the process of negotiating assumptions about language is more important than the product" (Matsuda 2014, 481), carefully describing the assessment practices a translingual writing curriculum should employ (Dryer 2016; Lee and Jenks 2016), and ethically investigating the translingual practices in multilingual communities (Bloom-Pojar 2018). The writing studies dispositions lens, then, reinforces the call for a more thoughtful and considered process for developing the "descriptive adequacy" applied linguist Li Wei (2018) describes as the first step in creating the knowledge necessary for a "perpetual cycle of theory-practice-theory" of translanguaging as a practical theory of language (12).

One of the primary challenges inherent in bringing complex theories of translanguaging as continued process into writing-classroom practice is that a translingual disposition resists simple definition and straightforward implementation. Lee and Jenks (2016) emphasize this key difficulty, noting, "Although composition can become a space that facilitates opportunities for students to 'do' translingual dispositions, these dispositions are constitutive of a constellation of highly complex sociocultural issues and experiences and therefore cannot be expected to be actualized or articulated in a preconceived and uniform manner" (319–320). In response to this challenge, we do not attempt to present in this collection a unified process for teaching translanguaging or a static and definitive catalog of translanguaging attributes. Rather, the range of terms in the work our contributors share highlights the complexity we are trying to showcase while providing pedagogies that develop a translingual disposition and are replicable and adaptable for a variety of learning opportunities in postsecondary, English-medium writing classrooms, writing centers, and writing programs populated by monolingual and multilingual students. By providing descriptive and reflective examples of the "changes being made at the organizational level to rethink the ways in which English is represented in US composition teaching, the design of composition and writing program curricula, and the preparations of (future) teachers of postsecondary writing" (Horner, NeCamp, and Donahue 2011, 271), this collection moves to fill the gap between the range of theoretical inquiry surrounding translanguaging and existing translingual pedagogical models for writing classrooms and programs in the United States.

Our contributors affirm that it is necessary to more fully engage pedagogies of translanguaging and translingualism because our legacy (and overwhelmingly monolingual) approach to English does not do what our increasingly multilingual student populations demand of it. And, while this collection aims to offer a variety of approaches to the teaching of diverse learners via a translingual disposition, it also moves to interrogate the affordances and constraints of translingualism as a pedagogical strategy through each chapter's inclusion of curricular strategies and specific writing assignments. As we note above, readers may identify some of the approaches to writing pedagogy described in each chapter, particularly those that engage critical pedagogies, as approaches to teaching writing they already employ. Clearly, asking students to investigate language ideology is not an innovative suggestion; however, we argue, a translingual disposition, when taught as a rhetorical strategy, reimagines traditional approaches to writing assignments and opens new spaces for student responses to them in important ways. What contributors to this collection bring to the table is the added notions that languages do not work in discrete systems, that we are always languaging, and that such negotiation is a central part of both monolingual and multilingual students' writing processes. To stress, these chapters contribute to the important conversation on the ways translanguaging has made its way into our writing classrooms.

The eleven chapters in this collection consider teacher, student, and institutional perspectives in the development and implementation of translingual pedagogies and are divided into two parts, beginning with translingual pedagogies enacted within first-year writing and ending with a consideration of translingual pedagogies in interdisciplinary contexts. In this way, the collection develops out of a focus on single classroom activities to a wider lens that considers translingual pedagogies across courses, writing centers, and writing programs. Each chapter offers detailed descriptions of translingual-oriented teaching, including an overview of the institutional context and linguistic makeup of both the department/program and participants (e.g., students, teacher-researcher, etc.); an analysis of the ways each approach fits into current theoretical conversations about translingual composing practices; descriptions of classroom practices and experiences; and considerations of the limitations, challenges, and uptake of the pedagogies offered. Additionally, chapters close with detailed appendices that provide assignment prompts, as well as other necessary information for readers to fully adopt and adapt these strategies into their own classrooms.

Part I, "Enacting Translingual Pedagogies in First-Year Composition," offers focused snapshots of work being done across a number of first-year writing courses in various US universities and colleges. These chapters are especially useful in that they offer a spectrum of both scaffolded and stand-alone assignments that engage a translingual disposition. The following paragraphs offer brief chapter overviews in order to orient readers to what contributions may be most useful to their own teaching.

The collection opens with Shyam Sharma's chapter, "Addressing Monolingual Dispositions with Translingual Pedagogy," which contends that the hegemonic proliferation of a Standard Written English dispositions in US writing programs, "the monolingual regime" (chapter 1), remains one of the central barriers to engaging pedagogies that invite and privilege translingual communicative competence. Sharma thus offers writing-classroom practice that positions "*translingual* pedagogy as a means toward larger educational goals," so that students understand they are not only simply indulging in non-SWE writing but learning to interrogate language and literacy practice and policy. Sharma emphasizes the need for both top-down and bottom-up promotion of a translingual disposition. Moreover, given the growing diversity of student populations across postsecondary institutions, this opening chapter is important in surfacing the various contexts where translingual pedagogies thrive due to emphasis on diversity of knowledge across cultures and societies, as well as rhetorical traditions and practices.

In chapter 2, "Criteria-Mapping Activities and the Transformation of Student-Teacher Relations in the Composition Classroom," Daniel Bommarito and Emily Cooney use criteria mapping (an adaptation of literacy mapping) to consider how classroom discussions of language differences can enhance students' agency and learning. Using this approach, the chapter emphasizes A. Suresh Canagarajah's description of the translingual negotiation entailed in any communicative act and employs Bob Broad's (2003) concept of dynamic criteria mapping to weave "the negotiation of language directly into the fabric of the curriculum. In this way, language negotiations are not an afterthought, tacked onto a 'language neutral' curriculum—rather, such negotiations *are* the curriculum." The chapter contends that this approach invites a recognition of linguistic diversity, makes this diversity visible, and allows for pedagogical flexibility.

In chapter 3, "Unity in Diversity: Practicing Translingualism in First-Year Writing Courses," Ming Fang and Tania Cepero Lopez present case studies of three instructors as they work to enact a translingual orientation in their first-year writing classrooms. Offering a descriptive analysis of instructor engagement with redesigned curricula, Fang and Cepero Lopez reiterate one of the premises in this collection: that there is no one way to foster a translingual disposition. Rather, there are key tenets that support translingual pedagogies, including holding "diversity as the norm, creating opportunities for linguistic negotiation, and encouragement of rhetorical dexterity." This chapter is a useful starting point for instructors who are developing translingual courses and assignment sequences. The authors examine how adaptation is an inherent tool in the development of a translingual disposition within a common course and offer personal adaptations "filter[ed] through the lens of each instructor's professional interests, as well as their personal linguistic and cultural background."

In chapter 4, "Keepin' It Real: Developing Authentic Translingual Experiences for Multilingual Students," Norah Fahim, Bonnie Vidrine-Isbell, and Dan Zhu bring together translingualism and neuroscientific approaches in order to surface connections between translingualism as a theoretical approach that views languages as fluid, and neurological studies that support the brain's movement towards fluidity across languages as it seeks optimization. The chapter presents a series of activities designed to allow students to define translingualism for themselves and make rhetorical decisions about their own access to their various linguistic resources. In this way, Fahim, Vidrine-Isbell, and Zhu advocate for learning environments where multilinguals can engage their different selves and linguistic repertoires, which in turn engages students' diverse languages and encourages students to practice their authentic multilingual voices.

In chapter 5, "An Integrative Pedagogy of Affirmation and Resource Sharing," Gregg Fields advocates for connecting translingualism to pedagogies designed to help students evaluate and reevaluate their linguistic resources, as well as the cultural and experiential knowledge that undergirds these resources. Fields argues that this approach, which is encapsulated in an integrative translingual pedagogy, leads to a pedagogy of affirmation, a linguistic healing of sorts, not just for traditionally defined bilingual, multilingual, and nonnative speaker students but even for students who traditionally are considered monolingual or native speakers. This chapter describes Fields's pedagogical moves and strategies in order to surface how instructor support and student engagement with a variety of linguistic resources invite students into a process of reenvisioning and reevaluation.

In chapter 6, "'Hay un Tiempo Y un Lugar Para Todo': Students' Writing and Rhetorical Strategies in a Translingual Pedagogy," Esther Milu and Mathew Gomes explore the redesign and implementation of a linguistic autobiography assignment. The authors position their research as a coming together of an "integrationist theory of translingualism and transmodality" and describe how this assignment positions students' language(s) and languaging as the central topic and site of inquiry. In examining student interaction with (and fulfillment of) this assignment, Milu and Gomes affirm and extend scholarship regarding the beneficial outcomes of pedagogies informed by transmodal and translingual theories of language and writing. Additionally, their chapter illustrates how inviting modal and linguistic experimentation can help students develop a translingual disposition as part of their rhetorical sensibilities.

Part II, "Enacting Translingual Pedagogies in Interdisciplinary Spaces," broadens the focus of the first section beyond first-year writing and, in one case, beyond the traditional US classroom. This section provides a wide range of translingual perspectives, including international contexts, multisited ethnography, writing center tutoring and training, and courses outside the first-year writing framework.

These chapters are especially useful in that they offer a kaleidoscopic cross-section of the work being done outside the first-year writing classroom. As editors, we suggest this second section is most useful in its attention to fluidity of engagement with a translingual disposition across learning contexts. Again, the following paragraphs offer brief chapter overviews in order to orient readers to what contributions may be most useful to their own teaching.

The second section begins with Mark Brantner's "Writing on the Wall: Teaching Translingualism through Linguistic Cityscapes." Brantner's study builds upon a literacy-autobiography assignment (similar to that discussed in Milu and Gomes's chapter); however, his chapter offers an interesting distinction from the work in Part I in that his research and teaching, while developing out of US theory and practice, is situated in an international context. In his examination of a literacy landscapes assignment, Brantner describes how translingual approaches can be positioned to invite students to explicate their own lived realities of linguistic division. This chapter's recognition of the mobility of resources students bring to their negotiation of linguistic heterogeneity provides a framework for faculty to ground their assignments, lessons, assessments, and teaching in the concrete conscious (and unconscious) practices students engage in.

Building upon the negotiative practices in chapter 7, Brice Nordquist's chapter, "Translingual Literacy and the Mobile Labor of Recontextualization," considers the value of understanding and tracing mobile literacies for both translingual theory and pedagogy across in-school and out-of-school contexts. Nordquist highlights that "linguistic mobilities necessitate perpetual translations. These translations involve not only linguistic transactions but also social, economic, geopolitical, and cultural transactions across asymmetrical relations of power" (chapter 8). This chapter emphasizes the mobility of meaning enabled via linguistic diversity and describes how a translingual disposition is able to illuminate the fluctuating, internally diverse, and intermingling character of languages.

In chapter 9, "Writing-Theory Cartoon: Toward a Translingual and Multimodal Pedagogy," Sonja Wang engages with a different student audience: college students enrolled in a bridge writing course. In this chapter Wang presents an assignment in which students are invited to draw writing-theory cartoons that represent key ideas, assumptions, and approaches they associate with experiences with multiple languages and literacies. Her analysis of student responses describes how the assignment creates opportunities for students to attend to the interrelationship of semiotic systems as part of the rhetorical repertoire essential for translingual negotiation. Like the work of Brantner and Norquist, Wang's assignment can be understood as inviting mobility through the opportunities created for students to reflect on language differences and translingual relationships in light of broader contexts of transnational experiences. These findings extend conversations in writing studies concerning the unique affordances of multimodality to develop metalinguistic awareness and translingual disposition, known contributors to successful writing practices.

Chapter 10, "Translingualism as Methodology for Peer Writing Consultants-in-Training," focuses on the ways translingual practices can be taken up in nonclassroom learning environments. The author, Naomi Silver, describes the introduction, and subsequent revision, of a unit on translingualism within a semester-long training course for undergraduate peer writing consultants. Like many of the chapters from Part I of this collection, Silver focuses on integrating translingual approaches within a mainstream, or traditional, writing studies context; within this chapter we see how translingualism can be offered as a module rather than the exclusive theme (as seen in Julia Kiernan's chapter [chapter 11]), and this addition of translingualism as a topic module also points to the elasticity of translingualism as a pedagogical approach. Also important to this chapter is the reasoning behind integrating translingualism; Silver characterizes the writing center as having "a strong commitment to social justice principles, which includes seeing students' language differences as resources to be mobilized in pursuit of their own communicative purposes."

The closing chapter, "A Framework for Linguistically Inclusive Course Design," also considers the role of translingual approaches in bridge writing programs. Julia Kiernan considers the pedagogical benefits and drawbacks of developing and implementing a semester-long transnationally themed writing course open to and accepting of translingual dispositions. Through exploring the linguistic gaps in current approaches to traditional curricular design, this research offers a framework for reassessing, reimagining, and redesigning writing pedagogy. An examination of student reflections points to the usability of linguistically sensitive curricula within US writing classrooms, particularly in terms of the placement of value on translingual competences, which in turn reflects a shift toward asset-based, culturally sustaining pedagogical practices.

NOTE

1. As editors, we recognize that the growing interest in and exploration of translingualism as a construct is linked to assumptions that undergird our collective understanding of complex languaging and literacy practices. We believe part of this exploration is the acknowledgment of the many points of contention surrounding translanguaging and a translingual approach from different lenses in rhetoric and composition (Bou Ayash 2013, 2015; Donahue 2013; Horner 2010; Horner and Kopelson 2014; Horner and Lu 2007, 2012; Horner et al. 2011; Horner, NeCamp, and Donahue 2011; Horner, Selfe, and Lockridge 2015; Jordan 2015; Lee and Jenks 2016; Lorimer-Leonard 2014; Lu and Horner 2013), second language writing (Leki 2003; Matsuda 2006, 2013, 2014; Matsuda and Matsuda 2010; Matsuda and Silva 2011; Silva 1993; Shuck 2010; Spack, 2004; Thaiss and Zawacki 2006; Zamel and Spack 2004), education (García and Wei 2014), and applied linguistics (Canagarajah 2002, 2005, 2006, 2007, 2009, 2011, 2013, 2018; Firth 1990, 2009; Firth and Wagner 1997; Kachru 1986; Kramsch 2018; Kramsch and Whiteside 2007, 2008; Park and Wee 2013; Wei 2018), as well as the points of conversion and shared stances toward opening our disciplinary languaging theories and practices beyond

an insistence on discrete language systems. While the contributors in this collection do not always reach back into this rich history, as editors, we fully acknowledge that without the work of those cited above, this collection, and the valuable insight of the contributors, would not be possible.

REFERENCES

Atkinson, Dwight, Deborah Crusan, Paul Kei Matsuda, Christina Ortmeier-Hooper, Todd Ruecker, Steve Simpson, and Christine Tardy. 2015. "Clarifying the Relationship between L2 Writing and Translingual Writing: An Open Letter to Writing Studies Editors and Organization Leaders." *College English* 77 (4): 383–86.

Bloom-Pojar, Rachel. 2018. *Translanguaging Outside the Academy: Negotiating Rhetoric and Healthcare in the Spanish Caribbean*. Champaign, IL: NCTE.

Bou Ayash, Nancy. 2013. "Hi-*ein*, Hi يني or يني Hi? Translingual Practices from Lebanon and Mainstream Literacy Education." In *Literacy as Translingual Practice: Between Communities and Classrooms*, edited by A. Suresh Canagarajah, 96–103. New York: Routledge.

Bou Ayash, Nancy. 2015. "(Re-)Situating Translingual Work for Writing Program Administration in Cross-National and Cross-Language Perspectives from Lebanon and Singapore." In *Transnational Writing Program Administration*, edited by David S. Martins, 226–42. Logan: Utah State University Press.

Broad, Bob. 2003. *What We Really Value: Beyond Rubrics in Teaching and Assessing Writing*. Logan: Utah State University Press.

Canagarajah, A. Suresh. 2002. *A Geopolitics of Academic Writing*. Pittsburgh: University of Pittsburgh Press.

Canagarajah, A. Suresh. 2006. "Toward a Writing Pedagogy of Shuttling between Languages: Learning from Multilingual Writers." *College English* 68 (6): 589–604.

Canagarajah, Suresh. 2007. "Lingua Franca English, Multilingual Communities, and Language Acquisition." *Modern Language Journal* 91 (1): 923–939.

Canagarajah, Suresh. 2009. "Multilingual Strategies of Negotiating English: From Conversation to Writing." *JAC* 29 (1/2): 17–48.

Canagarajah, Suresh. 2011. "Translanguaging in the Classroom: Emerging Issues for Research and Pedagogy." *Applied Linguistics Review* 2: 1–28.

Canagarajah, Suresh. 2013. *Translingual Practice: Global Englishes and Cosmopolitan Relations*. London: Routledge.

Canagarajah, Suresh. 2018. "Translingual Practice as Spatial Repertoires: Expanding the Paradigm beyond Structuralist Orientations." *Applied Linguistics* 39 (1): 31–54.

Donahue, Christiane. 2013. "Negotiation, Translinguality, and Cross-Cultural Writing Research in a New Composition Era." In *Literacy as Translingual Practice*, edited by Suresh Canagarajah, 150–161. New York: Routledge.

Dryer, Dylan B. 2016. "Appraising Translingualism." *College English* 78 (3): 274–83.

Firth, Alan. 1990. "'Lingua Franca' Negotiations: Towards an Interactional Approach." *World Englishes* 9 (3): 269–80.

Firth, Alan. 2009. "Doing Not Being a Foreign Language Learner: English as a Lingua Franca in the Workplace and (Some) Implications for SLA." *International Review of Applied Linguistics in Language Teaching* 47 (1): 127–56.

Firth, Alan, and Johannes Wagner. 1997. "On Discourse, Communication, and (Some) Fundamental Concepts in SLA research." *The Modern Language Journal* 81 (3): 285–300.

García, Ofelia, and Li Wei. 2014. "Translanguaging and Education." In *Translanguaging: Language, Bilingualism and Education*, edited by Ofelia García and Li Wei, 63–77. London: Palgrave Macmillan.

Gilyard, Keith. 2016. "The Rhetoric of Translingualism." *College English* 78 (3): 284–89.

Horner, Bruce. 2010. "From 'English Only' to Cross-Language Relations in Composition." Introduction to *Cross-Language Relations in Composition*, edited by Bruce Horner, Min-Zhan Lu, and Paul Kei Matsuda. Carbondale: Southern Illinois University Press.

Horner, Bruce, and Karen Kopelson, eds. 2014. *Reworking English in Rhetoric and Composition: Global Interrogations, Local Interventions*. Carbondale: Southern Illinois University Press.

Horner, Bruce, and Min-Zhan Lu. 2007. "Resisting Monolingualism in 'English': Reading and Writing the Politics of Language." In *Rethinking English in Schools: A New and Constructive Stage*, edited by Viv Ellis, Carol Fox, and Brian V. Street, 141–57. London: Continuum.

Horner, Bruce, Min-Zhan Lu, Jacqueline Jones Royster, and John Trimbur. 2011. "Language Difference in Writing: Toward a Translingual Approach." *College English* 73 (3): 303–21.

Horner, Bruce, Samantha NeCamp, and Christiane Donahue. 2011. "Toward a Multilingual Composition Scholarship: From English Only to a Translingual Norm." *College Composition and Communication* 63 (2): 269–300.

Horner, Bruce, Cynthia Selfe, and Tim Lockridge. 2015. "Translinguality, Transmodality, and Difference: Exploring Dispositions and Change in Language and Learning." Enculturation/Intermezzo. http://intermezzo.enculturation.net/01/ttd-horner-selfe-lockridge/.

Jordan, Jay. 2015. "Material Translingual Ecologies." *College English* 77 (4): 364–82.

Kachru, Braj B. 1986. "The Power and Politics of English." *World Englishes* 5 (2–3): 121–40.

Kramsch, Claire. 2018. "Trans-Spatial Utopias." *Applied Linguistics* 39 (1): 108–115.

Kramsch, Claire, and Anne Whiteside. 2007. "Three Fundamental Concepts in Second Language Acquisition and Their Relevance in Multilingual Contexts." *The Modern Language Journal* 91: 907–22.

Kramsch, Claire, and Anne Whiteside. 2008. "Language Ecology in Multilingual Settings. Towards a Theory of Symbolic Competence." *Applied Linguistics* 29 (4): 645–71.

Lee, Jerry Won, and Christopher Jenks. 2016. "Doing Translingual Dispositions." *College Composition and Communication* 68 (2): 317–44.

Leki, Ilona. 2003. "Living through College Literacy: Nursing in a Second Language." *Written Communication* 20 (1): 81–98.

Lorimer-Leonard, Rebecca. 2014. "Multilingual Writing as Rhetorical Attunement." *College English* 76 (3): 227–47.

Lu, Min-Zhan, and Bruce Horner. 2013. "Translingual Literacy, Language Difference, and Matters of Agency." *College English* 75 (6): 582–607.

Matsuda, Aya, and Paul Kei Matsuda. 2010. "World Englishes and the Teaching of Writing." *Tesol Quarterly* 44 (2): 369–74.

Matsuda, Paul Kei. 2006. "The Myth of Linguistic Homogeneity in U.S. College Composition." *College English* 68 (6): 637–51.

Matsuda, Paul Kei. 2013. "It's the Wild West Out There: A New Linguistic Frontier in US College Composition." In *Literacy as Translingual Practice: Between Communities and Classrooms*, edited by Suresh Canagarajah, 128–38. London: Routledge.

Matsuda, Paul Kei. 2014. "The Lure of Translingual Writing." *PMLA* 129 (3): 478–83.

Matsuda, Paul Kei, and Tony Silva 2011. "Cross-Cultural Composition: Mediated Integration of U.S. and International Students." In *Second-Language Writing in the Composition Classroom*, edited by Paul Kei Matsuda, Michelle Cox, Jay Jordan, and Christine Ortmeier-Hooper, 252–65. Boston: Bedford/St. Martin's.

Park, Joseph Sung-Yul, and Lionel Wee. 2013. *Markets of English: Linguistic Capital and Language Policy in a Globalizing World*. New York: Routledge.

Shuck, Gail. 2010. "Language Identity, Agency, and Context: The Shifting Meanings of Multilingual." In *Reinventing Identities in Second Language Writing*, edited by Michelle

Cox, Jay Jordan, Christina Ortmeier-Hooper, and Gwen Gray Schwartz, 117–38. Urbana: National Council of Teachers of English.

Spack, Ruth. 2004. "The Acquisition of Academic Literacy in a Second Language: A Longitudinal Case Study, Updated." In *Crossing the Curriculum: Multilingual Learners in College Classrooms*, edited by Vivian Zamel and Ruth Spack, 19–45. Mahwah, NJ: Lawrence Erlbaum.

Thaiss, Christopher J., and Terry Myers Zawacki. 2006. *Engaged Writers, Dynamic Disciplines: Research on the Academic Writing Life*. Portsmouth, NH: Boynton/Cook.

Trimbur, John. 2016. "Translingualism and Close Reading." *College English* 78 (3): 219–227.

Wei, Li. 2018. "Translanguaging as a Practical Theory of Language." *Applied Linguistics* 39 (1): 9–30.

Zamel, Vivian, and Ruth Spack. 2004. *Crossing the Curriculum: Multilingual Learners in College Classrooms*. Mahwah, NJ: Erlbaum.

PART I

Enacting Translingual Pedagogies in First-Year Composition

1
ADDRESSING MONOLINGUAL DISPOSITIONS WITH TRANSLINGUAL PEDAGOGY

Ghanashyam Sharma

INTRODUCTION

"I'm not interested in other languages," said an international student in a first-year undergraduate seminar titled Global Citizenship I taught a few years ago. "I need to learn better English." The class was discussing Carolyn Matalene's 1985 article "Contrastive Rhetoric: An American Writing Teacher in China." A native English-speaking domestic student responded in defense of learning translingual skills, drawing on Matalene's arguments about the benefits of learning about different rhetorical traditions, but the international, *multilingual* student was not convinced. He only wanted to improve his English.

Given the influence of the monolingual worldview on institutions' and students' definition of academic success, it is not surprising students want to improve their English and not consider developing skills in other languages as well. Even when students know the languages they use in everyday life give them access to more knowledge, relationships, and opportunities, they may view those languages as posing barriers in academic and professional domains. Thus, it is not students' linguistic identity or proficiency but instead their belief and disposition that impede their acceptance and promotion of translingual sensibility and competency. As such, this resistance is a pedagogical challenge to be addressed. Whatever their linguistic identities and experiences, and however they use languages outside school, students from many social, cultural, or national backgrounds typically find it hard to unlearn deep-seated monolingual beliefs about education and academic writing. Getting students to appreciate translanguaging as a norm and realize its value requires writing teachers to educate them about its intellectual, social, and professional benefits. As I argue in this chapter, writing teachers can best help students appreciate translingual skills if we approach these skills as a means for accessing different bodies of knowledge from different cultures and societies, for drawing on different rhetorical traditions and practices, and for learning about and using different perspectives on local as well as global issues.

I first address the tensions and dilemmas promoting translingual skills can cause within the current monolingual regime. Then I discuss the need to view *translingual* pedagogy as a means toward larger educational goals (beyond language awareness and sensitivity), especially in light of continued linguistic diversification of student bodies in the writing classroom. Using that broader perspective, I describe a few practical teaching strategies and activities from my classroom, responding to what A. Suresh Canagarajah (2013b) calls the "general feeling [among teachers] that theorization of translingual literacy has far outpaced pedagogical practices for advancing this proficiency in classrooms" (41). In doing so, I attempt to address three additional challenges I have faced in teaching and promoting translingual skills (and the opportunities I see for doing so):

1. Given that the monolingual disposition stems from powerful sociopolitical conditions in the world, how can we best foster appreciation—among students of all linguistic backgrounds and identities—for translingualism as a literacy skill in academe and a social/professional skill in the world beyond?

2. Considering that we teach writing to increasingly multilingual, globalized classes, what pedagogical approaches, strategies, and activities can we use for tapping into the languages and attendant rhetorical and epistemological resources our students bring into the classroom?

3. How can we promote translingualism as an educational goal among other stakeholders across our institutions and beyond?

Using assignments and activities involving global issues and citizenship as catalysts for linguistic, cultural, and educational border crossing, I discuss how writing teachers can productively confront the tensions between the idea of education as assimilation/belonging (university being a "community") and as navigating communities (university being a global "crossroads" of people and ideas). I conclude by briefly describing a three-pronged approach for promoting translingualism in academe and beyond.

CONTEXT AND PERSPECTIVE

Entering the classroom on Long Island after I moved from Kentucky to New York in 2012, I was unsure as to how I could put any multilingual scholarship or translingual theory into practice. When I asked a first-year writing class how many students were international, I encountered a confusing range of responses, reflecting the variety of linguistic and cultural identities of students. That diversity gradually inspired me to start drawing on both the scholarship I had studied and the life experiences I have had with different languages, cultures, and countries in my teaching. While I was born in a remote district in Western Nepal where most people only spoke the dominant Nepali language, I grew up learning nearly a dozen languages and being fluent in half of them. Throughout these linguistic experiences, ranging from languages I am fluent in to those in which I can only understand basic communication, I find my background provides unique opportunities for understanding diverse societies and cultures, for appreciating new perspectives on issues, and for exploring the nuance and complexity of ideas in context. With more diverse student demographics in New York, I am increasingly encouraged to foreground my students' knowledge and experiences of different languages, cultures, and countries as means for academic and intellectual growth.

The writing program and the university where I teach do not officially promote a translingual pedagogy, but they offer conducive environments for the promotion of translingual skills and their applications by their faculty. An increasing number of writing instructors in the program in writing and rhetoric at Stony Brook University (SUNY) have been advancing or responding to institutional interest in internationalization. We do so by adopting translingual-friendly pedagogies and through the use of global issues as the subject of reading, research, and writing in composition courses. Many writing-department colleagues have embraced the idea of bringing the world into the writing classroom through literary texts, research topics, and transnational/cross-cultural perspectives, as have many other colleagues across the university. We are connected to a multilingual and intercultural research center on campus and are strongly supported by the College of Arts and Sciences and the vice provost for Global Affairs and dean of International Academic Programs, himself a respected applied linguistics scholar. While slightly less than 20 percent of our nearly twenty-six thousand students are international by visa status (Fact Sheet 2018), there are no data about the linguistic makeup of the student body; however, the fact that roughly 60 percent of students are listed as nonwhite may indicate that the number of multilingual students is high. In the required writing courses I teach, many students from across the racial/ethnic and language identity spectrum describe themselves as multilingual. Students of all backgrounds also actively engage in clubs and organizations that focus on multilingual, transnational, and global-citizenship themes (I have been faculty advisor for some of them). One of the six units of the Undergraduate Colleges, run by the Department of Global Studies and Human Development, is global studies, where I often teach the course mentioned above. I have also developed and taught upper-division and graduate courses in rhetoric and writing across cultures. Thus, the institutional context, as well as my personal experiences, fosters my interest in translingualism that undergirds my scholarship, teaching, and service.

ADDRESSING THE CHALLENGES OF MONOLINGUAL DISPOSITION

Adopting practical pedagogical strategies for promoting translingual skills and dispositions requires addressing the dynamics of monolingualism. We must educate our students that it is not only by conforming to and mastering monolingual standards but also by developing and using translingual skills that they can exercise agency and power. Students need to understand that the mastery of Standard English and translingual skills are not mutually exclusive objectives. In this section, I draw on relevant scholarship in order to explain how the practical pedagogical strategies that follow in a later section are undergirded by an understanding of the power and agency students can exercise through both monolingual standards and translingual skills.

Scholarship about nonnative English speakers and writers often frames them as marginalized; their native English-speaking counterparts possess power, exercise more agency, and serve in gatekeeping positions (e.g., Horner and Trimbur 2002; Lillis and Curry 2010; Zamel and Spack 2006). This scholarship does so in order to describe and address consequential issues in academe and society. However, as some of the same scholarship also notes (especially Canagarajah 2009; Horner et al. 2011; Horner, NeCamp and Donahue 2011), nonnative English speakers and writers also seek or wield the same power, privilege, and agency in the process of learning and using English. Bruce Horner, Min-Zahn Lu, Jacqueline Jones Royster, and John Trimbur (2011), for instance, point out that individuals who are "identified by conventional standards as monolinguals might take a translingual approach to language difference . . . while individuals identifiable by conventional standards as multilingual with regard to their own linguistic resources might well approach language differences in ways at odds with a translingual approach" (311–12). That is, both translingual and monolingual choices—whether made within or across these linguistic identity positions or dispositions—can be strategies for exercising agency. In fact, the authors also add that agency manifests not only in deviations from the norm but also in all language acts the user makes deliberately; thus, conforming to conventional language standards does not mean a lack of agency nor the subordination of an individual's will to institutional demands as an unwitting, unagentive reproduction of dominant language norms.

Canagarajah (2006) similarly argues that a language user's decision to choose a "standard" grammatical structure can involve an act of exercising their agency; the decision to adopt monolingual standards is inherently "an ideologically favored option" (610) in their particular context and status in the discipline and the institution. This was the case with my multilingual student preferring a monolingual disposition. Instead of simply challenging monolingual disposition as uninformed or prejudiced, instructors should show students how they can improve target language by cultivating multilingual dispositions and engaging in translingual practices, as well as how they can exercise their intellectual agency and mobilize social/political capital by doing so.

While students know they can exercise power and agency by adopting monolingual standards, they may not be as aware they can also do so by drawing on translingual resources. Since monolingual discourses, beliefs, and practices about language and writing have fundamentally shaped academic practices and students' beliefs, it takes time and effort for teachers to educate students about the unique benefits of translingual competencies. Once students understand the benefits of not only mastering the dominant language but also being able to use others, most of them are eager to draw on, rather than suppress, translingual resources they have access to or can start acquiring through education. For instance, in one of my Global Citizenship classes, two students working on a group project, one from Guatemala and the other from rural Pennsylvania, had started the project with superficial points that generalized how people greeted in their communities/cultures (small talk and shaking hands respectively). When they came to my office for feedback, I asked them whether everyone in those cultures greeted anyone in the same way in every context. That simple pedagogical intervention prompted the students to explore the complexity and variability of outwardly simple communicative acts by context, relationship, power, and so on; they were not only able to bring languages and communication practices from their home communities into the classroom but were also able to do so in order to achieve a broader educational purpose, as I further discuss below.

At the end of the semester, a student in the same Global Citizenship class illustrated how translingual skills can serve as a powerful resource for communicative success inside and outside academe. A second-generation Indian American student described an intriguing incident involving a translingual communicative "crisis" in order to illustrate a sophisticated argument during a class presentation. Earlier that year, when his father asked him to pick up a relative from the airport, he had forgotten to ask who exactly the "auntie" was, so, as he approached the guest in a crowded airport lounge, he realized he didn't know the level of formality/respect his greeting needed. Should he touch her feet (meaning close relationship)? But doing so would be "too much" if the word *auntie* wasn't meant literally (as it happens in South Asia), or if the person was from the city, was highly educated, or might be embarrassed by his action in a public space "here in America." Or, should he just do the traditional namaste, and if so, how formally? Or, should he simply say hello? Unable to make the right decision within the few seconds available, he produced a combination of awkward gestures and sounds that were neither here nor there. Had his communication with his father happened in Hindi, the term *auntie* would have been far more specific; or if he could have understood the guest's words and gestures better, he would have gotten the cues there as well. Lacking linguistic fluency and cultural knowledge, he said, he had to resort to "dumb gestures."

Pedagogical interventions—such as requiring students to study language use in context, or to share and study how they communicate translingually—are necessary to foster critical thinking, as well as help students realize the agency and power they can exercise through translingual skills. But it is necessary to do so without inadvertently vilifying a monolingual disposition students may begin with or to which they adhere. Whether they speak multiple languages or only English, students should not be alienated or made uncomfortable about their views and dispositions regarding language (or culture and society for that matter). Even those who aren't at first attracted to the idea of drawing on different languages and bodies of knowledge might have something to contribute; some of them may learn or use translingual skills more passively than others, and some may see more social, economic, and cultural benefits than others in learning translingual skills. Some nonnative English-speaking students may never change their minds, insisting they have come to an English-speaking country to primarily improve their English as a marketable resource back home.

PEDAGOGICAL STRATEGIES, ASSIGNMENTS, AND ACTIVITIES

One of the simplest translingual activities I assign students in writing courses is to find and discuss words, idioms, and proverbs in different languages that are not easily translatable. Students who speak different languages offer examples for getting the conversation started; I also ask the class to find one or two items on the internet. For example, difficult-to-translate words and expressions are commonly searched and are useful resources when using the internet for brainstorming such topics. One site includes a list of words from languages from around the world. One example, the Spanish word *sobremasa*, refers to the moments after a meal when participants engage in food-related conversations. Discussions following this activity have included the difficulty of translation, the social realities or cultural values the words express or imply, language change, and technological advancements. To spice up the conversation, I often use examples of bad translation and local Englishes from websites like www.engrish.com; what usually begins with laughter often turns into serious conversations about translingual skills, cross-cultural communication, and broader social issues.

Reading and writing about or discussing literacy experiences is another set of activities that allows students to explore issues across cultures. I ask, "What do you call [e.g., *assignment*] in your home country?" With *assignment*, for instance, some students find out the word may only translate to "work" in some languages, losing the connotation of "giving" someone work to do; others add that the *practice* of writing assignments doesn't exist in the education system they came from. Students discuss contextual meanings of translated terms; for example, *tests* and *exams* are *given* by teachers and *taken* by students in South Asia, and issues like this give rise to robust conversations about education systems and teacher-student relationships. Domestic students help international students better understand academic terminology here in the United States, but as often, they become aware of issues they have never thought about. Some academic terms even prompt conversations about traditions and beliefs about knowledge in the broader society and culture. Especially with classes in which the majority of students are international, I use such activities to prepare for the academic transition essay, an assignment that allows students to share their experiences of transitioning to college (from another country or from high school). Students start by recounting an incident or process of learning about a new term or concept, go on to research the topic, and write about the term/concept/ practice by situating it in the broader culture and system of higher education. If they decide to compare issues between two countries or contexts, they must make sure not to criticize one side and praise the other (something international students are prone to do) but instead study specific issues in their full sociocultural and material contexts.

Further, if languages are tools for exploring ideas and crossing cultural borders, they can also be a means for reflecting back at what is more familiar. Borrowing the idea of "reflective encounters" from LuMing Mao (2003), I design activities that help students to think more critically about the primary language of class, English, in order to help them reflect on language use, rhetorical practices, and social issues in this language in the local context as well. For example, in a rhetoric and writing-focused graduate course, I engage students in reading about rhetorical traditions and practices across cultures, relating the readings to the current language policy in US academe. The benefits of the cross-cultural encounters and reflections are many. For instance, as one graduate student in a rhetoric course I teach within the teaching-of-writing certificate noted: "The solutions to our problems in teaching writing to all students, not just minorities, can be found by looking at other cultures. We . . . [can find] inspiration in the plethora of ideas and strategies that the world has already provided us with." Similarly, at the undergraduate level, whenever students engage in translingual activities, they learn how meaning is constructed and conveyed in other languages, how gestures and greetings express and maintain power relationships, and how seemingly universal concepts and practices can be translated by and into different communicative practices across contexts and cultures. As a student who interviewed her peers in three other countries for a research paper wrote, the experience of studying issues through the use of language in different societies and cultures can change one's "outlook on life in a way that I struggle to find the words to explain."

Moving closer to broader goals of the writing classroom, for which I am arguing translingual practice should be a means, I assign research papers in which students write about issues of global/transnational significance and/or consider any issue from transnational perspectives. Often extending from discussions about language, literacy, and educational systems, students explore their chosen issues in different contexts, offer multiple perspectives, and learn to appreciate different value systems—using their newfound perspectives to rethink/reflect on the local and familiar. For this research paper, students have written about transnational human trafficking, global climate change, unfair international treaties, cultural clashes, massive open online courses, global citizenship, and the United Nations. Both international and domestic students tend to be interested and engaged in this assignment; I usually start by assigning readings and responses on the broad subject area within which all students must develop their specific topics and arguments. As I offer below, I assign further work to scaffold students' research and writing process and engage extensive class discussions of the broader, shared subject. This assignment helps students recognize complexity, view the subject from different perspectives, and cultivate a sense of global citizenship. Let me share some of those scaffolding activities and follow-up assignments now.

A simple but powerful activity I use involves image searching a universal term on the internet. Students start this activity by writing down a word/concept that they think is absolutely universal (such as *beauty*). When we use the term *beauty*, for example, students find the results almost exclusively include women who are young, skinny, wearing makeup, and white. Some of them share more critical reactions: "Somehow terribly sad to look at," "Wow, that's what the internet thinks 'beauty' means!," and "I don't think this is what beauty means everywhere in the world." Typically, only one English term is involved in this activity, but it often leads to discussions about how the term/concept is understood across cultures and contexts. The activity also prompts discussions about the complexity of language, difference in societies' and cultures' understanding of seemingly universal concepts, and why internet algorithms "represent" ideas and images in certain ways. Often, the conversation becomes long, complicated, and even controversial and involves issues of racism, sexism and objectification of women's bodies, and homophobia. An important second part of this assignment is to ask students to "add a country or cultural or qualifier, and see what images come up." In one instance, a student added the word "Taiwan" and the result included "a lot of snakes." He went on to research the reason and share with the class how beauty is associated with snakes in some societies. Such class exercises help students open up and have fun while also learning different perspectives on important issues.

Many students simply call the writing class "English" class, and they are surprised when I tell them they can use other languages in the process and product of their writing. I tell students to consider using their home languages while taking notes, researching, reading, discussing their ideas with peers, developing outlines, and writing early drafts. While final drafts must be in English, allowing students to use their home language in the process can boost their confidence and understanding of the issue, often expanding the scope of their learning. Following the lead of other scholars (e.g., Canagarajah 2013b), I also encourage students to insert their voice in their own languages in the final draft, showing them how to do so rhetorically effectively (such as by providing the context and/or translating the text). Some students find sources and cite passages (typically along with translation) in another language; doing so seems to give them a greater sense of agency as researchers and writers. When students write about topics pertaining to a certain country or culture, I encourage them to search for sources from those contexts and in local languages. One student who cited a source in the Korean language and translated it for his readers here in the United States told me later he could neither have understood the issue nor convinced his audience as well as he had if he had not done so. Requesting students to read short passages in other languages during class discussion makes its own kind of impact. And I also ask students to compare how sentences are structured in different languages (showing them on the board or screen), which starts very productive conversations at the level of syntax and grammar.

I encourage students, while we recite and discuss texts in their home languages, to practice clear communication to their classmates, both those who do and those who do not share that language. In this way, students teach communicative practices. Canagarajah (2013b) highlights the communicative aspect of translanguaging when he notes that from a translingual perspective, it is "not sharedness or prior knowledge, but the way both interlocutors manage to co-construct meaning for an atypical item [or issue]" (7). When individuals are involved in conversation across linguistic borders, "they have to resort to diverse negotiation strategies for meaning-making. Meaning emerges from interaction, rather than being assumed or given" (71). The writing classroom allows students to take translanguaging one step further, even if they do not understand other students' languages, into discussing terms and concepts and perspectives expressed by words in different languages. Because most students are fluent in English as the shared medium of communication (the situation Canagarajah uses when making the above observation is of limited proficiency in a shared language on both sides), they are able to explore the issues involved quite extensively even as the participants might utilize only a few words from their languages. In one or two cases, students speaking the same languages completely switched into them (mainly Chinese, Spanish, and Hindi) during class discussions.

In contrast to my past assumption, I have observed positive responses (instead of discomfort) to students speaking different languages in the classroom. In fact, I was first prompted to encourage the use of different languages for comfort, convenience, or productive conversation after I heard one monolingual student whisper "Wow!" upon hearing me switch to Urdu to chat with a group of Pakistani students before class started. The incident reminded me of the scholarly conversations in writing studies, which, I argue, no longer views the two objectives of fostering translingual skills and mastering standard academic English as mutually exclusive. Canagarajah (2013b), for instance, suggests we can help students "bring their own languages in measured ways for significant rhetorical and performative reasons" (113). Translingual skills can help students exercise their agency to initiate change rather than wait for history to do it for them (113). Furthermore, situating the use and exploration of languages in broader contexts can tremendously enhance students' sense of agency, as well as their engagement in learning. As Koji Nakamura (2002) rightly points out, students are motivated to speak up when engaging with significant global and human issues. While some students show initial hesitation, once they develop a grasp on the issues, they become more invested in researching, taking a position, and considering complexities when they work with global/broader compared to local and personal issues.

Finally, when students begin to peer review their research essays, I take the opportunity again to reinforce translingual skills by encouraging them to appreciate differences in word choice and idioms, perspectives and assumptions, rhetoric and argumentation. I remind students such differences may have come from the different language and cultural backgrounds of their peers. I urge peer readers to not focus on standardizing the language and rhetoric of the text; I tell them to talk to the writer about the context and clarity of message. I also model translingually sensitive response as a reader myself; for instance, when international students meet with me to share their anxiety about language, I tell them to focus on their ideas and to compensate their linguistic challenges with research and reading, consultation and revision. Because nonnative speakers of a dominant language must be accorded additional space and flexibility, I encourage students to use their home languages for peer review if that is helpful.

BROADENING THE PURPOSE OF TRANSLINGUAL PEDAGOGY

Semester after semester, when I learn about the diverse backgrounds, value systems, skill sets, and experiences students bring into the classroom, I become aware of essentially two different views about the university. One is a traditional view that considers the university as a community, made up of insiders who, for instance, learn and use academic language as a default means of communication; this view defines academic success in terms of learned conformation to the monolingual norms and expectations of the community. The notions of disciplines, departments, discourses, and even courses and assignments are shaped by this dominant view of academe, and this view is in opposition to one that negates the alternative communicative academic resources that enrich institutions. The diversity of my students also reminds me that this view of the university has always been in tension with a second one, a crossroads of people and ideas that continually accepted outsiders throughout its history, including women, veterans, people of color, and international students. These outsiders have continued to unsettle existing norms and standards of language and discourse, often requiring the very purpose of education to be rethought. I consider that tension as productive, and I see translingualism as one of the most effective means of addressing it. Teaching and promoting translingual skills allows students to go beyond the standard linguistic norms, treating the university as a global crossroads of people and ideas. In this section, I further flesh out the pedagogical ideas underlying translingual strategies and activities I share in the previous section.

In spite of its popularity, the meaning of the term *translingualism* remains somewhat fuzzy; literature on its practical pedagogical application is still limited compared to theoretical discussions. In this chapter, I use the term *translingual* as a qualifier for describing teaching and learning approaches and activities that involve working with and across more than one language. Accordingly, I design and implement assignments and activities in order to treat languages and linguistic resources as windows into different bodies of knowledge, rhetorical traditions and practices, perspectives and value systems available in different cultures, communities, and contexts. Whether the assignments are as simple as discussing an "untranslatable" word from a certain language or as complex as writing a research-based essay on a translingual issue, I ask students to go beyond language into contexts, cultures, and other issues significant in higher education and the society and professions beyond. I treat the class as a multilingual community, as one where students who may speak distinct (often single) languages can use and share their languages and linguistic resources for learning about different societies and cultures. This means the class tries to go beyond the English language (and its varieties and variations) to focus on being a multilingual community and to study the multilingual society, professions, and world members of the class also inhabit and navigate.

For a variety of reasons, including the persisting monolingual disposition that must be tackled from within (Canagarajah 2013b), I certainly find it necessary to focus on the internal diversity of English. But I only consider Englishes as a starting point for helping students appreciate, practice, and develop translingual skills. It has been over two decades now since Min-Zhan Lu (1994) demonstrated some very effective ways of teaching translingual skills by using language variations within English (also see Canagarajah 2013b; Lu and Horner 2013). However, especially in light of the increasing number of languages spoken by students in classes like mine in New York, I find it necessary to go beyond this extended, intralingual practice of translingualism. By intralingual, I mean translingual practices within one named language, like English, for example. In my classrooms, focusing on varieties and variations of English feels like using a watered-down and insufficient pedagogy when I could/should be engaging students in communication and learning across borders of world languages. While the underlying dynamics of both intra- and interlingual border crossing (such as register and tone, features of discourses and genres, what Rebecca Leonard [2014] calls "rhetorical attunement") may be theoretically similar, I find it both possible and necessary to engage students in the translingual communicative practices they may be involved in outside academe.

Translingualism is an interesting subject whether or not different languages are involved. For instance, in *Translingual Practice*, Canagarajah (2013b) uses the term "translingual" to "capture the common underlying processes and orientations motivating [different] communicative modes" such as *code meshing, crossing, polyglot dialog*, and many other terms used by other scholars (such as *polylingual languaging, heterography, metrolinguistics,* and *plurilingualism*) (6). Focusing on processes and orientations helps us expand "the consideration to diverse other semiotic products beyond the code-meshed texts of multilinguals" (41). It also helps us realize how "voice, diversity, and hybridity find expression (perhaps more subtly) in texts that appear to be constructed in Standard Written English." This extended meaning of *translingual* shows how all of us are involved in translingual communication, which "finds representation in textual products with different types and degrees of language mixing" (41). However, my argument here is that even if there is a single student in class (or just the teacher) who speaks more than one language, it is possible to enact translingual learning across distinct languages—especially as long as English functions as a link language. Here are some of the strategies for realizing that possibility:

1. Treating the class as a community. When taking this approach, not all students must know more than one language. If one or more students (or the teacher) can share linguistic resources from non-English languages, the class can start crossing interlingual borders.
2. Engaging the class in collaborative translation as translanguaging. Students can use translated texts for achieving the educational objectives even without being able to communicate in different languages. Indeed, students can not only work quite productively with professionally translated texts but can also start the process with machine-translated language (though it remains primitive so far).
3. Helping the class use resources from different languages as means and occasions for learning. As I have highlighted and demonstrated above, using translingual activities as a means rather than end of learning best fits the writing classroom, motivates students, and also serves well to promote translingualism as an educational objective among other stakeholders.

Focusing on the interlingual sense of translingualism lends itself better to creating more concrete productive activities and assignments. It encourages students to take an extra step, looking beyond the borders of one language into the dynamics between and among languages—and thereby the contexts of different societies and cultures where particular texts/acts were/are used. It also allows them to better understand mobility and border crossing, tension and imbalance, power and agency in transnational and globalized contexts, including the globalized classrooms they are in. When they understand the intellectual and practical significance of using language to look beyond sociocultural and geopolitical borders, students best understand the value and practical significance of translingual competence. They respond better to pedagogical interventions when languages and linguistic resources are treated as a means of epistemological agency and also global citizenship—beyond just a linguistic skill.

I envision the ultimate objective of embracing translingualism as fostering students' educational and professional growth by promoting intellectual curiosity and interest in human issues across nations and cultures, in perspectives and value systems beyond geopolitical borders, and in global citizenship. Accordingly, the bases of most translingual activities and assignments (reading, research, discussion, and writing) in which I engage my students are *global issues* and *global citizenship*. To help students achieve the objective, students who speak two or more distinct languages contribute knowledge and experience about crossing geopolitical and cultural borders with those languages; students who do not speak more than one distinct language contribute no less by engaging in those activities while focusing on the issues and objectives of learning. If translingual activities enhance the quality of the former group's learning, they also broaden the scope of it for the latter. For any student, developing translingual competencies can be educationally most meaningful when they use languages as a means of inquiry into different value systems, as catalysts for intellectual inquiry with an openness of mind, and as opportunities for appreciating multiple perspectives when approaching complex issues (especially those that transcend national and cultural borders). Even when writing classes are not as "super-diverse" (Vertovec 2007; also see Hall 2009) as those some of us teach in and around larger global metropolises, students and teachers are likely to collectively use more than one distinct language in any classroom, more or less fluently. Even beyond the global metropolises, students ranging from those who use Indigenous languages at home, to the newly arrived international students, to multilingual children of immigrants and the multilingual "cosmopolitans" who have lived and studied in different countries, and to domestic multilingual students, an increasing majority of students speak more than one language. This reality makes it possible to introduce resources of more than one distinct language into class discussions, research, reading, writing, and oral presentation. As implied in the original use of the term by Steve Kellman (2000) and David Schwarzer, Melanie Bloom and Sarah Shomo (2006), translingualism can be a bridge between languages and cultures. And as Huang Tung-Chou (2010) further emphasizes by citing those authors, translingualism can be used to enable students "to express the funds of knowledge they possess . . . to thrive in a global community characterized by rapid cultural and technological change" (44); it need not be limited to teaching theoretical awareness of the complexity of language use.

Thus, I suggest writing teachers start by identifying the particular multilingual and translingual abilities and dispositions each class possesses. Doing so can help us determine the most appropriate starting points, topics of discussion, modes of collaboration and exchange, and so on. It is important that we translate theories to practice, avoid taking students' or other stakeholders' monolingual dispositions at their face value, and especially not vilify monolingual disposition among students. Instead, it is increasingly necessary and possible to engage in students' collective translingual skills and to do so for achieving broader educational goals and preparing students for increasingly multilingual settings in life and work.

CONCLUSION

The international student mentioned in the beginning of this chapter never changed his mind about his English-only interest. At the end of the semester, all his peers showed up to present their group projects a second time at the Undergraduate Research and Creative Activities symposium on campus; they were invited there to a special showcase of undergraduate student work hosted by the Multilingual and Intercultural Research Center on campus (along with a number of multilingual-themed sessions from various departments across campus). This one student wasn't interested because he seemed convinced that as long as he gained fluency in English, he could be successful, language-wise, in any place and profession.

Given the stranglehold of English monolingualism in US academe and society, as well as in the world at large, translingual communicative competence remains a hard-to-sell educational objective where this dominant "international" language is involved. So, the one skeptical student was part of a condition and reality that may often be insurmountable for educators and education. Also, even if we can successfully convince all students about the intellectual, social, and professional benefits of translingual skills and disposition, there are yet other stakeholders, agents, and forces that may undermine or even displace the entire educational mission undergirding translingual pedagogy. So, let me conclude by sharing a three-pronged approach for addressing the broader challenges without which the teaching and promotion of translingual skills in colleges and universities may be doomed to fail.

First, as I have already indicated above, I believe we should not only teach our students translingual skills but also educate them about these skills' educational, professional, and social uses and advantages. Here are some of the benefits I highlight with my students. Intellectually, an interest and ability to study and use language as a window into cross-cultural issues can help students become more informed about the larger world. Cultivating the sense of global citizenship can help them generate better ideas and perspectives for addressing challenges of life and society—whether local or cross-contextual. Professionally, such skills can help them better prepare for the diversified and globalized workforce and opportunities in it. For instance, Miguel Candel-Mora (2015) shows the relevance of such concepts as "intercultural teams, international meetings, geographical mobility, worldwide negotiations, and globalization" for professional engineers, indicating the significance of intercultural communicative competence in engineering courses (26). Claire Molina (2011) similarly highlights the importance of teaching and fostering "professionally-oriented translingual and transcultural competences" (1244) for today's students. Socially and culturally, translingual skills can help students better relate to people from diverse cultures and communities around them and around the world. Politically, in the broader sense, translingual skills can help them be better citizens of the world, a world where, for instance, the idea of "clash of civilizations" has morphed from a cynical political theory into an unfortunate reality.

Second, we must also inform and educate other stakeholders in the university and beyond because they shape the culture and environment in which translingual practices occur. We must inform and influence academic administrators, faculty colleagues, and others who shape or influence academic policy and curricula. Here too, the same theory of power and agency can help us understand people's perception about translingualism. In "A Theory of Power in Education," Nicholas Burbules (1986) states that "power is a relation that is not simply chosen (or avoided) but made more or less necessary by the circumstances under which persons come together" (97). He adds that circumstances involve "a presumption or expectation of certain roles that constrain the alternatives the [persons as] agents see as possible; or psychological traits—sometimes unconscious—that predispose persons to carrying out dominant or submissive positions in the relationship" (97). In order to teach translingual skills as an accepted educational goal, writing teachers must consider institutional context, engage institutional leaders, overcome barriers by promoting the benefits for students. Teachers' agency (as well as that of administrators) is inevitably tangled in the power structure of the institution and broader society where they function. Consequently, the best way to convey the benefits of translingual education is once again by focusing on the practical benefits, envisioning how translingual skills would be applicable in different disciplines and professions and in life and society beyond the classroom. University mission statements are awash with educational objectives of "internationalization" and developing "global" competencies (Tardy 2014). But when it comes to curricula and academic programs, academic services and resources, community engagement and professional development, few administrators and faculty across the disciplines promote different languages. Christine Tardy (2014) states, "The relative lack of institutional emphasis on language study in the face of a purported heightened interest in global awareness presents a somewhat surprising paradox" because the same institutions seem to not recognize language an "essential part of internationalization" (257). Enrollments in foreign languages are dropping, and so is the amount of resource allocated for language departments. Thus, it is necessary to promote the broader educational and social benefits of translingual competence among different stakeholders.

Furthermore, writing teachers who want to teach and promote translingual skills must also be aware of, and respond to, the broader social climate beyond academe. This strategy is an extension to what I have focused on in this chapter, but it seems crucial for teachers, as public intellectuals, to engage broader audiences on the issue of translingualism as a norm in a country like the United States. Here I am reminded of the strange case of Nepal, the country where I went to college and university and taught at different levels of education for more than a decade. In the past two decades, the quality of the country's education in the once-robust public-school system has dramatically deteriorated due to increasing popularity of expensive private English-medium schools, which have convinced the general public that private schools are better because they use English-only as the medium of instruction. Scholars and policymakers certainly understand the absurdity of that argument, but they are unable to counter the ever-growing demand for imposing English as the only medium in public schools as well. It is clear that doing so will only further undermine the quality of teaching and learning in already resource-poor public schools where most teachers have critically low proficiency in English, as well as make education unaffordable for more families. And yet, a range of factors, including globalization, emigration, the appeal of Western popular culture, and the explosion of information technologies, have all been prompting the society to adopt/impose English as a universal medium of education. Teaching alone cannot address the tangle of social/political forces in situations like that; the case of monolingual disposition as a default outlook on language in the United States is similarly challenging to tackle with classroom teaching alone.

It is also important to account for power dynamics in all contexts, ranging from the most specific context of the classroom to the broader sociocultural contexts of institutional policies/priorities, professional incentives, and global and geopolitical forces. If the contexts and power dynamics are ignored, the idea of teaching and promoting translingualism could turn into a temporary academic fad; practical pedagogies can be most effective when they are implemented for achieving broader educational goals and also when educators respond to larger sociopolitical realities.

Finally, when there is difference in perspective, understanding, or disposition toward multilingualism and translingualism, it is very important to take the resistance, opposition, and criticism with seriousness and respect. Imposing our views and ideologies about language might be temporarily successful, but doing so would also be counterproductive. As Horner et al. (2011) note, "The translingual approach [should encourage] reading with patience, respect for perceived differences within and across languages, and an attitude of deliberative inquiry" (304). We can maintain these qualities if we treat the class as a multilingual community instead of expecting every student to have the same level of understanding and interest of translingual activities and skills. If some students have not yet had the opportunity to appreciate the idea, or if they do not find it relevant or interesting, we should make sure not to alienate those students, even if we cannot convince or inspire them. While we should convey the rationales and show practical benefits, we must also acknowledge that translingual skills and disposition may not be equally relevant for all students and in all contexts and situations. After all, it would be ironic if we embraced or taught intolerance toward the student who wanted English only while seeking to diversify and enrich the learning experience for all students by using translingual methods and resources.

APPENDIX 1.A

A. Class Activities

1. TRANSLATION: Ask students to write down (or find on the internet) a word, idiom, or proverb each in the languages they know but cannot easily translate into English (or another language). Then ask them to share their approximate translation of the expression with a partner, discussing the challenge they faced while trying to translate. As a class, use the cases as occasions for discussing what the challenge reflects/implies about material or social realities and cultural values, language and social change, technological advancements, and so on.

2. ERROR ANALYSIS: Ask students to visit www.engrish.com and find the funniest but also most highly thought-provoking translation or spelling of English in another country. Why do they think the expression was translated or spelled that way? What can be learned from the translation about the language or context or culture?

3. STRUCTURE AND MEANING: After teaching sentence diagramming in English, ask students to do the same after translating the same sentences in other languages. Help them discuss how sentences are structured in different languages.

4. LOCALITY OF MEANING: Ask students to image search on google.com a word/concept that they think is absolutely universal (such as *beauty*). Then ask the class to draw inferences from the search result, listing the inferences on the board/screen for students to see. What cultures,

contexts, and ideas are represented and what are not? Ask students to add qualifiers having to do with different cultures and issues and discuss the difference in results.

5. ACCESS TO KNOWLEDGE: Encourage students to look for sources in other languages for research-based writing, asking them to consider what they gain or lose by doing so.

B. Research/Writing Assignments

6. ETYMOLOGY AND ADAPTATION: Ask students to research the history or etymology of a word or words that were borrowed from another language and may have been adapted to English. Using examples of words like *karma* or *renegade*, ask them to show how the words they choose take on new meanings in new social, economic, political, and cultural contexts.

7. CROSSING LEARNING CULTURES/CONTEXTS: Assign the academic transition essay, asking students to share their experiences of transitioning to college (from another country or from high school in the same country) with a focus on learning new terms and practices.

8. REFLECTIVE ENCOUNTER: After discussing LuMing Mao's article "Reflective Encounters," ask students to find "odd" language use (such as greeting, small talk, table manners, etc.) in another culture, then compare equivalent speech acts in their/another culture. Ask them to reflect on the potential strangeness of what is local or familiar to them.

9. TRANSNATIONAL ISSUES/PERSPECTIVES: Assign research papers in which students must write about issues of global/transnational significance and/or consider local issues from transnational perspectives. Some topics students can research include transnational human trafficking, global climate change, unfair international treaties, cultural clashes, massive open online courses, global citizenship, and the United Nations. Start by assigning readings and responses in a few areas and then scaffold students' research and writing process with activities and discussion to help them avoid making reductive arguments.

C. Teaching and Assessment Strategies

10. LANGUAGE CHOICE: Encourage students to use the language of their choice for taking notes, researching, reading, and discussing their ideas while developing written assignments or presentations. Allowing students to use their home languages for peer review and other collaborations can enhance motivation and understanding, thereby accelerating the pace of learning writing and improving languages (including English).

11. FOCUS ON STRENGTH AND PURPOSE: Urge students as peer reviewers to not focus on whatever is weak in early drafts, such as unedited or nonstandard English. Ask them to help their peer with the substance and clarity of message first.

12. AGENCY IN VARIATION: When assessing student writing or presentation, appreciate differences in word choice and idioms, perspectives and assumptions, rhetoric and argumentation. Help students make deliberate and meaningful decisions as they use or draw upon linguistic and epistemological resources from different backgrounds.

13. MULTILINGUAL COMMUNITY: Consider the class as a multilingual community and let students who only use one language be experts in that language. This allows the class to engage in collaborative translation as translanguaging.

14. BROADER PURPOSE: Give translingualism a broader purpose by using it to foster students' educational and professional growth, to promote intellectual curiosity and global citizenship, and to teach perspectives and value systems from beyond cultural and geopolitical borders.

REFERENCES

Burbules, Nicholas C. 1986. "A Theory of Power in Education." *Educational Theory* 36 (2): 95–114.

Canagarajah, A. Suresh. 2006. "The Place of World Englishes in Composition: Pluralization Continued." *College Composition and Communication* 57 (4): 586–619.

Canagarajah, A. Suresh. 2009. "Multilingual Negotiation Strategies of Negotiating English: From Conversation to Writing." *Journal of Advanced Composition* 29 (1–2): 17–48.

Canagarajah, A. Suresh. 2013a. "Negotiating Translingual Literacy: An Enactment." *Research in the Teaching of English* 48 (1): 40–67.

Canagarajah, Suresh. 2013b. *Translingual Practice: Global Englishes and Cosmopolitan Relations.* London: Routledge.

Candel-Mora, Miguel. 2015. "Attitudes towards Intercultural Communicative Competence of English for Specific Purposes Students." *Procedia—Social and Behavioral Sciences* 178: 26–31.

Fact Sheet. 2018. Stony Brook University. Accessed March 15, 2019. https://www.stonybrook.edu/commcms/irpe/fact_book/data_and_reports/_files/enrollment/FallProfile2018.pdf.

Hall, Jonathan. 2009. "WAC/WID in the Next America: Redefining Professional Identity in the Age of the Multilingual Majority." *WAC Journal* 20 (3): 33–49.

Horner, Bruce, Min-Zhan Lu, Jacqueline Jones Royster, and John Trimbur. 2011. "Opinion: Language Difference in Writing—Toward a Translingual Approach." *College English* 73 (3): 303–21.

Horner, Bruce, Samantha NeCamp, and Christiane Donahue. 2011. "Toward a Multilingual Composition Scholarship: From English Only to a Translingual Norm." *College Composition and Communication* 63 (2): 269–300.

Horner, Bruce, and John Trimbur. 2002. "English Only and U.S. College Composition." *College Composition and Communication* 53 (4): 594–630.

Kellman, Steve. 2000. *The Translingual Imagination.* Lincoln: University of Nebraska Press.

Leonard, Rebecca L. 2014. "Multilingual Writing as Rhetorical Attunement." *College English* 76 (3): 227–47.

Lillis, Theresa, and Mary J. Curry. 2010. *Academic Writing in a Global Context: The Politics and Practices of Publishing in English.* New York: Routledge.

Lu, Min-Zhan. 1994. "Professing Multiculturalism: The Politics of Style in the Contact Zone." *College Composition and Communication* 45 (4): 442–58.

Lu, Min-Zhan, and Bruce Horner. 2013. "Translingual Literacy, Language Difference, and Matters of Agency." *College English* 75 (6): 586–611.

Mao, LuMing. 2003. "Reflective Encounters: Illustrating Comparative Rhetoric." *Style* 37 (4): 401–25.

Matalene, Carolyn. 1985. "Contrastive Rhetoric: An American Writing Teacher in China." *College English* 47 (8): 789–808.

Molina, Claire. 2011. "Curricular Insights into Translingualism as a Communicative Competence." *Journal of Language Teaching and Research* 2 (6): 1244–51.

Nakamura, Koji. 2002. "Cultivating Global Literacy through English as an International Language (EIL) Education in Japan: A New Paradigm for Global Education." *International Education Journal* 3 (5): 64–74.

Schwarzer, David, Melanie Bloom, and Sarah Shomo. 2006. *Research in Second Language Learning*. Charlotte, NC: Information Age.

Tardy, Christine. 2014. "Discourses of Internationalization and Diversity in US Universities and Programs." In *Transnational Writing Program Administration*, edited by David Martin, 243–64. Logan: Utah State University Press.

Tung-Chiou, Huang. 2010. "The Application of Translingualism to Language Revitalisation in Taiwan." *Asian Social Science* 6 (2): 44–59.

Vertovec, Steven. 2007. "Super-Diversity and Its Implications." *Ethnic and Racial Studies* 29 (6): 1024–54.

Zamel, Vivian, and Ruth Spack. 2006. "Teaching Multilingual Learners across the Curriculum: Beyond the ESL Classroom and Back Again." *Journal of Basic Writing* 25 (2): 126–52.

2
CRITERIA-MAPPING ACTIVITIES AND THE TRANSFORMATION OF STUDENT-TEACHER RELATIONS IN THE COMPOSITION CLASSROOM

Daniel V. Bommarito and Emily Cooney

INTRODUCTION

In the introduction to *Literacy as Translingual Practice: Between Communities and Classrooms*, Suresh Canagarajah (2013) asks what meaning the prefix *trans* contributes when attached to *language*. Among its conceptual affordances, Canagarajah argues, the term *translingual* signals that the meaning of any discursive gesture is a product of the unique and dynamic circumstance in which it occurs. That is, meaning is an emergent property that derives from negotiations among interlocutors rather than only from adherence to preestablished formal structures. And the power to create meaning, furthermore, emanates from one's ability to participate with others in this complex negotiation process. Here is Canagarajah in his own words: "The term translingual enables a consideration of communicative competence as not restricted to predefined meanings of individual languages, but the ability to merge different language resources in situated interactions for new meaning construction. Competence is not an arithmetical addition of the resources of different languages, but the transformative capacity to mesh their resources for creative new forms and meanings" (2). In shifting attention toward interaction, Canagarajah emphasizes competence—that is, practical rather than propositional knowledge—and invites a reconsideration of how speakers and writers participate in the coconstruction of meaning. In effect, this shift toward interaction pushes teachers of writing to reconsider the ways they can help students not simply to comply with linguistic norms but also to participate in the very process of their negotiation.

The present chapter conceives of translingualism as a call to explore and make visible this highly situated negotiation process from a pedagogical perspective. Negotiating meaning through language norms is, of course, not a new concept in composition; however, we interpret Canagarajah's formulation of translingualism as asking compositionists to locate the spirit and practice of negotiation within language-rich environments, such as the multilingual writing classroom. In what follows, we detail two pedagogical strategies that seek to open up space for students with diverse language resources to recognize and participate in the negotiation of meaning by way of discussions of language norms. This type of pedagogical move, we believe, is one way (but certainly not the only way) to alter the balance of power in linguistically diverse classrooms and, ultimately, support the kind of agentive use of language promised by composition's renewed interest in language in the context of written discourse. Additionally, the activities in this chapter share features with work of assessment scholars who have made the negotiation of writing standards, conventions, and expectations central to classroom pedagogies (Inoue 2004) and part of a larger effort to "create opportunity structures for all students" (Poe, Inoue, and Eliot 2018, 16). Overall, this chapter offers examples of concrete activities used in the multilingual writing classroom, as well as a generative theoretical apparatus used to develop them.

CRITERIA MAPPING AS A CONCEPTUAL FRAME

We refer to the pedagogical activities detailed in this essay as *criteria-mapping activities*, a concept and practice adapted from Bob Broad's (2003) work on dynamic criteria mapping. In his monograph on program-wide writing assessment, *What We Really Value: Beyond Rubrics in Teaching and Assessing Writing*, Broad argues that traditional rubrics, in the "rush toward clarity, simplicity, brevity, and authority," make far-reaching claims about the values of a writing program without thoroughly investigating the validity of those claims (3). The traits of writing codified in a rubric and purported to comprise good writing are imported from some context far afield of the classroom in which they are used, representing a looming but often indecipherable view from nowhere. What is missing from such static, predetermined evaluative criteria found in a rubric, says Broad, are the voices of the writing teachers who use the assessment tools and whose determinations will have significant effects on the lives of the students being evaluated. Often, rubrics represent "not what instructors value in students' writing, but rather what someone believes the program's rhetorical values to be, or what someone wants them to be, or what someone wants people to believe them to be" (12).

For Broad, this leads to two related problems. The first problem is one of validity. Because the tools of assessment are not necessarily aligned with or derived from the context of instruction, it makes little sense to hold students accountable to them. If assessment is to be "relevant, valid, and fair," according to Broad (2003), "it must judge students according to the same skills and values by which they have been taught" (11). Leaving teachers' own values out of the assessment measure is likely to engender a division between what is taught and how it is evaluated. The second problem has to do with the way rubrics tend to restrict discussion. As Broad argues, "By predetermining criteria for evaluation, such a process shuts down the open discussion and debate among professional teachers of writing that communal writing assessment should provide" (12). In other words, because rubrics are seen as universally applicable arbiters of quality, the pressure is on the teacher-evaluator to conform to the values of the rubric rather than on the rubric to conform to the values of the teacher.

To resolve these problems, Broad devises a method in which the values of members of a writing program—those teachers performing assessments of students' writing—are elicited in a forum that includes members of the program community. Program teachers are asked to examine student writing and, rather than evaluate, identify what it is they value in it. The values shared by participants are captured and made visible to the rest of the group, a key move because the values become visible and, in a sense, communally owned. Inevitably, as in all cases of group analysis of writing, a variety of interpretations of the student writing result from this articulation of values. But instead of stamping out that variety—as one might in a typical norming session in which the rubric stands infallible—Broad asks that it be a source of discussion and debate. Once made visible to and discussed by the community, the values are eventually aggregated and provisionally codified in a way that more accurately represents the community's values to students through sound assessment tools.

We believe Broad's insightful analysis of rubrics and powerful approach to program-wide assessment has applicability inside the classroom, particularly with respect to the negotiation of language differences. The virtues of valid assessment and communal negotiation are, we think, in alignment with the general aims of scholars advocating a translingual orientation toward writing instruction—namely, the aims to treat language resources, in all their diversity, as attaining meaning through use and to help students use those resources in ways that afford agency and access in the ongoing negotiation of meaning. Furthermore, we understand these virtues to be at the core of pedagogies that seek to reframe student-teacher relations by giving students voice and stake in their own education. By framing translingual writing in terms of action, agency, and pedagogy, advocates of a translingual approach fall within the tradition of educators who view learning as the ability to access and contribute to the production of knowledge.

Through criteria-mapping activities, then, we see potential pathways into discussions of translingual pedagogy. One pathway is through a focus on the validity of rubrics used in writing assessment. From a validity standpoint, students must understand the terms and concepts by which they will be evaluated; however, rubrics are often rendered in the discourse of teachers, a discourse that may be detached from students' understanding and frame of reference. By inviting students into the development of the assessment measure—in much the same way teachers are invited to discuss program-wide assessment measures—we can take steps toward ensuring that students, particularly those for whom English is not a home language, understand and have more of a stake in the discourse of their own evaluation. Such a practice can be especially important given that many students may be unfamiliar with the expectations of US composition pedagogies. As Yuching Yang (2017) has found, some students who learn English as an additional language outside the United States are surprised writing in the United States is taught as a stand-alone subject for all students, including native speakers of English, and without explicit attention to language learning. Making expectations of the writing course and each writing assignment visible and negotiable can be of serious value for students who are unfamiliar with writing as distinct from language learning. Moreover, according to Broad (2003), "Assessments should *improve* performance," not simply serve as mechanisms for sorting and ranking (9; emphasis added). Inviting students to share in the development of such assessment tools can be a strategy for supporting ongoing writing development rather than judging post hoc the development a teacher hopes to have occurred.

Criteria-mapping activities as we conceive them open up a second pathway into translingual pedagogy by weaving the negotiation of language differences directly into the fabric of the curriculum. In this way, language negotiations are not an afterthought, tacked onto a "language-neutral" curriculum—rather, such negotiations *are* the curriculum. In other words, both activities we discuss are concerned with identifying the highly situated nature of meaning making and moving to the center the moments of negotiation that result. Achievement of such a pedagogy, we believe, relies not on *telling* students about negotiation and difference but on actually negotiating language, curriculum, and assessment with students. In short, this pedagogy aims toward, as Canagarajah puts it, developing competence through sustained practice. Ultimately, through criteria mapping, students are positioned to take active roles in developing awareness of the contingency of norms, developing strategies for negotiating them, and shaping the curriculum in formative ways.

Below, we describe two criteria-mapping activities that seek to render students' voices the basis of classroom dynamics. We see these activities as linked because they follow a procedure similar to the one outlined by Broad (2003): the activities (a) elicit ideas directly from students, (b) render those ideas visible so they can become grist for debate, and (c) use that thinking to shape the curriculum in some substantive way. Just as Broad considers program assessment to be incomplete without the voices of the teachers who are doing the assessment, we understand the writing curriculum to be incomplete without the voices of the participating students themselves.[1]

THE CONTEXT

We adapted Broad's notion of criteria mapping for two first-year writing courses designed specifically for linguistically diverse students. Both courses were delivered through the Department of English at Arizona State University (ASU)—a large, public US university, which serves mainly Arizona residents but also serves a large population of international students. We came to teach these first-year writing courses while enrolled as doctoral students in ASU's rhetoric, composition, and linguistics PhD program. As doctoral students new to teaching multilingual composition at ASU, we elected to enroll in a practicum offered through ASU's writing program in which writing teachers are mentored to teach courses for multilingual writers. As part of the practicum, we participated in weekly meetings with other teachers throughout the program, discussing literature on pedagogy and sharing teaching experiences during the sixteen-week term. The general structure of the curriculum, including the formal writing projects, was predetermined by the program administrator; however, teachers were invited to modify the curriculum as needed to develop daily lessons, activities, and assessments.

Dan taught ENG 107: First-Year Composition for Multilingual Writers, which was the first course of a two-course sequence of first-year composition (FYC). The class consisted of sixteen linguistically diverse students from China and Saudi Arabia and one student from Turkey. The major writing projects included a personal narrative on identity and representation, an analysis of creative risk taking in writing, and a researched analysis of transnational flow of some pop-culture phenomenon. Emily taught WAC 107: Introduction to Academic Writing for Multilingual Writers, which was designed for students who have relatively low placement test scores. Emily's class consisted of nineteen linguistically diverse students primarily from China, with others from Brazil, Korea, and the United Arab Emirates. The major writing projects included a literacy narrative, a descriptive essay on a community tradition, and a cultural critique of transnational food.

For both classes, in place of bound textbooks, we drew from a variety of online resources, including open-source digital texts, the Purdue Online Writing Lab, and other media related to language, writing, and topics linked to each writing project. The resources were used mostly as homework readings meant to prompt informal nightly writing assignments and in-class discussions. By the end of the semester, our students had crafted about fifteen pages of polished writing in formal projects and ten pages of informal writing in homework and in-class assignments.

ACTIVITY 1: THE RUBRIC AS DYNAMIC ASSESSMENT AND AGENDA SETTING

Dan's activity involved using a rubric as a heuristic to facilitate discussions with students about expectations and assessment criteria for the first formal writing assignment of the semester (see appendix 2.A for complete rubric). Additionally, class members' ongoing use and focused discussions of the rubric made visible divergent interpretations of it, which, once articulated, helped guide the direction of daily lessons. This activity mirrored in microcosm Broad's more general project of orienting a program around a shared articulation of values. Instead of an entire program, Dan's activity occurred within the bounds of a single section of multilingual composition.

The rubric was integrated into the classroom alongside the first formal writing project. Adapted from assessment criteria Dan had used in previous semesters teaching writing classes populated by mostly native English-speaking students, the rubric was described to the class as provisional—as a starting point for discussion—with the expectation that it would be modified for the multilingual audience as diverse interpretations of the rubric bubbled to the surface. Students were given the rubric and were asked to use it as a lens to analyze various samples of student writing from previous semesters, which Dan provided. This approach was intended to help students see the ways the terms signified, as the class linked the rubric's language to specific surface features of the sample texts.

After using the rubric to analyze and discuss sample student papers, the class was asked in subsequent meetings to turn their analysis to the writing of their fellow class members during peer review. This step aimed to help students bring an informed understanding of the terms of assessment into conversation with peers, those who had a clear stake in the ways those terms were understood and put to use. Along the way, students were encouraged to discuss with one another the terms of the rubric as Dan circulated throughout the room to prod and sometimes participate in those conversations.

The rubric was also used to facilitate discussions of drafts during student-teacher conferences. Prior to the conference, students were asked to engage with the rubric by marking any terms or phrases they did not fully understand and to bring the marked-up document to the conference prepared to discuss. During the conference, Dan drew on language from the rubric to talk with students about their written drafts. In that setting, students again experienced how the language of the assessment worked on a reader. For example, students commonly brought up terms that reflected Dan's singular perspective and his inevitably subjective readerly expectations. Such troublesome terms and phrases included statements like "the essay tackles an important issue" and the essay "finds a unique or interesting angle into the discussion." For these kinds of expectations to be met, they would have to be more clearly defined and illustrated. To be more clearly defined, a familiarity with Dan's frame of reference would be required, and thus so would explicit explanations and illustrations.

Other difficult terms signaled concepts incompatible with students' prior understandings. For example, the term "storytelling" was used in the rubric to refer to writing that did not reflect any strategic arrangement but followed a seemingly meandering "one damn thing after another" structure. Essays that followed this meandering pattern would be considered "weak," according to the rubric. But for some students, storytelling had associations that did not register as infelicitous or bad writing. In fact, since the writing assignment asked students to explore and describe personal experiences, storytelling seemed in a sense to be at the heart of the project. This opened up the possibility for discussions about how students understand stories, how they experience stories in their lives, and how stories might be used in different ways for different purposes. This type of confusion between teacher and student, subtle though it may have been, presented an opportunity for conversation beyond surface-level correctness or conforming to predetermined norms. It presented a way to negotiate linguistic representations of meanings tied to deeper, embodied experiences.

Some difficult terms students indicated were so foundational to the course they warranted the attention of the entire class. For example, multiple students indicated being unsure about the term "audience" in the rubric. Given that the composition course was grounded in rhetoric, the concept of audience was a key aspect of course outcomes. To address confusion about the concept of audience, Dan used a "collaborative planning" invention strategy (Flower et al., 1994) in which the class as a whole read and interrogated a single student's essay and asked probing questions about the writer's intended audience. The specific questions by real-life readers helped bring to life the notion of audience in a way Dan's rubric and prior instruction had not. Students also found it alarming that the rubric assumed writers had crafted each individual sentence of the final draft of the essay. To address students' surprise at the level of detail with which they had to consider their prose, Dan assigned a sentence-inventory task in which students chose two troublesome paragraphs in their own essays, listed each sentence as a single line in a new electronic document, and worked to clarify their claims, supporting information, and internal transitions and signposts. Both lessons, while not uncommon in writing classes, were important in this multilingual context for the way they allowed the curriculum to flex in response to students' voices.

Throughout this extended activity, students had a chance to become acquainted with the assessment tool, voice their own understanding, share that understanding with fellow class members, and participate in the collective negotiation of course expectations. A direct consequence of this activity was a curriculum that more accurately responded to the understanding and expectations of the students and the instructor. In the end, the rubric served various functions. At times, it was a hypothesis on Dan's part, a "working theory" (Flower 2002, 271) concerning what students knew, what Dan as the instructor could reasonably assess, and what students needed to improve at any given time. But as with any hypothesis, the rubric was subject to rivals and refinement, allowing Dan to learn from students and, with them, to modify expectations and goals. At other times, the rubric served as a conversation piece, a way to facilitate discussion about the assignment, the broader aims of the course, and the ways students could productively insert themselves into its proceedings. A crucial feature of the activity was that the pressure to conform cut both ways: students were pressured to adapt to the rubric as was the instructor to the students' feedback. The direction and magnitude of those pressures was directly influenced by ongoing two-way negotiation.

ACTIVITY 2: DEFINING AND (TASTE) TESTING AUTHENTICITY

Emily's activity was a communal negotiation of the term *authenticity* with students in her class, a process that resulted in a shared definition and set the stage for further scrutiny, critique, and development of the term's definition as students applied it in various contexts. The activity was the first step in a writing project that asked students to investigate the authenticity of a local restaurant's fare and to make a claim about that restaurant or the idea of authenticity using their firsthand experience as evidence. Students were invited to choose any restaurant they could easily visit from campus, but most chose to visit a restaurant that claimed to serve food from their home countries.

On the day she introduced the writing project, Emily wrote *authentic* on the board. All the students were asked to write down their own definitions of the word on a piece of paper. Some students used electronic translators, some discussed the meaning with a friend, and others wrote something down without consultation. Emily initially made a space for language negotiation by encouraging students to use their first language as a starting point; thus, prior to group negotiation of authentic, students had space to bring their own linguistic resources to bear on the task.

Emily then asked students to write their definitions on the board. When the board was filled, the class looked at the collection of definitions together to find similarities and differences. At this point, Emily's adaptation of Broad's criteria mapping was particularly helpful. By identifying similarities and differences, the class was able to list the criteria needed for a comprehensive class definition of authentic—that is, to list what they valued in a definition of authentic. Students then negotiated the criteria by arguing on behalf of their own definitions. To make room in the negotiation for the students who did not normally speak in class, Emily read their definitions aloud during lulls in the conversation and asked the authors to explain their reasoning, at times drawing on input from other members of the class in order to avoid foisting too much pressure on any one student. The result was a lively debate pitting what the class deemed necessary criteria against superfluous ones and discussion of what authentic means in different countries and contexts.

Several students made arguments for requiring not only that the food taste and look certain ways but also that the price and atmosphere of the restaurant reflect the places the food supposedly represents. Other students countered by saying authenticity should reflect the ingredients and tastes of the places where the food is served. By the end of the discussion, each student's definition had been considered and brought into the negotiation. As a class, students determined a provisional list of criteria any authentic restaurant must have in order to be considered as such. Most of the students took photos of the board, which was covered in definitions, links, and lists, in order to have a visual record of the shared criteria. Emily took one as well so she would be able to use that exact list of criteria in the grading process.

The agreed-upon definition of authentic served as a stable touchstone for Emily and the class when the students began testing and writing about their chosen restaurants. Students had a list to take with them to the restaurant, and they could go through each criterion point by point in their analysis. There was potential for a set of very similar essays because the stability of the class definition could have become rigid. Instead, Emily was happy to find, students seemed confident enough in understanding the key term and purpose of the assignment that they were willing to destabilize the definition in their final drafts. Many students stuck to the criteria established on the first day, but several concluded that while the restaurants they visited did not meet all the criteria listed, the criteria they did meet weighed more than the ones they did not. These students were purposeful in choosing to alter their definitions and were careful to detail in the descriptions why they made the choices they did.

In the end, this activity provided a chance for negotiation of the English language, but it also provided a chance for negotiation of the assignment itself. Emily found these opportunities challenging and enticing for two reasons. First, because the central focus of the assignment was on the word authentic, there was a need to discuss as a class what the definition of the term should be and how different definitions could be merged and negotiated into one. Second, because the assignment required language negotiation in order for students to be successful, Emily was able to facilitate a discussion using Broad's proposal as the basis for a dynamic mapping of the criteria for authentic and the assignment itself. By creating the criteria for what can be considered authentic, the students knew exactly what they were testing for their projects and that the other students were conducting the same test. This also meant any changes an individual student made had to be carefully explained. As the teacher, and soon-to-be evaluator, Emily knew everyone understood the assignment.[2]

OPPORTUNITIES FOR LEARNING AND ENHANCED PEDAGOGICAL DESIGN

In both activities, the negotiation of language played a central role in the unfolding of the curriculum. In activity 1, negotiation of evaluative terms found in the rubric spurred discussion of key concepts and expectations and influenced daily lessons. In activity 2, the negotiation of terms *was* the assignment, a writing project that lasted several weeks. As instructors, we are in a position to offer insight into the learning opportunities these activities provided and the ways they supported our pedagogical aims. Below, we list the opportunities we believe have surfaced as a result of adapting the idea of criteria mapping in the multilingual composition classroom.

First, students were alerted to the fact that words, when detached from context, are indeterminate and therefore in need of narrowing, testing, and careful explication. For example, Emily's class explicitly foregrounded the varied and messy significations of the term authentic. By making visible the students' multiple definitions of authentic and working together to pin down a tentative set of criteria (before explicitly testing it), students witnessed firsthand the capacious field of possibilities. Dan's class, when reading through the rubric, found themselves focusing on decontextualized and nebulous grading terms that needed additional context before students knew how to use them. By spending time gaining fluency in the discourse of the rubric, the class made explicit their concerns about how they were graded and had their concerns validated in the discussion of (and in) those terms.

Second, students practiced strategies for negotiating linguistic differences through their speaking and writing. For example, in activity 1, Dan's students worked orally with peers and with their instructor to describe how terms from the rubric aligned with (or failed to align with) textual features of written essays. In activity 2, Emily's students gained practice negotiating differences of meaning, orally at first and then in their formal written projects. In each case, students' own voices were injected into the conversation and genuinely engaged, leading to significant consequences in the context of instruction. In this way, language norms became not draconian regulations but tentative frames of reference, entry points into much more interesting and useful discussions of how language works and how students can wield their powers of negotiation more effectively.

Third, in both activities, assessment of students' writing was strengthened by a rubric that was tethered to the context of instruction in various ways. In activity 1, Dan's students had the opportunity to respond to murky terms abstracted in the rubric, and, therefore, assessment was part of the ongoing classroom conversation. In activity 2, by virtue of its initial design, Emily felt confident students understood the criteria of the assignment and how they wanted to approach it, and she felt more confident she could fairly judge how well individual students responded to the assignment because they had all negotiated its language. Furthermore, assessment was used as a way to improve performance rather than only as a summative judgment.

It is worth stating explicitly that our use of criteria mapping does not precisely correspond with Broad's. Broad's approach asks teachers in a writing program to examine student texts in an effort to identify and articulate the values of writing program teachers. Once identified, those values are then used to structure the assessments used throughout the program. Our approach is bounded by the classroom rather than an entire writing program, with the aim of inviting students (rather than program teachers) into the negotiation of values reflected in the discourse surrounding classroom assignments and assessments. Despite these different perspectives, we have found it fruitful to extrapolate principles and practices from Broad's work and to link them to Canagarajah's views of translingualism. By bringing criteria mapping into conversation with translingualism, our attention has been drawn to concerns shared by both lines of inquiry—including the instability of meaning as it emerges through negotiations among interlocutors and the need for pedagogies that accurately reflect how language is used and meaning produced, thereby helping ensure more valid, fair, and just classroom practices.

ADAPTING CRITERIA-MAPPING ACTIVITIES FOR INTEGRATED CLASSROOMS

Criteria-mapping activities can prove useful in a variety of classroom environments, but it may be the case that native English-speaking students are less inclined than language learners to adopt a critical orientation to language and meaning making. For example, adapting activity 1, Dan found native English-speaking students can feel all too comfortable with their working knowledge of the terms and concepts often found in rubrics—an unsurprising observation, perhaps, given many students' years of experience with standardized assessment conventions. Nonetheless, despite that prior knowledge (or perhaps because of it), students can find it challenging to discuss with precision particular discursive and textual features in relation to grading criteria.

To ensure students are making the most of the chance to negotiate a collectively developed rubric, then, Dan has found it helpful to push native English-speaking students to link specific features of their written texts to specific elements of the rubric, a process that has helped highlight misunderstandings and differing expectations that otherwise might have gone unnoticed. It may also be productive to ask students to develop the rubric themselves by reading sample essays and identifying values, much in the way Broad describes with teachers.

Adapting activity 2, Emily experienced more nuanced complications while teaching a class that included mostly native speakers of English and a sole bilingual student. Specifically, Emily's class struggled with tasks that demanded a high degree of metalinguistic awareness. When asked to create definitions of authentic, most students had difficulty conceiving of the term beyond its dictionary definition, and some went so far as to question the very usefulness of the activity itself. For many students, language and meaning were simply not subject to negotiation. Such monolingual assumptions influenced class discussions, as Emily found herself needing to work harder to elicit productive contributions from students. For example, because many in the class had trouble articulating unique definitions on their own, Emily encouraged students to seek established definitions across multiple dictionaries. This approach helped generate the variety needed to get a productive discussion off the ground and thus compose a shared definition of authentic.

Ultimately, adapting activity 2 for a different student population required that Emily shift its focus. For multilingual students, the assignment focused on practices that drew from a prior-existing metalinguistic awareness. For native English speakers, the assignment had to prioritize the process of dislodging entrenched monolingual assumptions by raising students' metalinguistic awareness. In fact, Emily found her multilingual students were uniquely advantaged because of their intuitive awareness of the provisional nature of linguistic norms. Teachers planning to adapt the activities described above would do well to note that students' different orientations to language norms may significantly affect the ways the assignment is interpreted and the outcomes that are possible.

CONCLUSION

Including students in the ongoing negotiation of assessment and assignment procedures seems to further the agenda Broad advocates—namely, increasing the quality of assessments by way of ground-up, democratic methods. In this way, we see the above activities as a logical extension of

Broad's project. The need for valid assessments comes into even sharper focus when we consider the increasing linguistic diversity of our composition classrooms. As more and more linguistically diverse students enter classrooms in English-dominant environments, it is crucial that teachers thoroughly and critically examine the beliefs and assumptions reflected in their pedagogical materials and the methods by which those intersect with the plurality of beliefs and assumptions represented by such linguistically sophisticated student populations.

APPENDIX 2.A

GRADING RUBRIC FOR MULTILINGUAL WRITING CLASS

Criterion #1: The essay advances a thesis about creative risk taking in writing
- Strong: The essay tackles an important issue related to creative risk taking and finds a unique or interesting angle into the discussion. The writer sticks closely to the thesis throughout, unless a deviation is warranted and clearly signaled.
- Adequate: The writer articulates a thesis or central claim, which serves as a guide for the piece as a whole. However, the writer may lose sight of the thesis at some points in the essay or may not make clear what is at stake.
- Weak: It is not clear what the essay aims to achieve, and there does not seem to be much at stake for the writer or reader.

Criterion #2: The essay uses summary and supporting evidence
- Strong: The writer grounds claims in quoted text from the published pieces under examination. Quotations are contextualized with rich background information and nicely tied back to the essay's thesis. The writer quotes selectively and strategically for high impact.
- Adequate: The writer grounds most key claims in quoted text from the published pieces under examination. Quotations may not be fully contextualized, putting too much of an interpretive burden on readers who may have to guess at meanings.
- Weak: Few claims are grounded in textual evidence. The writer shows little effort to contextualize quotations, perhaps out of inattention.

Criterion #3: The essay is strategically organized with an audience in mind
- Strong: It is clear that the writer has taken care to arrange the essay according to some logic, be it chronological, thematic, cause-effect, etc. That organization clearly helps to move the thesis along in a

deliberate way. Transitions and signposts are used effectively to link ideas, which an audience would find helpful.
- Adequate: The writer shows signs of having deliberately arranged the content of the essay, which facilitates reading for the most part. Paragraphs may have clear focuses, but be disconnected from one another or disjointed somehow. The essay would benefit from more attention to transitions.
- Weak: The essay does not seem deliberately structured with a reader or particular audience in mind. The writer may seem to slip into storytelling without a clear direction or purpose. Other types of arrangement are clearly possible but not explored by the writer.

Criterion #4: The manuscript is edited and polished for submission
- Strong: The final submission is cleanly formatted and edited. Most important, grammatical, mechanical, and formatting choices improve the reading experience. It is clear that the writer has attended to the text at the word level.
- Adequate: The final submission is deliberately formatted and edited. For the most part, grammatical, mechanical, and formatting choices do not take away from the message being conveyed. Some atypical surface-level features may be distracting rather than provocative.
- Weak: Grammatical, mechanical, and formatting choices suggest inattention, or even complacency, and may limit the ability of readers to follow along.

APPENDIX 2.B

IN SEARCH OF AUTHENTICITY IN TRANSNATIONAL FOOD RESTAURANTS

In the era of globalization, even food transcends regional, national, and cultural boundaries. In the process, however, recipes are modified to accommodate the local taste and the availability of ingredients. Restaurants that serve transnational food that originated in another country are abundant. Some of them claim to serve "authentic" food while others are unabashedly localized. Yet others market themselves as "fusion" restaurants, deliberately combining features of different traditions to create a new cuisine. One restaurant chain even serves "immigrant" Italian cuisine. In this project, we will critically examine the notion of authenticity. By taking a close look at the transnational flow of food and how different cuisines are transformed in the process, we will explore the following questions: Who can claim to be authentic and on what basis? Who decides what is authentic? How does the food industry use the notion of authenticity? How does the notion of authenticity affect you? Why does authenticity matter? What is authenticity anyway?

ASSIGNMENT

For this project, write a cultural-critique essay exploring the notion of authenticity—its possible meanings and significance—in today's global society. Your essay can take the form of a number of different genres, including a food-blog entry, a magazine article, a feature article in the lifestyle section of a newspaper. The appropriate length of the essay will depend on the genre you choose (and your instructor's guidelines). A cultural-critique essay is different from a restaurant critique: the focus is not to describe and evaluate the restaurant; instead, it focuses on the notion of authenticity—how it is defined and used as well as how it affects the restaurants, customers, and people who are associated with the country or culture.

To get started with your cultural critique, find a local restaurant that serves transnational food—anything from pizza and tacos to sushi and egg foo young. Then consider the following questions: What kind of restaurant is it? Is it associated with a country or ethnicity (e.g., Chinese) or a specific region or community within the country (e.g., Szechuan)? Is it a local restaurant or a chain restaurant? How does it play up or down the country or culture it is associated with and to what end? How do the quality and presentation of dishes compare to those served in the country of origin? Who prepares the food? Who serves it? Who comes to eat it? How does the restaurant describe itself in the literature—e.g., menus, signs, ads, and websites? What language is being spoken at the restaurant? What language is being used for the signs, menus, web pages, and other texts? How do customers and critics describe the restaurant and the quality of service and food in restaurant reviews? What do the local customers say about the restaurant and its food? What do people from the original country or culture say? What would you say?

To answer these questions, you will need to collect data from various primary sources. You can examine the website and ads for the restaurant to analyze how it markets itself. You can read and analyze various reviews and comments that are posted online. You can also visit the restaurant to observe the facility, people, and food. Consider taking pictures of the food, signs, and other objects to enhance the presentation of your ideas. You may also consider interviewing the restaurant owner and workers, as well as some of the customers. (Be careful not to interfere with the business.) Another possibility is to survey groups of people (e.g., customers who are not familiar with the country or culture, or those who are associated with the country or culture) about their views, preferences, and experiences with a specific restaurant or a cuisine.

LEARNING OBJECTIVES

In this project, you will learn to

- conduct primary research (e.g., observations, interviews, and surveys) as a source of knowledge;
- understand how values and practices transcend national and cultural boundaries;
- understand how cultural identities are represented and used to establish credibility (*ethos*) for businesses and how those uses might affect the image of the country or culture;
- describe cultural artifacts and practices to bring out their underlying values and assumptions;
- explore the significance of cultural values and assumptions;
- develop the awareness of your own language- and literacy-development processes.

PROCESS GENRES

Here are a few process genres that might help you develop ideas for the cultural-critique essay:

- a brief proposal stating which cultural site (i.e., restaurant) you are going to focus on as well as what kind of data are going to be collected and how;
- a field note describing the site of observation, various artifacts, people, and behavior in nonevaluative language;
- reflections and comments on the field note;
- an interview guide listing the main questions and possible follow-up questions you want to ask during the interview;
- interview notes stating the key information from the interviews and phrases that can be used in direct quotations;
- interview transcripts from audio- or video-recorded interviews (if any);
- photographs of cultural artifacts or practices.

AUDIENCE

The primary audience for this piece will be readers who are interested in concepts such as authenticity, identity, and ownership, as well as those who are interested in talking about food. They may also include people who are fascinated by different countries and cultures, or people who do not appreciate cultural differences but enjoy transnational food anyway. The audience could be your classmates who are also investigating the notion of authenticity in transnational food, but if you look around, you will find various knowledge communities where people ask these questions for various reasons.

GENRE OF CULTURAL-CRITIQUE ESSAY

A cultural-critique essay is a type of writing that generates insights into shared values and assumptions among a group of people by examining artifacts and practices that are associated with them. The most obvious examples of artifacts and activities are found in cultural festivals and holiday celebrations, as well as rituals such as weddings and funerals. Some of the most profound insights, however, are often hidden in ordinary activities, such as eating, shopping, and even sleeping.

A cultural-critique essay usually begins by introducing an artifact or practice and by posing a question or by stating a claim about its significance and meaning. The essay then provides an overview of the artifact or practice followed by descriptions of details that are related to the question raised in the introduction. Although a cultural-critique essay requires the ability to describe the artifact or practice, the description itself is not the most important part. The heart of the essay will be the discussion of the significance and meaning of the artifacts and practices. Through such analysis, the essay should reveal some of the tacit values and assumptions of a social group and discuss implications of those values and assumptions.

GRADING CRITERIA

- The writer focuses on the notion of authenticity through primary research into transnational food throughout the project.
- The introduction helps the audience become familiar with the artifact and/or practice being analyzed.
- The thesis makes a claim about authenticity based on the primary research and addresses the significance of the artifact's/practice's meaning and the shared values of those who use that artifact/practice.
- The writer uses the appropriate conventions for the genre they have chosen.
- The writer shares detailed examples from at least one primary source to support the claims made in the thesis.

- The body of the project discusses the values of the group that uses the artifact/practice and the implications of those values.
- The conclusion wraps up the project by reminding the audience why it is important and asking the audience to consider something new about authenticity through the lens of transnational food.
- The project is written in MLA format.

NOTES

1. It is important here to point out affinities between topics discussed here and research in composition studies that has addressed fairness and equity in writing education, particularly writing assessment. For example, Asao Inoue (2004) advocates a "community-based assessment pedagogy" that invites students to "take control of all the writing and assessment practices of the class, including . . . the creation of assessment criteria, rubrics, and writing assignments" (210). Elsewhere, Inoue (2014) argues that writing assessments in diverse college classrooms can be tools that push "the teacher and student to investigate, research, and negotiate the expectations of the local [Standard Edited American English] and the student's discourse, and even to question what 'error' means in each discourse" (346). Similarly, Mya Poe (2012, 2013) highlights the need for fairness in writing assessment, advocating classroom practices grounded in the rich complexities of local conditions. Becoming familiar with this research only after having developed the present chapter has led us to recognize deep resonances with the activities discussed herein, especially the importance of inviting students to negotiate the terms, and indeed the very purposes, of writing assignments and assessments.
2. For the sake of clarity, it may be helpful to note that Emily's class used criteria mapping in the early stages of the writing project to define and stress test a particular term. Emily did discuss grading criteria with her students during the drafting process, as is typical of her classes, but we do not emphasize those discussions here because they did not involve criteria mapping.

REFERENCES

Broad, Bob. 2003. *What We Really Value: Beyond Rubrics in Teaching and Assessing Writing*. Logan: Utah State University Press.

Canagarajah, Suresh A., ed. 2013. *Literacy as Translingual Practice: Between Communities and Classrooms*. New York: Routledge.

Flower, Linda. 2002. "Intercultural Knowledge-Building: The Literate Action of a Community Think Tank." In *Writing Selves/Writing Societies*, edited by Charles Bazerman and David R. Russell, 239–79. Fort Collins, CO: WAC Clearinghouse.

Flower, Linda, David L. Wallace, Linda Norris, and Rebecca Burnett, eds. 1994. *Making Thinking Visible: Writing, Collaborative Planning, and Classroom Inquiry*. Urbana, IL: NCTE.

Inoue, Asao B. 2004. "Community-Based Assessment Pedagogy." *Assessing Writing* 9 (3): 208–38.

Inoue, Asao B. 2014. "Theorizing Failure in Writing Assessments." *Research in the Teaching of English* 48 (3): 329–51.

Poe, Mya. 2012. "Fairness and Race in Digital Writing Assessment." In *Digital Writing Assessment and Evaluation*, edited by Dànielle Nicole DeVoss and Heidi A. McKee. Logan: Utah State University Press, Computers and Composition Digital Press.

Poe, Mya. 2013. "Re-Framing Race in Teaching Writing Across the Curriculum." *Across the Disciplines* 10 (3). https://clearinghouse.colostate.edu/atd/race/poe.cfm.

Poe, Mya, Asao B. Inoue, and Norbert Elliot, eds. 2018. *Writing Assessment, Social Justice, and the Advancement of Opportunity*. Fort Collins, CO: WAC Clearinghouse.

Yang, Yuching. 2017. "A Theoretical Framework for Exploring Second Language Writers' Beliefs in First-Year Composition." PhD diss., Arizona State University.

3
UNITY IN DIVERSITY
Practicing Translingualism in First-Year Writing Courses

Ming Fang and Tania Cepero Lopez

INTRODUCTION

With changing perceptions of language(s), literacies, and students, the tacit policy of English Only has been challenged and critiqued by many writing scholars (Canagarajah 2012, 2013; Horner and Lu 2012; Horner and Trimbur 2002; Jordan 2012; Matsuda 2006; Ramanathan and Atkinson 1999; You 2016). Consequently, many of us—writing scholars and instructors—have espoused the translingual approach to writing as one that values language diversity and emphasizes the fluidity, malleability, and discriminatory potential of languages. This approach foregrounds a more agentive use of multilingual repertoires, sensitivity to diversity of norms, and adaptability to change. However, as Dana Ferris (2014) notes, many discussions on translingual orientation remain largely philosophical rather than pedagogical. This chapter aims to contribute to the pedagogical discussion in translingual scholarship by providing a description and analysis of three cases of first-year writing (FYW) instructors who have redesigned their curricula and pedagogical approaches to better serve linguistically diverse students at Florida International University (FIU), the largest Hispanic-serving university in the continental United States. This chapter is also a response to the call for redesigning our curriculum for the multilingual reality (Jordan 2012) at this time of the "multilingual turn" (May 2014).

The redesign of the curriculum at FIU resulted from a faculty-development initiative within our mainstream writing program. As Paul Kei Matsuda (2006) points out, "The vast majority of US college composition programs remain unprepared for second language writers who enroll in the mainstream composition courses" (637), and ours was no exception. As a Hispanic-serving, majority-minority university, we have linguistically diverse writing classes, but most of our largely monolingual faculty had not been exposed to L2 research or L2 best practices.

DOI: 10.7330/9781646421121.c003

Our program viewed this mismatch as a deficiency to be addressed. Therefore, we drafted a proposal for a professional-development program for our writing faculty and teaching assistants with the goal of adapting our first-year curriculum to better serve multilingual students. After the proposal was accepted as part of our university's application for a Department of Education Title V grant, our program launched a multifaceted faculty-development plan in 2011, which consisted of several major components, including online curriculum resources, online training modules, the redesign of the graduate TA-training course, and a series of monthly faculty workshops. Each faculty workshop aimed to provide instructors with additional pedagogical tools to better serve our large population of multilingual students and covered topics such as rhetorical grammar, proofreading strategies, redesigning composition courses for the multilingual reality, treatment of errors, and responding to and assessing multilingual student writing.

In the course of our faculty workshops, we soon noticed that participants—a mix of full-time faculty teaching four writing courses per semester, with each course capped at twenty-five to thirty students, and adjuncts teaching multiple sections across several different local universities and colleges—were appreciative of any pedagogical strategies that helped them become more attuned to the needs of multilingual students, strategies that seemed to also make their teaching more efficient. In other words, the interest balance, perhaps out of sheer necessity, tipped to pedagogical practices rather than theoretical discussions. While in translingual scholarship the conversation has thus far moved from theoretical discussions to an analysis of how to implement pedagogical practices that accord with the translingual orientation, in our local community, the need for pedagogical practices that would assist instructors in meeting at least some of the challenges of teaching a diverse student body drove the conversation early on, with a later move to the theoretical rationale behind those teaching practices, which just happened to align with the translingual approach to writing instruction. Using this framework we started to read and focus on the translingual approach to writing instruction.

In the end, although at the programmatic level we did not intentionally advocate or candidly promote a translingual approach to writing instruction, we observed (and perhaps in some degree encouraged) what we perceived as a rather organic progression towards a translingual orientation in our FYW curricula. At the programmatic level, the push was for curriculum and teaching practices that would support the retention and graduation of our multilingual student population. As faculty members started to redesign their curriculum, each course took a unique shape, filtering through the lens of each instructor's professional interests, as well as their personal linguistic and cultural background. Last and perhaps most important, each curriculum redesign took a strengths-based approach that valued and used the diverse professional interests of our faculty and rich linguistic and cultural resources of our students as strengths and resources, creating more opportunities for both instructors and students to negotiate multiple linguistic resources, making use of any and all assets available to them. As we recreated our course designs, we worked to make our curricula more inclusive by expanding topic and assignment choices while also focusing on language and writing as the subject matter to explore in our classrooms.

In this chapter, we first contextualize the instructor cases by illustrating our institutional and pedagogical context; then, we review related literature and present our own story in relation to the current discussion of the pedagogical practice of translingualism. Following the literature review, we present specific instructor cases that illustrate how faculty took up a translingual approach and translated that into enacted classroom practices. Cross-case discussion is used to compare and contrast instructors' individualized interpretations and enactments of translingual pedagogical practice and the influence of the program initiative on the instructors' pedagogical choices. From our conversations and informal email exchanges with instructors, as well as from our careful review of their teaching materials, we acknowledge that in some cases they do not explicitly, or intentionally even, teach translingual practices or identify their teaching practices and curriculum designs as translingual; in such cases our intention has been to discuss how such practices may indeed be considered translingual and how they align well with the tenets of translingual practices, which, according to Suresh Canagarajah (2013), oppose "product-oriented, monolingual, and norm-based teaching" (7). We offer implications for teaching and faculty training before the conclusion of the chapter. Although we acknowledge that adopting a translingual orientation in teaching will probably continue to pose difficulties, we believe this chapter takes an active step in situating pedagogical implementations of translingualism.

AUTHORS AND INSTITUTIONAL CONTEXT

Both authors of this chapter are multilingual speakers who have worked as full-time instructors in the mainstream writing program at FIU. Our own identities certainly influence our work and the uptake of a translingual approach to writing, as well as our interpretation and analysis of the cases included in this chapter. As multilingual writers ourselves, we are sensitive to pedagogical practices that are inclusive and attentive to the needs of multilingual students. We also acknowledge that our subjective interpretive account does not completely capture the many multilingual realities of our teachers and students. Therefore, we present our own backgrounds for the readers' scrutiny.

Tania Cepero Lopez identifies as a Cuban exile and is a native speaker of Spanish. She left Cuba in 1998, at the age of twenty, and has lived in South Florida since then. In 2007, she earned her MA in English literature at FIU, where she was hired as a full-time instructor. Her experience as an ESL student and writing instructor was, however, somewhat atypical because she had acquired advanced English-language skills before coming to the United States; for example, she neither took ESOL classes nor spoke with a heavy accent. She did experience, however, cultural alienation and encountered the odd request to write in Standard English from faculty members who although well intentioned were not sure how to teach writing in English to an almost "accent-free" bilingual exile. But she also encountered mentors who helped her see her background as an asset rather than a barrier. When she became one of the few multilingual instructors in FIU's writing program, she found herself becoming a more patient reader, as well as a generous, compassionate educator, and was saddened by the pervasive view of ESL students as somehow deficient or unintelligent. But as a young faculty member at FIU, she had the opportunity to learn, from scholars like Paul Kei Matsuda and Dana Ferris, that many of the practices she had intuitively espoused were in fact considered to be both fair and effective for diverse student populations.

Ming Fang came to the United States for graduate study from China. As an international student and a native speaker of Chinese, she experienced the struggles and the triumphs with writing in English, which helped her sympathize and empathize with her multilingual student writers later when she became a writing teacher. Coming to the United States as a language learner, she first held true to the native-speaker Standard English ideal. Like many other language learners, she set her goals to reach native English-speaker levels of writing, trying to suppress her nonnative voice and strip off her accented writing. Like Tania, she also encountered many well-intentioned native English-speaking professors who tried to help her reach her goals, but unintentionally perpetuated the myth of Standard English (Matsuda 2006). Constantly realizing the gap between her own language competency and that of her native English-speaking peers, she felt disempowered, frustrated, and suffocated. It was not until she entered her PhD program that she gradually learned the value of her native language as a resource and her unique writing voice.

Our university, which is an urban, multicampus, designated Hispanic-serving institution (HSI) in Miami, serves over fifty-four thousand students. About 75 percent of our students are classified as members of a racial/ethnic minority. Hispanic students, in particular, comprise 67 percent of our student population. Our large first-year writing program offers over three hundred classes every year to over six thousand students. Despite this high percentage of multilingual students, we only have mainstream writing courses, with no ESL sections. Our mainstream classrooms, however, are not typically composed of native English speakers—the dominant prototypical students in composition studies. Instead, our mainstream students are diverse: most are bilingual.

Given our local context, we endorsed the National Council of Teachers of English's (NCTE) 2014 policy statement on Second Language Writing instruction, which states, in part, that universities must "recognize and take responsibility for the regular presence of second language writers in writing classes, to understand their characteristics, and to develop instructional and administrative practices that are sensitive to their linguistic and cultural needs." We also aimed to further what Bruce Horner (2006) discusses as a "radical shift from composition's tacit policy of monolingualism to an explicit policy that embraces multilingual, cross-language writing as the norm for our teaching and research" (570). The curricular change we discuss in the latter part of this chapter was propelled by the NCTE policy statement, as well as by the shifted view on the teaching goals and by the norm of teaching in FYW courses.

JOINING THE TRANSLINGUAL CONVERSATION

Bruce Horner, Min-Zhan Lu, Jacqueline Jones Royster, and John Trimbur (2011) began a significant theoretical discussion on the translingual orientation to writing instruction, which has been espoused by an increasing number of scholars for its strong appeals to the fluidity and malleability of languages, its advocacy of students' multiple languages as resources, and students' agentive use of those resources in constructing and negotiating meaning. This new theoretical orientation also successfully problematizes the status of English Only and brings new energy and dynamics into the composition classroom. However, many frontline teachers may still ask, "If we don't teach Standard English, what do we teach?" The theoretical discussion to date, although it has advanced our knowledge and understanding of the rich resources our students bring, does not clearly outline specific pedagogical practices.

We are glad to see some scholarly work that models translingual pedagogies (Canagarajah 2015; Sohan 2014); however, many questions practitioners deeply care about remain unanswered, including,

- What does the translingual movement mean for practitioners?
- In what way does the translingual movement solve real classroom teaching problems, such as giving effective feedback to students and teaching them basic rhetorical concepts?
- How can theoretical orientation guide our teaching of the multilingual class?
- How do instructors encourage students to translanguage? Or is it even beneficial to do so?

This chapter not only strives to respond to these questions but also uses individual instructor cases to explore how faculty understand and support language diversity in our classes and how they adapt the FYW curriculum to the needs of our multilingual students.

We offer three accounts of instructors who redesigned their courses to better serve multilingual writers and in the process moved towards a translingual approach to writing instruction that has benefited students as it pushes them to treat language as a living entity, one meant to be negotiated and innovated, not revered in its supposed purest forms. These accounts also help us understand the impact of our institutional efforts on better serving multilingual students.

The program effort on faculty development has resulted in enhanced faculty awareness that multilingualism is our norm and that it is a rich resource for teaching college writing rather than a challenge to be overcome. As our program director, Kimberly Harrison, concludes in her 2017 chapter in *Linguistically Diverse Immigrant and Resident Writers*, faculty have generally indicated more comfort with writing classrooms being spaces where multiple languages are legitimized for different learning purposes. This indicates a shift from thinking of writing classrooms as monolingual spaces occupied by nonnegotiable Standard English to spaces where various languages are allowed to mingle as students grow as writers and rhetors (196).

INSTRUCTOR CASE STUDIES

As we are most invested in exploring how individual instructors in a mainstream composition program understand and enact a translingual orientation in writing instruction, we chose three participants who we believe would best help achieve our goal. We took into consideration the participants' background: gender, education, language, and so on. We see them as representative of the writing instructors in our program and perhaps even of FYW instructors in general. In each case, we solicited teaching materials, including course syllabi, assignment sheets, and student work. As workshop organizers, we also noted their comments during workshops. Additionally, as their colleagues, we had the opportunity to talk with them frequently, either formally or informally, about their approaches to curriculum design, classroom practices, assignments, and so forth. These different channels of communication greatly facilitated our understanding of their perspectives and rationales of course design.

First Instructor: Tania Lopez

Tania, a researcher and participant in this project, began teaching FYW courses at FIU as a graduate teaching assistant in 2006. From her early days as a writing instructor, she understood ESL students could feel alienated by assignments that asked them to write about topics that presupposed a strong knowledge of US culture and found that focusing on discourse communities allowed for a more inclusive classroom experience for both native and nonnative speakers of English. While she was always personally invested in ESL writing instruction, she became strongly interested in translingual rhetoric after participating in the 2013 RSA Summer Institute workshop, "Shifting the Paradigm: Towards a Translingual Rhetoric of Writing," led by Suresh Canagarajah, Maria Jerskey, and Dorothy Worden.

Second Instructor: Nick Vagnoni

Born and raised in Key West, Florida, Nick, whose first language is English, started teaching writing and rhetoric at FIU as a graduate teaching assistant and later worked as a writing consultant at the Center for Excellence in Writing under the mentorship of Dr. Paula Gillespie, who has been nationally recognized as an advocate of using multiple languages when tutoring multilingual students. Although Nick is not a fluent multilingual speaker, he is committed to the teaching of multilingual students; it is precisely from this strong commitment that his interest in translingualism stems. Nick admitted that, because of his background in creative writing and literature, he did not have extensive knowledge about second language learning, which was a strong motivation for him to learn Spanish. He also wanted to experience learning a second language and what it feels like when two language systems coexist in the mind.

Third Instructor: Patsy Warman

Patsy, who self-identifies as a traditional monolingual speaker, began teaching the FYW sequence and worked as a writing center consultant during her graduate career. As a writing center consultant, she was also mentored by Dr. Paula Gillespie and presented a workshop on "Effective Practices and Theories of G1.5 and L2 Writing Consultants on a Diverse Campus." These teaching and tutoring experiences made her fully aware of FIU's cultural diversity, and her interest in translingualism stems from such awareness. She cares deeply about issues related to language differences and the specialized needs of multilingual students.

Though the small number of cases here cannot provide grand generalizations, they are of value in providing richer and fuller specifications, analyses, and interpretations of the complexities of how instructors create spaces in their courses to challenge standard-language ideology, hold the value of cultural and linguistic diversity, and encourage negotiation of language differences.

PRACTICING TRANSLINGUAL PEDAGOGIES: UNITY IN DIVERSITY

This section outlines how the instructors redesigned their first-year composition curriculum and classroom practices to better serve their diverse student populations. In this way, instructors either intentionally or unintentionally created spaces for a translingual approach to writing instruction that was uniquely personal yet grounded in similarly constructed translingual pedagogical principles.

Case Study 1: An Active Advocate for Translingual Teaching

Of all our instructors, Tania has most explicitly used a translingual approach in her curriculum design and writing instruction. In her syllabus for WR I,[1] she borrows from the 2011 work of Horner, NeCamp, and Donahue, explaining that writing and translingual rhetoric is the subject matter that students explore; she explains that the course will aim to further [the students'] knowledge and use of a translingual approach to writing which "sees difference in language not as a barrier to overcome or as a problem to manage, but as a resource for producing meaning in writing, speaking, reading, and listening" (Horner et al. 2011, 303). The syllabus also emphatically invites students to "read with patience, respect for perceived differences within and across languages, and an attitude of deliberative inquiry" (Horner et al. 2011, 304) as they explore the world through a translingual lens.

Tania's syllabus also demonstrates how she works to create opportunities for students to negotiate different linguistic resources and shuttle back and forth between languages or discourses. Instead of establishing a narrow topic focus, she allows students to "explore discourse practices in a discourse community of [their] choice and later practice writing in the discourse of that community." As a nonnative speaker/writer of English, Tania considers the concept of discourse communities an indispensable tool in writing instruction because no matter where we are from, no matter what language we speak in our *casa*, or home, all of us, without exception, navigate multiple discourse communities in our lifetimes. Her stated hope is that as students explore various discourse communities and their practices, they will "further [their] knowledge and use of a translingual approach to writing 'which sees difference in language not as a barrier to overcome or as a problem to manage, but as a resource for producing meaning in writing, speaking, reading, and listening'" (Horner et al. 2011, 303).

In conversations with colleagues, she often explained her goal was to help *all* her students develop translingual competence, to help them see communication as a constant shuttling between and across languages, as a constant negotiation and choice-making process that would have them either deviate from or conform to the dominant discourse within a specific discourse community. In other words, no language or variation is best or worst. They are all assets at our disposal to use or discard, or transform, or innovate.

In another FYW course, WR II,[2] Tania helped students develop translingual competence through grappling with key concepts such as "discourse community" and "discourse practices" (appendix 3.A). She also created opportunities for them to practice shuttling across and between languages, which Canagarajah and other translingual scholars have placed at the center of translingual literacy. Through asking students to "select a discourse community and possible research questions [they would] like to explore in relation to their discourse practices," with the instructor and classmates as their target audience, students were encouraged to use their home languages, mostly Spanish, for group discussions in class. Students were also encouraged to note any translingual practices of Miami local communities and how the discourse practices in students' chosen communities were influenced by different languages or different preferences of language use. Once students became familiar with their chosen community's discourse practices, they constructed a text that was meant for consumption within the community of their choice and were invited to use the existing linguistic resources they had discovered through research. These projects empowered students to enter a linguistically negotiated conversation, listen to multiple voices, and contribute new ideas while also adopting or deviating from what was considered conventional practices in their chosen community.

Tania's assignments and teaching practices indicate openness to individual choices and multiple learning styles. For most assignments, students were given several options in terms of subject matter and rhetorical choices and encouraged to explore their multiple literacies, translanguaging capabilities, and rhetorical sensibilities. Tania considers her pedagogical practices to be deeply influenced by the translingual orientation to teaching, in which students are encouraged to cultivate a sensitivity to linguistic diversity and a "disposition of openness and inquiry . . . towards language and language differences" (Horner et al. 2011, 311). The focus on translingual literacies as the main subject of discussion and research allows students to further develop not only their rhetorical sensitivity, but also what Canagarajah (2013) has called "sensitivity to similarity in difference" (9).

Case Study 2: Joining the Conversation about Language and Multilingualism

Like Tania, Nick believes in the value of students' language repertoire, the value of exploring language and communication issues in FYW courses, and the value of student agency in learning. As a trained creative writer and writing tutor, he has a strong understanding of writing as a process. However, compared with Tania, he does not explicitly identify his teaching orientation as translingual. Nick's curriculum design progressively became more focused on issues of communication, specifically multilingualism. As many translingual scholars have argued (Guerra 2016; Horner, Lu, and Matsuda 2010; Jordan 2012; Lu and Horner 2013), Nick believes multilingualism as a topic of conversation and research can help multilingual students develop both a sense of agency for their own writing projects and a heightened sense of rhetorical sensitivity.

The major projects in his WR I, for example, asked students to explore questions about intercultural or cross-cultural communication and multilingualism. His first writing project, the "Visual Rhetorical Analysis" (appendix 3.B), asks students to analyze two advertisements of their choice that "attempt to sell the same product to two different audiences" and encourages them to "consider ads that target audiences who speak different languages or belong to different cultures or races." In this project, students are sensitized to audiences with different language or cultural backgrounds. Multilingual students are given the opportunity to negotiate linguistic resources and cultural knowledge at their disposal as they choose a text and offer their interpretation of it. In other words, he created a space for students to explore language and cultural differences and then gave them license to negotiate and explain the different visuals as rhetorical artifacts in their rhetorical analyses. By creating this space for exploring differences, and by creating an opportunity for students to negotiate their multiple literacies, he showed them how the use of multiple languages in a classroom is a resource rather than a liability. He also instructed students on dominant discourse practices, as this assignment allowed them to practice composing the kind of thesis-driven, points-to-particulars analytical arguments favored in Western rhetorical traditions. In short, he allowed writers to use all the tools at their disposal as they tackled what in another pedagogical context might have been a difficult genre-focused, US culture– and Standard English–centric writing task.

Another major writing assignment in Nick's WR I course, the textual rhetorical analysis, gives students an opportunity to write on one of the following four opinion pieces about communication and language: *How Language Transformed Humanity* by Mark Pagel, *American "Multilingualism": A National Tragedy* by Franklin Raff, *"English Only" Laws Divide and Demean* by Warren J. Blumenfeld, and *The Right to Understand* by Sandra Fisher-Martins. In this assignment, students are asked to refrain from agreeing or disagreeing with the ideas presented and, instead, asked to "pay careful attention to what the text is trying to convince the audience of, who that audience is, what rhetorical strategies the author uses to persuade their audience, and whether or not [they] think the text is effective." In this way, Nick's assignment embodies Juan Guerra's (2016) version of translingualism, which does not expect students to produce writing that is code meshed but cultivates an awareness of what language does and a more complex view of language and communication. As students move across varied discourse communities, such an awareness helps students become more effective communicators in these communities. From reading, viewing, listening to, and examining works that focus on language and multilingualism, students adopt a critical language awareness (Guerra 2016). Just like Nick, as writing instructors, we want to cultivate among all our students the kinds of critical dispositions to language and a heightened sensitivity to varied rhetorical contexts that exist in students' lived experiences.

While this overview of Nick's course design suggests the alignment of his curriculum with translingual practices—inasmuch as he encourages students to question multiple views of multilingualism and language—it is his first-day icebreaker activity that best illustrates his use of translingual practices. In Nick's own words,

> After we've discussed their definitions of rhetoric for a little while, I tell them to get out a blank piece of paper and take five minutes to make a list of every word that they know. They give me weird looks, which is great. I remind them that no words are off limits, and if they speak more than one language, they should feel free to include words from other languages. After five minutes, they share their experiences in groups, first introducing themselves to one another, and then we discuss it as a class. I ask them how they made their lists, and then I ask them if they were successful in writing down every word they know. I tell them that there are lots of ways to think of rhetoric, but one way is to think of the choices that they make every time they use words (or don't). They're selecting from this vast collection of words every time that they speak, write, text, email, etc. Sometimes I also ask them how this list would have looked if they'd written it five or ten years ago, or how it might look ten years from now. I do this to get them to remember that their language has evolved—some students point out that they've learned English in the last five years; others point out that some words didn't exist five years ago. There's lots of different ways that this discussion can go, but it always seems to get students thinking about language and the choices that they make.

This activity shows Nick's respect for his students' native languages and diverse Englishes, but it also illustrates how he encourages them, kindly and patiently, to negotiate the many languages they use. Perhaps most important, this exercise reaffirms that multiple languages have a place in the writing classroom, that they are assets to use as *all* students strive to further develop their literacy in English. In other words, they are all English learners in their own individual way, and they can all be flexible, open, and active participants in this learning community (Kimball 2015). All students, the activity suggests, are life-long English-language learners and also life-long learners of multiple literacies. In short, this first-day-of-class ritual, very much like Nick's course design, fosters unity in diversity and deconstructs several monolingual orientation myths, such as one language equals one identity or languages are pure and separated (Canagarajah 2013, 20).

Case Study 3: Problem Solving with Paulo Freire
Patsy neither chose language and communication as the course focus nor explicitly engaged translingual practices in her course. This is not to say she is not concerned with monolingual hegemony or, specifically, multilingual students' learning needs; rather, she acknowledged some broad claims of the translingual orientation and designed her specific pedagogical practices based on the needs of the local students and her own professional interests in social justice issues. As a result, she created a WR II course[3] that encouraged students to explore and find solutions for significant problems of social and economic marginalization in their environments. She explained that her course guides students to see how positive changes in the world can be brought about through writing, and she empowers students to utilize writing to craft their own voices in their civic participation. We see how her personal interest in social justice and professional interest in the sociopolitical aspects of writing shape her take-up of a translingual approach in curriculum design and teaching.

In her course redesign, Patsy put her focus on moving beyond "the myth of linguistic homogeneity" (Matsuda 2006) and the dominant discourse of US college composition, which can alienate and marginalize multilingual students. For instance, when working with students, especially multilingual and minority students, Patsy encourages them to find, assert, and celebrate their own unique voices, even though they may also need to learn the "dominant syntax" to bring about changes in their world. As we see it, Patsy creates a focus on empowering multilingual students to recognize the power of their own language in writing.

By focusing on critical thinking in the WR II classroom, Patsy aims to enhance students' multicultural understanding and critical thinking, reading, and writing skills. She uses Paulo Freire's (1996) framework of sociocultural oppression to create a framework for students' research and problem-solving coursework. The focus on critical thinking and social problem solving is clearly explained in her syllabus: "*The term critical thinking is paramount [to this class]. It is not until we become strong critical thinkers—individuals who pose questions and challenge preconceptions—that we can become more powerful problem solvers and argument writers*" (emphasis added). The emphasis of the course design on students' critical thinking is also made clear in the classroom the very first week of class. Patsy explains that Freire's theory helps advance critical thinking: Freire wanted his students to become problematizers instead of memorizers. Freire opposed what he called "the banking method" of education, in which students deposit knowledge in their memory banks and then make withdrawals during exams. With Freire's problematizing method, students, instead of withdrawing knowledge from their memory bank, seek answers to significant questions. On one hand, Patsy helps students concretize important terms we emphasize in the composition classroom, such as *critical thinking*. Such terms are often considered vague and abstract by international students coming from a cultural background that may not encourage the same type of critical thinking, or by resident ESL students who are first-generation college students. On the other hand, by going beyond the banking method of education, Patsy does not simply deposit the conventions of academic writing into students' minds but rather invites her students to examine these conventions and the writer's choices with regard to language use. This approach aligns well with our positioning of translingual writing instruction, which asks of "writing not whether its language is standard, but what the writers are doing with language and why" (Horner et al. 2011, 304).

Throughout the semester, Patsy encouraged students to question power-relation problems in the communities they were familiar with and pushed them to problematize the sociopolitical injustice issues utilizing the concepts and knowledge they discussed and learned in Freire's *Pedagogy of the Oppressed*. She especially resonated with the translingual advocacy that all language practices, including writing, must be seen as "negotiations across asymmetrical relations of power" (Lu and Horner 2011, 586).

Although her course and assignment sheets do not seem to have overt translingual objectives (please see sample assignment in appendix 3.C), we argue she was teaching the course with translingual intentions to help students become more thoughtful about the use of language in understanding and negotiating power hierarchies. For instance, in her low-stake writing tasks, student writers were prompted to make connections between what they learned in Patsy's class and a situation outside the classroom they had experienced (appendix 3.D). The beauty of the assignment is that students found a locale where they could uncover their own voices and write about what was meaningful for them rather than being forced to follow the conventions of academic English. In these low-stake writing tasks, students' lived experiences were validated with Freire's work, which students were encouraged to use for meaning negotiation and meaning making. In our conversation with Patsy, she candidly explained, "[In order to] encourage students' authoritative voice in writing, I hope that in some way, I'm addressing the issue of linguistic social justice here. This is not just for our multilingual students, although, at times, they are the ones who are more vulnerable.

Monolingual students, too, may feel that they do not have enough linguistic resources to write with a strong voice." Patsy hopes to encourage a type of translingual thinking among students that makes it possible for them to learn what linguistic resources they possess and how they may deploy those resources in a meaningful way so they become flexible, open, and active civic participants.

Unlike Tania, Patsy did not explicitly introduce a translingual approach in her course. She also did not put language differences or the universality of linguistic heterogeneity at the center of her course as did Nick. Instead, her design gravitated to a focus on social injustice. Such design strengthens her commitment to supporting linguistically diverse students and developing receptive learning environments to create a space for students to explore communication "as negotiation socially across languages" (Kimball 2015, 68). Her course design aligns well with the core mentality of the translingual orientation: to approach students' linguistic resources positively and to empower students to be strong negotiators in power dynamics.

ADOPTION AND ADAPTATION

As we present the snapshots of these three instructors, we admit we have not presented the whole picture. Rather, we capture here only a part of their individual course designs, the part we hope helps to best illustrate the relevance of each instructor's pedagogical practices to translingual pedagogy. Although Tania, Nick, and Patsy all have their unique strengths and traits as teachers, the three cases we present here are not outliers. In other words, what they did before and after they entered their classrooms may well represent other writing teachers' curriculum redesign and teaching practices; for instance, they all

- empowered multilingual students to develop rather than suppress their voices in writing, a "difference-as-resource" perspective as explained by Canagarajah (2002, 13);
- actively tried to help students develop a heightened rhetorical sensibility that reflects a critical awareness of language as a contingent and emergent rather than as a standardized and static practice (Guerra 2016);
- validated what students bring into the writing classroom and encouraged them to do meaningful writing with what they bring in (Matsuda 2006);
- taught with a translingual attitude that clearly cherishes language diversity and encourages a more sophisticated view of language and literacy (Horner et al. 2011).

These actions and dispositions align with a translingual orientation to writing instruction in their positioning of linguistic diversity as the norm, creation of opportunities for linguistic negotiation, and encouragement of rhetorical dexterity by inviting students into the literacy practices of reading or writing nonstandard forms of English or non-English texts.

As Canagarajah (2015) explains, there is no predetermined pedagogy or specific prepackaged method for a translingual orientation in the teaching of writing. The differences between the cases make this evident. Although we were all influenced by the call from Horner et al. (2011), our implementation has varied. Each instructor's personal and professional interests strongly influenced which writing assignments they thought were meaningful, which paths they took in their course, which translingual principles they valued most, which recommendations made by the translingual scholars they resonated with most, and so on. In this way, a translingual orientation does not mean heralding a revolution that completely obliterates what we are or have been doing as literacy educators; gradual reforms to our curriculum and classroom practices grounded in sound translingual theory may go a long way in supporting students' language diversity as we continue to move away from a monolingual framework and linguistic homogeneity in writing instruction.

CONCLUSION

We hope this chapter, and the syllabi and assignments included, encourages writing instructors to explore and discover the linguistic strengths of their students and encourages them to negotiate with rather than simply surrender to the dominant discourse in academic or any other form of writing. Within this framework of translingualism, there lie many exciting possibilities for teachers to address language differences and celebrate language diversity in ways that work in their own teaching contexts. These case studies point to the benefits of introducing linguistic diversity to students and raising awareness of the multilingual reality of students' own writing contexts, thereby encouraging them to respond to these realities. As multilingual writing instructors ourselves, we feel intuitively drawn into this framework, which values language diversity and the agentive use of language resources. And, while Xuan Zheng (2017) states that translingual identities can be used as pedagogical resources to enact a translingual pedagogy, such translingual pedagogy should not be taken for granted with multilingual instructors. We argue that multilingual instructors and monolingual instructors may use different strategies that stem from their own educational and professional backgrounds. As our case studies indicate, writing instructors do not have to be multilingual to take a translingual approach. Translingualism is intrinsic to all writing and writers (Ray 2015). We encourage all writing instructors to rethink the goals for writing courses, invest in language differences, and conceive new strategies to dispel inaccurate, outdated views of language that may suppress student writers' voices.

To close, in this chapter we have outlined three cases of instructors implementing a FYW curriculum, and in doing so we have worked to achieve two major goals. First, by describing the adaptations to a "core curriculum" in an FYW program, we hope to encourage those frontline practitioners who are interested in enacting broad institutional changes to accommodate a translingual approach. By offering this chapter contribution we believe we are addressing timely and important questions, such as these two: (1) What is presently happening with the translingual approach—in any shape this might take—in our classrooms? and (2) What can we as composition instructors do to move from theory to practice if we believe in the benefits of a translingual approach to our multilingual students?

In doing so, we hope to contribute to the much-needed discussion of teaching strategies and pedagogical values of a translingual approach. Our diverse teaching context provides a good glimpse of what future US composition classrooms may look like, particularly in urban cities. National trends of Hispanic population growth indicate that the nation is becoming more like what we see today at FIU. The current 17 percent of Hispanic population is expected to grow to 31 percent by 2060. Our experiences can shed light on the phenomenon of teaching an increasingly diverse student population by taking the translingual orientation to writing instruction.

Second, going beyond the individual cases, we support the call for training mainstream composition teachers (Ferris, Liu, and Stein 2011; Matsuda, Saenkhum, and Accardi 2013) at the programmatic level. Today's mainstream classroom has become increasingly diverse, and composition teachers should develop their expertise in working with a diverse student body and learn to respect and approach students' diverse backgrounds positively. While we support the ideology of the translingual orientation, we also argue that the implementation of it can and must allow instructors to adopt different curriculum designs and practices so they can build upon their own strengths and enact translingual approaches that fit their own personal interests and professional backgrounds. As Horner et al. (2011) define, "A translingual approach . . . is about the disposition of openness and inquiry that people take toward language and language differences" (311). Through professional training, composition instructors with different professional interests may be able to find their own individually unique ways to foster such a disposition in their courses.

Having a translingual orientation in writing instruction does not simply mean explicitly teaching language difference, an area not all writing instructors feel competent or interested in teaching. As shown in the cases we present, the translingual paradigm can be translated into a wide range of distinct pedagogical practices: some encouraging students to use critical theory as a lens to examine social injustice issues and problematize power dynamics, making students aware of the different resources and outlets they have; some raising students' awareness of the multilingual spaces within which they live every day; some raising students' awareness of the contested privilege of Standard English and explicitly promoting language diversity.

Moreover, the traditional, common goals of writing and rhetoric courses—raising students' awareness of effective written communication and developing students' competence in crafting sound arguments—are retained in these instructors' courses. But new goals that would allow students to honor the power of all language users, to embrace language differences as resources, and to negotiate their own voices in writing are also enmeshed in the curriculum. This is how we interpret our colleagues' translingual approach to teaching linguistically diverse composition classes. It is built upon previous approaches that aim to empower multilingual students, such as the multilingual orientation and the critical-pedagogy orientation, but with an explicit agenda of encouraging and sensitizing students to a more complex view of language and languaging (what language does). Although efforts have been made to illustrate the pedagogical value of the new paradigm, continued discussion on how to translate the basic tenets of translingualism to classroom practices that would empower student writers to negotiate rather than conform to fixed, uniform standards should be encouraged. Also, if as Lu and Horner (2013) argue, "Difference is an inevitable product of all language acts. Hence, all writers face not the dilemma of whether to be 'different' in their writing, but the questions of what kinds of difference to make through their writing, how, and why" (585), the pedagogical practices that would encourage student writers to ponder these questions and make effective "difference" in their writing are well worth further discussion. The efforts made by the contributors of this collection must be extended.

More specifically, we call for pedagogical discussions to bring in student writers, whose "voices, needs, and perspectives," as Shawna Shapiro pointed to in a SLW-CCCC mailing-list discussion (October 1, 2015), "aren't often foregrounded in these conversations about both translingualism and SLW." A translingual approach aims to empower students to be more adept negotiators of language differences and more deliberative inquirers of written discourses. Therefore, the enrichment and development of this new paradigm call for a better understanding of students' perspectives. We believe a translingual approach, with its emphasis on the fluidity of languages and the value placed on students' different language resources, enhances students' rhetorical awareness of the different language resources at their disposal and supports students' learning of writing, especially for those multilingual students or students who are labeled *remedial* or ESL.

APPENDIX 3.A

TANIA CEPERO LOPEZ'S SAMPLE ASSIGNMENT SHEETS
UNIT 1: FOUNDATIONS OF WRITING AND RHETORIC

How to post questions and comments on this document:
1. Highlight the portion about which you have a question/comment.
2. Click on "Insert" tab.
3. Select "Comment."
4. Write text of comment.
5. Click on "Comment" to save post.
6. If you did not sign in before opening document, sign your name so that we know who wrote the comment.

What will you learn?

At the end of this unit, you should be able to

1. demonstrate familiarity with / understanding of rhetorical concepts including rhetoric, rhetorical situation, rhetorical purpose/aim, audience, genre, style, and document design;
2. purposefully incorporate quotations, summary, and paraphrase using attributive tags, quotation marks, and appropriate citation style;
3. employ revision and editing strategies appropriate to the audience and purpose.

How will you learn those skills?

Throughout the class, we will practice composing different types of texts (genres) for different audiences and purposes. This means that for every writing project, you will be provided a specific rhetorical situation to which you will respond with a text. Your work will be evaluated based on how your choices of subject matter, structure, style, and document design furthered or hindered your purpose for your target audience.

Rhetorical Situation 1

Purpose: Why are you writing?

Your purpose as rhetorical aim is to explain the most important rhetorical concepts and writing strategies you've learned throughout the unit. The idea is that as we move forward, your audience will be able to use this handout as a study aid.

Audience: Who are you writing for?

You, the writer in training, are your primary audience for this project inasmuch as you are designing a self-study aid, a text that will help you internalize this new rhetorical knowledge and vocabulary you will need to talk about and analyze texts produced by you and others—your peers and other more experienced writers. You should also keep in mind a secondary audience composed of your peers in this class and future ENC 1101 students.

Genre: What type of text will you build?

I'm charging you with composing a "Survivor's Guide to Writing & Rhetoric I." This brings certain genre expectations to the table. We will discuss this in more detail in class.

UNIT 2: READING RHETORICALLY: THE WRITER AS STRONG READER

How to post questions and comments on this document:
1. Highlight the portion about which you have a question/comment.
2. Click on "Insert" tab.
3. Select "Comment."
4. Write text of comment.

5. Click on "Comment" to save post.
6. If you did not sign in before opening document, sign your name so that we know who wrote the comment.

Objectives: What will you learn?

At the end of this unit, you should be able to

1. demonstrate familiarity with / understanding of rhetorical concepts including rhetorical situation, rhetorical purpose/aim, audience, rhetorical appeals, genre, angle of vision, reading against the grain;
2. recognize the rhetorical strategies and stylistic choices made by experienced communicators;
3. read and summarize another writer's argument succinctly;
4. articulate a clear perspective on the way the assigned text works rhetorically;
5. purposefully incorporate quotations, summary, and paraphrase using attributive tags, quotation marks, and appropriate citation style;
6. employ revision and editing strategies appropriate to the audience and purpose.

How will you learn those skills?

During the next few weeks, you'll compose a response essay, which is one of the most common genres in both academic and professional writing. For writers, the response essay has special value because it allows us to learn new writing strategies. Just like a mechanic might take a car apart to learn to build one, so must a writer learn to "read like a writer," paying close attention not only to what it is written but HOW it is written.

Rhetorical Situation 2

Genre

Your task is to compose what *The A&B Guide* authors call a "blended strong response" that combines reflection and rhetorical critique.

As reflection papers often do, your writing should be "more exploratory, open-ended, musing, and tentative" than a closed-form, thesis-driven argument (109).

As agreed by class, the response could be between 3 and 4 pages long.

What are you writing about?

You will choose **one** of the (translingual) literacy narratives provided below for your response:

Title	Author
"My English"	Julia Alvarez
"One Voice"	Susan Madera
"How to Tame a Wild Tongue"	Gloria Anzaldúa
"No Kinda Sense"	Lisa Delpit
"Superman and Me"	Sherman Alexie
"Mother Tongue"	Amy Tan
"The Absence of Writing or How I Almost Became a Spy"	M. Nourbese Philip
"Why I Write"	George Orwell
"Living in Tongues"	Luc Sante
"Primary Lessons"	Judith Ortiz Coffer

Full texts of all these narratives are posted on Blackboard's "Course Library."

Purpose

Your purpose in writing this response is twofold:

On the one hand, you should share with your readers "how the reading has affected you personally—what memories it has triggered, what personal experiences it relates to, what values and beliefs it has challenged, what dilemmas it poses, and so forth" (Ramage et al. 109).

On the other hand, you should also share with your readers your reaction to and analysis of this text **as a writer** in training. Your goal here is not to discuss every single choice, but rather, as Mike Bunn suggests, to "locate what you believe are the most important writerly choices represented in the text... to consider the effect of those choices on potential readers (including yourself)." As you write about the text as a writer, you can also reflect on "*different* choices the author *might* have made instead, and what effect those different choices would have on readers" (72).

Audience

In writing this response, you should aim to accomplish the goals outlined above for an audience of first-year composition students who may or may not have read or care about the text you are responding to and who may initially be undecided or against your views regarding this text's rhetorical effectiveness.

Document Design and Citation Style

Because we are now entering a more academic genre, I ask that you use either MLA or APA formatting and citation guidelines. Consult *The Everyday Writer* as needed.

Grading Criteria

As I grade your final draft, I will use this Scoring Guide.

How to collaborate in reading/comprehending this document:

As you read,

1. if any questions or comments come up that you'd like to address with the class, please insert them as comments on the Google document;
2. reply or comment on any other comments that your peers post (help each other understand the assignment's rhetorical context and the choices you should make as writers to succeed in this project).

WRITING PROJECT 3: RESEARCH REPORT

Assignment at a Glance: Compose a 4–5-page research report (RR) that presents your research findings to an academic audience in the field of composition/rhetoric.

Audience: Who are you writing for? As you write your research report, imagine that you are writing it for the readers of *Young Scholars in Writing*, which is, as its publishers explain, "a peer reviewed journal for undergraduates." You could also think of your readers as "young scholars" themselves. Young, in this context, "is not a marker of a scholar's age but rather of his or her experience with discursive inquiry in writing, rhetoric, and related topics" (*Young Scholars in Writing*). You can then assume that your readers will

1. have some interest in and knowledge of your research topic (discourse community/discourse practices) and
2. read your text strategically rather than linearly. This means that they'll most likely skim your report and then focus on those sections that seem most relevant to their own research interests (Ramage et al. 740).

Purpose: Why are you writing? In academic discourse communities, research reports are used to "share" new knowledge with other members of the community. Therefore, your RR should present a narrative of your research project, your research methods, and findings. Your main rhetorical aim is to inform, but you must also persuade your readers that your research is sound and worthy of their trust.

Genre: What should your RR include? What are the genre expectations here? As explained in the *A&B Guide to Writing*, research reports are one of the most commonly used genres in scientific research (737), but in the last few decades research reports have also become a common genre in the field of writing studies. Such reports usually combine empirical, online, and library research.

Your research report should have at least the following sections, which are typical in this genre:

Introduction	Explains the problem that has been investigated
Shows importance and significance of problem
Reviews previous studies examining the same problem (called a "literature review") and points to conflicts in these studies or to unknowns meriting further investigation
Poses the research question(s) that have been investigated
Presents researcher's thesis or hypothesis
Methods	Describes how study was done (enables future researchers to replicate the research process)
Discussion of findings	Presents the researcher's analysis of the results
Interprets and evaluates the collected data in terms of the original research question and hypothesis
Speculates on causes of findings
Shows applications and practical and theoretical significance of study
Usually includes a section pointing out limitations and possible flaws in the study and suggests directions for future research
Works Cited or References	Bibliographic listing of cited sources
For MLA guidelines see *The Everyday Writer*, pp. 427–473.
For APA guidelines see *The Everyday Writer*, pp. 479–510.

Learning Goals:

As you complete this project, you will learn to

- employ rhetorical appeals effectively to create presence for a problem;
- describe the problem in ways that appeal to the interests and values of the audience;
- write a strong thesis;
- synthesize the ideas of others into your own work through careful integration of sources;
- employ an effective document design using appropriate layout, clear headings, and visuals;
- use conventions of the discipline and/or target audience your project addresses;
- employ editing strategies appropriate to the audience and purpose.

Document Design: All drafts must follow field-appropriate citation and formatting guidelines. In comp/rhetoric either MLA or APA are widely accepted, so you can use either one. Consult *The Everyday Writer* for MLA and APA formatting and citation guidelines.

Important Deadlines:

Mon. July 29 @ 11:59 PM: Working Draft with Writer's Memo Due
Fri. Aug. 2 @ 11:59 PM: Final Draft with Writer's Memo Due in Assignment Dropbox.

Grading Criteria: Your final draft will be evaluated based on the following scoring guide:

Writer's Memo		
Very effective	Partially effective	Needs substantial work
Closely follows WM's instructions Demonstrates writer's developing self-awareness of their a. strengths b. weaknesses c. rhetorical sensitivity, and d. writing process	Meets most but not all of VERY EFFECTIVE criteria.	Meets very few or none of VERY EFFECTIVE criteria.
10 . . . 9	8 . . . 7 . . . 6 . . . 5	4 . . . 3 . . . 2 . . . 0

Subject-matter choice		
Very effective	Partially effective	Needs substantial work
The writer's research focus is appropriate for the rhetorical situation inasmuch as they have presented -a discourse community (not merely a community) as the focus on the research -clear research question(s), thesis and/or hypothesis about the discourse practices of that DC	Meets most but not all of VERY EFFECTIVE criteria.	Meets very few or none of VERY EFFECTIVE criteria.
10 . . . 9	8 . . . 7 . . . 6 . . . 5	4 . . . 3 . . . 2 . . . 0

Introduction		
Very effective	Partially effective	Needs substantial work
Explains the problem that has been investigated Shows importance and significance of problem Reviews previous studies examining the same problem (called a "literature review") and points to conflicts in these studies or to unknowns meriting further investigation Poses the research question(s) that have been investigated Presents researcher's thesis or hypothesis	Meets most but not all of VERY EFFECTIVE criteria.	Meets very few or none of VERY EFFECTIVE criteria.
10 . . . 9	8 . . . 7 . . . 6 . . . 5	4 . . . 3 . . . 2 . . . 0

Methods		
Very effective	Partially effective	Needs substantial work
Clearly describes how study was done (enables future researchers to replicate the research process)	Meets most but not all of VERY EFFECTIVE criteria.	Meets very few or none of VERY EFFECTIVE criteria.
10 . . . 9	8 . . . 7 . . . 6 . . . 5	4 . . . 3 . . . 2 . . . 0

Discussion of findings

Very effective	Partially effective	Needs substantial work
Presents the researcher's analysis of the results Interprets and evaluates the collected data in terms of the original research question and hypothesis Speculates on causes of findings Shows applications and practical and theoretical significance of study Usually includes a section pointing out limitations and possible flaws in the study and suggests directions for future research	Meets most but not all of VERY EFFECTIVE criteria.	Meets very few or none of VERY EFFECTIVE criteria.
15 . . . 14	13 . . . 12 . . . 11 . . . 10	9 . . . 8 . . . 7 . . . 6 . . . 5 . . . 0

Use of sources

Very effective	Partially effective	Needs substantial work
Writer demonstrates their ability to select, locate, and integrate sources rhetorically. This means that writer -uses sources to enhance the overall persuasive power of the report (this looks at both quantity and quality of sources used) -purposefully incorporates sources through effective summary, paraphrase, and quotation -uses attributive tags (e.g., according to) to separate their ideas from the source's to create context and shape reader's response to sources (A&B Guide 689–93) -cites sources following chosen citation style (MLA or APA) -has avoided intentional or unintentional plagiarism	Meets most but not all of VERY EFFECTIVE criteria.	Meets very few or none of VERY EFFECTIVE criteria.
15 . . . 14	13 . . . 12 . . . 11 . . . 10	9 . . . 8 . . . 7 . . . 6 . . . 5 . . . 0

Rhetorical knowledge

Very effective	Partially effective	Needs substantial work
Overall the writer demonstrates their growing rhetorical awareness by making choices about subject matter, structure, style, and document design that build ethos, pathos, and logos and thus further the author's purpose for the target audience.	Meets most but not all of VERY EFFECTIVE criteria.	Meets very few or none of VERY EFFECTIVE criteria.

10 . . . 9	8 . . . 7 . . . 6 . . . 5	4 . . . 3 . . . 2 . . . 0
Stylistic choices		
Very effective	Partially effective	Needs substantial work
The use of writing and rhetoric field-specific language builds ethos for the writer as a researcher in the field. Academic conversational tone/voice is appropriate for audience and purpose (author creates a persona that fits role as a researcher in the field of writing and rhetoric).	Meets most but not all of VERY EFFECTIVE criteria.	Meets very few or none of VERY EFFECTIVE criteria.
10 . . . 9	8 . . . 7 . . . 6 . . . 5	4 . . . 3 . . . 2 . . . 0
Mechanics/document design choices		
Very effective	Partially effective	Needs substantial work
The creation of meaning is not interrupted nor is the writer's ethos damaged by sentence, spelling, or punctuation errors. The writer builds ethos by following MLA or APA formatting guidelines for layout, font size and type, etc. The writer demonstrates genre awareness by using the expected layout features of research reports (e.g., subheadings clearly differentiating the different sections, double-spaced text, legible font size and type, etc.)	Meets most but not all of VERY EFFECTIVE criteria.	Meets very few or none of VERY EFFECTIVE criteria.
10 . . . 9	8 . . . 7 . . . 6 . . . 5	4 . . . 3 . . . 2 . . . 0

WORKS CITED

MacNealy, Mary Sue. 1999. *Strategies for Empirical Research in Writing.* New York: Pearson.

Ramage, John D., John C. Bean, and June Johnson. 2010. *The Allyn & Bacon Guide to Writing*. Customized for Florida International University. New York: Pearson Learning Solutions.

APPENDIX 3.B

NICK VAGNONI'S SAMPLE ASSIGNMENT SHEET
VISUAL RHETORICAL ANALYSIS

Length: Minimum 1,000 words

Value: 10% of final grade

Purpose: The goal of this assignment is to practice your ability to analyze—to break down and examine—the rhetorical techniques of two advertisements and present your analysis in a clear, specific, closed-form essay.

Assignment: Choose two advertisements (print or video) that attempt to sell the same product to two different audiences and write a thesis-driven essay that both describes the ads in detail and analyzes the rhetorical strategies they're using to sell their products to their audiences. For example, you might choose a car ad aimed at men and one aimed at women; a food ad aimed at teens and one aimed at parents; a clothing ad from the *Miami Herald* and one from *Cosmopolitan*. You might also consider ads that target audiences who speak different languages or belong to different cultures or races. Remember that your analysis should be organized around a thesis that makes a clear, specific claim about these ads. Perhaps you will explore why one ad relies on ethos while another relies mainly on pathos to sell similar products to different audiences. Or perhaps you can make a claim about what you think these ads say about the audiences or cultures they're trying to persuade. Make sure you have chosen ads you feel are complex, with many of the rhetorical elements we've discussed in class and in the readings, such as appeals to logos (logic), ethos (credibility), and pathos (emotions/values). What is each ad trying to get its audience to think and feel? Why?

Audience: Your audience should be your classmates and your professor, but you should assume that your readers have not seen the ads you're analyzing. With that in mind, your ad descriptions must be clear and vivid so that your readers can really understand the ads and the claims you're making about them. Don't be afraid to make strong, arguable claims about the ads, but remember to support those claims with evidence and logical thought. Don't just assume that your audience will know what you mean. Explain yourself.

To help form an arguable, interesting thesis, ask problematic questions about . . .

purpose and audience: Who is the intended audience for each ad? How do you know? What values does each audience hold? What might the context of the ad (where it appears) tell you about the audience?

use of type, layout, color, and image: What effects might these elements have on the ad's audience? What's the relationship between the images and the text?

the appeal to logos, the logic of the ad: Does the ad make sense? Does it have to?

the appeal to ethos and the credibility of the advertiser: Does the ad seem professional? Is it relatable? Is there a celebrity endorsement that might add credibility, for example?

the appeal to pathos: Does the ad try to evoke certain emotions or reinforce certain values? Why?

the effectiveness or ineffectiveness of the ad: Is it persuasive? Why or why not?

the advertiser's cultural perspectives: How does each ad reflect the culture or society that produced it? Does the ad include any popular culture references?

the angle of vision: Is there anything conspicuously absent from the ad? Why?

When evaluating your essay, I will consider the following:

Does the essay's introduction attempt to hook the reader and set up the analysis?

Does the essay contain a clear, specific, and arguable thesis?

meanings of images/text and possible effects on the target audience)?

Are both ads described clearly and thoroughly?

Does the essay supply detailed analysis that logically supports the thesis?

Is the essay clearly and logically organized?

Does the essay show evidence of thorough proofreading and editing?

APPENDIX 3.C

PATSY WARMAN'S SAMPLE ASSIGNMENT SHEET
WRITING PROJECT 2: EXPLORATORY WRITING (20%)

For your second assignment, you will write an exploratory essay. The exploratory essay is a thesis-seeking essay in which you explore—deeply— a problem you previously proposed related to the class theme of social injustice and marginalization. Rather than arguing a particular point of view, your objective in this assignment is to "wallow in complexity" and challenge the common ways of looking at a problematic social issue.

You'll begin, as much good writing does, with a question. You'll do research to come up with a (provisional, or temporary) answer. Then you will critique that answer—by reading against the grain, you will find flaws in the answer. Then you'll ask another question—a more complex question, based on your research and your rejection of your previous answer. You will attempt to answer that question, debunk that answer, and so on. The purpose here is not to find quick answers but to ask really good questions—and as a result, to probe a topic more deeply than you've ever done before. The work you complete in this assignment will be further utilized in your final essay of the semester.

This assignment asks you to fulfill two distinct rhetorical aims, and as such, contains features of both open- and closed-form writing. The first aim is to share the story of your research process. The exploratory essay documents the evolution of your thinking on the subject in a first-person narrative. You will describe your topic generation and initial impressions about the issue and take your reader through the steps of your source selection and evaluation. As you encounter each new source, you will illustrate any changes in your understanding of the issue. As the Allyn & Bacon chapter states, the essay is "easy to organize because it follows a chronological structure—but you will have nothing to say—no process to report—unless you discover and examine your problem's complexity" (472). So research, reflection, and good note taking are crucial.

The second purpose of this essay is to inform your readers about a specific sociocultural issue that draws their interest. Therefore, an important component of the assignment is conducting research. The sources you collect for this assignment must be evaluated, cited, summarized, and responded to. In total, you should use no fewer than *four credible sources* when writing this paper. These sources should illustrate the conversation on the issue from a number of varied angles of vision. For this reason, avoid researcher's bias during the selection process. To further enhance your appeal of ethos, use scholarly, peer-reviewed sources in addition to credible, popular texts. *You are required to utilize at least two scholarly texts, such as an academic thesis, peer-reviewed journal article, dissertation, or case study.* Also, you may use up to two popular media sources including newspaper articles, documentary films, video lectures, and well-respected websites. Search FIU Library's databases to locate appropriate sources. Avoid encyclopedic or "about-all" resources. Any questions about appropriate resources should be submitted to your instructor by email.

To complete this assignment, you will again be asked to work through a process of prewriting, drafting, and revision. Your research notes will take the form of detailed research logs in which you evaluate sources, summarize information, and provide your strong response to the source material.

Your essay should accomplish the following:

1. Wallow in complexity, using dialectic thinking to fully explore the topic.
2. Explore the topic in an evenhanded way.
3. Use sufficient research to adequately explore the topic.
4. Clearly and fairly summarize the research.
5. Synthesize the ideas of others into your own writing.
6. Show how the problem/question is interesting, problematic, and important.
7. Explain why your questions are not easily answered.
8. Use language and style appropriate to the subject and audience.
9. Document sources according to MLA or APA format.

📑 **Week 6**

Posted by 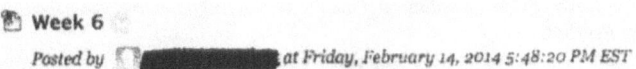 at Friday, February 14, 2014 5:48:20 PM EST

"With the establishment of a relationship of oppression, violence has already begun. Never in history has violence been initiated by the oppressed. How could they be the initiators, if they themselves are the result of violence?"

I think there is no more meaningful and exact sentence that describes what we are currently living in Venezuela. For those of you who don't know, the students in my country are taking the streets to protest against insecurity, rampant inflation, lack of opportunities, and diminishing quality of life, among others. They are against an oppressive government that has all the down radios and TV channels that oppose them. In order to repel the protests, they have cowardly used guns and prohibited artifacts against unarmed students. So far two students have been shot dead. There are thousands of photos and footage that proves this. Surprisingly, the government says the initiators of violence are the students.

As Freire says, since the first moment this oppressive relationship started, "violence had already begun." It was just a matter of time before these things happened. In a few words he clearly responds to their lies: "How could they be the initiators, if they themselves are the result of violence?"

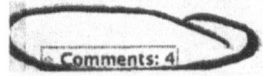

APPENDIX 3.D

SAMPLE STUDENT RESPONSE TO PATSY WARMAN'S INFORMAL ASSIGNMENT

NOTES

1. Writing & Rhetoric I (WR I). The first writing course in our FYW sequence, this course introduces students to the writing, reading, and critical-thinking skills required for college writing.
2. Writing & Rhetoric II (WR II). The second in our FYW sequence, this course puts a focus on student research-based writing.
3. She also teaches Writing as Social Action, an upper-level writing course in which she encourages students to take up an issue of social responsibility and to reflect, discuss, and write about that issue.

REFERENCES

Canagarajah, Suresh. 2012. "Toward a Rhetoric of Translingual Writing." *Working Papers Series on Negotiating Differences in Language and Literacy*. University of Louisville.
Canagarajah, Suresh. 2013. *Translingual Practice: Global Englishes and Cosmopolitan Relations*. New York: Routledge.
Canagarajah, Suresh. 2015. "Clarifying the Relationship between Translingual Practice and L2 Writing: Addressing Learner Identities." *Applied Linguistics Review* 6 (4): 415–40. https://transnationalwriting.wordpress.com/2015/09/20/canagarajahs-discussion-on-translingualism-extended-predraft-on-forthcoming-publication.
Conference on Composition and Communication. 2014. "CCCC Statement on Second Language Writing and Writers." https://ncte.org/statement/secondlangwriting/.
Ferris, Dana R. 2014. "'English Only' and Multilingualism in Composition Studies: Policy, Philosophy, and Practice." *College English* 77 (1): 73–83.
Ferris, Dana, Jeffrey Brown, Hsiang Liu, and Maria Eugenia Arnaudo Stine. 2011. "Responding to L2 Students in College Writing Classes: Teacher Perspectives." *TESOL Quarterly* 45 (2): 207–34.
Freire, Paulo. 1996. *Pedagogy of the Oppressed*. Rev. ed. New York: Continuum.
Guerra, Juan C. 2016. "Cultivating a Rhetorical Sensibility in the Translingual Writing Classroom." *College English* 78 (3): 228–33.
Harrison, Kimberly. 2017. "Re-Envisioning Faculty Development When Multilingualism Is the New Norm." In *Linguistically Diverse Immigrant and Resident Writers: Transitions from High School to College*, edited by Christina Ortmeier-Hooper and Todd Ruecker, 189–201. New York: Routledge.
Horner, Bruce. 2006. "Introduction: Cross-Language Relations in Composition." *College English* 68 (6): 569–74.
Horner, Bruce, and Min-Zhan Lu. 2012. "Translingual Literacy and Matters of Agency." Working Papers Series on Negotiating Differences in Language and Literacy. University of Louisville.
Horner, Bruce, Min-Zhan Lu, and Paul Kei Matsuda. 2010. *Cross-Language Relations in Composition*. Carbondale: Southern Illinois University Press.
Horner, Bruce, Min-Zhan Lu, Jacqueline Jones Royster, and John Trimbur. 2011. "Opinion: Language Difference in Writing: Toward a Translingual Approach." *College English* 73 (3): 303–21.

Horner, Bruce, Samantha NeCamp, and Christiane Donahue. 2011. "Toward a Multilingual Composition Scholarship: From English Only to a Translingual Norm." *College Composition and Communication* 63 (2): 269–300.
Horner, Bruce, and John Trimbur. 2002. "English Only and U.S. College Composition." *College Composition and Communication* 53 (4): 594–630.
Jordan, Jay. 2012. *Redesigning Composition for Multilingual Realities.* Urbana, IL: NCTE.
Kimball, Elizabeth. 2015. "Translingual Communities: Teaching and Learning Where You Don't Know the Language." *Community Literacy Journal* 9 (2): 68–82.
Lu, Min-Zhan, and Bruce Horner. 2013. "Translingual Literacy, Language Difference, and Matters of Agency." *College English* 75 (6): 582–607.
Matsuda, Paul Kei. 2006. "The Myth of Linguistic Homogeneity in U.S. College Composition." *College English* 68 (6): 637–51.
Matsuda, Paul Kei, Tanita Saenkhum, and Steven Accardi. 2013. "Writing Teachers' Perceptions of the Presence and Needs of Second Language Writers: An Institutional Case Study." *Journal of Second Language Writing* 22 (1): 68–86.
May, Stephen, ed. 2014. *The Multilingual Turn: Implications for SLA, TESOL and Bilingual Education.* New York: Routledge.
Ramanathan, Vai, and Dwight Atkinson. 1999. "Individualism, Academic Writing, and ESL Writers." *Journal of Second Language Writing* 8 (1): 45–75.
Ray, Brian. 2015. "'It's Beautiful': Language Difference as a New Norm in College Writing Instruction." *College Composition and Communication* 67 (1): 87–103.
Sohan, Vanessa. 2014. "Relocalized Listening: Responding to all Students' Texts From a Translingual Starting Point." In *Reworking English in Rhetoric and Composition: Global Interrogations, Local Interventions,* edited by Bruce Horner and Karen Kopelson, 191–206. Carbondale: Southern Illinois University Press.
You, Xiaoye. 2016. *Cosmopolitan English and Transliteracy.* Carbondale: Southern Illinois University Press.
Zheng, Xuan. 2017. "Translingual Identity as Pedagogy: International Teaching Assistants of English in College Composition Classrooms." *Modern Language Journal* 101 (S1): 29–44.

4

KEEPIN' IT REAL
Developing Authentic Translingual Experiences for Multilingual Students

Norah Fahim, Bonnie Vidrine-Isbell, and Dan Zhu

VIGNETTE: BONNIE'S STORY OF TRANSLINGUAL WRITING

It was 2010, the fall quarter at the University of Washington, Seattle, and my MATESOL program had introduced us to the intriguing concept of translingual writing. I am bilingual, and reading works from Juan Guerra, Gloria Anzaldúa, and Vershawn Young had left me dazzled at the idea of empowering my designated section of self-identifying multilinguals to embrace translingual writing. Seeing these well-known writers use translingual rhetorical choices to traverse their multiple voices as a strategy to embody their unique perspectives and shamelessly offer their non-English self to their readers left a profound impact on me, and I was set on imparting this gift to my students, as well as practicing it myself. Armed with examples, I brought illustrations to my classroom, explaining that a speaker of multiple languages could incorporate their other languages into a piece of writing. With excitement, I remember pointing to the homework for that evening and saying with a breath of anticipation, "Feel free to try out 'translingual approaches'!"

You might guess from your own experiences of pedagogy what happened. I definitely had an inbox full of essays—most of which contained multiple languages—but which seemed to be instances of code switching not based on intentional rhetorical choices. Some students switched to their L1 when they did not know a word in English. Others inserted their L1 but without sufficient context for the reader to deduce the major theme. Others wrote in their L1 and then used a dictionary to awkwardly translate it into their L2. Many students were incorporating their various linguistic resources, but they were not yet displaying what the published authors mentioned above were actively engaging. These published authors were liaisons of language who had a certain type of translingual writing that acknowledged their own blended personas and

DOI: 10.7330/9781646421121.c004

chose to perform these blended identities for their intended audience. Many of my students were not doing this type of writing. They were not yet questioning the interplay among identity, language, and audience, nor were they battling linguistic hierarchies or poetically expressing their empowered perspectives of the world. They were in my class to learn English and, to them, translingual writing did not feel like English.

INTRODUCTION

Bonnie's teaching story best captures a composition teacher's mixed feelings about translingual writing. On one hand, the intellectual value of translingual writing as a rhetorical choice is intriguing. When we read the aforementioned powerful pieces by renowned authors, especially when we observe how they freely and beautifully flow across languages to express their true selves, we become curious, and even enthusiastic, about the potential of this approach for our multilingual students. On the other hand, as it is a notion "still in search of its own meaning" (Matsuda 2014, 478), the term *translingualism* seems to lack defining boundaries or a clear articulation, which may have inflated its value in the field of writing studies to a certain degree. Additionally, race and power are embedded in languages; therefore, teachers who assume a classroom utopia where all languages are equal and each student holds an Americanized dream of individuality and self-expression may find themselves at odds with the realities of their multilingual students who do not wish to write in multiple languages or express a blended linguistic identity (Grollmus, Lovett, and Thu 2018). Worse yet, composition teachers can be overwhelmed with frustration over the limited pedagogical guidelines or sample practices based on this approach; as A. Suresh Canagarajah (2013) points out, "There is now a general feeling that theorization of translingual literacy has far outpaced pedagogical practices for advancing this proficiency in classrooms" (41).

These mixed feelings have prompted us (Norah, Bonnie, and Dan), as three composition teachers with over ten years of teaching experience and MATESOL backgrounds, to take a step back and reexamine the multilingual reality in our university's expository writing program (EWP), where a series of first-year composition (FYC) multilingual sections is offered to self-identified multilingual students. This chapter is based on our experiences teaching these multilingual sections in which we explored translingualism as movement across and through languages—not limited to mixing languages but extended to the critical work of contemplating cross-linguistic communication. For the sake of our pedagogy, we have found it helpful to define different types of translingualism in the composition classroom, and we will briefly include those definitions here. Further distinctions will be offered throughout the chapter. *Translingual work* we use to refer to the mental energy of translation. *Translingual negotiation* we use to refer to the work of contemplation and exploration of changes in syntax caused by grammar or word choice. Translingual negotiation is our attempt to describe Bruce Horner's, Min-Zhan Lu's, and others' work on addressing language difference and error in student writing (Horner 2016; Horner et al. 2011; Lu 1994). Finally, *translingual rhetoric*, a term expanded for our pedagogical purposes, we use to describe an intentional, stylistic, artistic use of linguistic resources to persuade, instruct, or express. We also found these three types of translingualism to lend themselves to particular assignments in distinct ways. Translingual work was particularly prevalent in the cross-language narrative and the research argument. Translingual negotiation was often seen within classroom discussions of editing, as well as the poetry assignment. Translingual rhetoric was commonly discussed in the cross-language narrative and the research argument. With each of these assignments, we included a reflection, which we labelled *self-analysis* in order to emphasize metacognitive reflection. These assignments and self-analysis often prime students to consider their own self-understanding as someone who is on a continuum between linguistically blended and linguistically compartmentalized. Throughout, the teacher promotes agency as students define translingualism for themselves and make rhetorical decisions about their own translingual process.

Our translingual pedagogy developed as an interplay among our research in applied linguistics, bilingual brain studies, and our daily classroom practices, each of which affirmed that multilingual individuals carry their distinctive cultural, social, and linguistic identities. Thus, we theorize translingualism should entail a space where each multilingual individual can recognize their multilingual identities, question the intersectionality of identity, emotion, and language, and explore how their own language use can reveal various intersections of these. As such, translingual-oriented multilingual classrooms are sites for conversations, self-reflections, engagements, and assignments that allow for student exploration of translingual writing. In this chapter, we offer two sites: a service-learning composition course taught by Norah and a writing-across-languages course taught by Bonnie. From these sites, we argue that translingual rhetorical approaches are not appropriate for all students due to the vast individual differences in language acquisition that impact their desire, writing style, and identity in English.

Specifically, site 1 provides a service-learning format that affords students opportunities to engage with their local multilingual community, where students can *begin* to have genuine conversations about their multilingual identities. Through individual reflections, in-class discussions, and main course assignments, students can come to a closer realization of their linguistic assets and insecurities. Site 2 seeks a deeper engagement and examination of students' own internal world by asking them to evaluate their own sense of self, emotions, and inner makeup, as well as their experience within the community, often providing stimulus for translingual negotiation and rhetoric. Within both sites, we offer course materials with explanation of possible adaptations. We also provide students' compositions to illustrate our gradual understanding of the complexity of students' multilingual identities. We argue that *translingual rhetoric* is distinct from the *translingual work* and *translingual negotiation* many multilinguals do when they contemplate communicative implications across languages. Furthermore, we argue that translingual rhetoric—the artistic, stylistic choice to blend linguistic and cultural knowledge into a composition—is not for all multilingual students, and that we as teachers should "keep it real" by allowing diverse responses to translingual approaches, which may or may not represent a desire for fluidity across languages (Bou Ayash 2016).

INSTITUTIONAL CONTEXT

Our practices are situated at the University of Washington, a large state-funded university in the Pacific Northwest. The university's expository writing program (EWP), which is under the English department, offers more than four thousand students each year an array of FYC courses, which meet a shared set of outcomes while allowing for varied approaches, settings, themes, and materials among instructors. With a sharp increase in international undergraduate enrollment, a 66 percent increase over the last six years or a 218 percent increase over the past decade (as of 2016), the EWP added multilingual sections to its FYC series to better meet the writing needs of the influx of international students (EWP 2016). These multilingual sections share the same learning outcomes and workloads as regular FYC sections while offering smaller student/teacher ratios to allow more scaffolding and more language support. It is worth noting that the program's intention to adopt the term *multilingual* was an effort meant to shift the program from a deficit model or a support model (previously listed as ESL) to one that embraces students' multilingual assets—an intent that tends to align with the trends of translingualism. Though the word *multilingual* was not at first familiar to some students and staff members, this theory shift on a program level had somehow planted the seeds of translingual approaches.[1]

Interestingly, although these multilingual sections are primarily designed for international students, in reality, since students are registered on a self-identified basis, these sessions have attracted many noninternational students, or domestic multilinguals. As a result, the general makeup for these self-selected multilingual courses is international students whose first language is not English, domestic students whose home language is not English, and self-identifying multilinguals who choose not to order their languages (e.g., a trilingual student with a Mandarin-speaking mother and English-speaking father who grew up in a Spanish-speaking neighborhood of Houston, Texas). In addition to English, students in these courses speak Mandarin, Spanish, Tamil, Hindi, Korean, Russian, Vietnamese, Thai, Ukrainian, Cantonese, Arabic, Japanese, Portuguese, French, Malay, Turkish, Tagalog, and Asante Twi.

This unexpected accommodation has reflected what we call the "multilingual reality" of the student population in our university, which has fortunately enriched our understanding of students' multilingual identities and thus stimulated fruitful practices to address and accommodate the needs of both international and domestic multilinguals. It is important to note that our pedagogical practices are situated in a program where both international and domestic multilinguals are welcomed in our multilingual classrooms. We sense it is important to provide this information to clarify the term *multilingual*, which we refer to in this chapter, with no intention to deliberately differentiate or assimilate these two groups.

SITE 1: RECOGNIZING MULTILINGUAL IDENTITIES THROUGH COMMUNITY ENGAGEMENT

In this section, Norah shares her experience teaching a service-learning FYC course designed specifically for *self-selecting* multilingual domestic and international students. While not possible for all multilingual courses, we offer this service-learning course case study as a starting point for teachers to provide students with contexts that allow for a stronger sense of initiative and confidence regarding their multilingual identities. What is offered here is a service-learning FYC course that takes multilingual students into local communities. As will be demonstrated in examples of the students' work that follow, in some cases, the interactions and emotions students experienced during their volunteer work encouraged them to investigate shifting language norms within their local community. In other cases, through real interactions within their local multilingual communities, students began to realize that language use is in constant flux and that their multiple-language usage could be displayed as an asset. This realization is a *first* step towards establishing translingual approaches in the FYC classroom, as students are more willing to share and engage with experiences that relate to their multilingual identities.

A service-learning composition course is similar to FYC courses in terms of course objectives, assignment requirements, and production of the final course portfolio. When offering this multilingual service-learning course, we described it to students as "a class focused on improving your academic writing skills and connecting coursework with life experience through serving with community-based organizations." We framed this course as an excellent opportunity to have real stakes students can identify with when working on their class assignments. It is necessary to point out what made this service-learning course distinct: all service-learning contexts, as detailed below, were specifically selected to allow for more engagement with other multilinguals within the local community.

In order to better tailor students' experiences, it is best to work in collaboration with a university-based organization. To offer our multilingual students these specifically tailored volunteer experiences, Norah worked closely with the University of Washington's (UW) Carlson Leadership and Public Service Center (CLPSC) to find relevant volunteer positions that would allow students opportunities to feel more comfortable with their multilingual identities crossing languages within their translingual identities, as they would be working closely with a multilingual local community. Norah selected the theme literacy and education in the United States since all multilingual students have reference points of different models of learning and education regardless of their language backgrounds. Students were required to complete at least twenty hours of volunteer work offering services related to literacy and education. In order to help Norah's students find more contexts where they could make use of their multilingualism, the CLPSC suggested a number of organizations within the Seattle area that were known to have higher multilingual local populations. For example, the International District served as a suitable context where several students volunteered at the After-School Tutor for Chinese & Vietnamese English Language

Learner (ELL) Students at the Chinese Information and Service Center. Other students volunteered as assistants by working closely with teachers in Franklin High School's ELL program, which was known to have students with a diverse range of home languages (including Somali and Arabic). Another group of students volunteered at the local Boys & Girls Club of America, as well as the Study Zone in local libraries, where they helped run after-school programs. Given that these organizations were all based in local areas with high immigrant/local multilingual populations, Norah's multilingual students reported several opportunities to make use of their L1 to form rapport with the students they worked with. In designing this course, our intention was that multilingual students feel supported and safe since their volunteer work was directly related to their coursework and was carried out with local community agencies partnering with their university (see appendix 4.A) while utilizing their multilingual resources.

Students' Perspectives

At the start of this service-learning course, several multilingual students expressed concern through their written reflections (see appendix 4.B for prompt) about their responsibilities as volunteers. Since English was not their L1, they were worried about tutoring middle or high schoolers and whether the children they worked with would "make fun of their English" or not. Through an in-class discussion, Norah prompted students to talk through whether they had the same concerns after two weeks of volunteer work. The discussion that ensued was illuminating and marked a moment of genuine learning. To be more specific, here is a reflection by an international student, Bo: "The children are all nice and patient. They always explain the words I can't understand and they often ask me to teach them words that have the same meanings in Chinese. It is a really wonderful progress since we can all learn new things." Bo's community-based experience encouraged him to see his multiple languages as an asset, a characteristic to embrace.

Another student, Shelley, encouraged by Bo's comments, narrated that instead of simply helping a middle schooler with her homework, Shelley ended up replying to the student's numerous questions about the different languages Shelley spoke (Mandarin, Japanese, and English). Although the majority of the conversation was in English, through this service-learning encounter, Shelley attributed more positive experiences to her multilingualism; it was an asset and not a reason for holding her back, as she initially believed. She was also able to use her L1, Mandarin, to explain a homework assignment to a student who also spoke Mandarin at home. Such a moment, as explained by Canagarajah (2009), allows for speakers to "stick to their linguistic peculiarities and negotiate intelligibility through difference" (18); in these moments, such unique usage of phrases and expressions becomes a common resource between speakers. The service-learning site became a place for genuine interaction with others and social bonding. As such, this naturally occurring encounter, made feasible through a service-learning class format, allowed for a potential translingual moment when multiple languages coexisted and aided a moment of learning.

Towards a Translingual Disposition

During a whole-class discussion, after group presentations on their final project (see sample project assignment in appendix 4.C), students shared their personal reflections as the quarter neared an end. One student, Hoda, an Arabic-speaking student who arrived in the United States with her family as a middle schooler, shared with the class a poignant memory from her first few years in the United States. She explained, "My brother and I were the only *brown* kids at school. We did our best to hide the fact that we spoke another language besides English. We wanted to fit in." Hoda then paused and said that now it is different. She explained she has come to realize English is no longer the norm based on her service-learning experiences with the diverse student population she worked with during the middle-school afterschool program. She noted that the classroom population she worked with had a more diverse range of backgrounds than her old school. Several of Hoda's classroom peers seconded her opinion, saying that within a few years, the norm could be that encounters with US-based academic institutions would no longer solely be based on the so-called academic English standard. Such in-class conversations produce pedagogical moments for instructors and students to discuss differences in language use and, as explained by Aimee Krall-Lanoue (2013), open up the opportunity to discuss not only which forms of English are dominant but, more important, also how English is used and what really constitutes error in writing.

In other instances, students utilized their first languages when working with middle schoolers who shared the same L1. It is important to note that the community agencies we collaborated with served a multilingual and multicultural community, so students had greater opportunities to utilize their multiple languages. Following frequent in-class discussion of the goings-on in their service-learning encounters with multilingual community members, Norah's students were more willing to consider their multilingualism as an asset that would favor them socially and academically on the long run in an ever-changing fast-paced multilingual world. Monolingualism no longer must be the norm. It is helpful to bear in mind that this discussion could have likely yielded much more student engagement and a development in their understanding of their sense of multilingualism had we had the luxury of more time—a ten-week class is only a starting point. Admittedly, not all FYC instructors can afford to handle the time-consuming logistics of a service-learning course. Therefore, we offer an alternative assignment format in appendix 4.D that serves as a starting point to help multilingual students volunteer at local organizations that serve immigrant communities who share a common L1 or L2.

Through the contexts of such community-based engagement, students are able to build confidence in their multilingual identities, which is a crucial step that aids in paving the way for a successful translingual experience later in the classroom. For example, Hoda's reflection earlier allows for what Bruce Horner, Min-Zhan Lu, Jacqueline Jones Royster, and John Trimbur (2011) refer to as "the disposition of openness and inquiry that [students] take toward language and language difference" (311), which in our experience allows for students to cease hiding their L1 competency and instead use it as a valid asset for course research. Once this realization occurs, instructors and students can begin having genuine conversations about the nature of multilingual identities and how students can best make use of translingual practices for better learning experiences. The unique context of a service-learning course is that it offers multilingual students the chance to engage directly with local multilingual community members. These experiences, and the emotions associated with them, can help students reexamine their multilingual identities through in-class group discussions as well as individual reflections. The advantage here lies in offering students real-life contexts where their usage of multiple languages becomes socioculturally situated and unforced.

Pace and Student Readiness

Despite stories of success, not all students had positive experiences when exploring their multilingual identities. Another student, Ning, provided a heartfelt reflection, which presents a case for students who embrace the belief that English has the monopoly on success:

> Chinese is my first language. During the tutoring volunteer work, I feel much more confidence about my English speaking. Children do not care a lot about how well I can speak English. But sometimes I have to say a word several times so they can understand. But they may lost interest on me and keep doing their work. That make me a little bit sad. One time a girl said that I have a weird accent of speaking English. At first I felt heart broken. But then I realize that only when I speak English fluently just like a native speaker then can I be recognized by others. That become my motivation to improve my speaking.

Unlike previous students' reflections in which they took up their multilingual sense of identity and embraced their usage of Mandarin as their L1, this student is struggling. This student gives in to *his* reality caused by linguistic homogeneity. Before Ning had a chance to embrace his multiple identities, he felt silenced. However, these different student experiences demonstrate it is necessary that students become comfortable with their multilingual identities first.

Multilingual self-identification, blended linguistic performances, and critical examination of language crossing are areas of contemplation grounded in an awareness and conceptualization that cannot be taught or implemented in a few weeks. We advocate that before rushing into any teaching of translingual rhetoric, a teacher's aim should be to create spaces for reflection on community engagement and help keep the discussions real so students can gain better awareness of their multilingual assets and feel empowered. This is reminiscent of what Kris Gutiérrez refers to as the "Third Space," which is "a transformative space where the potential for an expanded form of learning and the development of new knowledge are heightened" (quoted in Guerra 2012, 29–39). The suggested writing assignments, in-class reflections, and discussions mentioned in the sample-materials section at the end of this chapter encourage students to engage within the local community and allow for this "transformative" and exploratory space on their own terms and comfort levels. Scholars and instructors interested in implementing translingual work in their future classrooms should be mindful that translingualism as a practice begins at the core of a writer, in moments when they grapple with cross-language use, the intersectionality of their own identities, and the very nature of translingualism as a theoretical construct.

SITE 2: WRITING ACROSS LANGUAGES

The goal of site 2 is to provide students an opportunity for a deeper engagement with and examination of their own internal world through translingual work, negotiation, and rhetoric. These assignments call on the students' intrapersonal and metacognitive skills, asking them to evaluate their own sense of self, emotions, and inner makeup, as well as their experience within the community. Though appendixes 4.E and 4.F offer detailed prompts and lesson plans, we will briefly synopsize the overall structure of the translingual pedagogies shown here, offering their intended purposes, as well as examples of their implementation with analysis. All pedagogies originated from a language-attachment-theory (LAT) paradigm (Vidrine-Isbell 2018), which is a hybridized neuroscientific framework for language teaching that posits socioemotionality and social bonding as catalysts for language acquisition in the brain (Vidrine-Isbell 2017). The following pedagogies are founded on this structure: introduction of a cross-language concept (i.e., Sapir-Whorf hypothesis, social-gate hypothesis), study of the concept through readings, individual self-analysis, and community sharing. In these pedagogies, cross-linguistic studies are integrated into the creation of activities in which students are asked to explore how they experience emotions and their own identities in their languages. What has resulted are the following series of pedagogical assignments, which, student evaluations report, have broadened their cross-linguistic awareness and understanding of their own identities. Below, I (Bonnie) overview each assignment, offering analysis of student examples.

Cross-Language Narrative: Description and Overview

The first pedagogical assignment is cross-language narrative writing, which affords the opportunity to practice both translingual work (TW) and translingual rhetoric (TR). In this pedagogical practice, students encounter the concept of affect socialization (Pavlenko 2013), an idea that assumes that when a person acquires a language, they also gain socialization into the language's culture, learning how to feel and think about the world. Next, students read research and essays on this concept, such as work by Aneta Pavlenko (2008), in which she refers to Elena Korenea's experience with the word *frustration* as a word without direct translation into Russian (151). Using these readings, students self-reflect and analyze their own cross-language experiences in three spaces—alone/freewriting at home, one on one with a classmate, and in larger class discussion (see appendix 4.E). These reflections and stories are then shared in group discussions and written about as arguments for or against the presence of the concept of affect socialization within their individual, multilingual experience. For this step, students use their knowledge to complete one of two assignments.

Cross-Language Narrative: Option 1 (Translingual Rhetoric) and Option 2 (Translingual Work)

The first option, one more suitable for translingual rhetoric practice, asks students to complete a personal argument essay similar to the genre of the examples (e.g., Gloria Anzaldúa, Manuel Muñoz, Amy Tan, etc.), in which the author argues an original claim that results from critically analyzing their own narrative. Students are given the choice to incorporate multiple languages, as well as cite from various non-English sources. Because these narratives are crafted into personal arguments, students often practice translingual rhetoric, blending their own linguistic and cultural knowledge into a personalized writing style.

The second option, designed for translingual work, asks students to write an autobiographical narrative in two of their languages and to use analytical research skills (Koven 2007) to perform self-analysis on the differences and similarities that exist between their languages. From these self-analyses, students begin to experience awareness of how language, culture, and identities intertwine and/or compartmentalize within themselves. For the scope of this chapter, we focus our analysis and student examples on only this option.

Cross-Language Narrative: Examples and Analysis

A student's linguistic background, particularly how and if their development of self occurred within a language, often determined the option chosen, as well as the manner in which the assignment was completed. For example, in option 2 (translingual work), students using direct translation between narratives instead of those using two new narratives often related to their acquisition background. A Korean English student who had come to the United States in childhood completed his story first in English and then in Korean—without looking at the previous story for translation. His stories, which were based on the same memory, were about visiting Korea and awkwardly trying to express respect through Korean honorifics. After writing each, he analyzed and compared each version in a reflection. Here, the student wrote about his increased formality and an odd impulse to see the event from a Korean point of view when writing in Korean. He explained that his English version was easier to write, as the topic was about not feeling truly part of his home culture. Here, his translingual work is extended into personal analysis of how language influences his emotions and identity in various ways. This self-reflection was shared with classmates, some of whom shared similar experiences of no longer feeling a link to their heritage languages due to extended time in the United States. This unique experience when shared in group offered the student greater awareness of his split identity, and as a result, he expressed the desire to be "more Korean" and seek out relationships from his home culture.

To contrast, some students do not experience differences between their L1 and L2 when doing the translingual work of option 2. For example, when completing this assignment, a Chinese English student wrote easily in his L1, Chinese, a story about expressing love, but he went through the process of direct translation into English for his L2 version of the story, looking at the original Chinese version and translating word by word. When interviewed later, he described that he only used English for school work and that his friendships, community, and relationships in the United States were with others who spoke his L1, Chinese. In addition, he had spent most of his life in China and was new to the United States, here only to complete university and then return to life in China. Therefore, his awareness was that his identity was more singular than multiple and that he would simply translate his thoughts into English for academic and professional purposes. For some students, particularly those who were forced to learn English in stressful educational environments, there was desire neither to blend linguistic resources for rhetorical purposes nor to act as a liaison between the two languages or cultures (Motha 2014).

To understand why the manner of assignment completion relates to linguistic background, it is helpful to consider a prominent issue in bilingualism—the degree of integration or separation of the two languages in a bilingual brain.[2] Studies from the last decade (Buchweitz and Prat 2013; Isel et al. 2010) more heavily support the understanding that in proficient bilinguals, semantic neural overlap exists. This means the brain has optimized in such a way that it recruits similar areas of the brain for semantic processing (shared concepts and shared cortical tissue). In less proficient bilinguals, different language-processing areas of the brain are used, likely accounting for translation to the first language (Green and Abutalebi 2008). This degree of convergence of brain networks for bilingual conceptual processes depends upon the individual differences that occurred in the course of acquisition and ultimate attainment of the L2. We see this exemplified in the above two examples. For the Korean English student, who used only the memory of the story to write across languages, there is more evidence for a shared common conceptual system, while in the Chinese English student, who went word by word through his L1 story to translate it into English, there is more evidence for the separation of languages in the bilingual brain.

Though as teachers we cannot peer into our students' brains to confirm, there are interesting correlations in the self-analyses and linguistic autobiographies. In the above cases, the Korean English writer describes an earlier age of acquisition, significantly more L2 social identification, and more desire to integrate both languages than does the Chinese English student. In the Chinese English student's case, translingual rhetoric does not match the students' purpose, desire, or sense of self, making a translingual work option more appealing.

By offering options in the cross-language narrative writing assignment, teachers can notice how a student's linguistic background impacts their identity and provide spaces for self-reflection on the relationship between the L2 and their understanding of self. Unlike my initial teaching attempts to scaffold TW, TN, and TR (with translingual rhetoric being the pinnacle of translingual writing), best practice is to promote agency in a student's linguistic journey, understanding that individual differences exist in both the brain and soul of bilinguals. Therefore, giving assignment options often allowed students to enter into translingualism in their own way, and for many, this became a process of moving among all three types of translingualism (translingual work, translingual negotiation, translingual rhetoric).

Cross-Language Poetic Writing: Description and Overview

A second pedagogical approach is cross-language poetic writing, in which students explore the concept of cross-linguistic differences in identity and emotion (Pavlenko 2001, 2007). Students read and engage translingual poetry, stories, or letters from multilingual authors and then write a creative piece of their own choice (see appendix 4.F). The aim of this assignment is to allow students to discuss their experiences in light of others, define translingualism for themselves, and consciously decide if crossing languages in translingual rhetoric fits their mode of creative self-expression. Reading published pieces from bilingual authors often primes students to discuss their own experiences of identity and language. For instance, the author Rhina Espaillat wrote a poem incorporating her L1 into her L2 (see appendix 4.F) in order to give readers a glimpse of her linguistic autobiography. Students can read and analyze poems like hers in groups, creating their own definitions of translingual rhetoric and exploring their own experiences in comparison with the writer. One student explained having a story opposite Rhina Espaillat's: "Since I never grew up speaking English, I never experienced prejudice or difficulties because of language." Other students recounted stories of feeling similar to the author, while still others explained the pressure from their parents to learn a language no one around them spoke. These discussions and engagements with texts ask students to explore their own linguistic backgrounds and experiences within their languages. Through recounting stories (Cozolino 2013), students gain heightened awareness of when, where, and how their languages traverse. Recognizing these instances of overlap primes the readers to decide whether or not translingual rhetoric is an appropriate approach for composing a piece that reflects their own style, voice, and language history.

Cross-Language Poetic Writing: Options (Translingual Work, Translingual Negotiation, Translingual Rhetoric)

After this textual engagement, students are invited to write their own creative piece with the goal of self-expression (Hanauer 2010). This open prompt encourages students to interpret the assignment broadly, using computer code, visual images, music, Chinglish, Spanglish, and Ebonics. With translingualism being in a state of pedagogical experimentation, we did not feel the need to draw boundaries between multimodality and translingualism. Interestingly, students naturally entered into the different types of translingualism—some used the word-by-word direct translation method between their poems (translingual work), others added English rhymes but repeated the ideas between their L1 and L2 poems (translingual work / translingual negotiation), and still others created a single mixed-language poem reflective of their identity (translingual rhetoric). Though the final product varied, the content of the poems in the majority of cases dealt with translingual negotiations that explained to the audience (instructor) cross-linguistic differences in emotion and the relationships tied to those languages. Some examples included explanations of saying *I love you* / 我爱你, a culturally difficult phrase to say in Chinese (Deweale 2008), explanations of learning the L2 emotion of homesickness (nhớ nhà) / loneliness in a profoundly new way, and explanations of linguistic choices used to navigate disempowerment.

Cross-Language Poetic Writing: Examples and Analysis

Memories, emotional experiences, and the human relationships connected to each are unconsciously wired into a language during encoding, creating socioemotional differences across linguistic identities (Pavlenko 2001, 2005; Schumann 1997; Vidrine-Isbell 2017). In our context, students who felt drawn to a translingual rhetoric/negotiation had more L2 socioemotionality, linking human interaction with the English language (example 1 below), whereas students whose English education consisted of book memorization and translation methods tended to choose translingual work/negotiation. In self-analysis, translingual work/negotiation writers often described lack of emotional force in L2 expression and cross-linguistic differences in emotional expression while translingual rhetoric/negotiation writers discussed language-bound pressures, prejudices, and significant L2 relationships. For example, a Mexican American student wrote a translingual rhetoric poem about insecurities between her linguistic identities and the social pressures she experienced in various stages of life. Here is an excerpt of her poem:

> Insecurities
>   I think about how
>   When I was younger
>   I would dance to the beat
>   of *Jarabe Tapatío* music.
>   I would twirl my *China Poblana* dress
>   And the heel of my shoes would gracefully tap the floor.
>   "*Hablo español*"
>   "*Soy Mexicana*"
>   I would tell people.
>   Why else would I dance a traditional Mexican dance?
>   I think about how
>   In middle school
>   *Todo cambio*
>   "You're not Mexican enough"
>   "*Gringa*"
>   "Think you're better than us now?"
>   Suddenly I was
>   *Insegura*
>   *Muy muy*
>   *Se le crea*
>   Too good for them.
>   Why did my ethnicity matter?
>   My language?
>   Being bilingual was a curse.

This translingual rhetoric writer describes an early acquisition of both languages in social contexts, and her poem continues to recount her journey through high school and into university by showing the various English and Spanish voices that shaped and challenged her. Her poem is cyclical in that her early memories of pride in her Mexican culture return in university, with more acceptance of having multiple, changing identities within one body. In her analysis, she mainly discusses personality shifts experienced between languages. The translingual rhetoric seen here differs from the other two types of translingualism in that the writer is intentional, stylistic, artistic in her use of linguistic resources to express her journey to resolve competing linguistic identities.

In contrast, another student, completing the same assignment using translingual work and translingual negotiation, wrote her poem three times—in Chinese, in English, and in poem form in English only. This writer had recently come to the United States, and her poem exemplifies her work of translating her memories into a new language.

> **Chinese version:** 月那次与家人分别时的心情，回忆起来不免还是有些伤感，外婆握着我的双手强忍泪水的画面历历在目。凌晨五点，天还没亮，我们就准备出发去机场。关上房门时我在心里默念着要开心地走，不能在外婆面前掉眼泪。可当我想笑着和外婆道别时，她紧紧地握住了我的手，想说要我一路平安，好好照顾自己，可却哽咽着没把话说完，只是握着我的手久久没有放开。在她的眼里我看的了从来没有见过的不舍和心酸。

> **English version:** I can never forget the time when I said goodbye to my grandma as I left China and came to Seattle. The emotion that burst out in my heart was so strong that I can still feel it when I recall that memory. It was 5 a.m. when the sky was not bright yet. I was checking with my luggage and was going to the airport and took the flight to Seattle. I was thinking about being happy and not drop my tears in front of grandma, but when she hold my hand tightly, I could not help crying. Grandma was support to say "safe and sound, and take good care of yourself," but she was choked with sobs and could not manage to say the whole sentence. I saw the sadness in her eyes that I had never seen before.

Here, translingual work and negotiations begin. In her analysis, she describes the lack of emotional force she feels her words portray in English—the loss of emotional meaning between the two (translingual negotiation) and the desire to find the perfect English word for her Chinese (translingual work). In this case, her memories, the words used, and the person she is communicating with all happened in Chinese—making her body encode these into her implicit memory in Chinese. In her self-analysis, she explains, "When I wrote the story in English, I can hardly find a word other than sadness to represent the feeling when someone leave but you don't want him/her to leave, and the feeling of letting someone go when you have already being accompany for several years. Chinese enable me to express my feeling more precisely and actually feel it when I am writing. However, English does not give me that kind of arousal." The experiences that shaped this writer (identity, emotions, and memories) were not those of an English speaker; therefore, in a new environment with English as the medium of instruction, she practices sharing herself through translation. She negotiates the changes in meaning, the loss of emotional connectedness, and the grammatical differences that occur. This hardworking student, then, moves into her final goal—a poem in her second language.

> Farewell
> Sun had not rise,
> Lights had not shine.
> But I had to take a flight.
> To a place I chose to thrive.
>
> It was the first time,
> That I was on my own ride,
> Not willing to turn my back,
> But I had to say goodbye.
>
> At the door side,
> Grandma hold my hand,
> Trying to say a word,
> But stopped by tears in eyes.
>
> Hey grandma,
> Take good care of your life,
> I will be fine.
> Farewell, and goodbye.

In this poem, the student is playing with poetic devices in the new language. She uses repetition of the sound /aɪ/ at the end of lines, imagery of darkness, and line breaks for emphasis. She is still playing in her new language—in translation, negotiations, and sharing herself with her writing community. A desire to mix languages as a means for self-expression (translingual rhetoric) seems unnecessary, as the self she must express has developed in the socioemotional context of China.

CONCLUSION

Individual differences that greatly impact translingual pedagogy exist within our multilingual populations. First, the degree of integration or separation of each language varies within the brain, changing the way conceptual knowledge is processed across languages. Second, memories and emotions are simultaneously encoded during language acquisition, altering the experience of remembering, writing, and developing identity across languages. Third, and perhaps most important, human experiences (L1 and L2) are connected to both language acquisition and identity. These relationships shape the way the brain organizes languages and the identities performed in these languages. These individual differences create a complexity for translingual pedagogy that requires teachers to develop spaces for open engagement with assignments. Bonnie extended the terms *translingual work* (TW), *translingual negotiation* (TN), and *translingual rhetoric* (TR) to help organize some of this complexity, and since then, we have found it easier to understand why a certain type of translingualism is chosen over another. Factors such as age of acquisition, social engagement, and the amount of use influence the neural representation of concepts in the brain. In addition, individual stories, identities, and emotions also intersect and collide within the same body, demanding that translingual insight be unique to each student. This chapter argues that translingual rhetorical approaches are not suitable for all multilingual students. Teachers must respect students who may not be drawn to translingual rhetoric and be careful not to create a hierarchy in their composition class—with translingual rhetoric valued over traditional writing approaches. Translingual work, translingual negotiation, and the use of translingual rhetoric are all equally valuable activities that may be practiced and discussed in the classroom with the objective that students thoughtfully engage with their own individualized cross-linguistic choices.

In regard to classrooms containing both monolingual and multilingual students, we call for further pedagogical research specific to these classrooms. Because our specialization has been in courses where students have a high fluency in more than one language, we acknowledge the need for tested pedagogies in contexts with mixed monolingual and multilingual groups. Additionally, many multilingual students in our courses offered stories about language discrimination that might not have been offered in a class discussion with a mixed group. Exploring what it means to traverse languages with groups who self-identify as highly fluent in more than one language allowed us as teachers to experiment with translingual practices specific for bilinguals and multilinguals. From the twenty-four-plus multilingual courses we have taught, we have discovered the need within this population to discuss topics of linguistic hegemony and emotionally harmful experiences that have happened, often in naturally occurring moments of translingualism. Pedagogically, discussions of topics regarding movement across languages prime students for grappling with translingualism as a theory and practice. For example, introducing debates such as the Neo-Sapir Whorf hypothesis (Pavlenko 2005), personality shifts in language use (Koven

2007), emotions across languages (Chamcharatsri 2013), and issues of language and race (Motha 2014) have inspired self-exploration across languages. We see these internal questions and community discussions as an important part of translingualism in practical classroom application because movement across languages benefits from an awareness of the rhetorical and personal consequences of those linguistic choices.

In the appendices that follow, we offer specific assignments for multilingual classrooms interested in service learning and writing-across-languages courses. In each, we address limitations and ways to adapt these assignments, and we clearly acknowledge these assignments are aimed at a population that self-identifies as using more than one language in daily life. Though we agree with the critique of conventional multilingualism as "plural monolingualism" (Bou Ayash 2016) and acknowledge the agency of both mainstream and nonmainstream learners to remake standardized forms and language representations (558), we nevertheless report on translingualism from a bilingual and multilingual framework, which is slowly shifting within our university.[3] We also acknowledge difference in privilege and consequence between mainstream and nonmainstream students' linguistic backgrounds, which warrants acknowledgment and respect. Translingualism must, in practice, be careful that moving "beyond" the multilingual framework does not also mean ignoring the cross-linguistic differences multilinguals experience due to their fluency and sociocultural histories. Furthermore, we admit the ease in teaching to flatten language difference (Gilyard 2016) and the difficulty of assessing languages not our own (Lee 2016). To address the first issue, we have attempted to prioritize students' autobiographies and agency in the curriculum, as well as name and discuss experiences of "sameness-of-difference" (Gilyard 2016). To address the second, we have asked other multilingual teachers to define or check the languages we are not familiar with, or we have looked up words in new languages for ourselves.

We also join with those students who complained that "translingualism does not feel like learning English." But translingualism is beyond English—it is about the power all languages possess to change our thoughts, our emotions, and potentially ourselves. In these spaces of open dialogue, engagement, and introspection, teachers invite students to explore translingualism and explore their own complex identities, deciding for themselves whether a translingual rhetorical approach helps them be true to their own voice. As we might say in the classroom, it is all about "keepin' it real" or 做真实自我 (zuò zhēn shí zì wǒ) or نوكن صادقين (nakoon sadeqeen) or *ser tú mismo*.

APPENDIX 4.A

SERVICE-LEARNING COURSE START-UP KIT

This start-up kit is aimed to help teachers as they design their service-learning courses.

1. Select Course Theme

    In the instance of our course designed specifically for multilinguals, we selected the theme literacy and education in the United States since all students have a reference point of different models of learning and education. Other course themes might include citizenship and immigration, where students can volunteer at organizations that serve newly arrived immigrants, or food and community, where students learn about social and economic dynamics related to food and volunteer at local food banks or community centers. It is important to select a course theme that increases multilingual students' chances of their various languages.*

2. Set Up Course Logistics

    Students are required to complete at least twenty hours of community-based volunteer work in organizations that deal with similar issues. For example, some of my students volunteered at the local Boys & Girls Club of America, where they helped in the running of some after-school programs, and others worked with after-school tutoring programs at the Chinese Information and Service Center (CISC). Other students volunteered as tutors at local libraries' Study Zones, and another group of students acted as assistants to high-school and middle-school instructors teaching multilingual students. All of these volunteer opportunities were organized by the University of Washington's (UW) Carlson Leadership and Public Service Center (CLPSC) (http://depts.washington.edu/leader).

    Note to instructor: When setting up your service-learning FYC class, it's important to remember that these contexts are far more likely within the local multicultural and multilingual communities that offer genuine spaces where students can make use of their multiple languages in a naturally occurring context.

3. Timeline

    Students only began their community-based work during their second week of courses, after they had gone through an orientation run by the CLPSC and then a second orientation at their community agency of choice. Therefore during the first days of class we discussed and worked closely with texts that related to our course theme so students could link topics discussed in class to their experiences while volunteering. Consequently, students' community-based work and experiential learning eventually became one of the course texts and a form of primary research that they could use in their assignments and class discussions and that counted towards part of their participation grade. Other logistical information includes getting weekly brief feedback on your students' commitments from the community-agency site supervisors.

*Special thanks to Elizabeth-Simmons O'Neill, Suhanthie Motha, Sandra Silberstein, and Lillian Campbell in the University of Washington's expository writing program for their consultation.

APPENDIX 4.B

GUIDELINES FOR IN-CLASS DISCUSSION AND REFLECTION

These guides are provided to students after their first weekly visit to the community center they signed up for. This becomes a weekly writing prompt to encourage students to reflect on their experiences and learning in relation to course texts but at times to their language usage as well, depending on each student's experience.

SAMPLE SERVICE-LEARNING REFLECTION QUESTIONS

By now you should have at least started your orientation, and some of you have started your volunteering already. Please write a paragraph explaining your experience so far and any thoughts you would like to reflect on. Also, has anything you have done so far during your service learning resonated with any of our course texts or in-class discussions?

1. If you did not grow up in the United States, has participating in community service impacted your understanding of Seattle/US culture? If so, how?
2. If you grew up in the United States, do you think you learned more about the immediate culture of your organization/school? If so, how?

Questions following several visits to volunteering site (after students have established rapport with local community):

1. What did you think about using your service learning for practicing composition?
2. What was it like to be a mentor to children and teach English even though it was not your first language?
3. Some students say that service-learning composition courses fight against a tendency for entering multilingual undergraduates to isolate themselves from local community integration. Do you think this is true? Why or why not?
4. What do you think are the benefits of a multilingual service-learning course?
5. Has service learning been a generally positive, neutral, or negative experience for you? Can you explain/tell stories about your answer?

APPENDIX 4.C

SERVICE-LEARNING ASSIGNMENT

Curriculum Artifact for Your Organization

Note to instructor: As students begin to learn more about their organization, in groups of two or three they present a project they could potentially make use of at their volunteer organization. Using these artifacts depends on the consent of the volunteer organizations, which are often ready to accept alternative resources from volunteering students.

ASSIGNMENT PROMPT

Now that you've had a chance to read into scholarship on literacy learning and investigate literacy practices at your organization, this is your chance to create an artifact for your volunteer organization based in your research. The audience for this artifact might be your students, staff members, community members at your organization, or parents. Artifacts might include

- a lesson plan for a classroom or after-school activity (try to think about how this activity might make use of volunteers as well);
- an assignment or activity that engages students in learning something new (again, try to think about how this activity might make use of volunteers as well);
- an informational text for teachers or staff at your organization to share your learning about literacy and how it might be relevant to them (this could be a video, brochure, poster board, website, etc.);
- an informational text for parents of the children at your organization to share your learning about literacy and how it might be relevant to them (again this could be a video, brochure, poster board, website, etc.);
- an informational text for future volunteers at your organization to share your learning about literacy and how it might be relevant to them.

In addition to creating your curriculum artifact, you will write a 3- to 4-page double-spaced letter to the director of your organization explaining why this artifact should be put to use. Base your claims in findings from both your field research and the scholarly work you have read about literacy learning.

This should include:

Context: Provide background on who you are and your research into literacy learning and your organization.

Argument: Why should the organization use your artifact? Why is it a useful source for your particular audience?

Minor Claims: Explain specific choices you made in your artifact.

Evidence: Draw on findings from your field research (using summary and quotations) and scholarly research to defend artifact choices.

Stakes: Why is it important for your organization to use this artifact?

APPENDIX 4.D

SAMPLE ALTERNATIVE ASSIGNMENT

Investigating Your Local Community

Note to instructor: For example, in order to fulfill a qualitative research data component of a paper (through surveys or interviews), students can self-select to volunteer at local organizations that serve immigrant communities who share a common L1 or L2. In the case of our class, several students interviewed senior citizens at the Chinese Information and Service Center (CISC) that serves Seattle's Asian community who are most in need. Local and international students who had a knowledge of Cantonese were able to conduct interviews in both English and Cantonese.

ASSIGNMENT PROMPT

Topic

In this individual research project you will continue to pursue and refine your line of inquiry as you investigate your community based on original research through interviewing people directly involved in the community. You will also draw conclusions about the nature and limitations of this qualitative research method.

Guidelines

- Begin with the research question(s) or topic(s) you have developed and, as with the other methods for this project, be open to redefining those questions as you complete research in preparation for your interview, and then transcribe and analyze the interview itself.
- The focus of your project will grow out of topics related to the course theme, your own areas of expertise and interest, class readings and discussions, your initial research on the community's history, and the lines of inquiry identified within your community group.

Remember, during the interviewing process you are encouraged to use your L1 and/or any other languages you prefer (remember your journal entries after each interview).

- Your individual project will need to be 5 pages describing and analyzing what you have learned about the community based on an in-depth interview with local community members.
- You can have the option to include additional primary documents from local organizations, from the person you interview, or other resources (pending a discussion with instructor).
- During the research process you are likely to revise (re-see) your research question as the data you collect shape your understanding of both the method you are using and the community you are studying.
- Your Essay 2 should create an argument about your community based on your presentation and interpretation of your research evidence—answering the questions or drawing conclusions about the specific issue(s) you set out to investigate—and should also reflect on the nature and limitations of what you learned by using this method.
- In addition to your 5-page analysis, attach a transcription of your interview (at least 3 pages, single-spaced text, double spaced between questions and responses) and a Works Cited list including all sources you consulted in devising your research questions.

Format

5 pages of your own writing, double-spaced TNR 12, 1" margins, in addition to title page, Works Cited (MLA format), and appendices of relevant primary materials (census data, newspaper articles, interview transcripts and photos, etc.)

APPENDIX 4.E

CROSS-LANGUAGE NARRATIVE WRITING LESSONS

Note to instructor: Studying narratives across languages is a productive way for multilingual students to approach academic writing in a manner that engages their own stories and identities. In this appendix, instructors introduce students to the concept of *affect socialization*, offer students narratives by multilinguals, and encourage students to practice skills such as genre analysis and rhetorical awareness on the pieces of writing.

SOURCES FOR MULTILINGUAL NARRATIVES

- Gloria Anzaldúa: Anzaldúa, G. (1999). *Borderlands / La frontera* (2nd ed.). San Francisco: Aunt Lute Books.
- Helen Kim: In Danquah, M. (2000). *Becoming American: Personal Essays by First Generation Immigrant Women* (1st ed.). New York: Hyperion.
- Manuel Munoz: Munoz, M. (2007, August 01). "Leave Your Name at the Border." *New York Times (1923–Current File)*, p. A19.
- Amy Tan: Tan, A. (1990). *The Joy Luck Club* (1st Ballantine Books ed.). New York: Ivy Books.

SOURCES FOR CROSS-LANGUAGE NARRATIVE ANALYSIS:

- Koven, M. (2007). Selves in Two Languages: Bilinguals' Verbal Enactments of Identity in French and Portuguese (Vol. 34). Amsterdam/Philadelphia, PA: John Benjamins.
- Koven, M. E. (1998). Two Languages in the Self/The Self in Two Languages: French-Portuguese Bilinguals' Verbal Enactments and Experiences of Self in Narrative Discourse. *Ethos* 26(4), 410–455.

Note to instructor: Reading, analysis, and class discussions should allow students to discuss content, personal responses, organization/structure, and rhetorical strategies.

Reading and Response Assignment:

Step 1: Read and annotate selected sections from the chosen article. Freewrite about your personal experiences (similar to or different from the author's) and reflect on the reading.

Step 2: Meet with partner (online or in person) to discuss their understanding of the author's claims and personal experiences and thoughts in connection to author's ideas.

Step 3: Together with partner, write a paraphrase of section you found interesting and post it online along with one well-thought question.

Step 4: Together, respond to at least two other groups' online posts.

Note to instructor: Allowing three spaces for engagement—alone, with a partner, and online class discussion—usually increases comfort level with the content and primes students for public engagement during class discussion. Also, online engagement with others (sharing likes / seeing who commented on your post) helps build class community.

NARRATIVE WRITING ASSIGNMENT

Following this analysis, students are encouraged to perform their own genre analysis of one of the above models and then write their own narrative. Depending on the genre chosen, these narratives can have elements of argumentation or resemble a creative, autobiographical narrative. Teachers can design this assignment in multiple ways. Two assignment samples and prompts are presented below:

First, teachers could allow this assignment to be an informal personal-argument essay (much like Amy Tan's), in which the students are creating an original claim from their narratives. This focuses more on developing writing outcomes such as argument development, claims, and nuanced writing. I have used this format for English 200-level courses.

Prompt for Option 1: Genre Analysis and Personal-Argument Essay

Pre-step: Read and annotate. Read and annotate Amy Tan's essay "Mother Tongue" (note to instructor: this can be changed to any of the multilingual essays of the student's choice), trying to highlight the main claim, support for the main claim, subclaims, support for the subclaims, and any hedging you notice.

Step 1. Genre Analysis. Write a one-page single-spaced analysis explaining the structure, the evidence that supported the author's main ideas, and the conventions of this genre, the personal essay. In addition to analyzing the argument, use the questions below to analyze the genre. Sample questions can be:

- What is the tone?
- Does the author use dialogue?
- Does the author use descriptions that appeal to the 5 senses?
- How do small anecdotes function in the essay to prove the author's point?

The aim of this assignment is to demonstrate understanding of the following outcomes displayed in the author's writing. How does the author . . .

- employ style, tone, and conventions appropriate to the demands of a particular genre and situation?
- demonstrate the ability to write for different audiences and contexts, both within and outside the university classroom?
- demonstrate a clear understanding of their audience, and are various aspects of the writing (mode of inquiry, content, structure, appeals, tone, sentences, and word choice) addressed and strategically pitched to that audience?
- articulate and assess the effects of their writing choices?

Step 2. Personal Argument. Using your one-page analysis, begin to design your own personal essay following the genres in our examples. What could your life argue for or against? What characters and places will you describe? What anecdotes will support your claim?

The aim of this assignment is to demonstrate your ability to display the following outcomes in your own writing: Does your writing . . .

- employ style, tone, and conventions appropriate to the demands of a particular genre and situation?
- demonstrate your ability to write for different audiences and contexts, both within and outside the university classroom?
- show a clear understanding of your audience, and are various aspects of your writing (mode of inquiry, content, structure, appeals, tone, sentences, and word choice) addressed and strategically pitched to that audience?
- demonstrate your ability to articulate and assess the effects of your writing choices?

Second, teachers could allow this to be an opportunity for students to write an autobiographical narrative in two languages and compare their identity, writing style, and self-expression across their languages using research-analysis skills found in Michéle Koven's work (1998, 2007). For this assignment, students will need to read excerpts of the above-mentioned research articles and consider how researchers analyze narrative before applying these critical-thinking skills to their own narratives. The goal would be to rhetorically analyze their own writing across languages to gain more metacognitive knowledge of their identity and writing in each. From these self-analyses, students begin to experience awareness of how language, culture, and identities intertwine and/or compartmentalize within themselves. I have used this format for English 100-level courses. See prompt below.

Prompt for Option 2: Cross-Language Narrative

Write a story in two of the languages you speak (one of the languages you choose needs to be English). You will write for 10 minutes in one language, and then again for 10 minutes in the other. After you write, put the narratives side by side. Next, you will take out a new sheet of paper for a metacognitive analysis. Take these stories and analyze them using metacognitive analysis. For this metacognitive practice, think about your rhetoric, your self, your own identity and how it changes or does not change. (Note to instructor: Students are given about 10 minutes to jot down initial thoughts for their metacognition. For homework, they write a one-page single-spaced paper in which they analyze their self and their writing in each language.) Here are some questions to guide the metacognitive writing practice:

- What do you notice is different between the two languages?
- What do you notice is similar?
- Did you feel different writing in each language?
- Which language do you prefer to express the story? Why?
- How does your tone, word choice, and style show your identity and position to your audience in each?

For a more academic skill-based lesson, teachers can include the readings from Koven (1998, 2007) and require students to engage in an informed self-analysis and synthesis.

APPENDIX 4.F

CROSS-LANGUAGE POETIC WRITING LESSONS

Step 1. Introduce Concept. Cross-linguistic differences in identity and emotion is the concept introduced in this lesson. This concept has been studied across fields of second language writing. Here are two sources for the concept of cross-linguistic differences in identity and emotion:

- Pavlenko (2001): Pavlenko, A. (2001). "In the world of the tradition, I was unimagined": Negotiation of identities in cross-cultural autobiographies. *International Journal of Bilingualism* 5(3), 317–344.
- Pavlenko, A. (Ed.). (2006). *Bilingual minds: Emotional experience, expression, and representation* (Vol. 56). Multilingual Matters.

In addition to students looking at the concept academically, students explore creative writing by multilingual writers. Showing students that multilinguals might use code mixing or code meshing to express a multilingual identity might be an important step in the process of language pedagogy. The sources below are creative-writing pieces and creative academic pieces in which writers engage multilingual topics. Students choose two sources for multilingual poetic expression from this list:

- Rhina Espanaliit, "Bilingual/Bilingue"
- Lydia Kim, "I miss you"
- Vershawn Young, "Your Average Nigga"
- Gauri Shinde, "English Vinglish"
- Juan Guerra, "From Code-Segregation to Code-Switching to Code-Meshing: Finding Deliverance from Deficit Thinking through Language Awareness and Performance"

Step 2. Freewrite Self-Reflection. Students freewrite on the question How do these expressions of identity and emotion compare or contrast with your own? and share with partner.

Step 3. Small-Group Discussion. In a small group, students can share their thoughts on these questions:

- What is translingual writing?
- What are the different reasons authors use it?
- How does the writing style demonstrate their personal identity?
- Consider your own identity and story. Would using a translingual writing approach fit your own purposes? In what cases would translingual approaches fit (not fit)?

Step 4. Creating Your Own Piece. Following discussion and analysis, teachers can invite students to create their own creative-writing piece, discussing a topic of their choice. Consider allowing multimodality to be enmeshed with the writing to allow students with various resources more liberty.

PROMPT FOR CREATIVE WRITING

For this assignment, consider two of the above readings as creative-writing pieces from multilinguals. You will notice other languages than English mixed into the publication. You may decide as you create your creative piece that you would also like to use all of your linguistic resources to express yourself or you may decide that you prefer to use only English. The only requirements are that you must (1) understand the reasons for your choice to include or exclude translingual approaches and (2) use at least 150 words in your creative writing. Sample genres include poetry, story, letter, playwriting, and song. Following this assignment, our class will hold a public reading in which students will be asked to show their work in a community setting.

PUBLIC READING

Because this assignment often results in meaningful work for students, instructors can offer a public reading or community-sharing event as part of the course. Students should be encouraged to share but allowed to choose a segment from another class writing assignment to read if they feel their creative piece should remain confidential.

NOTES

1. As we wrote this chapter in 2016, the EWP had been working towards moving beyond the term *multilingual students* and transitioning to the term *translingual students*. The EWP's leaning towards addressing translingualism had gone through different stages. In fall 2010, the term *translingualism* was first introduced to incoming TAs, who teach the bulk of FYC courses, during ENGL 567, the main pedagogy course offered to all incoming TAs. However, as of fall 2016, the term *translingualism* was introduced to new TAs on the very first day of their one-week orientation at the start of the quarter. This decision was guided by the belief that talking about diversity first "opens up the possibility of acknowledging a wide variety of student incomes, backgrounds, experiences, needs" (EWP assistant director, pers. comm.), which sets the tone for allowing different kinds of diversity, including linguistic diversity, to be more central to the EWP's philosophy. Second, by introducing translingualism to new TAs at the very start, and by sharing exhibits of student writing that demonstrated such instances of shuttling between languages, the EWP made it possible for TAs to envision different ways to bring such pedagogies into their classroom. During the TA orientation, the EWP was also keen to point out that such a shift in language use is also "something that happens for students within one language—even for students just composing in English (i.e., varieties of English, multimodality, etc.)" (EWP assistant director, pers. comm.). A pedagogical concept like translingualism also opens up room for relevant discussions with students on the benefits and necessity of shifting rhetorically within a text.
2. *Bilingualism* is used here to indicate a focus on two languages. "Bilingual" participants may have more than two languages.
3. As we publish this chapter in 2021, we have all departed from the institution's EWP and moved on to new institutions and hence cannot report on the most recent programmatic changes in TA professional development.

REFERENCES

Bou Ayash, Nancy. 2016. "Conditions of (Im)Possibility: Postmonolingual Language Representations in Academic Literacies." *College English* 78 (6): 555–77.

Buchweitz, Augusto, and Chantel Prat. 2013. "The Bilingual Brain: Flexibility and Control in the Human Cortex." *Physics of Life Reviews* 10 (4): 428–43.

Canagarajah, Suresh. 2009. "Multilingual Strategies of Negotiating English: From Conversation to Writing." *JAC* 29 (1/2): 17–48.

Canagarajah, Suresh A. 2013. "Negotiating Translingual Literacy: An Enactment." *Research in The Teaching of English* 48 (1): 40–67.

Chamcharatsri, Pisarn Bee. 2013. "Emotionality and Second Language Writers: Expressing Fear through Narrative in Thai and in English." *L2 Journal* 5 (1): 59–75.

Cozolino, Louis. 2013. *The Social Neuroscience of Education: Optimizing Attachment and Learning in the Classroom.* New York: W. W. Norton.

Dewaele, Jean-Marc. 2008. "The Emotional Weight of I Love You in Multilinguals' Languages." *Journal of Pragmatics* 40 (10): 1753–80.

EWP. 2016. Composition and Writing Courses and Support Resources for International and Multilingual Students and Their Teachers at the University of Washington. English Department. Accessed September 18, 2016. https://english.washington.edu/sites/english/files/documents/ewp/mllewp2014.pdf.

Gilyard, Keith. 2016. "The Rhetoric of Translingualism." *College English* 78 (3): 284–89.

Green, David W., and Jubin Abutalebi. 2008. "Understanding the Link between Bilingual Aphasia and Language Control." *Journal of Neurolinguistics* 21 (6): 558–76.

Grollmus, Denise, Sara Lovett, and Sumyat Thu. 2018. "Anti-Racist Translingual Pedagogy and Positionality for WPAs and Instructors." Panel conducted at the Conference on College Composition and Communication, Kansas City, MO, March.

Guerra, Juan C. "From code-segregation to code-switching to code-meshing: Finding deliverance from deficit thinking through language awareness and performance." *61st yearbook of the Literacy Research Association* (2012): 29–39.

Gutiérrez, Kris D. 2008. "Developing a Sociocritical Literacy in the Third Space." *Reading Research Quarterly* 43 (2): 148–64.

Hanauer, David Ian. 2010. *Poetry as Research: Exploring Second Language Poetry Writing*. Vol. 9. Amsterdam: John Benjamins.

Horner, Bruce. 2016. "Addressing Language Differences and Error in Student Writing." Workshop Presented at the Writing Program of Seattle Pacific University, Seattle, WA.

Horner, Bruce, Min-Zhan Lu, Jacqueline Jones Royster, and John Trimbur. 2011. "Opinion: Language Difference in Writing: Toward a Translingual Approach." *College English* 73 (3): 303–21.

Isel, Frédéric, Annette Baumgaertner, Johannes Thrän, Jürgen M. Meisel, and Christian Büchel. 2010. "Neural Circuitry of the Bilingual Mental Lexicon: Effect of Age of Second Language Acquisition." *Brain and Cognition* 72 (2): 169–80. https://doi.org/10.1016/j.bandc.2009.07.008.

Koven, Michèle. 1998. "Two Languages in the Self/The Self in Two Languages: French-Portuguese Bilinguals' Verbal Enactments and Experiences of Self in Narrative Discourse." *Ethos* 26 (4): 410–55. https://doi.org/10.1525/eth.1998.26.4.410.

Koven, Michèle. 2007. *Selves in Two Languages: Bilinguals Verbal Enactments of Identity in French and Portuguese*. Studies in Bilingualism 34. Amsterdam: John Benjamins.

Krall-Lanoue, Aimee. 2013. "'And Yea I'm Venting, But Hey I'm Writing Isn't I': A Translingual Approach to Error in a Multilingual Context." In *Literacy as Translingual Practice: Between Communities and Classrooms*, edited by Suresh Canagarajah, 228–34. New York: Routledge.

Lee, Jerry W. 2016. "Beyond Translingual Writing." *College English* 79 (2): 174.

Lu, Min Zhan. 1994. "Professing Multiculturalism: The Politics of Style in the Contact Zone." *College Composition and Communication* 45 (4): 442–58.

Matsuda, Paul K. 2014. "The Lure of Translingual Writing." *PMLA* 129 (3): 478–83.

Motha, Suhanthie. 2014. *Race, Empire, and English Language Teaching: Creating Responsible and Ethical Anti-Racist Practice*. New York: Teachers College Press.

Pavlenko, Aneta. 2001. "'In the World of the Tradition, I was Unimagined': Negotiation of Identities in Cross-Cultural Autobiographies." *International Journal of Bilingualism* 5 (3): 317–44.

Pavlenko, Aneta. 2005. "Bilingualism and Thought." In *Handbook of Bilingualism: Psycholinguistic Approaches*, edited by Judith F. Kroll and Annette M. B. De Groot, 433–53. Oxford: Oxford University Press.

Pavlenko, Aneta. 2007. *Emotions and Multilingualism*. New York: Cambridge University Press.

Pavlenko, Aneta. 2008. "Emotion and Emotion-Laden Words in the Bilingual Lexicon." *Bilingualism: Language and Cognition* 11 (2), 147–64.

Pavlenko, Aneta. 2013. "The Affective Turn in SLA: From 'Affective Factors' to 'Language Desire' and 'Commodification of Affect.'" In *The Affective Dimension in Second Language Acquisition*, edited by Danuta Gabry-Barker and Joanna Bielska, 3–28. Bristol: Multilingual Matters.

Schumann, John. 1997. *The Neurobiology of Affect in Language*. Malden, MA: Blackwell.

Vidrine-Isbell, Bonnie A. 2017. "The Impact of Social Bonding and Socioemotionality in Adult Language Learning: Blending Applied Linguistics and Neuroscience." PhD diss., University of Washington.

Vidrine-Isbell, Bonnie A. 2018. "Language Attachment Theory: The Possibilities of Cross-Language Relationships." In *Contemporary Perspectives on Cognition and Writing*, edited by Patricia J. Portanova, Michael Rifenburg, and Duane H. Roen. Fort Collins, CO: WAC Clearinghouse.

Young, Vershawn. 2007. *African American Life: Your Average Nigga: Performing Race, Literacy, and Masculinity*. Detroit, MI: Wayne State University Press.

5
AN INTEGRATIVE TRANSLINGUAL PEDAGOGY OF AFFIRMATION AND RESOURCE SHARING

Gregg Fields

FROM CONTEXT AND CONTACT TO INTEGRATION

The ethnic and linguistic sociocultural context of the composition classroom in the United States can create or reinforce unnecessary constraints about what languages, resources, and pedagogies should be used in a particular classroom (Inoue 2015; Pratt 1991). Too often, both students and well-meaning instructors, myself included, let these constraints create false circumscriptions, subconsciously foregrounding socially constructed divisions that reinforce SWE—sedimented white/Western English—and negate the existing linguistic resources of a diverse population of college students (Gates 1988; "Test on Street Language," *New York Times*, April 17, 1983). Further, students and instructors may be socially conditioned or "disposed to recognize [certain linguistic elements] as belonging to disparate spheres" (Lu and Horner 2013, 600). Using a translingual pedagogy in an integrative way facilitates a greater sharing of resources and changes how instructors and students view the linguistic knowledge they possess, individually and corporately. As this collection attests, translingual scholarship regularly asserts the need for students' nonnormative, nonsedimented forms of English to be seen as resources and not deficits (Horner et al. 2011, 303) and as sophisticated attempts to negotiate meaning across socially constructed divisions (Canagarajah 2009, 2013). For this reason, I use *integrative* as a way to represent the combining of various resources across these socially constructed boundaries, leading students to draw together their individual resources rather than segregate or compartmentalize these resources. Further, through the use of *integrative*, I intentionally attempt to draw on the connotative historical associations with *integration* as a signifier.

In order to build on the idea that students possess unique educational and linguistic resources that preexist their presence in first-year composition (FYC), I expand on the aspect of translingual pedagogy that engages those resources and gives greater value to the student's preexisting linguistic repertoire. The aim of this chapter is to provide tangible assignments that can lead students to reenvision and affirm their own linguistic repertoires. To accomplish this, the chapter first articulates how translingual concepts reorient a vision of linguistic knowledge as ultimately and uniquely individualized but also partially overlapping with various sedimented, normative indexicalities. Envisioning linguistic knowledge as uniquely individual, yet often overlapping, helps instructors and students value the writer's existing resources, as well as places for growth. The chapter then anchors translingualism to an integrative pedagogy of affirmation—teaching students to cross the mental borders in their minds, integrate socially separated resources, and bring the full body of their owned language to bear in their writing. In presenting this pedagogy, I provide instructors with a few classroom practices—a tested class activity and a scaffolded formal project—that help students reenvision their own linguistic resources. Accompanying a clear description of the curricular items, the chapter also includes a metanarrative of student reactions and realizations often expressed both during and after engaging in the activity. While the student data included below are from a first-semester college writing course designed specifically for international students (ENG 107) from a large research institution in the southwest United States, I have also used these same assignments in mainstream writing classrooms (ENG 101), as well as in developmental/basic writing courses at a local community college (ENG 091) to help students think beyond the linguistically and culturally circumscribed, United States–situated college writing classroom. This form of integrative translingual pedagogy works to enhance students' "language egos" (Brown 2007, 72), reinforce their existing linguistic resources, and create space for students to share their personal resources within and across socially constructed circumscriptions of the writing classroom.

AUTHOR'S SITUATED CONTEXT

When asked why I find translingual concepts and pedagogies of affirmation so important, I often struggle to communicate the parts of my own layered experiences that pressurize my engagement with these topics. As strange as it may seem, I see hundreds of faces from my past: many are my students, obviously, but there are also *mi abuelas de la cocina* at the McDonald's restaurant, where I worked in high school and my early college years, who first taught me to speak the "broken" Spanish I used years later to communicate with contractors and day laborers in southern California while working construction and finishing my bachelor's and master's degrees. Seeing how others spoke with and treated many of these primarily Spanish-speaking workers led me to look for ways to positively acknowledge their linguistic resources and identities, and a few offered to teach me a little of their Spanish if I taught them some of my English. These experiences partially guided my decision to focus on L2 writing, intercultural communication, and translingual concepts as I moved into my master's program.

As I began teaching first-year writing (FYW) at that time, affirming language diversity became more important. My first section of FYW, which was made up of twenty students, was quite diverse: four international students from Iran, Bahrain, and China; a dozen students who had Spanish or Tagalog as a home or heritage language; and a few domestic monolingual students. Since that first class, I have taught various forms of FYW and have worked in writing centers at a community college and two state universities in both California and Arizona. In these experiences, I have continued to work with both international students (from twelve to fifteen different countries and equally varied linguistic backgrounds), as well as domestic / Generation 1.5 students (to complicate this terminology, see Matsuda and Matsuda 2009) with varieties of Spanish or local tribal languages as part of their various linguistic repertoires. Most of my classes have continued to be blended classrooms where it has seemed vital to help students to not only value their own individual knowledge, language, and experience repertoires but also see their fellow students' repertoires as resources.

POSITIONING AND INTEGRATIVE TRANSLINGUAL PEDAGOGY

As a place to begin, the negotiation model offered by Suresh Canagarajah (2009) is taken up in the title of this work and describes a "shuttling between [or across] languages," helps us see language resources refocused, even recentered, within the individual language user and then adapted and applied to a variety of contexts. More declaratively, as Angela Creese and Adrian Blackledge (2015) assert, "meaning-making is not confined to the use of languages as discrete, enumerable, bounded sets of linguistic resources. Rather, signs are available for meaning-making in communicative repertoires (Rymes 2010) that extend across languages and varieties" (21). However, students often struggle to decompartmentalize their knowledge (Lu and Horner 2013), get stuck in a monolingual or multilingual framework (Horner, NeCamp, and

Donahue 2011), or have difficulty seeing beyond a bifurcated, divided, even schizophrenic view of their own *linguocultural* identities (Anzaldúa 2007; Leki 1991; Pavlenko 2006; Zentella 2014; Yang 2010).

Attempts to use what I am calling an *integrative translingual pedagogy* to heal this perspective have been initiated in a variety of realms. For instance, David Schwarzer (2009) elevates the idea of "Teaching the 'Whole' . . . Learner," giving very practical techniques for changing the learning environment to accommodate the "whole" learner. Proponents of differentiated instruction, Alice Quiocho and Sharon Ulanoff (2008) elevate the individual's skills/resources/needs and attempt to expand instructors' views of their students. However, while whole-learner and differentiated-instruction approaches help students decompartmentalize their learning experience, the translingual approach pushes these ideas further into the epistemic and cognitive areas, encouraging instructors and students to integrate (as I term it) language, knowledge, life experiences, and language identities. Each of these resources invigorates pedagogical attempts to help students reappraise their language and knowledge resources.

This reappraisal of individual knowledge and language resources possesses potential for even greater impact when we consider how "language [can be] seen as a window into identity" (Trent 2015, 45). Understanding the interconnectivity among language, knowledge, and identity helps students value their own diverse accents and move beyond "self-perceived deficiencies" or "in-between-ness" (Zawacki and Habib 2014, 201; Roberge 2009, 5). Moreover, interconnectivity complements instructor attempts to affirm, heal, and recompose student perspectives of self away from disassociated linguistic identities and toward an affirming and integrative translingual pedagogy. In this way, students can then engage with all their various linguistic resources as personal property, part of a toolbox of resources owned and articulated according to the student's needs as they enter new and varied rhetorical contexts.

THEORETICAL APPROACH: A TRANSLINGUAL EPISTEMOLOGY

This translingual pedagogy asks us to show students that linguistic knowledge should not be compartmentalized and, moreover, that whatever linguistic knowledge a language user possesses is a resource. It shifts away from deficit models, negative language transfer, and interlanguage perspectives that tell language learners "You don't know enough" and do not celebrate the new knowledge if it does not match normative language use (even though it may still be intelligible and communicative).

And so, while much emphasis thus far in translingual scholarship has focused on translingual practices, encouraging negotiation and the fluidity of language resources, these practices are external expressions of an internal mindset about language and knowledge resources. And, while these tangible practices and productions are important, if students do not ascribe value to the whole of their knowledge and language, they will struggle to draw on these resources to negotiate meaning or code switch because they mentally background these resources, deeming them less legitimate.

I came to this thinking by way of Gloria Anzaldúa's words—some of which I incorporate in the introduction of this chapter—because her expression gives key insight into the reappraisal function of an affirming translingual pedagogy. When Anzaldúa (2007) declares, "I am my language. Until I can take pride in my language, I cannot take pride in myself. Until I can accept as legitimate . . . all the other languages I speak, I cannot accept the legitimacy of myself" (81), she provides a mindset for engaging with one's individual language repertoire. First, she uses the singular form, "my language," as a marker of individual ownership, but she also uses the plural form, "all the . . . languages I speak." Through the plural usage, she references external languages, the socially constructed units, what might be considered big-L Languages—Spanish, English, French, or even language varieties like Chicano Spanish or British English or American English. When she says "all the languages I speak," she communicates the struggle to associate an internal amalgam or composite repertoire of resources with the external social schema or categorization. Supporting this idea, Creese and Blackledge (2015) describe the phenomenon, saying, "Translanguaging leads us away from a focus on languages as distinct codes to a focus on the agency of individuals engaged in using, creating, and interpreting signs for communication" (26). So when we describe translingual writers as shuttling between or across languages, we are saying they use their *internal individual amalgamated* resources to negotiate across *externally constructed* borders, which is the primary essence of this translingual distinction.

To clarify this in my own classroom, I describe language in three parts as Language, languages, and (L)anguage. Big-L Language (Language) is the larger socially sedimented construct; little-l languages (languages) are smaller subsets or spatial-temporal cross-sections of a language in use (Lu and Horner 2013) that still remain externally reinforced through social practice; and (L)anguage represents the complete linguistic repertoire of the individual language user. Anzaldúa says "I am my language," and I would resignify it as "I am my (L)anguage," which represents the composite of all the pieces or facets of her languages she speaks. This representation helps differentiate between external, socially constructed divisions and an internal communicative repertoire. This internal communicative repertoire of (L)anguage is essential to the pedagogy I describe in this chapter. Further, it is what I attempt to affirm, legitimate, and reascribe value to for my students through the classroom practices, activities, and assignments below. We should encourage language users, writers, and students to value their own their resources—including that individual composite (L)anguage, which is so often tied to their histories and identities—as effective and useful parts of themselves.

However, when these relationships are not understood clearly or when sufficient confidence in the perspective is not present, writers tend to pull the external socially constructed borders inward and create wall-like internal compartments. These constructed compartments then set up "a counterstance lock[ing] one into a duel" (Anzaldúa 2007, 100) or duality, leading to various degrees of internal linguistic separation (Pavlenko 2006). When the separation of linguistic resources is then transferred to one's identity, then suppressing facets of one's (L)anguage becomes a suppression of parallel facets of one's composite identity (Cummins 2011; Pennington 2015; Trent 2015), as seen in part through Anzaldúa's (2007) tension, as well as her assertion that "ethnic identity is twin skin to linguistic identity" (81). Yet, understanding an affirming translingual pedagogy "resist[s] the more . . . compartmentalized identities" derived from external monolingual perspectives (Bou Ayash 2013, 98).

Thus, legitimating a student's linguistic resources through a pedagogy reliant on an integrative translingual pedagogy removes the pressure of an external, constructed monolingual norm in which the Language or languages are often perceived as segmented, fragmented, and lacking cohesion; instead, this affirming pedagogy brings these languages into cohesion within the student's personal (L)anguage. Where a student's (L)anguage overlaps with others, the student finds external cohesion to match their internal cohesion, but when their (L)anguage does not line up with others, they can draw on external translingual practices to address the fluid needs of a negotiated situation without delegitimizing their own resources. The student can draw on these resources because the act of ownership—the student's possession of these various linguistic resources, their (L)anguage—gives their Language a unique individualized legitimacy distinct from the external Language or languages of the larger community and other members, which may be externally or socially delegitimated. Therefore, through this integrating and affirming pedagogy, teachers can lead students to recognize and enact agentive ownership of their (L)anguage independent of Language or languages enacted by others around them.

This articulation of an integrative translingual pedagogy, inasmuch as translingual concepts change the way we use language to negotiate meaning, also have epistemological implications that change the way we approach that which we have come to know, are coming to know, and will come to know, including what we think and know of ourselves. Going one step further, this integrative pedagogy helps students decompartmentalize internal resources so they can reintegrate and take ownership of their linguistic knowledge. Teachers can encourage the development of this translingual thinking by affirming existing linguistic resources and encouraging students to integrate their languages into their (L)anguage.

ENACTING AN INTEGRATIVE TRANSLINGUAL PEDAGOGY OF AFFIRMATION

Enacting an integrative pedagogy involves engaging students in decompartmentalizing language and knowledge, taking the whole of who they are as possessing potential to enhance their academic work. As Schwarzer (2009) describes it, the whole-language / whole-learner approach "encourages the teacher and the learner to look at language not in segments but as a whole. In whole language, all language skills are *integrated*, class participants learn about the cultures of their peers and their communities, social rules are openly discussed, and class activities incorporate the students' knowledge and talents" (28; emphasis added).

With their varied backgrounds, students have much to offer their fellow students if they see these other resources as valid. While we can acknowledge the student's whole language, we also must make clear why they experience dissonance in certain social settings while providing this affirmation. When teachers enact the pedagogy I am suggesting, they affirm their students' linguistic identity and encourage their students to see their own personal resources and the resources of others as valid. The following classroom practices, activities, and assignments are designed to lead students toward this epistemologically integrated perspective, particularly in regards to their language resources, but teaching students to be integrative with linguistic resources also equips them to value their composite identity and other types of knowledge and experiences in a similar fashion.

SWEAT THE SMALL STUFF: ESTABLISHING AN AFFIRMING TRANSLINGUAL ATMOSPHERE THROUGH EVERYDAY CLASSROOM PRACTICES

Simple everyday practices become a crux of classroom practice if we are to be successful with the often more obvious major projects or curricular innovations. Instructors must establish an environment conducive to challenging linguistic ideologies through everyday classroom gestures as much as the major organizational units. Indeed, I have seen positive reactions to simple, small adjustments to how I engage with my students and their (L)anguage, and I have seen students visibly relax and become more talkative as a result of a few small moves applied consistently. To warm students to the idea of a classroom that emphasizes a linguistically integrative and affirming translingual pedagogy, I use a few practices regularly to reinforce the valuing of students' less normative indexicalities. Simple adjustments to how I open a class on the first day include non–Standard Written English (SWE) examples, responses to student in-class questions of "right" or "wrong" practices, and feedback designed to positively reinforce students' (L)anguage and knowledge resources and affirm their composite identities.

First, drawing from my experience with Spanish-speaking contractors, I continue to develop my knowledge of greetings in my students' various Languages. From *ohayo gozaimasu* (おはようございます) to *marḥaban* (مرحبا), I have been known to greet my students in Arabic, Chinese, Spanish, Japanese, and Californian "Bruh" language from the first day of class. My intention with these greetings is to put students at ease, exemplify the acceptance of other languages in my writing class, and activate that portion of their (L)anguage they tend to background when entering an "English" classroom at a college or university in the United States. Second, if I see students struggling to get ideas on paper in English during freewriting activities, drafting along the way, I suggest using writing in whatever other languages they feel comfortable with (Elbow 1999). Third, when teaching about writing systems as a way to enhance linguistic transfer even for primarily monolingual US students, I use examples from Spanish and African American Vernacular English (AAVE) to compare aspects of language like word order, SVO or SOV, and verb conjugation: including phrases like *te quiero* or *You don't know who you is* can be effective as well because these phrases have already been partially incorporated into everyday English usage, so normative monolingual students can anchor concepts alongside those students with a more varied linguistic repertoire. These daily habits or practices create an atmosphere that ascribes value to languages other than the normative SWE.

Beyond these, I also regularly look for opportunities to allow students "to position themselves as authoritative experts" (Pavlenko 2006, 19) through presentations that do not just allow, but also encourage, students to use their (L)anguage in the classroom and to be *linguocultural* informants to the rest of the class and sometimes other students on campus. One assignment asks students to create pop-up museum-style presentations based on essays about cultural sayings, which they later display in public spaces around campus (this assignment is discussed in more detail later). Even in class, if students mention terms I or other students are unfamiliar with, like an alternate formal greeting, or if a student is translating key words from an activity for another student, I ask them to write these expressions on the dry-erase board with an English definition. These sorts of classroom practices help establish the presence of other languages through audibility and visibility. Speaking these out or publishing them on the whiteboard lends these nonnormative resources legitimacy and acknowledgment of value.

Finally, through shifting the way I respond to questions about good, right, or correct writing practices away from yes or no answers, I have made it a habit to emphasize context and hedge statements, saying things like, "In the U.S. academic writing environment, [this thing] is often done [this way]." And in giving feedback to students, I use phrases that discuss the effectiveness or ineffectiveness of a particular construction or rhetorical move, and I couch my responses in discussions of convention for a particular audience rather than whether something is good or bad writing or right or wrong. These sorts of classroom practices regularly surprise students—whether I am displaying my own attempts to learn or allowing them to present something from their own backgrounds to add to the resources of others and make more audible or visible their own (L)anguage. This surprise is for good reason; not only do some of these activities make facets of student (L)anguage more public and shareable, but they are each a way of developing an affirming atmosphere and gradually normalizing my students to the varied linguistic resources present in the classroom and beyond it.

A TRANSLINGUAL CLASSROOM ACTIVITY

Beyond these classroom habits of integration and affirmation, progress continues to be made in pedagogy that validates writers in our classrooms. One could point to Mary Louis Pratt's (1991) classic contact zone/safe-house pedagogy, designed to facilitate the challenging of dominant norms, which led her students to more critically approach the tension of cultural and linguistic dialectics and instantiations of power; and later, Paul Kei Matsuda and Tony Silva's (1999) course design allowed students to act synergistically as mutually benefitting cultural and linguistic informants. These pedagogical instantiations, along with more recent code-switching activities highlighted in Canagarajah's monograph (2013), give us, as instructors, resources to draw on. My own classroom activity (appendix 5.A) and more formal writing assignment (appendix 5.B) described below should be seen as just that, tools adaptable to instructor goals and student needs.

A Color by Any Other Name—Building a Lexicon

This activity can be effective as a *linguocultural* ice breaker earlier in the semester to expand students' thinking surrounding cultural and linguistic resources. It might also be effective in preparing students for working with peers, as they learn to take advantage of alternative resources or perspectives. I use the activity in the context of a FYW classroom, but it could be applicable to intercultural communication courses. One could even use this activity in business environments as a team-building exercise.

Detailed Description

I ask students to examine their own individual lexicons by focusing on a seemingly elementary topic (I use color words) that, when interrogated, is clearly complex. When students can see how complex a seemingly simple aspect of language can be, they begin to comprehend the complexity of their own larger linguistic repertoire. I like to use color words because students can work with familiar subject matter; even monolingual domestic students can draw on high-school Spanish or French resources when pressed. So, I introduce the prompt, "Record every color word/descriptor that you know on a blank sheet of paper." At the instructor's discretion, students could either work in silence without sharing or take the liberty to discuss with neighbors if necessary—sometimes these interactive conversations can display the rich possibilities of interpretation. Throughout this process, I have heard students ask questions about hyphenating colors and using modifiers (light, dark, neon, etc.) and discuss what criteria count for the activity with one another. Figure 5.1 depicts a few of the final color lists of some of my international students, but the process of developing these lists can also be very beneficial for affirming student resources.

After the initial listing, I have students pair up, share lists, and then write reflectively on differences and similarities of their lists, as well as

An Integrative Translingual Pedagogy of Affirmation and Resource Sharing   135

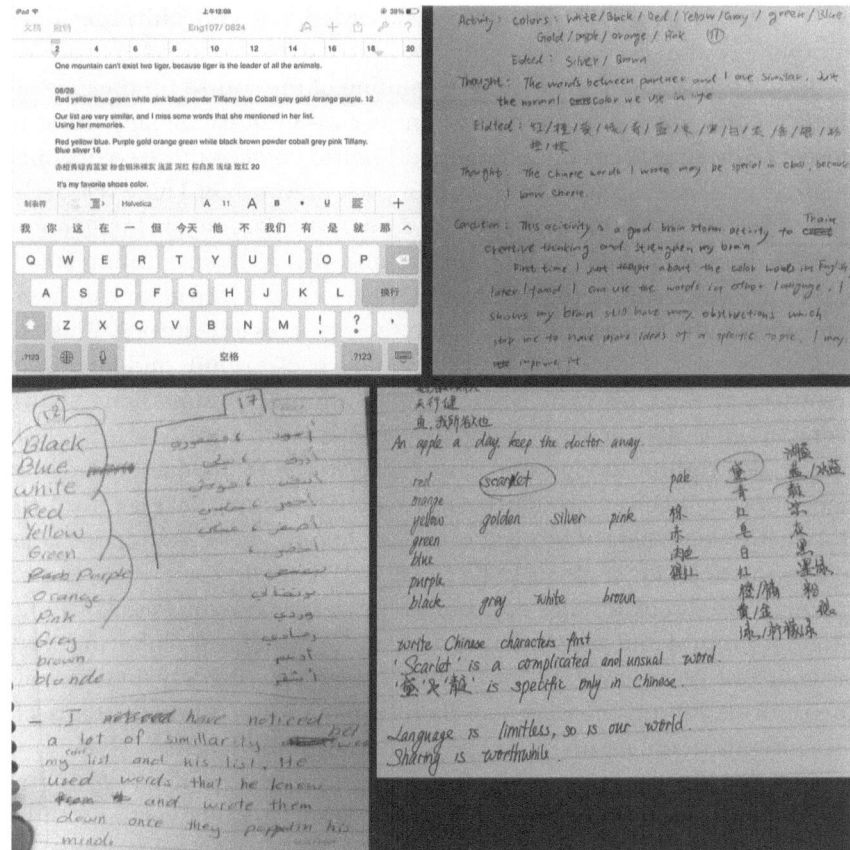

Figure 5.1. A representative sampling of student responses to the color activity in a FYC course for international/multilingual students.

the techniques they and their partner used to develop the list. After a few minutes of reflective writing, we share and compare as a class. In terms of the origins of their ideas, many students initially say they just wrote what came to mind; when pressed, they realize there was an internal process for drawing out their language resources. For instance, science majors reveal they started with ROY.G.BIV (an acronym for the color spectrum privileged in physics courses), or other students mention thinking about the rainbow or car colors or sports teams for inspiration, to name a few: one student even attempted to focus on colors by "remember[ing] fruits" (Student K). As students share and compare, their reflections note the initial similarity but also indicate surprise at the variety, and they have expressed that "shar[ing] the solution from each other is good" (Student G), acknowledging and affirming one another's resources.

Because I use this activity at the beginning of the course (in the case of the ENG 107 course, the third fifty-minute class session), initially, the students consistently focus on sedimented English colors—those colors one might experience as part of a twenty-four pack Crayola box. I have yet to see more than one student per class offer a Spanish, Chinese, or Indigenous word or two from Yaqui or Hopi in the first pass of brainstorming color words. This moment of the activity is key because the instructor can then open a dialogue and ask students about their choices to write only English words even though they have other language backgrounds and linguistic resources at their disposal. Students may volunteer assumptions about being in the United States or being in a class with the title ENG or English in the description along with *writing/composition*. Sometimes, students need more guidance through these issues. The instructor may need to discuss the legitimate rhetorical tendency toward these assumptions, as well as the need for students to be aware of that tendency.

Once the discussion has concluded, the instructor can return to the original prompt and ask students to continue listing *every* color in every language or representation they can think of. Even the way they lay out the information on the page can be informative and a potential aspect for students to reflect upon. I have seen many students create some sort of partition on the page—skipping a space, drawing a line, starting a new column—before starting the next list. Students seem to consistently break English words and Spanish, French, Arabic, or Chinese words/scripts/characters into separated areas on the page visually instead of viewing these linguistic resources as unified, at least initially.

After having students reenvision their color resources, I also like to ask them how they came to the colors they listed from other languages. This interrogation can lead to various discussions depending on the demographic of the class. The first response is often that students simply translated—"green" for *verde*, "pink" for *rosa*, "red" for *rouge*, and the like, which can also allow the instructor to discuss types of translation and whether word-for-word translation is accurate. Is "pink" really the same as *rosa* in all contexts, or does it have different connotations in different contexts? This type of discussion provides an opportunity to discuss translation programs, dictionaries, and other resources writers may attempt to use to make their writing more effective in varying rhetorical and linguistic contexts. Nevertheless, students who are particularly proficient in other languages as part of their individual (L)anguage often have more complex answers leading to discussions about "dark red" not translating directly to *sangria* or the metaphorical nature of Chinese color characters. For students, these discussions add another layer of complexity to the originally perceived-as-simple topic of color.

Nearing the end of this in-class activity, I ask students to begin copying their individual lists into the public space of a chalkboard, whiteboard, or online discussion forum. As students' lists emerge into the public space, mixing their (L)anguage with the cross-sectional languages of the classroom, the instructor can work through discussions of overlapping elements or unique resources that have now been shared in the common space. Students may vocalize various values toward language or their interpretation of the assignment to rationalize, justify, or interpret the sparse or expansive nature of their own lists juxtaposed with their classmates'. Student comments like, "Oh, I didn't know that was okay" or "I put this word because I thought . . ." act to open up discussions about what should count as a linguistic resource and criteria for its effective use. These discussions may lead to deep-rooted sociocultural assumptions about language, or they could inspire students to be more open to innovative linguistic practices, often both at the same time.

As a final step, students could (free)write again, reflecting on the activity as a whole and its possible repercussions. Instructors could even scaffold this activity with a larger reflective essay, possibly on linguistic practices in the media, in their homes, in work environments, and so forth. Ultimately, by allowing students' resources to be publicly shared and discussed along with the thought processes connected to enacting those resources, students become more aware of options that exist beyond their own. This reflective process begins to break down assumptions about what is acceptable and what counts as a linguistic resource generally or in specific contexts. Students can begin to understand how all their life experiences and linguistic resources can be drawn on and can enhance their writings. The purpose is to help students realize the breadth of their linguistic resources in this single, partitioned section of their lexicons. Further, by pushing students to the boundaries of themselves in this single, often-simplified area of color, the instructor equips them to do so in other areas. Students can begin to see the various possibilities they possess not only on a lexical or morphological level but also on syntactic, semiotic, and rhetorical levels.

THE MORE FORMAL SCAFFOLDED PROJECT

Because I often use the color activity early in the semester, it acts as an effective way to introduce larger, more complex writing assignments designed to lead students to a greater understanding of their own resources, languages, and (L)anguage. In this section, I describe a larger curricular sequence of essays designed to guide students into a deeper understanding of the personal and social meanings of a single cultural saying from their own (L)anguage repertoire. Through this eight-week sequence, students learn to reappraise the variety of resources they each possess while also deepening their awareness of how language can change meaning over time and in different sociocultural contexts. Students begin to see how words come to mean, and they ultimately analyze the broader implications of a single phrase. Students are introduced to integrative translingual thinking inferentially through the scaffolded analytical work on this five-part project briefly outlined below (see appendix 5.B for a more complete description of the various parts of the project).

In an eight-week sequence of assignments, students write in a variety of genres, moving from personal narrative to definition to deeper analysis, shifting from the individual to the social and from reporting to reflection. In the midst of the essays, they also use a variety of media. The structuring of the assignment sequence follows two commonly acknowledged pedagogical principles—Piaget's self-to-social trajectory of development and Bloom's taxonomy of cognitively scaffolded activities, moving from report to analysis to application and performance—and these principles overlap with the integrative model, helping students translate their identities and repertoires across those self-to-social and cognitive porous boundaries through the progression of assignments. Further, drafts along the way intentionally incorporate alternate modalities as part of the scaffolding to help students remix their language resources as they remix genres and content presentation. Because students are asked to first tell of their own personal experience with a saying, they explore why the piece of language or cultural saying is meaningful and holds personal value. This exploration draws their focus to the value imbued in the language they own. Many students choose proverbs of encouragement from family members or, more often with domestic students, politically/racially charged language, which has led past students to critically consider the larger social implications of that language.

For some, this exploration of language links to memories of family and encouragement to work hard; in one essay, a student shared a Chinese farming metaphor equivocal to "no pain, no gain": "I saw my grandpa was still farming under the burning sun. I asked him why he farmed tenaciously at there. He told me that '一分耕耘, 一分收获' and taught me this saying is important, so I need to remember it." The student went on to share how this expression kept showing up throughout his life as mentors tried to encourage him to be successful. Through this personal memory, this student—and similarly other students—supplied personal meaning and appraisal to pieces of his own language. As students expand their knowledge of the saying's history and social relevance through part 2 and part 3 of the project, that personal ownership can help affirm their own value and relevance as language users and possessors of their pieces of language. When students choose non-English resources like this, they often provide their own translation of a phrase without initially including the original Arabic or Chinese or Spanish saying. They are often surprised they would be allowed to include even glossed non-English signifiers. The students' surprise in these situations has given me the opportunity in one-on-one conferences to reinforce the importance of valuing those backgrounded pieces of the student's (L)anguage. In this more personal part 1 of the assignment sequence, students begin the process of reappraisal and, through the sharing process with other classmates, are introduced to the meaningfulness of language beyond common denotations, those relationships and experiences often associated with our "twin-skin" identities.

In part 2 and part 3, students shift focus from their internally meaningful personal experiences to the external sociocultural and historical developments of those phrases. They are asked to orient their chosen piece of language historically, to provide the common social definition and background, reporting how the language might have shifted or changed or in some cases what has led to its broader cultural uptake within specific subcultures. One student used the Chinese saying " '做在前头, 不吃苦头' (do things ahead of time so that you will not taste the bitterness later)" that he learned from his mother to open up a critique of how different cultures value time or time management. He provided research on both Japanese and Brazilian cultures to orient the saying to this cultural approach to time. Another student focused on the English shorthand YOLO, moving from its role as a simple confidence booster used by his friends while skateboarding to the hyperinstantiated value in the United States that led to the death or injury of certain celebrities known for using this saying. Yet another student focused on the proverb "a man is as old as he feels, and a woman is as old as she looks" to illuminate her family's push against cultural norms as she was growing up by encouraging her to finish her college education in engineering. The writer ultimately used the critique of this saying to affirm her role as a female scholar and engineer; she even emphasized the importance of remixing this language to affect change in cultural perceptions of different genders, offering the replacement saying, "A person is as old as he/she feels!" Students in parts 2 and 3 of this sequence are led to examine and analyze the link between their individual language resources, histories, or personal meanings and the larger sociocultural interpretations or nuances of those sayings. Through this process of analysis and examination, students can begin to internalize and more positively reaffirm the relationships among those internal resources and external socially constructed meanings.

For the final portion of the sequence, students create a presentation meant to depict each part of the larger project. Students then create a pop-up museum of language and present to one another and passersby in a public area on campus. This final step of the project helps students not only mentally shift from personal to social but also display that work publicly. This pop-up language museum of sorts provides students the ability to publicly display their work, which creates motivation through the authentic audience and situation. Also, by specifically connecting to the affirmation and reappraisal of their own linguistic resources, students take a personal part of their language repertoire and teach it to others in this public forum. And in this forum, students do not simply provide a denotative anchor; they provide their own personal connections as well as the larger history as mini-subject-matter experts on the piece of language they have studied. Through this culminating presentation, students can develop confidence and take the personal value of a piece of language and potentially shift the external value of that saying through their own narratives and analysis. Adding another layer to this benefit, final presentations incorporated a multimodal component, which enabled students to link audio pronunciations of the students' pieces of language. This was able to make this project a useful venue for code switching or remixing, providing opportunities to create more porous borders between socially constructed language boundaries.

DESCRIPTION, ADAPTATION, AND APPLICATION OF IDEAS

Using activities like those offered here, I attempt to guide my students toward more effective external language use after helping them reappraise the various resources they possess so students can be introduced to the value of their own individualized linguistic repertoires, their (L)anguage, which often gets backgrounded or even devalued.

Other instructors can borrow, adapt, or dismember the above curricular items as they see fit to accomplish the goal of affirming students' linguistic resources by leading them to integrate linguistic knowledge and experiences rather than bifurcate these resources. As Anzaldúa (2007) observes, this bifurcation leads to a delegitimizing and devaluing of the student's unique linguistic repertoire. I have found myself more successful when introducing broad language themes essential to an integrative translingual pedagogy if I emphasize Rogerian practices and question asking (e.g., Why might the United States not have an official language? What state-level legislation has affected the local context? What factors complicate these sociopolitical factors?) while also being prepared to give some of the linguistic political history of the nation or region. If introduced more directly, the tensions of a contact zone may flare, in the very ways Pratt emphasizes (1991). Writing studies must continue to articulate multiple rhetorical options for minimizing or deescalating these tensions to a manageable simmer so intellectual, social, and emotional identity work can be accomplished effectively.

CONCLUSION

One key premise of this chapter rests on the idea that knowledge and linguistic resources, while often compartmentalized into socially constructed categories that become mentally and culturally sedimented, are actually capable of travelling across porous category membranes—a linguistic or cognitive osmosis of sorts. Along these lines, an integrative translingual pedagogy encourages learners to bring all past knowledge and linguistic resources to bear when attempting to address the challenges of academia and life in general, but students can often maintain a reticence in this area linked to constructions of self and identity along with incumbent low appraisals of those same resources, leading them to a habit of backgrounding certain knowledge and language resources, as well as the identity cross-sections connected to those resources.

For this reason, one primary goal I maintain for the duration of my time with my students is to give them the ability to see those knowledge resources as accessible rather than compartmentalized, as adaptable and fluid rather than static and fossilized, but most important as possessing greater significance and value. I want students to have a right to their own language and knowledge, but I also attempt to help them reappraise those resources at a higher value: and beyond the self-reappraisal, I want students to extend that revaluing beyond their own resources to the resources of their fellow students.

To accomplish this goal, I have attempted to enact and articulate an integrative translingual pedagogy, hoping to draw out and affirm the students' complete language profile connected to their complete life experiences: with school, with work, at home, in relationships, in sports or other extracurricular activities. This pedagogy aids students in (re)discovering and recontextualizing their own knowledge so they can foreground their linguistic resources from those past-experience venues to address the challenges of academia. Through this pedagogy of affirmation, students can address these challenges as more unified selves, not singular selves; as unified composite selves with multiple facets. And so, while the primary goal of this chapter is equipping fellow instructors in their endeavors to deliver an affirming pedagogy through practical implementations—and I do give concrete techniques and activities—that pedagogy rests on a specific foundational perception of learning and knowing and coming to know, a perspective both cognitively and linguistically integrative.

APPENDIX 5.A

BRIEF OUTLINE OF THE COLOR ACTIVITY

- (3–5 minute) Prompt students: "Record every color word/descriptor that you know on a blank sheet of paper."
- (2–3 minutes) After students have expended their immediate possibilities, have students pair up and compare lists.
- (1–2 minutes) Have students write reflectively, comparing their own list and techniques for discovering words with those of their partner.
- (1–2 minutes) Ask for a few students to read what they wrote/share what they discovered.
- (2–10 minutes) Rarely will more than one student deviate from writing their (E)nglish-only color words. If one or two students did incorporate words that most would consider to be from another Language, ask the other students in the class how this example opens up their own lexical lists and discuss the social assumptions and linguistic implications.
- (2–3 minutes) Reintroduce the prompt emphasizing "EVERY color word."
- (2–6 minutes) At this point, some students may think along the lines of direct translation (Pink = Rosa, Red = Rouge, etc.). This could open up a larger discussion about whether students see these colors as possessing the same texture or not. For example, do "pink lips" convey the same image as "rosa lips" or "lips the color rosa"?
- (2 minutes) Have four to six volunteers copy their lists onto the chalk/whiteboard.
- Ask students to discuss similarities and differences.

- Finally, have students (free)write for a few minutes on the implications of these similarities and differences and the activity as a whole. What lessons do we take away from the activity?
- Come back together as a class and have students share their perspectives.

APPENDIX 5.B

WRITING PROJECT 1

Cultural Saying / Proverb / Expression Analysis

FINAL DUE DATE: WEEK 8

Part 1: Cultural Saying Personal Narrative (700+ words)
> Create a video that tells the story of your relationship with your saying.

Part 2: Cultural Saying History/Definition Essay (800+ words)
> Create a poster/timeline image out of history/definition.

Part 3: Cultural Saying Deeper Analysis/Argument (~5–6 pages or 1,500+ words)
> Create an outline/PowerPoint presentation as draft of Part 3.

Part 4: Reflective Essay (1–2 pages)

Part 5: Synthesized Presentation of Project: Public Poster / Presentation Activity

THE OVERALL PURPOSE

This project is designed to help us gain a critical perspective of the language(s) we use and a better understanding of how language works: where language comes from, how it connects to identity, and why the words we use can have such great impact on how we see the world and each other. I intend for you to gain a deep understanding of a piece of language to better see the complexity of our words in general. You will then share this piece of your language repertoire with the rest of the class.

THE MISSION AND GAME PLAN FOR THE OVERALL PROJECT

Ultimately, in Part 3, you will write an analysis paper examining a single piece of language.

- Pick any piece of language, any cultural expression/saying/proverb, that interests you (and that you think you can develop into a 5-page analysis). This expression could be from any language: Chinese,

Arabic, English, Spanish, German, French, etc. You could use an expression from one of your academic courses, from a song you know, from an ancient text, or even from a book, show, or movie. Pick something that is meaningful to you personally.

- For example: "ethos," "containment theory," "c'mon son," "get wit it," "nefarious," "wedo/[güero]," "swag," "indubitably," "mon petit chou chou," "bae," "I'm all thumbs," "now we're cooking with fire."

- Discover your chosen expression's source, meaning, history, and tension. You might ask yourself . . .
  - Where and when is this language most likely to be used? Why? Does it connect to a specific geographic location?
  - Who is most likely to use this expression? A particular ethnicity, social class, or age demographic?
- Finally, your job is to analyze how all this background information may change or display what people think, why they think it, and how this piece of language then could represent the person who uses it.

PART 1: PERSONAL CONNECTIONS TO LANGUAGE

Part 1.A: Personal Narrative Essay

The best projects begin with a meaningful connection between the writer and his or her topic. This part of Project 1 should help us to see your personal connection to your expression.

For this first step, you will need to pick any cultural expression, saying, or proverb that has some meaning for you, and then you will describe/narrate that story for us, your audience. Basically, tell us what your expression means for you and why it matters to you.

- Is there a memory connected to this expression? Maybe something from your childhood or adolescence?
- Is the piece of language new to you, but you can see the importance of understanding what it means? What is your initial impression of what it means or why it is important?

Part 1.B: Video Draft of Your Narrative

To help you tell the story of your saying, you will:

- Create a 2–4 minute video.
- Include underscoring/a background track.
- Change camera shots or incorporate images/effects at least every 20–30 seconds.
- Optional: You could also include sound effects or anything else that might enhance the video.

You are required to spend only an hour and a half of time on this portion, but you can choose to spend more time than that if you wish.

PART 2: CULTURAL SAYING'S SOCIAL HISTORY/DEFINITION ESSAY

Part 2 moves beyond your personal connection and involves researching the history of the term, often described as an etymology.

Part 2.A: The Essay

- What is the common definition of the saying? (You should cite sources.)
- Help us understand the origin or birthplace of the expression.
- Who said it first?
- When did it change? Why?
- Help us understand how the larger society views and has viewed your saying.
- Find 4–8 sources from which to create a timeline/history.

Part 2.B: The Poster/Timeline Project

- Create a one-page timeline or poster/cheat sheet with images to help us understand what you have discovered about your saying.
- Use 3–9 images.
- Use in-text citations for your sources.

Take some time to think about design or layout. What will make this more interesting and informative for the viewer?

PART 3: DEVELOPING A DEEP CRITICAL ANALYSIS

The Overall Purpose description for the project leads us to this analytical essay.

Options for This Project

- Pick a single cultural text (book, song, music video, etc.) that uses your saying and deeply and critically analyze its use in that text.
- Is it used to demean women through humor? Does your saying create some sort of sociopolitical or socioeconomic tension? How does it change from your personal experience with it?

- Remix your history to create a deep critical analysis of the saying's language use over time.

Reminder of Basic Requirements for Part 3 (see overall project description)
- Write a 5–6-page analysis paper (1,500+ words).
- Use MLA format.
- Use a 5-question survey to poll at least five different people about your expression.
- Use at least 4 outside sources.

PART 4: SELF-REFLECTIVE ANALYTICAL ESSAY

For this part of Project 1, you will think back/reflect analytically not on the content (the what) of your project or essays but rather on the process of learning and writing (the how). You will act as your own systems analyst to determine and evaluate practices that were more helpful or more effective vs. practices that were less helpful or ineffective.

PART 5: POP-UP MUSEUM: SYNTHESIS AND PUBLIC PRESENTATION OF WRITING PROJECT 1

You will look back at the first four parts of the larger Writing Project 1 including the various alternate writing genres (video, infographic/timeline poster, outline presentation, etc.).

You will then create a united presentation of all parts of the project. This synthesized presentation should be turned into an e-portfolio or a trifold presentation board. (If you use an e-portfolio, you may bring your own laptop with a PowerPoint presentation and a cheat sheet for your audience with a link to the portfolio.)

REFERENCES

Anzaldúa, Gloria. 2007. *Borderlands/La frontera: The New Mestiza*. 3rd ed. San Francisco: Aunt Lute Books.

Bou Ayash, Nancy. 2013. "Hi-ein, hi ني or ني hi? Translingual Practices from Lebanon and Mainstream Literacy Education." In *Literacy as Translingual Practice: Between Communities and Classrooms*, edited by Suresh Canagarajah, 96–103. New York: Routledge.

Brown, Douglas H. 2007. *Teaching by Principles: An Interactive Approach to Language Pedagogy*. 3rd ed. White Plains, NY: Pearson Education.

Canagarajah, Suresh. 2009. "A Rhetoric of Shuttling between Languages." In *Cross-Language Relations in Composition*, edited by Bruce Horner, Min-Zhan Lu, and Paul Kei Matsuda, 158–83. Carbondale: Southern Illinois University Press.

Canagarajah, Suresh. 2013. *Literacy as Translingual Practice: Between Communities and Classrooms.* New York: Routledge.
Creese, Angela, and Adrian Blackledge. 2015. "Translanguaging and Identity in Educational Settings." *Annual Review of Applied Linguistics* 35: 20–35.
Cummins, Jim. 2011. "Identity Matters: From Evidence-Free to Evidence-Based Policies for Promoting Achievement among Students from Marginalized Social Groups." *Writing & Pedagogy* 3 (2): 189–216. https://doi.org/10.1558/wap.v3i2.189.
Elbow, Peter. 1999. "Inviting the Mother Tongue: Beyond 'Mistakes,' 'Bad English,' and 'Wrong Language.'" *Journal of Advanced Composition* 19 (3): 359–88.
Gates, Henry Louis, Jr. 1988. *Signifying Monkey: A Theory of African American Literary Criticism.* New York: Oxford University Press.
Horner, Bruce, Min-Zhan Lu, Jacqueline Jones Royster, and John Trimbur. 2011. "Opinion: Language Difference in Writing: Toward a Translingual Approach." *College English* 73 (3): 303–21.
Horner, Bruce, Samantha NeCamp, and Christiane Donahue. 2011. "Toward a Multilingual Composition Scholarship: From English Only to a Translingual Norm." *College Composition and Communication* 63 (2): 269–300.
Inoue, Asao B. 2015. *Antiracist Writing Assessment Ecologies: Teaching and Assessing for a Socially Just Future.* Fort Collins, CO: WAC Clearinghouse.
Leki, Ilona. 1991. "Twenty-Five Years of Contrastive Rhetoric: Text Analysis and Writing Pedagogies." *TESOL Quarterly* 25 (1): 123–43.
Lu, Min-Zhan, and Bruce Horner. 2013. "Translingual Literacy, Language Difference, and Matters of Agency." *College English* 75 (6): 582–607.
Matsuda, Paul Kei, and Aya Matsuda. 2009. "The Erasure of Resident ESL Writers." In *Generation 1.5 in College Composition: Teaching Academic Writing to U.S.-Educated Learners of ESL,* edited by Mark Roberge, Meryl Siegal, and Linda Harklau, 50–64. London: Taylor & Francis.
Matsuda, Paul Kei, and Tony Silva, 2011. "Cross-Cultural Composition: Mediated Integration of U.S. and International Students." In *Second-Language Writing in the Composition Classroom,* edited by Paul Kei Matsuda, Michelle Cox, Jay Jordan, and Christine Ortmeier-Hooper, 252–65. Boston: Bedford/St. Martin's.
Pavlenko, Aneta, ed. 2006. *Bilingual Minds: Emotional Experience, Expression, and Representation.* Clevedon, UK: Multilingual Matters.
Pennington, Martha C. 2015. "Teacher Identity in TESOL: A Frames Perspective." In *Advances and Current Trends in Language Teacher Identity Research,* edited by Y. L Cheung, S. Said, and K. Ben Park, 16–31. New York: Routledge.
Pratt, Mary Louise. 1991. "Arts of the Contact Zone." *Profession* 33–40.
Quiocho, Alice L., and Sharon H. Ulanoff. 2008. *Differentiated Literacy Instruction for English Language Learners.* New York: Prentice Hall.
Roberge, Mark M. 2009. "A Teacher's Perspective on Generation 1.5." In *Generation 1.5 in College Composition: Teaching Academic Writing to U.S.-Educated Learners of ESL,* edited by M. M Roberge, M. Siegal, and Linda Harklau, 3–24. New York: Routledge.
Rymes, Betsy R. 2010. "Classroom Discourse Analysis: A Focus on Communicative Repertoires." In *Sociolinguistics and Language Education,* edited by Nancy H. Hornberger and Sandra Lee McKay, 528–46. Avon: Multilingual Matters.
Schwarzer, David. 2009. "Best Practices for Teaching the 'Whole' Adult ESL Learner." *New Directions for Adult and Continuing Education* 121: 25–33.
Trent, John. 2015. "Towards a Multifaceted Multidimensional Framework for Understanding Teacher Identity." In *Advances and Current Trends in Language Teacher Identity Research,* edited by Y. L. Cheung, S. Said, and K. Ben Park, 44–58. New York: Routledge.
Yang, Jung. 2010. "Lost in the Puzzles." In *Reinventing Identities in Second Language Writing,* edited by Michelle Cox, Jay Jordan, Gray G. Schwartz, and Christine Ortmeier-Hooper, 51–53. Urbana, IL: NCTE.

Zawacki, Terry Myers, and Anna Sophia Habib. 2014. "Negotiating 'Errors' in L2 Writing: Faculty Dispositions and Language Difference." In *WAC and Second-Language Writers: Research Towards Linguistically and Culturally Inclusive Programs and Practices*, edited by Terry Myers Zawacki and Michelle Cox, 183–210. Fort Collins, CO: The WAC Clearinghouse. https://doi.org/10.37514/per-b.2014.0551.2.07.

Zentella, Ana Celia. 2014. "TWB (Talking While Bilingual): Linguistic Profiling of Latina/os, and Other Linguistic Torquemadas." *Latino Studies* 12 (4): 620–35.

6
"HAY UN TIEMPO Y UN LUGAR PARA TODO"
Literacy Autobiographies and the Cultivation of Translingual Rhetorical Sensibilities

Esther Milu and Mathew Gomes

INTRODUCTION

For more than sixty years, scholars in rhetoric, composition studies, and sociolinguistics have insisted upon the need to thoroughly address and support linguistic diversity in college writing courses. The changing demographics in US postsecondary institutions, characterized recently by increasing enrollments of international students and multilingual students, continue to foreground the continued importance of pedagogical attention and support for linguistic diversity. In this context, translingualism represents one of the most recent theoretical and pedagogical responses. While translingualism has been theorized differently in various fields, this chapter describes a pedagogy that supports a wide range of multilingual and multimodal capacities and emphasizes working across languages and modalities (Canagarajah 2013a; Horner et al. 2011; Horner, NeCamp, and Donahue 2011; Horner, Selfe, and Lockridge 2015; Pennycook 2007). The pedagogy we describe assumes languages are always evolving, fluid, and interacting with each other to generate new meanings and grammars and that language is one among many modes of communication. Moreover, in analyzing language, scholars have argued that written, visual, oral, performative, embodied, and tactile, among other modes, work together in making meaning (Horner, Selfe, and Lockridge 2015; Pennycook 2007).

In this chapter, we describe the outcomes from a literacy-autobiography (LA) assignment. Analyzing texts from a spring 2014 course taught by Esther, we identify three specific outcomes of the LA assignment that affirm and extend current research on translingual rhetorical sensibilities (Guerra 2016), which include the cultivation of translingual rhetorical dispositions. Evidence of these dispositions emerged from students' considerations of how meshing linguistic and semiotic resources in their writing was culturally and rhetorically situated.

CONTEXT
Authors' Institutional, Educational, and Linguistic Backgrounds
Esther is from Kenya, a country where translingualism is a practice of everyday life. Her first language, or mother tongue, is Kikamba, which she speaks with family, friends, and members of the Kamba ethnic community. She obtained her elementary, high-school, and undergraduate education in Kenya, where she learned additional languages like Swahili and English. Swahili is Kenya's *lingua franca* and is taught as a mandatory subject to all students from first grade through twelfth grade. English is the official language of instruction and business.

Esther joined graduate school at Michigan State University in 2010, and like many "nonnative" speakers of English started experiencing the everyday microaggressions and discrimination based on her accent and very Kikamba-Kiswahili influenced English. This discrimination was not something she had experienced in her previous schooling, and from these experiences she felt the pressure to assimilate and write in Standard American English (SAE). However, the more she strove to sound and write like a "native" American English speaker, the more voiceless and less authentic she felt. Graduate school introduced her to research on language diversity and the various pedagogical approaches that have been proposed in the field over the years. In reading about translingualism, she felt this is the approach that best represents the kind of multilingualism she practices (or embodies) in her everyday language use. She then became interested in learning ways of bringing her own languages to her academic writing and helping her students do the same. The course we describe represents Esther's effort to bring her own translingual rhetorical sensibilities to a first-year writing (**FYW**) course she taught in spring 2014.

Matt's first and primary language is American English. This was the language he spoke in his household growing up; it was the language he spoke in school; it was the first language he learned to read and write in. However, in the Central Valley of California, where he grew up, there is a much wider range of languages in circulation, especially Spanish, Hmong, Laotian, Tagalog, and Vietnamese. When he began teaching writing in his hometown, Matt became concerned with how to support the wide linguistic capacities of his students and began studying the literature around code switching, code meshing, and translingualism.

His interest and belief in the need to support linguistic diversity persisted through graduate school, where he encountered an audience of multilingual students with international citizenship. His experiences teaching both domestic and international multilingual students have led him to reaffirm his belief that writing pedagogies should be intentional and attentive to differing language needs and desires of differently situated students. When Esther first proposed teaching her FYW with a translingual orientation toward the curriculum, she asked Matt to help develop assignments and research various aspects of the class, including students' writing.

Institutional and Pedagogical Context

Esther's FYW course took place at Michigan State University (MSU). MSU is a unique site for looking at translingual practice, particularly given its long history of global outreach and international student recruitment (Smuckler 2003). MSU's Office for International Students and Scholars (OISS) (2014) recently indicated that 14.5 percent of the student body is comprised of international students, with many of them coming from China, Korea, Saudi Arabia, and India. These changing demographics have foregrounded the diversity of MSU's linguistic landscape. Within such a space, an attention to the changing landscape of linguistic and rhetorical practices, and pedagogical strategies for engaging those practices, is particularly important.

We found much support among our colleagues at MSU. At the time of Esther's course, we found ourselves among teachers who have recognized the linguistic diversity of the campus and have described commitments to linguistically inclusive and translingual pedagogies (De Costa et al. 2017; Cushman 2016; Fraiberg 2010; Gonzales 2015; Kiernan 2015; Limbu 2012). These commitments are significant given the campus's growing linguistic diversity.

Therefore, in line with our commitment to linguistic diversity, we designed a course in which translingual theory informed the content and the pedagogy. The course was grounded in the assumption that students integrate diverse linguistic and semiotic resources in their everyday communication, and as teachers, we should respect, honor, and provide a space to harness the power of those resources in academic writing. These principles informed course readings, assignments, instruction, and assessment; as we describe in further detail, we believe this course helped students develop translingual dispositions as part of their rhetorical sensibilities. We show some of the outcomes from

Esther's translingual LA assignment, in which students (1) cultivated textual-negotiation strategies; (2) identified rhetorical practices as culturally situated; and (3) articulated cultural rhetorical principles.

INTEGRATIONIST APPROACHES TO TRANSLINGUAL COMPOSITION

The topic of translingual writing has received considerable attention since Bruce Horner, Min-Zhan Lu, Jacqueline Jones Royster, and John Trimbur's (2011) call to end the monolingual norm and the myth of linguistic homogeneity (Matsuda 2006) that has characterized the field of US college composition for many years. Horner et al. (2011) argue for a translingual paradigm that aims to "(1) honor the power of all language users to shape language to specific ends; (2) recognize the linguistic heterogeneity of all users of language both within the United States and globally; and (3) directly confront English monolingualist expectations by researching and teaching how writers can work with and against, not simply within, those expectations" (305). More recently, scholars and teachers in college composition and sociolinguistics have adopted translingual practices in an effort to "challenge structuralist conceptualizations of language as discrete, bounded, impermeable, autonomous systems, conceptualizations that unfortunately (1) privilege linguistic codes over nonlinguistic ones, and (2) contribute to the hierarchization and separation of languages, leading some languages and their corresponding users to be valued more than others" (De Costa et al. 2017, 464). Further, there have been calls to adopt a translingual approach, not just to languages and modes but also to contexts, meanings, genres, disciplines, localities, and research traditions (Gonzales 2015; Horner, NeCamp, and Donahue 2011; Leonard and Nowacek 2016).

Translingualism has further been defined and theorized in relation to transmodality. One approach has been to make a distinction between the multilingual/multimodal and translingual/transmodal dyads. Alastair Pennycook (2007) observes that the former focuses on plurality of languages and modalities by treating them as separate and discrete entities while the later posits that in the contexts of global communication, languages, modes, cultures, and bodies cannot be treated as separate. Similarly, Bruce Horner, Cynthia Selfe, and Tim Lockridge (2015) have argued that, while translingualism and transmodality are very similar concepts, they have been theorized, researched, and taught separately to the "impoverishment" of both. In the last few years, a number of scholars and teachers have taken this integrationist approach to language and modes in their theorizing and pedagogy (see De Costa et al. 2017; Gonzales 2015;

Shipka 2016). Our chapter contributes to the emerging integrationist theory of translingualism and transmodality. We demonstrate how our students meshed languages and modes in their compositions while showing awareness of how their practices were culturally and rhetorically situated.

Another approach towards advancing the theorization of translingualism/transmodality has been a consideration of the affordances of the prefix *trans* as used in both concepts. Translingual scholars see *trans* as one way of countering the additive or segregationist approaches towards languages and modalities—instead favoring the integrationist approach. Suresh Canagarajah (2013a) notes that the prefix *trans* requires us to see all communicative acts as involving more than the use of words. Hence, in analyzing any language or communicative practice, one must consider how, in addition to linguistic resources, various semiotic resources that involve the use of symbols systems (e.g., icons, images, color) are used in a text; the different modalities (aural, oral, visual, and tactile channels) involved; and the ecologies, or the social and material context, of language use. Similarly Horner, Selfe, and Lockridge (2015) consider the "trans" prefix "as an alternative meant to focus on cross-language and mode work and the need for negotiation" while Pennycook (2007) sees the prefix "trans" taking "us beyond the 'posts' and the 'critical', and as an overarching framework, it pulls together numerous 'trans' concepts like transgression, transculturation, translation, transtextuality, transmodality among others" (37). Like these authors, we see affordances in the prefix and find it turns our attention repeatedly toward the contexts in which people make rhetorical decisions about language and modality.

Given these theoretical developments, there have begun to emerge some classroom-based examples that showcase the outcomes of integrationist approaches toward languages and modes and that demonstrate the direct benefits of a translingual approach to *all* students. Laura Gonzales (2015) in her study with L1 and L2 students shows how they combined and crossed a variety of languages and modes to communicate. She, however, argues that L2 students demonstrated an "advanced expertise and rhetorical sensitivity when layering meaning through multimodal composition." Julia Kiernan (2015) shows the benefits of a pedagogical approach that invites second language learners (SLLs) to combine multimodal and translingual writing practices within first-year writing courses. Such benefits include students being more engaged compared to composition classes that favor traditional print texts. In De Costa et al. (2017), Steven Fraiberg and Xiqiao Wang conducted similar studies to demonstrate the benefits of leveraging home languages and a variety of semiotic resources drawn from L2 students' social and material cultures. These studies showcase translingualism benefiting L2 learners; yet all language users, including self-identified monolinguals, are implicated in these approaches.

Some of the outcomes of a translingual pedagogy beneficial for students identifying as monolingual or multilingual include opportunities for creativity (Seloni 2014), as well as criticality (Stewart and Hanson-Thomas 2016). Canagarajah (2013b) has argued that a translingual pedagogy can help students practice specific textual-negotiation strategies. However, Juan Guerra (2016) has cautioned that translingual pedagogies falter when they place focus on code meshing rather than on the cultivation of rhetorical sensibilities. While Jerry Lee and Christopher Jenks (2016) insist it is difficult to come up with a prescribed set of beliefs, they agree translingual dispositions generally involve an openness to language diversity (see also Horner et al. 2011). Gonzales's (2015) research shows that translingual pedagogical approaches can help writing instructors teach genres as socially situated and fluid.

PEDAGOGICAL ENACTMENT OF A TRANSLINGUAL LITERACY AUTOBIOGRAPHY

Esther's class was linguistically diverse. A survey administered at the beginning of the course showed many students identified as multilingual (52 percent) in addition to English speaking; many students spoke Chinese (24 percent) and Spanish (24 percent); a smaller number spoke Arabic (4 percent) and German (4 percent). Within such a landscape, the need for a writing course supportive of linguistic diversity and informed by current translingual theory was apparent to Esther and Matt. In consultation with the writing program administrator at the time, Esther designed a course that would allow students to practice and experiment with integrating various languages and modes into their compositions, while Matt served as a researcher who administered several surveys to Esther's students, collected and analyzed their written work, and conducted individual student interviews.

The MSU first-year writing (FYW) curriculum has a set of common learning goals based in "inquiry, discovery, and communication." These goals represent three linked purposes the program believes writing can serve: to guide inquiry, to articulate new knowledge, and to communicate to specific audiences. While all instructors work toward these goals, they are afforded the academic freedom to design and teach FYW courses in line with their own theoretical and pedagogical commitments.

Table 6.1. Participants, national origins, and language fluencies

Participant	Country	Language
Jessica	United States	English
Neal	United States	English
Ahmed	Saudi Arabia	Arabic; English
Gabriel	United States	English; Spanish
Xiang	China	Chinese; English

While Esther invited students to produce texts that integrated multilingual and multimodal elements throughout the entirety of her FYW course, the assignment we focus on here is the literacy-autobiography assignment. We have chosen to analyze the LA because Esther's experience reflected Canagarajah's (2013b) claim that the LA genre—perhaps more than other assignments—can encourage students to translanguage while also allowing for personal and creative expression (47). Moreover, Canagarajah argues that the LA assignment reveals practices of producing and interpreting code-meshed texts. Esther made similar observations—on the surface, the texts students produced for the LA contained more code-meshed textual features than other assignments. However, after reflecting on our pedagogical design, we believe the assignment reveals more than practices of reading and writing code-meshed texts; it also helped students develop a set of what Guerra (2016) calls "rhetorical sensibilities." Therefore, we emphasize how outcomes of the LA included code-meshed products *and* indications of translingual and transmodal rhetorical sensibilities.

We include work from five students: Jessica, Neal, Ahmed, Gabriel, and Xiang. Jessica and Neal, domestic monolinguals, both received educations primarily in English and spoke English in their homes but were excited by opportunities to approach, practice, and reflect on rhetorical practices beyond Standard Written English (SWE). Gabriel identified as a multilingual domestic student who received instruction in English in school and Spanish at home with his grandmother's help. Finally, Ahmed and Xiang both identified as international students, from Saudi Arabia and China respectively, with educational backgrounds that exposed them to multilingual learning environments.

Enactment

In spring 2014, the common FYW curriculum at MSU asked students to theorize, research, write, and reflect about literacy in all of its core assignments. These literacies included personal literacies, cultural literacies, disciplinary literacies, and multimodal literacies. Esther saw the first assignment in this curriculum, the LA assignment, as one in which students could be encouraged to practice translanguaging and code meshing in addition to reflecting on their language practices. Typically, the LA assignment invites students to consider past and present events and practices associated with literacy, to consider the relationship of these to their lives now, and to imagine literacy as encompassing a broad range of practices.

It is within this curricular context that we saw an opportunity to experiment with translingual writing by redesigning the LA assignment, by making language (in addition to literacy) the subject of inquiry. We wanted students to make an explicit connection between their literacy and language histories and development. In table 2, we provide short excerpts of the LA assignment description from the department alongside our redesigned version. In contrast to the common version of the assignment, Esther's redesigned LA description asked students to mesh linguistic and semiotic resources in a four- to five-page essay accompanied by a one-page reflection memo explaining their composing process, as well as their rhetorical, linguistic, and semiotic choices. This reflection was guided by a heuristic recommended by the MSU FYW program to help students think about the five major components of literacy: invention, arrangement, revision, style, and delivery (**RAIDS**) (see appendix 6.A).

Esther's pedagogy was guided by two themes: practice and experimentation. The themes cohere with Horner, Selfe, and Lockridge's (2015) call for teachers to experiment with translingual/transmodal composition and to encourage their students to do so. As such, students were informed of the experimental nature of the pedagogy and the different ways they would be able to practice and experiment. The students also had the option not to practice or experiment.

Since the pedagogy was experimental, and not all students wanted to participate, Esther feared the students might translanguage in ways incomprehensible to other students. She therefore asked them to compose to an audience whose members consider themselves English monolinguals. She wanted to ensure students (1) were conscious of their linguistic and semiotic choices; (2) demonstrated "rhetorical sensibility" (Guerra 2016) as they translanguaged in their writing; and (3) "develop[ed] a reflective awareness of writing as they wrote their pieces" (Canagarajah 2013b, 47). Nevertheless, as we reflect on Esther's decision to prescribe an English monolingual audience for the

Table 6.2. Comparison of literacy autobiography prompts

FYW Program LA description (2012 version)	Esther's translingual LA assignment (Spring 2014)
... In this project, you'll write about your own experiences with literacy, broadly defined. The purpose of the project is to invite you—now that you're in a new place in your educational career—to make sense of significant literacy-related events in your life and to consider how they might be relevant to how you use and/or think about literacy now.	... since language plays a significant role in [y]our literacy acquisition, you will write your story of literacy development along with your story of language learning/development. By examining your language-learning histories, current language use, and practices, you will tell a story of how the language(s) you use have contributed and continue to contribute in your development as a reader or writer. Your narrative should show the relationship between the two.

Source: FYW TA Workshop Powerpoint presentation.

students, we wonder whether it might have scared some of them away from translanguaging.

Esther scaffolded this assignment with activities and classroom discussions aimed at helping students develop a translingual orientation to language and literacy. The first week was characterized by discussions on readings that offered a different orientation to dominant and Western understandings of literacy. These included Julie Lindquist's "Elements of Literacy," Laura Bohannan's "Shakespeare in the Bush," and Alberto Manguel's "Reading Ourselves and World Around Us." In week two, the class discussed readings that demystified and challenged the myth of monolingualism and monomodality. The readings included Scott Wible's "Rhetorical Activities of Global Citizens," which helped frame discussion on the need for multilingual competencies in global contexts and in the twenty-first century. Students also watched Patricia Ryan's TED talk "Don't Insist on English" and Jay Walker's "The World's English Mania," which further explore and challenge the prestige status of the English language locally and globally. Students read the "Skin We Ink" by David Kirkland, a text that combines written and visual modes to describe the literacy practices of one black male (see appendix 6.B); the students analyzed the multimodal nature of the text they had initially considered monomodal.

As they read and responded to these texts, students were asked to consider the different resources they use when they communicate in different contexts. One of the approaches Esther used to help students discover their translingual resources was to invite students to journal for one week, tracking their everyday language use in diverse places and spaces (home, school, church/mosque, workplace, the streets, Twitter, Facebook, blogs, or any spaces they practice literacy). Every day, students wrote a one-paragraph reflection of what languages and semiotic resources they used, how, when, and where. Esther then asked students to share individual definitions of language based on their journaling activities and observations.

Through this process, students began to see language as including a wide range of semiotic resources including images, symbols, gestures, and colors. Many students, though not all, began to see how they engaged in some level of multilingualism and/or their potential to create hybrid texts. For example, in his reflection memo, Neal, a monolingual domestic student, wrote, "I ultimately realized with the journal entry all the languages I had used per day. I never thought that there was a different language that I talk to my parents and friends via social network, e-mail, text messages, etc. It was crazy how I reflected upon this. That's the funny thing about language is that you don't know what different language types you use throughout your day. It just comes naturally. It was very interesting to see how my language changed throughout my day and this helped influence my writing process on this topic." This journaling process also helped some students generate ideas for their LA assignments.

For the next two weeks, students drafted and revised their LAs based on the feedback they received from their peers and Esther. Students read language and literacy autobiographies by major language scholars like Geneva Smitherman, who draws linguistic resources from Ebonics and Standard Written English (SWE), and Gloria Anzaldúa, who draws from SWE and Spanish (see appendix 6.B). The students were reminded that the texts were models—to help them see the different rhetorical strategies the authors used. Students were encouraged to come up with their own situated strategies of representing their language and literacy histories, interests, and identities. The outcomes of this practice included the development and articulation of some translingual dispositions, which we describe in detail in the following section.

"HAY UN TIEMPO Y UN LUGAR PARA TODO": THE RHETORICAL SENSIBILITIES CULTIVATED BY THE TRANSLINGUAL LITERACY AUTOBIOGRAPHY

Like Canagarajah (2013b), we believe the LA can encourage translanguaging. However, we also believe it can help students cultivate translingual rhetorical sensibilities. Specifically, we found students' work demonstrated several notable outcomes supporting their development of translingual rhetorical sensibilities; examples from Jessica, Ahmed, Gabriel, Xiang, and Neal show three such outcomes:

1. recognized and engaged many translanguaging strategies
2. identified cultures and communities as sites of rhetorical practice
3. articulated specific cultural-rhetorical principles from their language backgrounds

These outcomes suggest the LA offers opportunities for students to explore and articulate possibilities of rhetoric beyond the vocabularies and techniques offered by traditional SAE rhetorics and can help them cultivate a translingual rhetorical sensibility.

Recognizing and Engaging a Wide Variety of Translanguaging Strategies

The products of students' rhetorical negotiations were, in some cases, code-meshed texts, which often indicated students' openness to linguistic diversity (Horner et al. 2011).

Among self-identified multilingual students, we observed the practices of code meshing, translation, and the interrogation, or making sense, of semiodiversity. These students—Ahmed, Gabriel, and Xiang—code meshed using Arabic, Spanish, Chinese, and English. Since the LA explicitly invited students to use all the languages in their repertoire, the self-identified multilingual students took up the challenge to test their translingual fluency by incorporating their home languages in their English texts. As their reflective memos revealed, they discovered they could effectively compose in two or more languages and that language differences were not a hindrance to meaning. For example, Gabriel wrote, "I used the strategy of writing in both English and Spanish to show that they can mix well and still be understood." This outcome supports the claim that multilingualism is not a hindrance to meaning and communication even in contexts where monolingual norms are expected (Horner et al. 2011). Gabriel's comment further reveals that students have multilingual rhetorical competencies even as they enter our classrooms.

Since our pedagogy followed an integrationist approach to languages and modes, our analysis of code meshing went beyond analyzing the meshing of linguistic resources to include semiotic resources. In addition to languages, many students integrated linguistic and semiotic resources in their LAs, including rhetorical choices involving colors, images, gestures, symbols, pictures, and special characters. Sometimes, students translanguaged across multiple modes at once. For example, Jessica included an image of a quote she has tattooed on her side: "*We are all in the same game, just different levels. Livin' in the same hell, just different devils.*" The inclusion of this image can fall into visual, written, performative, embodied, and tactile modes.

In addition to code meshing, students also engaged in other translanguaging strategies, such as translation. However, what we found really interesting about the students' code-meshing choices were their final translation decisions. Xiang and Gabriel demonstrated heightened rhetorical sensibility and agency in making decisions about what to translate or not to translate. In some instances, for the untranslated linguistic items, students provided contextual cues through explanations and definitions to help the reader understand what they were trying to communicate. In other instances, the students deliberately chose not to translate, explain, or define their translanguaged items. Xiang observed, "[Because] some words cannot be translated to English, I wrote Chinese instead. I use many internal feeling while I am describing the situation." For example, he chose not to translate the title of his LA: "爱你曾经恨过的." As readers, we were compelled to consult resources outside the text to understand the meaning of his title. In reading his narrative, we realized he was very aware of his decision not to translate since the title captures and frames his entire narrative: the love-hate relationship he has had with his English teachers.

Similarly, Gabriel chose not to translate or explain some of his Spanish words and phrases because he was "trying to show that you don't need to know a certain language to understand literature." Both Xiang's and Gabriel's deliberate choice not to translate some of their linguistic items shows potential for code-meshed writing to encourage readers and listeners to develop a translingual disposition towards texts written in multiple languages. Gabriel's explanation of his decisions, especially, remind us of the claim that Min-Zhan Lu and Horner (2013) make, that the translingual approach to the LA assignment provides opportunities for rhetorical agency. In this moment, both we the readers and Gabriel the writer are compelled to focus attention on the matter of rhetorical agency; Gabriel challenges us as readers while simultaneously challenging himself to make conscientious and purposeful rhetorical decisions that invite us into his purpose. Translingual writing, then, creates opportunities for teachers and students to be more tolerant of language differences (1) because it provides opportunities for students to pursue such moments of rhetorical agency and (2) because it invites audiences and teachers to read such moments of rhetorical agency with generosity and attention toward understanding.

Translanguaging strategies, as revealed in students' narratives, were part of their language and literacy learning histories. Ahmed, a multilingual international student, reflected on how his parents translated Disney movies from English to Arabic to help him learn both languages. As he grew older, he started watching untranslated US movies, which not only improved his English literacy but also helped him develop a translingual disposition toward listening, reading, and understanding different English accents. Similarly, Gabriel discussed how his grandmother taught him by switching between Spanish and English, thus allowing him to gain literacy in both languages. Teachers interested in teaching translingual pedagogy should realize students already possess these literacies and strategies, but there is a need to create spaces and opportunities for students to practice and experiment with said strategies.

Ahmed used the LA assignment to interrogate the diversity of English and diversity of meanings in English and Arabic. He identified the subtle differences between British English, the version he learned in Saudi Arabia, and American English, the version he used for the LA assignment. Further, he explored the diversity of meanings in some English and Arabic words, phrases and sayings:

> In fact, movies helped me a lot to catch phrases and words that has actually a different meaning in the dictionary but they are used to match a specific meaning in the sentence, such as saying "Get off my back" which means to get off someone's back in literal meaning, but the actual meaning is to stay away from someone or to stop following them. Arabic has some similar type of sentences that are said differently than they are meant, such as saying ام فـوشت رش meaning that no harm comes to you, but it's used to tell someone that he's crazy and that you don't agree with him.

In this passage, Ahmed demonstrates an awareness of his own textual negotiative strategies and how these are affected by transmodal receptive activities, like watching films. While a textual encounter with the phrase *get off my back* may for a viewer produce some cognitive dissonance, Ahmed's comment reminds us that this phrase benefits from the visual context movies afford. Watching movies, then, was transmodally implicated in Ahmed's English-literacy development. Moreover, we see in this passage Ahmed articulating an awareness of culturally situated phrases and words—such as "Get off my back"—and understanding that such phrases exist both in English and in Arabic. Ahmed's observation, we argue, demonstrates some awareness of the underlying fluidity of language across contexts. Thus, code meshing, translation, and engaging in semiodiversity are some of the translanguaging strategies that became visible because our redesigned LA explicitly asked students to not only write in multiple languages but also to make language the topic of inquiry. Therefore, an

LA assignment that explicitly asks students to interrogate their language-learning histories has the potential to also help them discover, or become more aware of, their translingual literacies and consequently engage in more nuanced language-difference negotiation practices.

Identifying Cultures and Communities as Sites of Specific Rhetorical Practices in Monolingual Situations

We found that some students used the LA assignment to reimagine the landscape of their literacy practices and to identify when and how communities develop specific rhetorical practices. We saw this was especially important when students identified American English as their primary language. Jessica, for example, identifies as a white, midwestern woman who was "raised to speak English and . . . friend-to-friend dialogue or otherwise known as 'slang.'" Jessica's LA was immediately interesting, however, for its integration of photographs. These photographs included images of her family, her friends, and her teammates. Arguably, Jessica engaged in translanguaging and transmodality, predominantly through the integration of these photographs.

However, more interesting to us were the functions of these photographs within Jessica's assignment. To each of these photographs, Jessica connected narratives about formative and significant rhetorical practices. For example, accompanying several pictures of Jessica with her close friends were descriptions of the way this particular group communicates.

> When I am with my friends, we do not think about being proper and formal. . . . Our generation has made so many different forms of words that it is just what we are all used to. When texting, we have a constant group chat going. . . . There are even some things in my group of friends that only we know. For example, when one of us six girls gives attitude, more than likely, somebody will text a snowflake picture. For my group of friends, this symbolizes the word "chill." This means we are telling each other to lose the attitude but in a nicer way. We call those inside jokes.

This small excerpt has several layers of rhetorical considerations, which we found worth unpacking for students who identified as monolingual. Having previously identified as monolingual, Jessica was compelled to turn her attention toward the function of visual and symbolic interactions and recognize these elements as a piece of her repertoire of semiotic and rhetorical assets.

Like the photographs Jessica integrated into her LA, the emoji she writes about could be viewed as a form of translanguaging using visual media. More interesting to us, however, were Jessica's explanations of the rhetorical affordances of the emoji. For example, she mentions that the group of friends uses "inside jokes" to convey information in such a way that "only we know" what is being communicated. While the "inside joke" limits the audience for whom this emoji would have a precise meaning, Jessica also indicates that the emoji presents an additional affordance for delivering messages to that audience. Jessica explains that her friends considered the snowflake emoji as a "nicer" version of the message they wanted to communicate—"chill." In this way we see how connecting communication strategies to cultures and communities grounds these strategies in community aims and values.

Jessica's LA made similar observations about the rhetorical strategies she used with other communities—her family, her volleyball team, her classmates, and teachers from secondary school. The essay led Jessica to conclude, "I am not monolingual and nobody in this world is, but at least bilingual. There are so many forms of language and literacies that people do not even realize. This goes for culture too. . . . Language can be expressed in numerous ways it is just opening your eyes to see all of the different forms." In Jessica's description we see the LA as especially important for "opening [the] eyes" of students who perceive themselves as having limited experience with language difference. While we detect in Jessica's conclusion a problematic conflation of language and modality (Matsuda and Jablonski 2000), we appreciate that Jessica came away with the lesson that even when she communicates in English, her practices combine translingual and transmodal forms of communication. Moreover, many of these students, like Jessica, connect these practices to community-based rhetorical exigencies.

Jessica's LA submission highlights one aspect of rhetorical sensibility that was among the outcomes of the LA assignment. In her LA and subsequent reflection, Jessica articulated and demonstrated how her own rhetorical practices were culturally situated, culturally specific, and multimodal. Moreover, her very localized description of texting conventions within her specific group of close friends echoes the assertions of Gonzales (2015) and Anis Bawarshi (2016) about the fluidity of genre since Jessica recognized how the genre conventions of individual text messages were linked to specific community expectations. We believe the LA assignment might encourage a variety of students to engage the unique facets of rhetorical practice that are a part of everyday lives, even among "monolingual" communicators, such as the use of pictures, emojis, document design, and fashion.

Articulating Cultural Rhetorical Principles

A third major theme present in students' LA assignments was an articulation of specific cultural rhetorical principles. According to Phil Bratta and Malea Powell (2016), one hallmark of cultural rhetorical analysis involves the ability to "build meaningful theoretical frames from inside [a] particular culture." In other words, some students situated their work within particular cultural communities (as Jessica did); some students were also able to speak in detail about rhetorical practices meaningful to that cultural community. In this sense, we observed students speaking from within their own communities to articulate the rhetorical principles that constitute those communities. We believe this is a translingual disposition to the extent that all communication, particularly in global contexts, cannot be separated from peoples' cultures, bodies, experiences, and histories (Pennycook 2007).

In this section, we focus on examples from Ahmed's and Gabriel's LA assignments and reflections. Both Ahmed and Gabriel, as multilinguals, worked to articulate rhetorical principles that emanate from their communities, and especially their families.

In his LA paper and subsequent reflection, Ahmed demonstrates an understanding and belief that literacy and its acquisition are culturally situated, describing that his own language development entwined among language, religion, and pragmatism. According to Ahmed, his parents were both fluent in English and Arabic and believed it was important that Ahmed learn to practice and speak Arabic well. Ahmed writes,

> [My parents] also wanted me to be better in speaking Arabic, as I must know how to read Quran (the book of Islam). It's really important for every Muslim to read Quran in Arabic, even if they didn't speak the language; they had to at least learn to. Nevertheless that Quran now has been translated to other languages, but its [*sic*] never as correct as when reading it in Arabic. Many sentences cannot be translated into English, as English doesn't have translations for some Arabic words, unless you make a sentence translation for that word. Like the word كادف, it doesn't have any straight up translation and you find this word in a lot of Arabic words, that word means (to give with all your heart), close to sacrifice but not, since sacrifice means تضحية in Arabic.

Ahmed's explanation of his parents' motivations explains how Arabic plays a role in sustaining culture and religion to the extent that the language conveys precise and distinct concepts from the possible translation options Ahmed believes are available. This culturally sustaining impetus was part of the exigency for Ahmed's literacy learning. At the same time, Ahmed describes pragmatic reasons that fueled his English-language development. Ahmed writes he was compelled to learn English so he would be able to understand English entertainment, such as Disney films. He also describes traveling with his parents and experiencing English as a lingua franca of that travel experience, writing that "everywhere we went we had to speak English, no matter what language they praised, English was the way to communicate." Thus, Ahmed noted both personal and pragmatic exigencies for learning English.

Similarly, Gabriel described in detail some of the rhetorical practices meaningful to his family; his LA focused extensively on how and why his grandmother taught him Spanish and English simultaneously before he began formal schooling. Gabriel writes, "My grandmother taught me letters and words and would have me practice them in English and Spanish. She would also have me write down *parablas* in both English and Spanish. She thought it was very important that I learn how to read in Spanish and English so she would she would read me children books in Spanish and English. Once I started school *mi abuela* made sure I stayed disciplined in Spanish." While Gabriel utilizes several translanguaging strategies—including code meshing of Spanish, English, and images—these two Spanish *parablas, la lengua guarde el pescuezo* (the tongue guards the throat) and *hay un tiempo y un lugar para todo* (there is a time and place for everything), were also remarkable examples of the outcome of articulating specific cultural rhetorical principles. Gabriel drew together two Spanish *parablas* to articulate fundamental rhetorical principles underpinning his experience within his Mexican American family. These two *parablas* served as central themes in Gabriel's work. The latter, Gabriel explained, was his grandmother's rationale for teaching him Spanish and insisting upon his speaking it: *hay un tiempo y un lugar para todo*—there is a time and place for everything, both English and Spanish.

Similarly, *la lengua guarde el pescuezo* (the tongue guards the throat) served several rhetorical purposes in Gabriel's LA. As Gabriel elaborated in his reflective memo, he began writing with this phrase in mind. In his final reflection on this phrase, Gabriel writes, "I always assumed [my grandmother] told me this to keep me out of trouble. However as I grew up I realized that she told me this so that I would continue my Spanish speaking and never forget about it. She wanted to ensure that I am the only person in control of what I say and how I say it. My tongue guards my throat and I am free to talk however I want to." We were particularly impressed by Gabriel's explanation of the dual meaning of the phrase, which, on the one hand, serves as a warning to speak cautiously but on the other is an affirmation of his multilingual capacity and rhetorical agency. Particularly in the face of an educational culture that taught Gabriel only "the American way," these two *parablas* form the basis for an important rhetorical lesson his grandmother tried to teach both Gabriel and his father: their family would grow up speaking both Spanish and English freely, knowing there were occasions in which both would be important.

Taken together, Ahmed and Gabriel's LA assignments and reflections offer examples of how students use this assignment to articulate cultural rhetorical principles, theories of language, and rhetoric. Their descriptions of the exigencies for their literacy learning and rhetorical principles allow us to better understand these students and their cultural "systems, beliefs, relationships to the past, practices of meaning-making, and practices of carrying culture forward to future generations" (Bratta and Powell 2016). To that extent, we believe that when used toward the outcome of articulating cultural rhetorical principles, the translingual LA assignment has the additional opportunity to support culturally sustaining pedagogies by scaffolding an asset-based learning experience that supports linguistic, literate, and cultural pluralism and equality (Paris 2012). Teachers interested in cultivating a translingual rhetorical sensibility should take an asset-based approach to learning that allows and encourages students to interrogate the historical, cultural, religious, and political factors surrounding all the languages they bring to their translingual experience. In doing so, students will demonstrate critical language awareness as they translanguage in their writing.

CONCLUSION

In this chapter, we have described the LA as a valuable assignment for our own courses when they have been oriented around translingual theory and the practice of translanguaging. This assignment, which invites students to consider language and literacy broadly, and reflect on critical moments in their lives associated with literacy, has yielded a number of outcomes for us as scholars and teachers committed to linguistic diversity. More specifically, we've found some particularly beneficial outcomes include recognizing and engaging a wide range of semiotic resources; identifying cultures and communities as sites of rhetorical practice; describing particular and divergent values around literacy and literacy acquisition; and articulating specific cultural-rhetorical principles to guide rhetorical agency. Thus, the focus of the assignment is not merely on producing a code-meshed text but also on cultivating the rhetorical sensibilities Guerra (2016) argues are critical for college writing classes to teach.

Such affordances, we believe, can begin to challenge the dominant, monolingual, monomodal, alphabetic, product-oriented writing practices prevalent in FYW classrooms. One such affordance is that assignments like the LA can help make good on the theoretical distinction of *trans* by genuinely inviting students to consider moving across languages and modalities in their composing in ways that extend beyond the traditional approaches to the LA in our curriculum and in ways that honor their cultural and linguistic backgrounds.

APPENDIX 6.A

LANGUAGE AND LITERACY AUTOBIOGRAPHY ASSIGNMENT DESCRIPTION

According to Ulla Connor, "A literacy autobiography is an account of significant factors and events that have contributed to your development as a reader or writer" (41). Oftentimes, we don't stop to reflect how certain persons, events, practices, or experiences in our lives have played a role in shaping the literate persons we are today. This assignment asks you to do that. And since language plays a significant role in our literacy acquisition, you will write your story of literacy development along with your story of language learning/development. By examining your language-learning histories, and current language use and practices, you will tell a story of how the language(s) you use have contributed and continue to contribute in your development as a reader or writer. Your narrative should show the relationship between the two.

INVENTION ACTIVITIES

- Look back . . .

    Since this is an autobiography, it will involve a lot of reflection. Consider for example (1) what significant people in your life have played a role in your language and literacy development, e.g., teachers, parents, siblings, peers, etc., or (2) what events, experiences, places, things you've read, neighborhoods, standardized testing, cultural practices, language norms and policies, monolingual/multilingual settings, migration, technology, books, newspapers, social media, etc., have shaped your literacy-development journey.

- Track your language practices . . .

    You will keep a language log for one week where you record and reflect on your everyday language practices in diverse places/spaces where you practice literacy. These could include home, school, church/mosque, workplace, the streets, Twitter, Facebook, blogs, etc.

You will track what languages you use each day while speaking and writing in these different places. At the end of each day, you will write a one-paragraph reflection on what languages you used that day, how, when, and where.

GUIDELINES

You should be able to demonstrate a self-reflection and an awareness of the significance of the persons, events, and factors you write about and show how they contributed to your development as a reader or writer. You should particularly show the relationship between your language learning/histories/practices/experiences and your literacy development. Your essay should draw readers' interest and should provide relevant supporting details. You may also use other features of narration like dialogue and description.

LANGUAGE USE

You will write in some or all of the languages you know or use. And since communication goes beyond using languages, feel free to use other writing/symbol systems you know or use.

AUDIENCE

You will be writing to an audience that considers itself "English monolinguals." We will read language and literacy autobiographies by Geneva Smitherman and Gloria Anzaldúa. From these samples, you will see examples of various linguistic and rhetorical strategies multilingual writers use when they combine several languages in their writing. However, you are encouraged to come up with your own situated strategies of representing your language and literacy history.

MEMO

The final paper should be accompanied by a one-page (single-spaced) memo where you reflect on your writing process using the heuristics of RAIDS (see Jane E. Aaron, *Little, Brown Compact Handbook,* 7th edition).

This assignment will have two phases: a rough draft for peer review is due 01/23. Final draft and a memo are due on 01/28. Upload in Dropbox in Desire2Learn. The length of your final paper should be 4–5 pages.

APPENDIX 6.B

SELECTED READINGS RELATED TO THE LA ASSIGNMENT (IN ORDER)

1. Lindquist, J., and D. Seitz. 2008. Introduction to *The Elements of Literacy*, edited by J. Lindquist and D. Seitz. New York: Longman.
2. Bohannan, L. "Shakespeare in the Bush." *Natural History*. http://www.naturalhistorymag.com/editors_pick/1966_08-09_pick.html.
3. Manguel, A. 2011. "Reading Ourselves and World Around Us." In *Reading and Writing Literacies*, edited by N. Dejoy, C. Craig, S. T. Lessner, and B. J. Williams, 15–17. New York: Pearson.
4. Kirkland, D. 2009. "Skin We Ink: Conceptualizing Literacy as Human Practice." *English Education* 41 (4): 375–95.
5. Wible, S. (2013). "Rhetorical Activities of Global Citizens." In *Literacy as a Translingual Practice: Between Communities and Classrooms*, edited by A. S. Canagarajah, 39–46. New York: Routledge.
6. Ryan, P. 2010. "Don't Insist on English." TED video, 10.19. http://www.ted.com/talks/patricia_ryan_ideas_in_all_languages_not_just_english.html.
7. Walker, J. 2009. "The World's English Mania." TED Video, 4:16. http://www.ted.com/talks/jay_walker_on_the_world_s_english_mania.html.
8. Smitherman, G. 1999. "From Ghetto Lady to Critical Linguist." In *Talkin That Talk: African American Language and Culture*, 1–12. New York: Routledge.
9. Anzaldúa, G. 1987. "How to Tame a Wild Tongue." In *Borderlands/La frontera: The New Mestiza*, 53–64. San Francisco: Spinsters/Aunt Lute.

REFERENCES

Bawarshi, Anis. 2016. "Beyond the Genre Fixation: A Translingual Perspective on Genre." *College English* 78 (3): 243–49.

Bratta, Phil, and Malea Powell. 2016. "Introduction to the Special Issue: Entering the Cultural Rhetorics Conversations." Enculturation 21. http://enculturation.net/entering-the-cultural-rhetorics-conversations.

Canagarajah, Suresh. 2013a. *Literacy as Translingual Practice: Between Communities and Classrooms*. New York: Routledge.

Canagarajah, A. Suresh. 2013b. "Negotiating Translingual Literacy: An Enactment." *Research in the Teaching of English* 48 (1): 40–67.

Cushman, Ellen. "Translingual and Decolonial Approaches to Meaning Making." *College English* 78 (3): 234–42.

De Costa, Peter I., Jyotsna G. Singh, Esther Milu, Xiqiao Wang, Steven Fraiberg, and Suresh Canagarajah. 2017. "Pedagogizing Translingual Practice: Prospects and Possibilities." *Research in the Teaching of English* 51 (4): 464–72.

Fraiberg, Steven. 2010. "Composition 2.0: Toward a Multilingual and Multimodal Framework." *College Composition and Communication* 62 (1): 100–126.

Gonzales, Laura. 2015. "Multimodality, Translingualism, and Rhetorical Genre Studies." *Composition Forum* 31. https://compositionforum.com/issue/31/multimodality.php.

Guerra, Juan C. 2016. "Cultivating a Rhetorical Sensibility in the Translingual Writing Classroom." *College English* 78 (3): 228–33.

Horner, Bruce, Min-Zhan Lu, Jacqueline Jones Royster, and John Trimbur. 2011. "Opinion: Language Difference in Writing: Toward a Translingual Approach." *College English* 73 (3): 303–21.

Horner, Bruce, Samantha NeCamp, and Christiane Donahue. 2011. "Toward a Multilingual Composition Scholarship: From English Only to a Translingual Norm." *College Composition and Communication* 63 (2): 269–300.

Horner, Bruce, Cynthia Selfe, and Tim Lockridge. 2015. "Translinguality, Transmodality, and Difference: Exploring Dispositions and Change in Language and Learning." Enculturation/Intermezzo.

Kiernan, Julia E. 2015. "Multimodal and Translingual Composing Practices: A Culturally Based Needs Assessment of Second Language Learners." *Journal of Global Literacies, Technologies, and Emerging Pedagogies* 3 (1): 302–21.

Lee, Jerry Won, and Christopher Jenks. 2016. "Doing Translingual Dispositions." *College Composition and Communication* 68 (2): 317–44.

Leonard, Rebecca Lorimer, and Rebecca Nowacek. 2016. "Transfer and Translingualism." *College English* 78 (3): 258–64.

Limbu, Marohang. 2012. "Teaching Writing in the Cloud: Networked Writing Communities in the Culturally and Linguistically Diverse Classroom." *Journal of Global Literacies, Technologies, and Emerging Pedagogies* 1 (1): 1–20.

Lu, Min-Zhan, and Bruce Horner. 2013. "Translingual Literacy, Language Difference, and Matters of Agency." In *Literacy as a Translingual Practice: Between Communities and Classrooms*, edited by Suresh Canagarajah, 26–38. New York: Routledge.

Manguel, A. 2011. "Reading Ourselves and World Around Us." In *Reading and Writing Literacies*, edited by N. Dejoy, C. Craig, S. T. Lessner, and B. J. Williams, 15–17. New York: Pearson.

Matsuda, Paul Kei. 2006. "The Myth of Linguistic Homogeneity in U.S. College Composition." *College English* 68 (6): 637–51.

Matsuda, Paul Kei, and Jeffery Jablonski. 2000. "Beyond the L2 Metaphor: Towards a Mutually Transformative Model of ESL/WAC Collaboration." *Academic Writing* 1. https://wac.colostate.edu/aw/articles/matsuda_jablonski2000.htm.

Office for International Students and Scholars. 2014. Statistical Reports. http://oiss.isp.msu.edu/about/statistics.htm.

Paris, Django. 2012. "Culturally Sustaining Pedagogy: A Needed Change in Stance, Terminology, and Practice." *Educational Researcher* 41 (3): 93–97.

Pennycook, Alastair. 2007. *Global Englishes and Transcultural Flows*. New York: Routledge.

Seloni, Lisya. 2014. " 'I'm an Artist and a Scholar Who is Trying to Find a Middle Point': A Textographic Analysis of a Colombian Art Historian's Thesis Writing." *Journal of Second Language Writing* 25 (1): 79–99.

Shipka, Jody. 2016. "Transmodality in/and Processes of Making: Changing Dispositions and Practice." *College English* 78 (3): 250–57.

Smuckler, Ralph H. 2003. *A University Turns to the World: A Personal History of the Michigan State University International Story*. East Lansing: Michigan State University Press.

Stewart, Mary Amanda, and Holly Hansen-Thomas. 2016. "Sanctioning a Space for Translanguaging in the Secondary English Classroom: A Case of a Transnational Youth." *Research in the Teaching of English* 50 (4): 450–72.

PART II

Enacting Translingual Pedagogies in Interdisciplinary Spaces

7
WRITING ON THE WALL
Teaching Translingualism through Linguistic Landscapes

Mark Brantner

INTRODUCTION

Translingual studies often traces students' linguistic abilities, histories, and practices of negotiating classroom communities and making meaning. They often, also, examine the ways writing courses and programs sponsor students' compositional strategies. And they primarily focus on programs and classrooms from the United States in an attempt to challenge what Paul Kei Matsuda (2006) calls the "myth of linguistic homogeneity" (638). Understanding the rich resources students bring to negotiating linguistic heterogeneity rightfully undercuts the deficit models that presuppose students' inability and, often, express hostility toward encountering difference. Further, the focus of empirical studies on students' strategies enables faculty to ground their assignments, lessons, assessments, and teaching in the concrete conscious and unconscious practices students engage in.

Without challenging or undercutting the value of these student-centric introspective and analytical studies, this paper adds to translingual discussions by describing the ways translingual pedagogies inform an assignment sequence that operates outside the focus on student practices, outside the first-year composition (FYC) classroom, and outside the United States. I believe that expanding the purview of translingual approaches and pedagogies can offer methods for developing students' abilities to critically engage their communities and the environments in which their translingual strategies and attitudes have developed. In other words, this paper outlines the ways a translingual pedagogy might foster a form of critical literacy. Gary Anderson and Patricia Irvine (1997) have given us a working definition of the concept. They write that critical literacy is "learning to read and write as part of the process of becoming conscious of one's experience as historically constructed within specific power relations" (82).

DOI: 10.7330/9781646421121.c007

The assignment I describe in this chapter brings together ideas from translingual and critical-literacy pedagogies and from emerging studies of linguistic landscapes. Specifically, the linguistic landscape assignment I outline asks students at the National University of Singapore to examine how the complex cultural, economic, and political diversity of Singapore's multilingual and urban linguistic landscape sponsors particular literacy practices at the expense of others. The primary learning outcome for the assignment is for students to investigate the ways their abilities to read and write in English, in their mother tongues, or even in their familial dialects or languages are, in part, regulated by the spaces they inhabit, spaces historically constructed and subject to specific power relations. As students become cognizant of regulated languages within regulated spaces, they develop the kinds of critical literacies advocated by Anderson and Irvine. Students come to see the ways power structures physically organize languages within their landscape and regulate, or at least prime, their language use within it. In connecting critical literacy to translingual practices, students recognize that their strategies for communicating across linguistic differences are not simply instances of personal choice. More importantly, students grasp that historical and power relations regulate not only linguistic differences but also the strategies they use to communicate across them.

EDUCATIONAL LANDSCAPE

Over 150 years old and with approximately thirty-five thousand students across thirteen faculties and schools, the National University of Singapore is Singapore's oldest and largest institution of higher education. It is consistently ranked among the top twenty-five institutions in the world and among the top three institutions in Asia by QS University rankings and the *Times Higher Education* World University Rankings. I teach in the University Scholars Programme (USP), which is an independent interdisciplinary academic program. Essentially equivalent to an honors college in the United States, USP draws students from seven of the university's thirteen faculties. USP graduates receive a certificate and earn honors in their home departments and faculties. Students accepted into USP usually have graduated at the top of their junior college or polytechnic and have scored in the top percentiles on their A-level exam. USP's curriculum has three tiers, the Foundation Tier, Inquiry Tier, and Reflection Tier. The assignment I describe and my course are taught as part of the Inquiry Tier. But to note, in the

Foundation Tier, essentially their first year, students take a quantitative reasoning module (QR), an interdisciplinary history of ideas module, and a small seminar-style first-year writing module called Writing and Critical Thinking (WCT). This module, originally modeled on the Harvard College writing program, takes an interdisciplinary, thematic approach to teaching academic writing. Thus, when I meet these students, at the Inquiry Tier stage, I assume they have already taken the QR and the WCT modules. Specifically, the assignment discussed here is offered in a class called the Politics of Language and Literacy in Singapore.

The entire Inquiry Tier module is based on the work of the new literacy studies group and takes its direction from sociocultural and multidisciplinary studies of literacy. The module has three projects. The first is an ethnographic study of literacy practices within a literacy event. In this assignment, students document the ways people use texts to accomplish particular purposes within particular discourse communities. One student, for example, recorded the ways a parishioner translates an English sermon into Mandarin during a church service, and another student documented how a young woman uses Chinese calligraphy to participate in cultural celebrations. This first assignment challenges students' understanding of literacy as a purely cognitive ability, which can be tested through Singapore's high-stakes examinations, and pushes them to understand literate action is situated and purposeful. Importantly, the first project stresses that literacy is a practice that enables people to participate as members of a community and to accomplish shared activities within those communities.

The course's second project, which is the focus of this essay, asks students to investigate a portion of Singapore's linguistic landscape (see the project's assignment sheet in appendix 7.A). Through their investigations of linguistic landscapes, students investigate official regulations and uncover unofficial conventions and strategies their communities use to negotiate linguistic diversity in Singapore's highly multicultural context. Projects have included a survey of the three terminals at Chiangi International Airport, a study of the emergence of Bangla among restaurants and shops in the Little India district, and the documentation of heritage initiatives in Telok Ayer, a district designated by Sir Stamford Raffles for Singapore's Chinese community.

In addition to developing a translingual approach that analyzes material communal practices, this assignment investigates a nation that takes linguistic heterogeneity as a central tenet of its national identity. Singapore has four national languages, Mandarin, Tamil, and Malay, which serve as mother-tongue languages, and English, which serves as an interethnic transactional language and connects Singapore to global markets. However, various Chinese dialects, Indian languages, and Singlish complicate this official linguistic picture. Within this linguistically rich cultural landscape, Singaporean students develop a rich set of linguistic resources in their daily lives. Singapore has adopted a bilingual education policy in which all citizens take courses in English and their mother tongue. Further, many students live in flats in which multiple languages are spoken by parents and grandparents. A common result of this complicated linguistic heterogeneity is that Singaporean students are unconsciously adept at negotiating language diversity, which remains the norm.

However, students see this negotiation, whether conscious or unconscious, as a product of individual capacities, abilities, and, most commonly, individual choice. Let me give you an example. This linguistic landscape assignment is part of my Politics of Language and Literacy in Singapore module, but I did not initially include a linguistic landscape assignment. Instead, I began the module with a literacy narrative. A young Malay woman's narrative made me see the importance of this particular assignment. This young woman wrote eloquently about the accolades she had won during her secondary education regarding her abilities to write in and speak *Bahasa Melayu* (Malay). She wrote poetry and spoke with her family in her mother tongue. However, during her time at the university, she no longer felt particularly adept with Malay. Her narrative concludes with a resolve that if she wants to maintain her Malay, and its link to her ethnic identity, she needs to use it more often. Many other students, especially Chinese and Malay students, have expressed similar sentiments. Their abilities to converse in their mother tongue, they believe, depends on their conscious choice to use the language.

What this commonplace causal conclusion misses and what, I think, the ideas from critical literacy and new literacy studies help students see is that their abilities to use their languages rest, in part, on the regulations and conventions that govern the appropriate use of their mother tongue in social, academic, economic, and familial spaces. More important, I believe, this assignment helps them see that these rules of propriety are embedded in and constructed within historical and material power relations and are literally concretized in the walls around them. Students don't simply invent their strategies for negotiating linguistic differences ex nihilo; instead, they may internalize the regulations and conventions that govern social discourse and that structure the language as it appears in public spaces.

After hearing my student's pangs of guilt over what she saw as her own failing to choose to use her mother tongue, I developed a linguistic landscape assignment that demonstrates that the choice to use a language and the strategies for writing and speaking across languages follow rules that can be uncovered from the patterns of language use in public spaces.

As an American and a US-trained practitioner-scholar working in Singapore, I had to quickly become acquainted with some of the linguistic histories of both the country (through studying language and educational policies) and its people (through collecting literacy narratives, which can be found at the Digital Archive of Literacy Narratives at The Ohio State University). I believe the assignments in this course honor the expertise of my students who are Singaporean or have lived in Singapore for several years. It allows them to share with me the histories and the knowledge they've accumulated through their lived experiences. I learn a great deal from them, their stories, and their knowledge of local spaces. At the same time, my expertise in literacy studies challenges their understanding of these lived but often unanalyzed experiences. In short, I explain early on that I am an expert in some aspects of the module and they are experts in other aspects. Working together, everyone learns but in different ways. Finally, few of these kinds of studies had been conducted at the time of teaching this module, so I also pointed out to students that we were engaged as a group in authentic research that could revise these theories in light of Singaporean literacy practices.

LINGUISTIC LANDSCAPES

The study of linguistic landscapes (LL) began as a subfield of sociolinguistics but is burgeoning into a rich interdisciplinary field in its own right, cutting across applied linguistics, sociolinguistics, sociology, language planning, and cultural studies. Linguistic landscapes map language contact and reveal how unequal distributions of linguistic resources become concretized within situated linguistic and literate actions. Although LL studies examine locations of different scales (street, neighborhood, town, city, nation) and public and private spaces (science lab versus public square), most LL studies focus on the urban environment, leading Florian Coulmas (2008) to call it the "linguistic cityscape" (14) and Durk Gorter (2013) to call it the "multilingual cityscape" (191). In their seminal study, Roderigue Landry and Richard Bourhis (1997) succinctly define these landscapes: "The language of road signs, advertising billboards, street names, place names, commercial shop signs, and public signs on government buildings combine to form the linguistic landscape of a given territory, region or urban agglomeration" (25). Although their definition names a handful of specific types of signs, more recent studies have greatly expanded the objects that fall under examination.

Early studies employed a quantitative approach. Peter Backhaus (2007), for instance, recorded signs adjacent to Tokyo's circular Yamanote train line. Backhaus canvased Tokyo's major neighborhoods, and the study offered a systematic framework for calculating the distribution of languages and scripts in the city. The study revealed the exchanges among languages and scripts on signs and showed a multilingual Tokyo that was changing in accord with globalization, world Englishes, and migration. Similarly, Thom Huebner's (2006) study of Bangkok, Thailand, reveals the impact of world Englishes as Bangkok's linguistic landscape shifts from incorporating more Chinese to more English. More important to my module, the study reveals the ways Bangkok's signs can be understood as demonstrating code-meshing strategies such as lexical borrowing, syntactic and orthographic mixing, and pronunciation. These strategies speak to the influence of English on the Thai language system and reveal the strategies Thais use to negotiate linguistic differences.

Other studies take a more qualitative approach. Eliezer Ben-Rafael (2008), for instance, draws from gestalt theory to see the LL not as a series of countable signs but as perceptible wholes, geographic centers such as downtowns or shopping centers, where actor-created signs dynamically interact with more permanent architectural and natural features. Further, even among the actor-created LL, actors produce signs for different reasons. Thus, Ben-Rafael offers four sociological structuration principles: (1) drawing on the work of Irving Goffman, he posits the "presentation of self" principle, which accounts for how actors create signs that differentiate themselves from their competitors in the LL; (2) the "good reasons" principle, which addresses the audience's sense of propriety and desires; (3) the "collective-identity" principle, in which actors signal that they belong to a particular group identity (in Singapore, a food shop may signal it's Halal); and, (4) drawn from Pierre Bourdieu, the "power-relations" principle, which highlights language policies' and governing bodies' roles in regulating or restricting LL signs or the languages that appear on those signs.

Although the study of LL has become a burgeoning subfield in its own right, linguistic landscapes have remained rather invisible to rhetoric and writing scholars. Ben-Rafael (2008) offers us a great point of entry, however. He writes, "LL can be referred to as symbolic construction of the public space as it is the languages it speaks out and the symbols which it evinces that serve as the landmarks of this space where 'things happen' in society" (41). Drawing on gestalt theory and envisioning the linguistic landscape as a "symbolic construction of the public space," Ben-Rafael authorizes rhetoricians to use their full toolbox to study such symbolic constructions. His four structuration principles can be integrated with rhetorical concepts. For instance, the sociological principle "presentation of self" aligns nicely with aspects of rhetoric's treatment of ethos. Offering broader implications for our field, Bernard Spolsky (2008) argues that the differences between the LL's visible language may or may not be in accord with the space's spoken language, and thus most LL studies actually reveal aspects about a location's literacy practices (29).

The studies discussed above offer, primarily, a synchronic portrait of language in contact. However, it is important, especially when studying historically layered spaces, to take a diachronic approach (Blommaert 2013). Writing about Sydney, Australia, Alastair Pennycook and Emi Otsuji (2015) suggest LL research can reveal the diachronic movement of literacy and language practices. They write, "Here we see the intertwined-ness of historical migrations and everyday practices of multiplicity through eating, shopping, entertaining, consulting and grooming. The layers of linguistic landscapes need to be understood not so much in terms of static physical emplacements, but rather as the mobilization of history through everyday practices" (155). This approach is crucial to a cityscape, such as Singapore, where rapid urban development coincides with heritage preservation initiatives.

Gorter (2013) concludes that "[the] results of linguistic landscape research offer fresh perspectives on issues such as urban multilingualism, globalization, minority languages, and language policy" (205). However, it is the contention of this chapter that linguistic landscape research can also frame perspectives on translingualism, pedagogy, rhetoric, and writing. For instance, the assignment I outline here focuses less on students' individual language resources, which many translingual pedagogies rightly foster. Instead, a study of the linguistic landscape opens opportunities for students to critically engage and reflect on the situated use of their language resources and literacy practices. What are the most common visible language conventions within a space? Who controls or regulates the visual language within a space? How might the linguistic landscape prime students to use particular practices and language resources at the cost of others? How do they perpetuate or challenge those conventions and for whose interests?

TEACHING THE LANDSCAPES

The assignment asks students to analyze the linguistic landscape of some area within Singapore. The assignment's sequence contains five weeks of instruction. These five weeks are usually divided into two two-week instructional units divided by a semester-break week, which gives students a chance to go into the city to collect data.

In the first two weeks of the assignment sequence, students follow the lead of early sociolinguistic analyses of linguistic landscapes. They focus on what to count as a sign, what logic delineates an area of study, and what they will count as linguistic markers. During this period, we read early linguistic landscape studies, attending to the methodology sections, the kinds of questions these studies attempt to answer, and the ways these studies count the various languages present in landscapes. Early studies focused on counting densities of various languages. For example, Huebner (2006) studied the densities of Thai, English, and Japanese in several Bangkok sectors.

Before I introduce the assignment, I generally collect data from the section of campus dedicated to the University Scholars Programme (USP). USP maintains two two-story buildings, which house classrooms and faculty offices, one one-story multipurpose hall/gymnasium, and significant portions of a large dormitory. Although most of the dormitory is dedicated to USP, it also houses international students, and its cafeteria is shared with a neighboring dormitory/residential college. Following the lead of the studies we will read, I take photos with my phone of all the signs that decorate the outside of these areas. I always make sure to photograph repetitive signs, such as exit signs, signs visible within USP's space but located outside its boundaries, signs that are multilayered or that have been augmented, and other possible examples of writing, such as packaging boxes or bags of chips. Then I share this data with students through an Instagram account.

On the first day, we read an introduction to LL and examine the data I've collected. The goal for the first day is twofold: introduce aims, goals, and methods of LL studies and introduce rhetorical theories that might be applicable. To accomplish this, I ask students to work in groups to develop criteria for evaluating signs and the space. Students are immediately confronted by the nature of signs and their durability, as well as their relations to the concrete spaces they occupy. First, students must decide whether a sign visible within USP but attached to a neighboring building should count as a member of their data set and how much of the shared dormitory and cafeteria should count as USP space. Second, they must develop a rationale based on their aims, goals, and methods for analyzing collected data. Toward the second goal, I ask students to examine USP's signs to analyze how USP presents its ethos to the public. They draw on this research question as they analyze the signs and the language on them. Students must decide how to examine the visible languages along with commonplaces we use to describe our programmatic identity (e.g., three giant signs tell students "Be Curious," "Be Critical," and "Be Engaged"). Last, students must decide how much to incorporate repetitive, campus-wide directive signs, such as exit signs.

After providing students with experience in analyzing a data set from USP's LL, students collect their own data sets. In groups, they go to areas known as hawker centers, which are large public food courts all over the island. There, they test their methods for defining signs, delineating borders, and determining linguistic markers. We spend two or three class meetings working with the material they have collected at the hawker centers. Although the focus of this task helps students engage the deceptively complex issues that surround collecting signs, delineating borders, and determining linguistic use, we also follow early sociolinguistic models, so students count the various official languages of Singapore and look for dialects or other languages. Students begin to see the concrete numerical ways languages are distributed in their daily lives. Every study I have seen so far has demonstrated, without question, the dominance of English in the Singaporean cityscape. Students return to class with their data sets, and we repeat the analytical exercise we did for the USP LL. Each group posits its own question. Then, they must see how their methods for collection align with their design for analysis. During this time, I do not lecture but set the parameters for their study, and they work in groups. I visit each group to answer questions and make sure they're on the right trajectory. The groups must collect their data via some form of social media so the data sets from hawker centers can be visible to everyone in the class.

After each group has analyzed its own data set, we troubleshoot some of the recurrent questions that face multiple groups. These most often relate to multilingual signs, multilayered signs, and signs that incorporate words and images. Students immediately encounter problems with simply counting the languages on signs. How will they count signs with traditional Chinese characters and pinyin? How will they count signs, especially those advertising food, that mix languages? We use Huebner's study of Bangkok (2006) to discuss these issues surrounding multiple languages on signs. On many signs in Singapore, the languages remain distinct, especially in official "top-down" (Ben-Rafael et al. 2013, 14) signs. In these cases, we discuss font size and order of languages to highlight the relative value and power of the individual languages in public spaces. But many "bottom-up" signs (Ben-Rafael et al. 2013, 14), those signs made by individual hawkers, use various strategies of code meshing within specific chunks of text. Huebner (2006) points out that many Thai public signs play with lexical borrowing, syntactical borrowing, and pronunciation within linguistic units to communicate within and across language communities. Students betray official state ideological stances when they expect the languages to be kept fully distinct. In other words, students expect signs to be multilingual and to switch between distinct linguistic codes and national languages, but they do not expect the messiness they encounter when they find signs that mesh linguistic codes. For example, they are unsure how to count a sign that reads, "We sell the best nasi lemak in Singapore."

In addition to linguistic code meshing, students immediately encounter another translingual strategy. Specifically, hawker centers combine linguistic and visual resources. Signs often display an image of each dish, a number, and the name of each dish, most often in English and one or two other languages. This mix of linguistic and visual resources can be quite complex. Does the sign use Chinese characters or Hanyu Pinyin Romanization (pinyin)? Should they count the name of Malay dishes in Romanized script as English or Malay, especially when other dishes on the same sign describe the food rather than show a name.

Through their analyses, students immediately recognize hawker-center LLs contain more languages than the university campus. This opens up discussions of audiences, purposes, and language policies. For example, we share our hawker-center data as a class in order to see the relative differences in language density among the different centers as they cater to different populations—local, tourist, Chinese, Malay, or Indian. This introduction of the rhetorical dimension of language use becomes the focus of the second half of the assignment cycle. We also address the differences in purpose between hawkers selling food within a local context and the purposes of signs at a university that sells itself as "A Leading Global University Centered in Asia." Students begin to see that the larger purposes of a localized hawker center differs greatly from a university that seeks to take on a larger role in the globalization of higher education. The former is freer to address a local audience using the linguistic resources available to the local context, but the latter must marry its purposes with languages that circulate both locally and internationally, in this case English. This point also sheds light on issues regarding language policies. Different organizations at different levels regulate language use on the university campus and in hawker centers.

By the end of the second week, students have analyzed a given data set and created their own in groups. Before the semester break, I ask students to develop a research question and identify an area of Singapore to study. All students must post their questions and reasons for choosing their locations on NUS's course-management system, and each student must peer review two other students' posts, helping to refine their classmates' questions and delineate spatial boundaries. I review everyone's posts and directly email students who seem to be having difficulty. I only post to the online forum to address large-scale recurrent problems. Finally, students are given the option to work individually or in groups. They often find that they want to work on similar spaces or that that they have overlapping questions. I only suggest that the data collection and analysis must warrant a team effort. During the semester break, students do fieldwork and collect their photos from their locations.

Following the break, we work as a class to troubleshoot and support students' projects. While the readings in the first two weeks lay out sociolinguistic methodological models, the readings in the second two weeks provide us with sociological and rhetorical modes of analysis that highlight critical approaches to ideology, social structures, and cross-linguistic communication within those structures. I give some minilectures, but the primary objective of each class is to work on the project and to troubleshoot with classmates. I must note that I offer optional readings from Ron Scollon and Suzie Scollon's (2003) excellent *Discourses in Place: Language in the Material World*, and that I deliver daily minilectures on methods of analyzing individual signs. For instance, it is significant in Singapore that English is most often the top language on a sign or in the largest font. Also, hawker centers rely on the composition of their signs to help negotiate linguistic difference. For instance, a photo of the dish is large and central with a number, the dish's name in transliterated English where necessary, and the name is in Malay, Chinese, or Tamil scripts. Further, the readings in this second half pull from rhetorical theory, literacy studies, translingual theory, and sociology to reveal the material, literally concrete, ways communities negotiate, contest, foster, and suppress language diversity and local literacies. Supported by the readings from this unit and the previous unit, we shift our discussions from methods of collection to focus on modes of analysis. Having documented Singaporean literacy practices in the previous unit, students have encountered Deborah Brandt's (1998) term "literacy sponsor" as well as Alanna Frost's (2011) "literacy steward." In the first unit, students have generally understood these terms as individual people, schools, or the government who act consciously to support or, apropos of Singapore, regulate their literacies.

This assignment and our readings challenge students to broaden their understanding beyond individual actors making conscious decisions to the ideological domain. Marián Sloboda (2008), in particular, makes this claim explicit in the reading "State Ideology and Linguistic Landscapes." Marián Sloboda defines ideology as a process of recycling a large number of signs such that they mutually index each other. Drawing on three Eastern European countries, Sloboda shows that communal meanings are produced when large groupings of signs index each other and reference explicit or implicit state ideologies. Such a "stratified pattern of social meaning" exists in the material landscape, called "topos of memory," and offers people a set of meanings to orient themselves toward in communication (174). Sloboda's reading is provocative, yet its focus on ideological "patterns of social meaning" misses a crucial element of translingual theory, that is, strategies of negotiation. In short, Sloboda offers us an opportunity to shift focus from the patterns of meaning to the patterns of practices we see. Just as Sloboda suggests people orient themselves toward the linguistic landscape's ideological messages when they converse with others, I believe taking a translingual approach to the linguistic landscape allows us to realize people adopt and adapt the translingual strategies they encounter in the LL as they communicate within and across linguistic borders. In synthesizing Deborah Brandt, Alanna Frost, and Marián Sloboda, students begin to see that a cityscape is not simply a random collection of individual and disconnected signs. They begin to see that material signs and material language practices index (in Charles Peirce's sense) the rules that govern how Singapore negotiates linguistic differences in public spaces (Scollon and Scollon 2003).

OTHER LANDSCAPES

The assignment I've described here is, frankly, situationally specific. The normal four-modular-credit courses, with one hundred–minute class sessions, and the nature of USP's status as, essentially, NUS's honors college, allow for the demanding amount of work I've described above. Further, prevailing language policies, state-sponsored ideologies, and bottom-up practices sponsor a complex linguistic landscape that meshes multiple linguistic codes. And the country's rich multicultural history fosters an ethic of communicating across linguistic differences. Although I imagine it might be difficult to fully imitate this assignment in many other locations where the LL is more monolinguistic, including parts of the United States, I believe this assignment illustrates that students' attitudes toward linguistic differences and their strategies for communicating across these differences stem in no small part from the linguistic landscapes of their material cultures. So just as the multilingual language practices analyzed in the Singaporean cityscape can help students think about strategies such as code meshing, the more monolingual linguistic landscapes of some cities and small towns can reveal a dearth of communal resources for negotiating differences. This kind of study equally reveals the presence and the absence of such strategies.

A criticism that might be leveled against linguistic landscape studies points to the focus on writing at the expense of the languages spoken within a space (Spolsky 2008). In Singapore, signs are likely in English, but it is not uncommon that the primary language spoken within a space is a mother-tongue language. This assignment and LL studies more generally could be improved by pedagogies and studies of locations' soundscapes. Furthermore, these studies can be enriched by related methodologies such as interviews and ethnographic observations to examine how people create, display, or interact with the signs and the spaces they occupy. It is not uncommon that individual bottom-up signs counter policies designed by corporate owners or governmental regulators. Investigating the motives of communication within a given space could reveal interesting tensions between individuals and communities, among different communities sharing space, and between communities and regulating literacy sponsors. Further, ethnographic observation can reveal how the language in their spaces shapes people's interactions. Such studies could be relevant to critical-literacy studies, on the one hand, and possibly to business communication, on the other.

Linguistic landscapes studies can be adapted to questions about material practices that differ from the aims and goals of studying the linguistic issues addressed above. For instance an assignment could ask students to examine the ethos of a location, such as a coffee shop, community center, church, or campus sporting event. Taking seriously the ways banal practices and symbolic topoi "locate the subject in a particular place and time" (Dickinson 2002, 23) allows rhetoricians to examine the situated rhetorical construction of self. Further, language in spaces and on signs is often gendered, raced, and classed. LL studies that ask students to address these issues reveal issues of power in a culture but also the concrete control over localized spaces. And students could study the environmental messages on signs or even the environmental impact of material signs themselves.

HORIZONS

Singapore's national and cultural identities are deeply entwined with its multicultural, multireligious, and multilingual histories. Even the Singapore National Pledge, in both its English and Malay versions, emphasizes unity regardless of linguistic differences. The pledge celebrates four national languages, English, Malay, Tamil, and Mandarin, and vernacular languages, such as Hokkien, Cantonese, Hindi, Punjabi, Tagalog, and French, among others, that are spoken by citizens, permanent residents, long-term residents, and tourists. But more important, it calls for people to communicate across linguistic differences to work together in shared purposes. The pledge fosters an ethic of translingual communication that strives to negotiate linguistic differences. And some of the strategies people use to communicate across these differences are literally visible and sometimes concretized in Singapore's linguistic landscapes.

At the same time, the linguistic landscape is governed by formal regulations, such as national language policies and hawker-center regulations, and informal conventions, such as a sense of propriety or strategies that appeal to particular audiences. Brandt (1998) and Frost (2011) teach us that informal conventions and formal rules act as "sponsors" and "stewards," shaping situated language use. Sometimes when my Malay-speaking student walks into a space where only English and Mandarin are visible, she "chooses" to rely on her English to communicate. This assignment argues that her decision to use her mother tongue stems in no small part from the ways the concrete material culture of Singapore fosters particular language uses in particular locations, and this process is cued visually by the landscape. In short, the landscapes we inhabit help us develop the strategies, or lack thereof, for negotiating linguistic differences; at the same time, the visual landscapes cue us to rely on particular linguistic resources at the expense of others. The assignment I've described here, designed for my Politics of Language and Literacy in Singapore for the University Scholars Programme at the National University of Singapore, strives to help students develop critical literacies that look past the writing on the wall to see the power relations such writing indexes.

APPENDIX 7.A

ASSIGNMENT SHEET
Linguistic Landscapes

In this unit, we will be examining Singapore's linguistic landscape. The study of linguistic landscapes has been developed in the field of sociolinguistics and generally studies the interactions among languages that occur within a delineated public space. In their seminal study, Landry and Bourhis (1997) write:

> The language of road signs, advertising billboards, street names, place names, commercial shop signs, and public signs on government buildings combines to form the linguistic landscape of a given territory, region or urban agglomeration. (25)

In this unit we will be looking at sociolinguistic and sociological approaches to the study of linguistic landscapes. We will also be attempting to develop rhetorical approaches to data analysis (currently, there are no published rhetorical studies in this field). We will examine the linguistic landscapes of several locations in Singapore.

METHODS

To accomplish this study, we will use photographs of Singaporean spaces. Use your handphones to take photos, and collect and collate them through either Instagram or Pinterest. Remember to consider the following:

- What counts as a sign?
- What boundaries form the public space?
- How will you collect the images? Store them?
- Who produced the signs?
- Who is the audience for the signs?
- What are the signs made of?

You will want to make sure that you are able to choose a small enough delineated space such that you are able to collect enough images without becoming overwhelmed. You will quickly find that a space contains more signs than you initially guessed—many of our model studies collected hundreds, even thousands, of pictures. If you'd like to canvass a larger space, you may work in groups. We will mimic the methods of collection that are described in our readings.

ANALYSIS

You may choose to follow a sociolinguistic analysis (Spolsky), sociological (Ben-Rafael), or rhetorical study. In all cases, take notice of the languages that are present and not present and consider the ways in which the scripts and images on the signs engage linguistic differences.

FORMATTING

The formatting of the project should reflect the best way to offer the analysis of your data to your audience. Also, be sure to take note of the different ways in which sociolinguists, sociologists, and rhetoricians offer a thesis, present evidence, and analyze data. Make sure that your method of analysis matches the recognizable presentation among members of the discipline. Consider the following:

- Interview: How might you present it? Transcripts? Audio? Video?
- Photograph: How might you present it? Separate links? Embedded images? Appendices?
- Video: Web?
- Copies of a text: Copies? Appendices?
- Object: Photographs? Oral presentations?

The delivery of an argument to an audience depends on the recognized patterns of delivery, the type of evidence, and audience. I'm open to multiple ways to make an argument. In your prospectus, you will explain how and why you will deliver your argument.

Papers should follow standard MLA formatting guidelines: http://owl.english.purdue.edu/owl/resource/747/01/.

If you choose a social scientific approach, you may follow standard APA formatting guidelines: http://owl.english.purdue.edu/owl/resource/560/01/.

APPENDIX 7.B

ASSIGNMENT SCHEDULE AND READINGS

WEEK 1

A:	Gorter	"Introduction"; "Conclusion"
B:	Huebner	"Bangkok's Linguistic Landscapes"

WEEK 2

A:	Backhaus	From *Linguistic Landscapes* (Tokyo 1)
B:	Backhaus	From *Linguistic Landscapes* (Tokyo 2)

WEEK 3
SEMESTER BREAK: NO CLASSES
WEEK 4

A:	Ben-Rafael, Shohamy, et al.	"Linguistic Landscape as Symbolic Construction"
	Ben-Rafael	"Sociological Approach to the Study of LL"
B:	Sloboda	"State Ideology and LL"
		Draft Project 2/Peer Review

WEEK 5

A:	Spolsky	"Prolegomena to a Sociolinguistic Theory of Public Signage"
B:		Presentations

REFERENCES

Anderson, Gary L., and Patricia Irvine. 1993. "Informing Critical Literacy with Ethnography." In *Critical Literacy: Politics, Praxis, and the Postmodern*, edited by Colin Lankshear and Peter L. McLaren, 81–104. Albany: SUNY Press.

Backhaus, Peter. 2007. *Linguistic Landscapes: A Comparative Study of Urban Multilingualism in Tokyo*. Clevedon: Multilingual Matters.

Ben-Rafael, Eliezer. 2008. "A Sociological Approach to the Study of Linguistic Landscapes." In *Linguistic Landscape Expanding the Scenery*, edited by Elana Shohamy and Durk Gorter, 40–54. New York: Routledge.

Ben-Rafael, Eliezer, Elana Shohamy, Muhammad Hasan Amara, and Nira Trumper-Hecht. 2013. "Linguistic Landscape as Symbolic Construction of the Public Space: the Case of Israel." *International Journal of Multilingualism* 3 (1): 7–30.

Blommaert, Jan. 2013. *Ethnography, Superdiversity and Linguistic Landscapes: Chronicles of Complexity*. Clevedon: Multilingual Matters.

Brandt, Deborah. 1998. "Sponsors of Literacy." *College Composition and Communication* 49 (2): 165–85.

Coulmas, Florian. 2008. "Linguistic Landscaping and the Seed of the Public Sphere." In *Linguistic Landscape Expanding the Scenery*, edited by Elana Shohamy and Durk Gorter, 13–24. New York: Routledge.

Dickinson, Greg. 2002. "Joe's Rhetoric: Finding Authenticity at Starbucks." *Rhetoric Society Quarterly* 32 (4): 5–27.

Frost, Alana. 2011. "Literacy Stewards: Dakelh Women Composing Culture." *College Composition and Communication* 63 (1): 54–74.

Gorter, Durk. 2013. "Linguistic Landscapes in a Multilingual World." *Annual Review of Applied Linguistics* 33: 190–212.

Huebner, Thom. 2006. "Bangkok's Linguistic Landscapes: Environmental Print, Codemixing and Language Change." *International Journal of Multilingualism* 3 (1): 30–57.

Landry, Rodrigue, and Richard Y. Bourhis. 1997. "Linguistic Landscape and Ethnolinguistic Vitality: An Empirical Study." *Journal of Language and Social Psychology* 16 (1): 23–49.

Matsuda, Paul Kei. 2006. "The Myth of Linguistic Homogeneity in U.S. College Composition." *College English* 68 (6): 637–51.

Pennycook, Alastair, and Emi Otsuji. 2015. *Metrolingualism: Language in the City*. New York: Routledge.

Scollon, Ron, and Suzie Wong Scollon. 2003. *Discourses in Place*. New York: Routledge.

Sloboda, Marián. 2008. "State Ideology and Linguistic Landscape." In *Linguistic Landscape Expanding the Scenery*, edited by Elana Shohamy and Durk Gorter, 173–88. New York: Routledge.
Spolsky, Bernard. 2008. "Prolegomena to a Sociolinguistic Theory of Public Signage." In *Linguistic Landscape Expanding the Scenery*, edited by Elana Shohamy and Durk Gorter, 25–39. New York: Routledge.

8
FOLLOWING LABORS OF RECONTEXTUALIZATION
Toward a Pedagogy of Translingual Mapping

Brice Norquist

INTRODUCTION

A translingual orientation is an orientation to spatiotemporal mobilities. As people and texts move—from moment to moment and over the courses of their lives, across modes and media and from one place to another—they make and remake languages. Min-Zhan Lu and Bruce Horner (2013) explain, "[Languages] are constantly in movement and rebirth through the labor of those recontextualizing them" (599). This labor is habituated and thus often invisible. It is also obscured by monolingual ideologies and through mechanisms of standardization that present academic and professional languages as fixed and bounded entities (Nordquist 2014). In other words, we are blinded by automaticity and dominant representations of homogeneity. Consequently, one of the greatest challenges of translingual writing pedagogy is learning to pay attention to labors of recontextualization and to the ways these are taken up by students with different histories, bodies, expectations, and desires (Gilyard 2016).

Perhaps because the field of rhetoric and composition is still predominantly text centered (Brandt 2018), our pedagogies tend to begin with discursive evidences of translingual labor—linguistic blends in the lyrics of a rap, the lines of poem, a student essay, an academic article, or a conference call for papers. We assign Anzaldúa, Smitherman, Silko, and Tan to highlight possibilities for rhetorical action through translanguaging. And we apply theories of linguistic heterogeneity to illuminate and make sense of these discursive practices. In other words, we extrapolate labors of recontextualization from texts.

But as Paul Prior (2004) asserts, texts are only synecdoches for distributed and complex processes: no matter how insightful the interpretation, "a text does not fully or unambiguously display its history" (171).

Like the translingual practices of the writers mentioned above, the literacies and languages of our students emerge from multigenerational and embodied movements, frictions, and stoppages across geographic and cultural borders, identities, stages of life, digital networks, and institutions. Translingual literacy is a condition and consequence of bodies in motion.

To account for labors of recontextualization that materialize in translingual texts, we must pay better attention to entanglements of linguistic and embodied mobilities, what Suresh Canagarajah (2018) refers to as "spatial repertoires." By encouraging students to attend to such entanglements in their own lives, we might help them pursue opportunities for agentive language practice. To recognize opportunities for agency, students need a sense of the field of possible trajectories and their own abilities to move alongside, against, or around the paths of others and seemingly stable structures. In other words, they must have a sense of their own possible mobilities. It is the agencies enacted in students' intertwined embodied and linguistic mobilities that I seek to better understand in this chapter. By tracing out entanglements of student mobility and exploring their pedagogical implications, I consider how foregrounding patterns, representations, and practices of movement might reorient our attention to translingual practice.

Through activities that attend to the ways individuals and groups traverse and connect scenes of literacy in their everyday lives—activities associated with what I refer to as *translingual mapping*—students and teachers might pursue two key objectives of translingual pedagogy. First, we can seek better understandings of how literacies produce, maintain, and transform material places and social relations across lines of race, gender, class, language, ethnicity, nationality, and more. Second, we can recognize openings for agentive action, or ways to appropriate, resist, and alter dominant discourses, genres, and ideologies through literacy and language practice. By tracing entanglements of linguistic and embodied mobilities, students and teachers can come to see how their own practices both accommodate and resist dominant forms.

To demonstrate how translingual mapping might work in writing classes, this chapter translates between methodological and pedagogical interventions. In the first part of the essay, I present a range of methods used to follow students' material and linguistic mobilities—time-space mapping, mobile observation, and screen recording—and show how these methods reveal labors of recontextualization only partially represented in translingual texts. The second part considers how these methods can be adapted by students and teachers in writing courses to document, represent, and adapt translingual literacies. Overall, I'm interested in what we and our students can learn about relations among social and cultural mobilities and translingual practice by following the material movements of people and texts.

SNAPSHOTS FROM A MOBILE ETHNOGRAPHY

The following representations of research and student practice come from a multisited ethnography in which I followed eleven students through their final year of high school and across subsequent years in colleges, universities, and/or full-time jobs (Nordquist 2017). The study began at a public high school in Louisville, Kentucky, which I call Hughes. The school is known for the diversity of its student body. While Hughes is located in an affluent, predominantly white neighborhood in East Louisville, the Jefferson County Public School System (JCPS) buses large numbers of students from economically depressed, predominantly minority neighborhoods to the school, contributing to a population in which 64 percent are students of color and 74 percent qualify as "economically disadvantaged."[1] Hughes also has a large contingent of English-language learners. During the 2011–12 school year, over 6 percent of the total student population was labeled "limited English proficiency" and enrolled in the school's English as a Second Language Program (Jefferson County Public Schools).

I spent approximately four months at Hughes as an in-class tutor before developing research questions and goals. During this time and after the study officially began, I observed classroom practices; listened to students' and teachers' concerns about past, present, and future literacy demands; participated in class discussions when invited; and talked with students about literacy practices in and out of school. I read essay drafts and assignment prompts and provided feedback. I attended faculty and school-board meetings, school assemblies, and sporting events. I learned what I could from students, teachers, staff, and material surroundings about the practices that constituted scenes of writing at Hughes and about the institutional, social, cultural, and historical influences shaping these practices.

To challenge perceptions of bounded classrooms and institutions and divides between secondary and tertiary education, and to better understand how students connected literacies and identities across scenes of writing, I traced their patterns of movement in classes, traveled with them to school and work in cars and on buses, walked with them through hallways and across campuses, and navigated digital environments alongside them. In this chapter, I focus on threads of movement traced in processes of *going along* with three participants. Katherine, the first student mentioned below, is a second-generation Mexican American honors student who struggled to reconcile disjunctions between preconceptions and realities of academic literacies in her movement from high school to community college. Nadif, a first-generation Somali immigrant, moved to Louisville from the world's largest refugee camp in Dadaab, Kenya, and from Hughes to the University of Louisville. Finally, James is an African American student I followed into full-time employment after graduation when his access to higher education was blocked by a number of institutional and economic barriers. Intersections and divergences among Katherine's, Nadif's, and James's trajectories reveal how language and literacy practices shape and are shaped by ideologies, experiences, and habituated practices of and desires for mobility.

MOVING ACROSS CLASSROOMS AND CITIES

One method participants and I used to follow these trajectories was time-space mapping. As a method of classroom observation oriented to mobility, our maps charted circulations of bodies and texts around classrooms; patterns of interactions among students, teachers, and objects; and the timing of these interactions.

Figure 8.1 traces the bodily and textual movements of Katherine over the course of a single period of Advanced Placement English Literature and Composition. Students in this class are arranged in a circle to encourage discussion, and the teacher (represented as a circle herself) takes a spot alongside the students. I've drawn a box around the X marking Katherine, and I've represented myself with a triangle. After a brief discussion of a previously introduced essay assignment (having to do with Oscar Wilde's *The Picture of Dorian Gray*), the period is devoted to drafting and workshopping student essays. The dotted lines in the sketch designate the trajectories of Katherine's essay draft, hand delivered in sections to peer reviewers (and myself) in exchange for portions of their essays. The solid lines designate her continual movements across the room to confer with the teacher and to consult a stack of writing guides and reference books. Each line is marked with the approximate temporal window in which these exchanges occurred.

Like every map, this one misses most of the practices constituting the scene. Katherine's microbodily movements are not represented, nor are the expectations, perceptions, and desires conditioning her

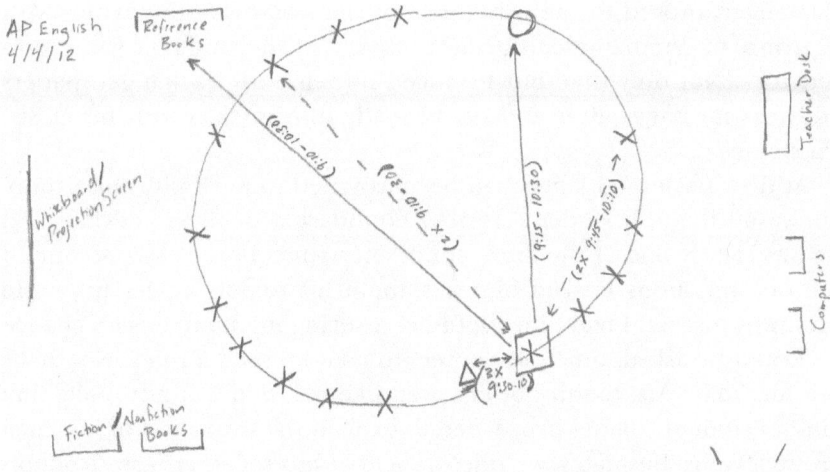

Figure 8.1. Katherine's bodily and textual movements during a single period of AP English Literature and Composition. The circle represents the teacher, the triangle represents me, and each X represents a student with the boxed X representing Katherine.

practice. The map does not show the anxiety and support she feels as she moves toward the teacher, the frustration and boredom of thumbing through an MLA style guide, the pleasure and vulnerability of exchanging texts and ideas with classmates, or the restlessness of sitting still. As a participant-observer, I tried to capture what I could of these dimensions of her practice in field notes, follow-up interviews, photographs, and in the collection of artifacts, but, of course, these methods also fall well short of a "full picture."

Despite their limitations, time-space maps did turn up significant patterns of mobility over time. Like the maps of transport planners, sketches of classroom activity highlighted the importance of quotidian routines, participants' allocations of time, and access to and usage of materials. Aggregating the content of these maps also revealed student relationships formed through ongoing collaborations across time and space. Tracing the threads of these collaborations became a central concern of the project.

For example, mapping classroom mobilities and talking through these maps with research participants helped me notice unique associations across racial, cultural, and linguistic differences in one of the regular English classes I observed. After several weeks of working with students in the class, I began to notice patterns of exchange in which James, who almost exclusively socialized with his African American classmates, moved to the other side of the classroom to partner with a group of Vietnamese, Burmese, and African students for group activities. Not only that, but I noticed he regularly exchanged papers and text messages after and occasionally during class with his "ESL" classmates.

At first, I assumed James had been assigned to work with this group. He wasn't the only student crossing boundaries for these activities and he was clearly one of the more confident writers in the class, so one of the first questions I asked him was about his role as a peer tutor. He promptly insisted I had him confused, assuring me there was no chance he would be asked, much less agree, to take up such a role: "No, that's not me, man. Ms. Smith doesn't even like me, and I'm not really that kind of student." James proceeded to explain the formation of his small group: "We're busmates, we ride the school bus together from Iroquois [his neighborhood in South Louisville]."

As we continued to develop our conversations about these collaborations over time, James described how he was initially hesitant to engage in conversation with his busmates because he assumed their language differences would put too much strain on their exchanges: "I knew most of them [ESL students] from classes, but never really talked to them because I didn't think I could understand them. And I didn't think they could understand me either."

When I asked how his attitude and practice on the bus began to change, he admitted that, at first, he asked busmates to share their homework, specifically reading-review and math worksheets from which he could easily copy answers. However, over a period of time, he began to recognize reciprocation as a shared expectation of the group and started helping his busmates meet the demands of the Standardized English required in their papers. James was good at accommodating the standards of academic discourse presented in his classes, and this ability quickly made him a valuable member of the bus collective comprised primarily of English-language learners. On trips I observed, James could hardly keep up with the demand for his feedback. Completed and partial worksheets, essay drafts, and word puzzles circulated over vinyl seats to James's spot, and one ESL student after another slid in beside him to consult and then slide back out.

While it would be easy to dismiss James's initial forms of participation in these collectives as common instances of cheating, the development of his role in the relationships and shared efforts of this group signals a much more complex and pedagogically valuable set of tactics employed to exploit gaps in institutional strategies of control and containment.

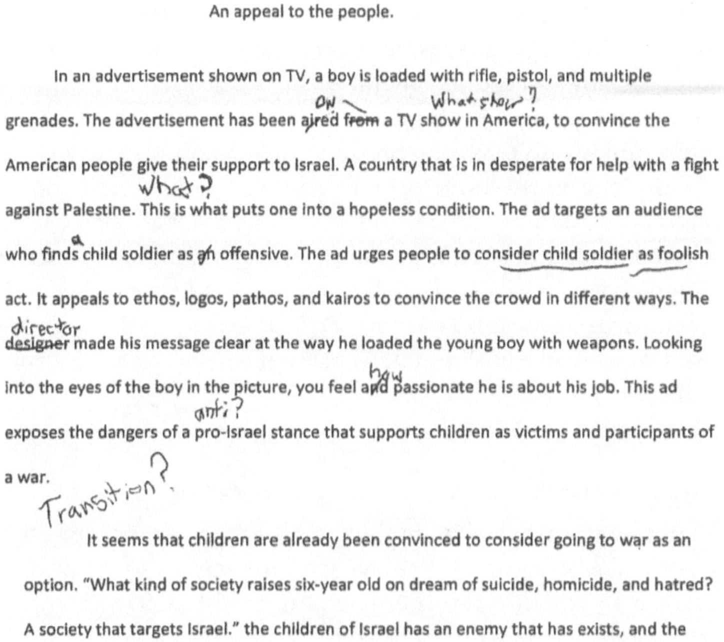

> An appeal to the people.
>
> In an advertisement shown on TV, a boy is loaded with rifle, pistol, and multiple grenades. The advertisement has been aired ~~from~~ [On] [What show?] a TV show in America, to convince the American people give their support to Israel. A country that is in desperate for help with a fight [What?] against Palestine. This is what puts one into a hopeless condition. The ad targets an audience who finds child soldier as ~~an~~ [a] offensive. The ad urges people to consider child soldier as foolish act. It appeals to ethos, logos, pathos, and kairos to convince the crowd in different ways. The [director] ~~designer~~ made his message clear at the way he loaded the young boy with weapons. Looking into the eyes of the boy in the picture, you feel a~~n~~[how] passionate he is about his job. This ad exposes the dangers of a pro-Israel stance that supports children as victims and participants of a war. [anti?]
>
> [Transition?]
>
> It seems that children are already been convinced to consider going to war as an option. "What kind of society raises six-year old on dream of suicide, homicide, and hatred? A society that targets Israel." the children of Israel has an enemy that has exists, and the

Figure 8.2. Draft composed by Nadif for AP English and marked by James on the bus ride to school.

These tactics are especially pronounced in James's collaborations with Nadif, who had come to rely on James's feedback on most all of his writing for school. In figure 8.2 is a draft composed by Nadif for AP English and marked by James on the bus ride to school.

As evidenced in this excerpt, James's review of Nadif's work goes beyond surface-level corrections to include the sort of formative commentary we might associate with genuine investment in the meaning-making processes of Nadif's composition. In this way, their collaboration involves the pedagogical value of peer review often promoted and pursued in writing classes. However, this review could not have occurred within the confines of the school because Nadif and James were separated into different tracks of study: Nadif into advanced placement and James into regular (read remedial) courses.

Despite institutional, linguistic, and cultural divisions, the students comprising this bus collective made use of their daily patterns of embodied mobility, coordinated via linguistic and literate mobilities, to share tasks and resources across space and time, bodies, texts, and objects. These collaborations not only occurred beyond the confines of containerized classrooms or schools but also helped reconstitute classrooms, schools, languages, and literacies by marshaling mobilities circulating within and around them. As demonstrated in James's movement across the space of his English class to resume work with busmates that began and would continue on their daily commutes to school or in the influences of impromptu peer reviews on Nadif's academic essays, languages and literacies are always distributed across space-time and among individuals and objects in places that cross-cut, intersect, diverge, and align with one another. Translingual pedagogies attentive to labors of recontextualization follow threads of such distributions to account for collaborative and translingual histories of writing processes and their materializations in essays like Nadif's.

MOVING IN DIGITAL AND NONDIGITAL SPACES

My second case involves a mobile technology more cutting edge than a school bus. Figure 8.3 shows screen shots from a text message conversation in which Katherine is chatting with a friend during her intermediate-level composition class at community college.

As she participates in face-to-face peer review with a partner in class, Katherine is simultaneously engaged in the exchange excerpted below and is contributing to a Facebook group chat. Her peer-review partner is also multitasking—peer reviewing with Katherine and texting her own messages throughout the class period.

In this portion of a conversation that spans approximately twenty minutes of a fifty-minute class and includes over fifty individual messages, Katherine is fielding school-related questions from a friend and classmate. Up to this point, the exchange has covered a wide range of topics, from weekend plans to South Korean pop music to, finally, schoolwork. The friend, represented in grey text bubbles, is expressing her anxiety about end-of-term deadlines. In the screenshot on the left, Katherine is attempting to assuage her friend's anxiety by reassuring her of the time she has to finish assignments and by offering to help her with work she is unable to complete because she lacks internet access at home.

In the screenshot on the right, Katherine is providing an overview of an essay assignment for a shared introductory psychology course and is teasingly fending off requests to offer more information about the essay. After sending the basics of the assignment, her friend asks her to continue: "Siguele mija siguele (go on, girlfriend, go on)." To which Katherine responds, "Y te lo mande (I already sent it to you).

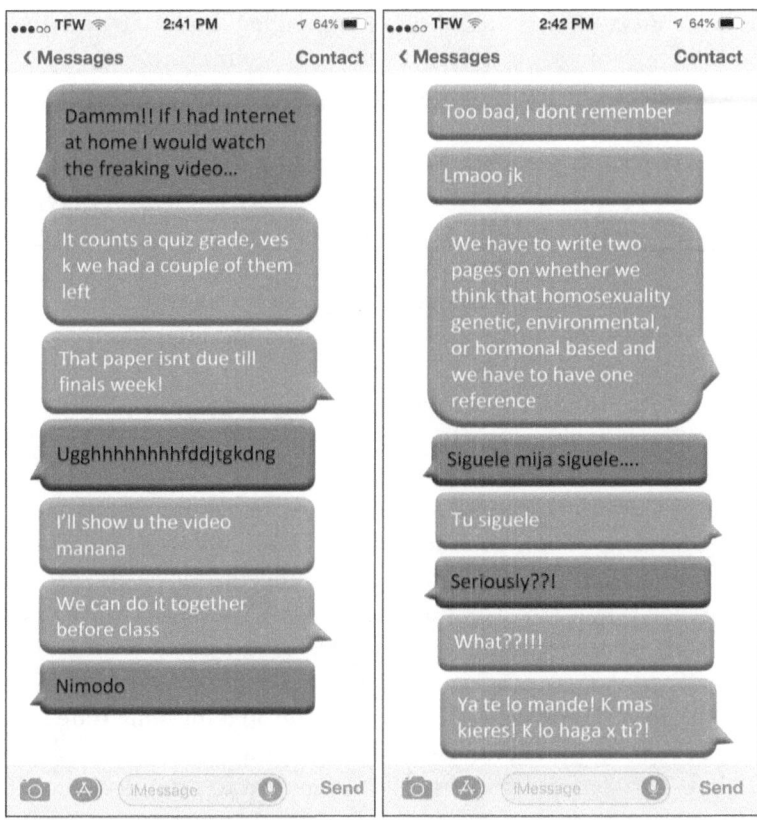

Figure 8.3. A text message conversation between Katherine and a friend that took place while Katherine is in her composition class.

K mas kieres (what more do you want?). K lo haga x ti (What? Do you want me to do it for you too?)."[2] Discussing the language of this exchange and explaining her need to translate, Katherine asserts, "Just like in English there is text language, this is the same in Spanish. To be specific, this conversation is in Spanglish, so it has its own slang. The K stands for Que because my friend and me know English and Spanish—the sound is the same. X in Spanish is times, which is por. For example one times one would be uno por uno. The sentence correctly is supposed to be Que lo haga por ti, and it is said sarcastic." In many ways, this translingual exchange works like the mobile collectives James, Nadif, and their classmates cocreate on the school bus. Through a similar process of negotiation around forms of collaboration, Katherine and her friend partner with their devices to share resources and school work across languages and contexts.

Perhaps most interestingly, these entangled material and linguistic mobilities reorganize the space-times of Katherine's, James's, and Nadif's presences, as their interactions in scenes of writing are mediated by and connected to a host of other meetings. Among other things, this simultaneity creates possibilities for translingual and transmedia negotiations in scenes otherwise demarcated by institutionalized languages (i.e., Standardized English) and literacies (academic and discipline specific). But as I previously suggest, these negotiations tend to go unnoticed by teachers and students themselves because they are habituated and because dominant assumptions of monolingualism condition perceptions and practices in K–16 schools.

When I asked Katherine if she blended Spanish and English in her writing or in class, she said, "No, never." When I tried to reconcile this response with her text exchanges, she said, "Well, that's not really writing." And when I asked whether she thought texting influenced her academic writing or her interactions in school, she laughed and said, "Only in ways that get me in trouble." Katherine does not count her translingual labor as labor because she is conditioned to ignore or avoid it in pursuit of a monolingual standard for presumably isolated and individually authored academic texts. Translingual pedagogies attentive to labors of recontextualization—to the making and remaking of languages through material and representational movements across space-time—encourage students like Katherine to attend to the simultaneity of their literacy practices and to the languages and texts that emerge from these entanglements.

PEDAGOGIES OF TRANSLINGUAL MAPPING

To attend to material and embodied dimensions of composing, many researchers and teachers turn to methods of mapping (Arnold, NeCamp, and Sohan 2015; Clarke 2002; Ivanič et al. 2009; Leander and Rowe 2006; Mannion, Ivanič, and the Literacies for Learning in Further Education [LfLFE] Research Group 1 2007; Reynolds 2004; Taylor 2017; Taylor and Hall 2013). Mapping affords not only a method for representing connections across space-time and practice but also for composing representations of translingual labor that can be read alongside representations offered by other maps. Multiple and layered mapping processes can provide different interpretations, and therefore different maps, of the practices under investigation.

Prior's (1998) concept of "chronotopic lamination" provides a good starting point for imagining how entanglements of embodied and linguistic mobilities can be mapped by teachers and students. Prior presents the concept as a tool for attending to "the dispersed and fluid chains of places, times, people, and artifacts that come to be tied together in trajectories of literacy" (Prior and Shipka 2003, 181). To recall such trajectories, Prior and Jody Shipka (2003) ask undergraduate and graduate research participants to draw scenes of writing a specific text—the place(s) where they wrote, resources they used, the people involved, activities that accompanied the writing, and their feelings during this process. In a follow-up drawing, participants trace the origins of a project; people, texts, and experiences that have shaped the project over time; a history of drafts, responses, and revisions; and accounts of shifting feelings about the project (182). Through these mapping exercises and attendant interviews, Prior and Shipka's participants reflect on their struggles to communicate ideas, the motivational and affective forces influencing their decisions, the intricate coordination of schedules and activities for writing, and the ways they tune in to and (re)structure their writing environments.

While these maps show the complexity of distributed writing across space-time, they do not represent the linguistic mobilities involved in these distributions. When asked to reconstruct their literacy trajectories from memory, Prior and Shipka's participants recall intertwined spatiotemporal, material, and cognitive processes but not instances of language contact and negotiation. Again, this is likely because translingual practice is automatic and obscured by monolingual ideologies. But sorting through layers of space-time forming and formed by literate activity should always turn up linguistic frictions and mobilities. We navigate chronotopic laminations—simultaneities of contexts—through translingual literacies. Like Katherine, if we are not attuned to these simultaneities and the linguistic versatilities required to maintain them, we tend to reconstruct accounts of composing that fit dominant expectations. Labors of recontextualization are simplified or erased to preserve illusions of autonomy—spatial, temporal, linguistic, and authorial.

To help students recognize their own and others' labors of recontextualization, translingual mapping asks them to supplement retrospective accounts of literacy trajectories (e.g., literacy narratives, maps, portfolios, etc.) with documentation of *in situ* practice. In other words, the pedagogy asks them to notice their own language practices in the present, not necessarily through lenses of translingual theory (at least not initially) but through methods of linguistic (auto)ethnography and critical geography. To compliment retrospective accounts of literacy trajectories, students document *in situ* practices with methods featured in the first half of this chapter: time-space journals, mobile observations and interviews, screen recordings, photos, audio, and video. For example, the assignment offered in the appendix to this chapter asks undergraduate writing and rhetoric majors in an upper-level course I developed at Syracuse University, *Networking Literacies*, to create mobile literacy journals using a shared mobile observation app called EthOS (ethosapp.com). In the course, students used the smartphone app to document their own daily literacy practices and collect literacy artifacts with photos, text, audio, and video and to represent (map and translate) these practices and artifacts in shared workspaces. Students in the class used the app to not only collaborate with each other but also to work with students in an upper-level literacy course taught by my colleague at the time, Tom Fox, a professor of English at California State University, Chico.

Students in our connected classes shared data and analysis gleaned from their mobile methods on interactive platforms such as blogs, digital archives, or Google MyMaps. In this way, students' maps include literacy artifacts that serve as guideposts—student, teacher, and institutional texts; images; video; audio; graffiti; posters; social media; text messages; and so forth—with reflective commentary or annotation connecting one guidepost to another and, thus, illuminating the map.

For instance, the screen shot in figure 8.4 from a project composed in Google MyMaps offers an example of how students might represent literacy or text trajectories; attach literacy artifacts and representations of practice to particular geospatial points or routes; and layer or rectify multiple maps to investigate overlaps and divergences. In this project, the student considers erasures of businesses, bodies, languages, and cultures through processes gentrification in New York City and attaches his reflections to particular location markers on a digital street map. Through some combination of written reflections, past and present photos, and short videos of literate activity and screen recordings, such translingual mapping projects offer multiple and often conflicting perspectives of literacy and language practices emerging from and propelling movements across space-time.

By mapping interconnected literacy practices onto representations of material places and trajectories (city maps, bus routes, school blueprints, campus maps, and so on) and attaching artifactual representations to markers of these locations, students might better understand and communicate the ways places in and out of school shape and are shaped by the trajectories of literacy coursing through them. As Nedra Reynolds (2004) suggests, such projects encourage students to "engage more fully with the geographical construction of difference—especially as it

Figure 8.4. Screenshot from a project composed in Google MyMaps depicting the erasures of businesses, bodies, languages, and cultures through the gentrification of New York City.

influences texts and discourses—and begin to consider teaching and learning, reading and writing, from the standpoint of moving through the world: through forms of walking, mapping, and dwelling" (138).

Relations among geographic and linguistic constructions of difference can be further explored as students and teachers read their literacy maps in light of "official," institutional representations of literacy development—standards and assessments, program outcomes, evaluations, curricula, and degree plans. On both secondary and tertiary levels, this process of reading individual maps alongside and against institutional depictions of progress, such as the Common Core Standards, can reveal patterns of inclusion and exclusion, access and denial, embraces and threats, and other means of creating and policing social and institutional boundaries.

In the case of James and Nadif described above, translingual mapping could provide opportunities to share literacy practices over time and across academic tracks. James's and Nadif's maps might highlight differences in the types and quantities of tasks assigned in their high-school courses, texts used to facilitate such tasks, teacher and peer support and feedback, material resources provided, and so on. After reflecting on the ways the boundaries creating and maintaining these differences assign them particular identities and interpret and measure their language and literacy practices, James and Nadif could read the similarities and differences depicted in their individual maps in the context of the Common Core Standards as an idealized map of their supposedly shared practices and experiences. Translingual mapping would ask them to work together to trace out the ways their practices accorded with and diverged from the standards.

By making the boundaries that define and delimit their work and identities more apparent, James and Nadif could join their critical perspectives to reflect on and critique their own geographic and institutional situatedness and, subsequently, to develop additional tactics for responding to this situatedness by exploiting possibilities for movement within apparently closed systems. In other words, by engaging in processes of collaborative map making and reading, James and Nadif might come to better understandings of how meanings are made through linguistic mobilities and boundaries. By studying their own literacies across space-time in relation to standardized representations of these literacies, new patterns of containment and conformity (Giroux 2010) and also of innovation, resistance, and transformation may become visible to students and teachers, patterns that indicate literacy's present and potential roles in maintaining and challenging social divisions.

MAPPING TRANSLATIONS

By mapping (tracing and annotating) literacy practices across space-time, students and teachers create opportunities to reflect upon the ways literacies, languages, and meanings are reordered, networked and translated across locations and identities. Translingual mapping highlights how linguistic mobilities necessitate perpetual translations. These translations involve not only linguistic negotiations but also social, economic, geopolitical, and cultural transactions across asymmetrical relations of power. In this way, meaning is made, exchanged, and transformed through entanglements of embodied and linguistic mobilities.

For Claire Kramsch (2006), this "traffic in meaning" is precisely what language teaching should consist of so language competence is measured not as the capacity to perform in one language in a specific domain but rather as "the ability to translate, transpose and critically reflect on social, cultural and historical meanings conveyed by the grammar and lexicon" (103). From this perspective, language and literacy teaching is indelibly tied to translation and a diversity of meanings (Pennycook 2008, 34).

Translingual mapping attends to this traffic in meaning by challenging students to reflect upon the ways simultaneous literacy trajectories require constant translations of meaning across identities, languages, texts, cultures, discourses, media, and localities. The approach focuses on the ways participation in rhetorical circulations (Chaput 2005; Edbauer 2005) requires literate and linguistic facility within and across diverse languages, markets, discourses, and texts. While translations of meanings are always already reproducing and transforming scenes of writing across contexts, translingual mapping also encourages students and teachers to account for this traffic by making use of the mobilities circulating within their ostensibly bounded classrooms (Leander, Phillips, and Taylor 2010).

We can return to the face-to-face-to-interface mobilities Katherine practices in her community college writing class to demonstrate how this traffic in meaning might be illuminated and reflected upon through translingual mapping. Recognizing students will likely not share all the mobilities that intersect with and diverge from their physical presences in class, nor should they be compelled to, they can be asked to map the literacies they engage in (and feel comfortable sharing) over the course of a single class period along with the contexts these practices connect and help constitute.

Figure 8.5 is a map Katherine and I developed together to represent the scene of writing presented in the case of her classroom multitasking. In this map, simultaneous exchanges—peer review, essay, text-message conversation, and Facebook chat—serve as primary nodes. Branching off from these guideposts are localities and texts evoked and identities and languages performed in each exchange. Of course, these branches are not comprehensive; they represent a small number of associations Katherine and I decided to trace out.[3]

The map reveals Katherine's peer-review session as mediated by a number of texts (light blue)—written and spoken feedback, her own and her partner's essays, and the text messages interrupting and augmenting their face-to-face interactions. The identity (in green) she performs in this exchange is different from those she takes up in other exchanges; while she is friendly and compliant, Katherine also communicates verbally and physically that she is only marginally invested in the activity, a level of investment that seems to match her partner's. The language she and her partner use to discuss their essays approximates the slightly elevated conversational English used by the teacher of the course, and the only locality referenced (dark blue) in this particular exchange is the classroom itself.

As this map demonstrates, the possible influences shaping and shaped by Katherine's contributions to this peer-review activity and the larger scene of literacy are relatively easy to trace out. A more difficult, but perhaps more productive, task is creating opportunities for her to

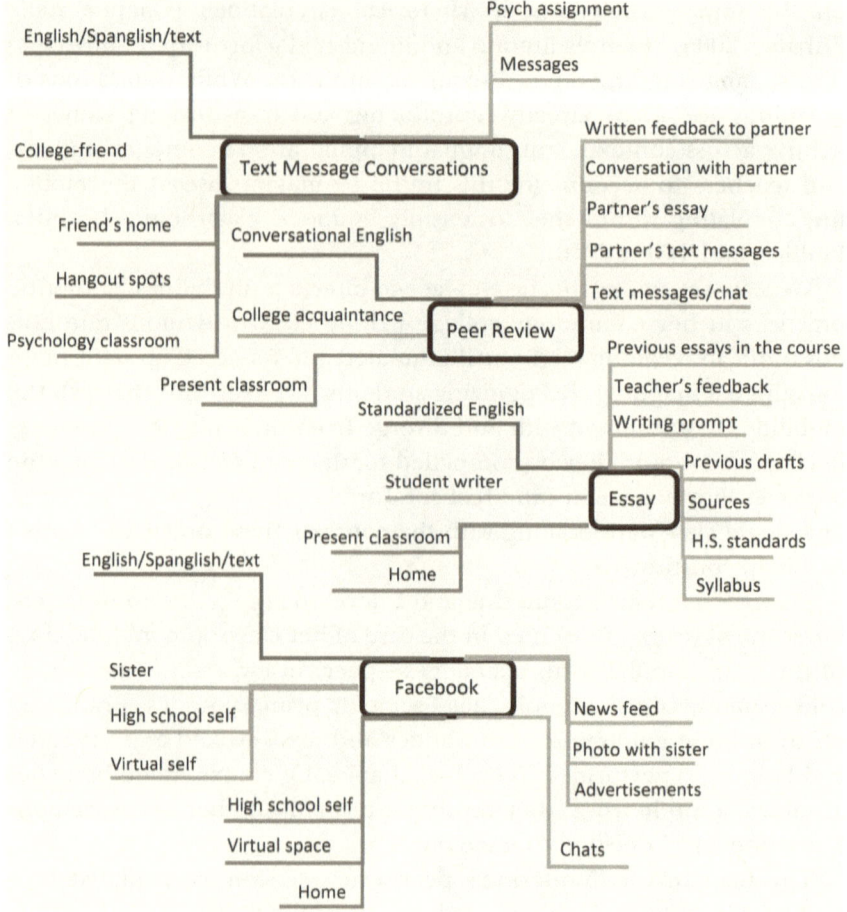

Figure 8.5. A map representing the scene of writing presented in Katherine's classroom multitasking.

reflect on and make new meanings from transactions and translations within and across exchanges. In other words, after mapping associations that comprise these primary exchanges, an extended translingual mapping exercise would ask Katherine and her classmates to consider how one seemingly discrete exchange shapes and is shaped by another. For instance, Katherine might consider how her text-message conversation, which spans the duration of the peer review, influences the oral and written feedback she provides her partner and the identities or languages she performs in the session. Reading her text messages alongside her written review might help Katherine recognize similarities and differences in the ways she positions herself, frames her commentary, draws upon diverse language resources, and so on.

After considering the relations among these similarities and differences, Katherine could attempt to translate meanings across exchanges by investigating the ways meanings are lost, changed, and gained in translations of her peer-review comments into the Spanglish of her text messages or by considering how the content and tone of her text conversation would change if it were conducted face to face in the context of her writing classroom. This practice of translating across differences might highlight the influences enabling and constraining her identities, languages, and literacies. And through this process of identifying affordances and constraints, she might locate possible agencies or ways to exploit and create openings for new mobilities and, thus, new processes of meaning making within and across contexts.

To add a final dimension to this traffic in meaning, Katherine and her peer-review partner could exchange maps to consider similarities and differences in the meanings and realities they construct through processes of map making. Again, this process of translingual mapping might allow students to share critical perspectives and develop tactics for contesting institutional constraints and expanding and creating possibilities for movement. Of course, these activities could also, and often do, fall flat. While it's useful to think through how Katherine and her classmates might take up such assignments, such processes seldom unfold in the ways I've outlined here. Katherine and other students could find more interesting ways to engage in translingual mapping, or they could decide to reject these activities outright.

Regardless of how they play out, pedagogies attentive to labors of recontextualization, such as translingual mapping, focus on how to best enable students to negotiate the demands of concurrent and often conflicting contexts, challenging them to identify, reflect upon, and employ language and literacy choices to achieve personal, civic, educational, and professional objectives across scenes of literacy. Such pedagogies approach students not as novices faced with tasks of conforming to the demands of specific scenes of literacy but rather as agents continually reproducing and remaking themselves, the scenes, and the discourses they cocreate through entangled literacies and mobilities. To help them realize the agencies that emerge from their language and literacy practices, such pedagogies seek to create opportunities for students to recognize and reflect upon the ways their translingual literacies both accommodate and transform conventions of discourse, genre, and discipline, as well as social relations within and across places.

APPENDIX 8.A

NETWORKING LITERACIES COURSE DESCRIPTION

How do we move through and connect places and processes of writing in our everyday lives? In this course, we'll map our own and others' interconnected practices of writing in and out of school and follow movements of texts across media, languages, and contexts. We'll experiment with methods for following and representing trajectories of writing across space and time. Engaging in different ways of narrating and visualizing writing trajectories will provide us opportunities to consider how literacies, languages, and meanings are ordered and reordered, networked and translated across locations and identities.

Here are some objectives we can begin with and revise in our investigations:

- better understand how composing practices are both located in place and actively produce place
- map multiple, and oftentimes overlapping, places where composing occurs
- observe and represent the various materials and supports (both human and nonhuman) people employ while composing texts
- trace the dynamic, emergent, distributed, historical, and technologically mediated dimensions of composing practices
- better understand composing as an embodied activity
- reflect on our own research practices and the implications of these practices for meaning making

PROJECT 3: MAPPING PROCESSES

Step 1

For the final project of the course, we'll work in pairs or individually (your choice) and employ mixed qualitative methods to trace a process of composing across space and time. You can choose to document and analyze the dynamic, emergent, distributed, historical, and technologically mediated dimensions of your own or someone else's composing process. Either way, you'll need to map the composing process for a single project from start to finish using the methods we've read about and practiced over the course of the semester, and you'll need to share your research in progress in our EthOS mobile observation app. Here are some methods you might consider employing to trace the literate activities bound up in processes of composing:

- time-space journaling
- audio and/or video journals or observations

- photo documentation
- geolocation journals

Step 2

Once you've collected and analyzed data through a series of analytic memos (see schedule attached), you'll choose a digital platform (website, blog, Google MyMaps, etc.) to help readers/viewers visualize the literate activity constituting the process you've traced.

Step 3

The final stage of this project involves connecting to colleagues in Chico. As a reminder, here's what Brandt and Clinton have to say about comparative ethnography in "The Limits of the Local":

> The concepts offered here are particularly amenable to comparative ethnographic study. They can help us to consider how and how much local literacies involve importing and exporting literacy across contexts as well as the role of things in managing these movements. Which contexts principally import and from where? Which principally export and to where? Which maintain, so to speak, a balance of trade? We can compare sponsorship patterns across contexts as well, measuring the relative power of sponsors between one context and others, the ideological burdens or costs to the sponsored in particular contexts, as well as changes in sponsorship patterns over time. (353–54)

You just completed a small ethnographic-like project (or many of you did). Look through yours and/or a colleague's project from Chico and **describe a "comparative ethnographic study" that might be done**.

- How might the themes and/or approaches of these studies relate to each other?
- What might situating these studies in relation to each other reveal that individual studies couldn't reveal on their own?
- What shared literacies are exported and/or imported into these projects?
- What sorts of literacy objects do they have in common and how do these objects shape the literacy practices under consideration?

NOTES

1. In 2007 the US Supreme Court struck down Louisville's voluntary school integration program for using race as a factor in school assignments. Louisville's integration plan now uses socioeconomic status as a measure to achieve diversity (Lewin, *New York Times,* June 29, 2007).

2. Katherine translated these texts during an interview focusing on these and other examples of text-message conversations she engaged in while in class.
3. Moreover, the identities, languages, localities, and texts referenced here are not singular or static.

REFERENCES

Arnold, Lisa, Samantha NeCamp, and Vanessa K. Sohan. 2015. "Recognizing and Disrupting Immappancy in Scholarship and Pedagogy." *Pedagogy* 15 (2): 271–302.

Brandt, Deborah. 2018. "Awakening to Literacy circa 1983." *College Composition and Communication* 69 (3): 503–10.

Canagarajah, Suresh. 2018. "Translingual Practice as Spatial Repertoires: Expanding the Paradigm beyond Structuralist Orientations." *Applied Linguistics* 39 (1): 31–54.

Chaput, Catherine. 2005. "Rhetorical Circulation in Late Capitalism: Neoliberalism and the Overdetermination of Affective Energy." *Philosophy and Rhetoric* 43 (1): 1–25.

Clarke, Julia. 2002. "A New Kind of Symmetry: Actor-Network Theories and the New Literacy Studies." *Studies in the Education of Adults* 34 (2): 107–22.

Edbauer, Jenny. 2005. "Unframing Models of Public Distribution: From Rhetorical Situation to Rhetorical Ecologies." *Rhetoric Society Quarterly* 35 (4): 5–24.

EthOS Ethnographic Observation System. n.d. Accessed August 30, 2016. https://www.ethosapp.com/.

Gilyard, Keith. 2016. "The Rhetoric of Translingualism." *College English* 73 (3): 284–89.

Giroux, Henry A. 2010. "Dumbing Down Teachers: Rethinking the Crisis of Public Education and the Demise of the Social State." *Review of Education, Pedagogy and Cultural Studies* 32 (4): 339–81.

Ivanic, Roz, Richard Edwards, David Barton, Marilyn Martin-Jones, Zoe Fowler, Buddug Hughes, Greg Mannion, Kate Miller, Candice Satchwell, and June Smith. 2009. *Improving Learning in College: Rethinking Literacies across the Curriculum*. London: Routledge.

Jefferson County Public Schools. n.d. *2012–2013 Data Books*. Division Data Management, Planning and Program Evaluation. Accessed August 31, 2016. http://assessment.jefferson.kyschools.us/DataBooks1213/High_Data_Book.html.

Kramsch, Claire. 2006. "The Traffic in Meaning." *Asian Pacific Journal of Education* 26 (1): 99–104.

Leander, Kevin, Nathan C. Phillips, and Katherine Hendrick Taylor. 2010. "The Changing Social Spaces of Learning: Mapping New Mobilities." *Review of Research in Education* 34 (1): 329–94.

Leander, Kevin M., and Deborah Wells Rowe. 2006. "Mapping Literacy Spaces in Motion: A Rhizomatic Analysis of a Classroom Literacy Performance." *Reading Research Quarterly* 41 (4): 428–60.

Lu, Min-Zhan, and Bruce Horner. 2013. "Translingual Literacy, Language Difference, and Matters of Agency." *College English* 75 (6): 582–607.

Mannion, Greg, Roz Ivanič, and the Literacies for Learning in Further Education (LfLFE) Research Group 1. 2007. "Mapping Literacy Practices: Theory, Methodology, Methods." *International Journal of Qualitative Studies in Education* 20 (1): 15–30.

Nordquist, Brice. 2014. "English *Only* through Disavowal: Linguistic Violence in Politics and Pedagogy." In *Reworking English in Rhetoric and Composition: Global Interrogations, Local Interventions*, edited by Bruce Horner and Karen Kopelson, 49. Carbondale: Southern Illinois University Press.

Nordquist, Brice. 2017. *Literacy and Mobility: Complexity, Uncertainty and Agency at the Nexus of High School and College*. New York: Routledge.

Pennycook, Alastair. 2008. "English as a Language Always in Translation." *European Journal of English Studies* 12 (1): 33–47.

Prior, Paul A. 1998. *Writing/Disciplinarity: A Sociohistoric Account of Literate Activity in the Academy*. Mahwah, NJ: Lawrence Erlbaum.
Prior, Paul A. 2004. "Tracing Process: How Texts Come into Being." In *What Writing Does and How It Does it: An Introduction to Analyzing Texts and Textual Practices*, edited by Charles Bazerman and Paul A. Prior, 167–200. Mahwah, NJ: Lawrence Erlbaum.
Prior, Paul, and Jody Shipka. 2003. "Chronotopic Lamination: Tracing the Contours of Literate Activity." In *Writing Selves, Writing Societies: Research from Activity Perspectives*, edited by Charles Bazerman and David R. Russell, 180–238. Fort Collins, CO: WAC Clearinghouse.
Reynolds, Nedra. 2004. *Geographies of Writing: Inhabiting Places and Encountering Difference*. Carbondale: Southern Illinois University Press.
Taylor, Katie Headrick. 2017. "Learning Along Lines: Locative Literacies for Reading and Writing the City." *Journal of the Learning Sciences* 26 (4): 533–74.
Taylor, Katie Headrick, and Roger Hall. 2013. "Counter-Mapping the Neighborhood on Bicycles: Mobilizing Youth to Reimagine the City." *Technology, Knowledge and Learning* 18 (1–2): 65–93.

9
WRITING-THEORY CARTOON
Toward a Translingual and Multimodal Pedagogy

Xiqiao Wang

INTRODUCTION

This chapter both describes and investigates a multistage language-reflection assignment that asks students to theorize their own languaging practices. The assignment and the action-research project planned alongside it are the products of my response to two exigencies that compel reconsiderations of writing pedagogy in light of broader changes in US institutions of higher learning. The first exigency points to the changing demographics of US universities, where the steady increase of international students over the past decade has brought the population to a record high of more than one million students in 2016 (Opendoors 2016). Like many institutions of higher education across the United States, the public university where this pedagogical innovation is situated has witnessed a rapid and drastic increase of international students: from 5 percent to 8 percent each year for each of the past five years so that as of 2015, international students constituted 13 percent of the entire undergraduate student body.

The communicative contexts of these students are marked by characteristics that conventional writing classrooms are not used to, including the diverse, multilingual backgrounds of the students, the diaspora communities they occupy, the transnational affiliations they maintain through the mediation of digital technologies, and the constant cross-border movements of bodies, goods, and information that characterize their experiences. As important agents shaping and shaped by these transnational processes, universities are responsible to develop pedagogical practices sensitive to students' knowledge, engage their participation, and address the daily challenges they face in and out of college classrooms.

The second exigency is theoretical and disciplinary in nature, as it arises from an identifiable gap between recent advancement towards a translingual stance on writing and the lack of pedagogical enactments of the theory. In recent years, scholars have challenged the narrow conception of languages as discrete entities and literacy as bound to a print-based medium, opening up space for expanded notions of language use and literacy practices as multilingual, multimodal, multisensory, and multidimensional (Canagarajah 2007). However, theoretical inquiry into the internationalization of composition has just begun to motivate practical strategies that incorporate translingualism into first-year writing courses (Kiernan, Meier, and Wang 2016). In this chapter, I offer one such pedagogical approach to suggest how teachers can build on the rich linguistic and semiotic repertoire of ELL students. Further, observing my own practice as part of an action-research project, I offer an analysis of how playful encounters with multimodality during the writing process are particularly important for ELL students as they learn to theorize multilingual experiences and translingual relationships.

I start this chapter by reviewing the literature on translingualism, with a particular focus on existing scholarship that offers pedagogical recommendations for enacting translingualism. I then present a description of the assignment as situated in the context of a bridge writing course at a large public midwestern university in the United States. Finally, drawing on exemplary cases from a corpus of artifacts and interview data collected from a cohort of forty-four students, I describe how a writing-theory-cartoon assignment affords opportunities for translingual and metalinguistic work. As analysis of student work shows, students use the assignment to reflect on multilingual experiences, to formulate and articulate informal theories of translingual relationships, and to perform agentive literacy identities.

TOWARDS A TRANSLINGUAL AND MULTIMODAL FRAMEWORK

This assignment, with its emphasis on negotiation across languages and modes, reflects shifts toward a translingual view of languages in literacy education and writing studies. This view challenges the monolingual ideology that conceives languages as "discrete, stable, internally uniform, and linked indelibly to what is held to be each writer's likewise stable and uniform location and social identity" (Lu and Horner 2013, 583). Rather, it recognizes the inherent fluidity and variation of languages (Horner et al. 2011) and argues that language competence is performed through participants' negotiation with fluid, hybrid codes and constant "shuttling" between communities and cultures (Canagarajah 2006; Pennycook 2007). In this view, languages and language varieties constitute an integrated linguistic repertoire that can be selectively reconfigured to fulfill the needs of communicative situations.

If we see language use as "traffic in meaning," where one engages in the passing of "ideas, concepts, symbols, [and] discourses" (Pennycook 2008, 33), it is necessary to consider English in the context of and in relation to other languages and modes. That is, it is important to attend to the interrelationship of semiotic systems as part of the rhetorical repertoire essential for translingual negotiation. Scholars have offered transmodality as a lens to examine all communicative practices as inherently heterogeneous, affective, bodily, and material, highlighting the role various texts, tools, strategies, practices, and human and nonhuman tools play in supporting and constraining communicative acts (Gonzalez 2018; Horner, Selfe, and Lockridge 2015; Shipka 2016). As such, both translingualism and multimodality encourage us to view writing as socially situated, emergent, and negotiated rather than as static, rule-driven phenomena. As new literacy scholars have argued, print-based notions of literacies are inadequate in accounting for the ever-changing forms and functions of literacies, therefore compelling an expanded conception that attends to other modes, including visual (Kress and van Leeuwen 2006), auditory (Halbritter 2006; Selfe 2009), gestural (Prior et al. 2006), and spatial codes (Leander, Phillips, and Taylor 2010), as well as other forms of digital literacies (Lankshear and Knobel 2007), such as instant messaging (Lee 2007; Lewis and Fabos 2005), multimodal storytelling (Gilje 2011; Hull and Nelson 2005; Vasudevan, Schultz, and Batemen 2010), and fanfiction writing (Black 2006; Jacobs 2007). Indeed, to be literate in terms of such emerging cultural practices, one must be a selective user of semiotic resources and literacy technologies through contingent, self-initiated learning. An important part of the learning involves one's ability to "translate" meaning across modes and to reconfigure an integrated repertoire of semiotic resources to achieve what Glynda Hull and Mark Nelson (2005) call "semiotic fullness" (244). In this regard, the argument made here is consonant with the emphasis on meaning negotiation by translingual theorists.

Researchers have observed how digital technology and multimodality can be harnessed to reinforce the development of literacy competence in both home language and English. Drawing on their studies of the translanguaging practices of elementary-school students, Patricia Velasco and Ofelia García (2014) encouraged teachers to make use of drawings, videos, and so on to engage multilingual students beyond the earlier years of literacy learning. Jim Cummins (2006) engaged culturally and linguistically diverse students in the creation of multimodal, multilingual identity texts, allowing them to construct knowledge in meaningful ways. Others have argued that expertise garnered through digital-literacy practices could help students forge empowering identities (Black 2007; Hull and Katz 2006; Yi 2008). Weaving together and extending these insights, I propose a pedagogical approach that enacts translingual and multimodal emphasis as a means of supporting multilingual writers' development of a translingual disposition.

Responding to the observation that "theorization of translingual literacy has far outpaced pedagogical practices for advancing this proficiency in classrooms" (Canagarajah 2013, 41), this chapter suggests that writing teachers recognize, valorize, and build on the communicative repertoires of students and their families (Hornberger and Link 2012; Velasco and Garcia 2014) by encouraging critical analysis and visual representation of their informal theories about multilingual experiences and translingual practices. The assignment recognizes translation and negotiation of meaning as operating in all communicative acts and seeks to help students develop a disposition of openness and inquiry toward language and language difference (Lu and Horner 2013). In practice, the assignment engages ELLs in collective consideration of translanguaging practices through the medium of cartoon drawings.

CONTEXT

The curricular redesign described in this chapter occurred in a bridge writing course (entitled Preparation for College Writing, subsequently referred to as PCW) at a large public midwestern university in the United States, which currently serves approximately nine hundred first-generation, heritage-language, and English-language learners, with the majority being Chinese and others from such countries as South Korea, Saudi Arabia, and Thailand. Student placement is determined by standardized testing scores (e.g., SAT and TOEFL) that do not meet the threshold determined by the university. Required of most international students prior to taking first-year writing, this course is key to students' formal introduction to language practices at the university.

Framed as a collaborative action-research project, the broader project involved a team of teacher-researchers, whose immediate goal was to implement curricular changes within our individual classrooms and broader goal was to revise an existing monolingual model of teaching. As a methodology, action research is defined as comparative research based within social action, leading to recommendations for change (Lewin 1946; McLaren 2007). Situated within a broader program-wide initiative on pedagogical innovation, this research focused on critical reflection upon our own pedagogical practices through monthly pedagogical workshops and collaborative reading of scholarship, which guided both collaborative development and revision of core assignments.

Central to this pedagogical innovation has been the concern to develop theory-informed pedagogies that treat students' repertoires of linguistic and semiotic resources as assets and their composing processes as sites of inquiry and learning. Learning objectives for the bridge writing course include using inquiry as the backbone of writing, treating one's cultures and languages as resources for learning and sites of inquiry, and determining goals and strategies for one's own learning through preflection and reflection. More specifically, the new course initiatives highlight students' ongoing negotiations of languages, cultures, and genres (Canagarajah 2006). One such pedagogical initiative uses a translation narrative assignment to engage students in individual and collaborative translation of cultural texts and reflection on translation processes and strategies (Kiernan, Meier, and Wang 2016). The writing-theory-cartoon assignment described in this chapter stemmed from this pedagogical work.

In order to analyze the pedagogical affordances of the assignment, I collected and analyzed a corpus of forty-four student artifacts generated in the spring and fall of 2014, with each student sample including two drafts of writing-theory cartoons, written explanations of cartoon design, a reflective essay, and a discourse-based interview, which all created opportunities for students to clarify and articulate their informal theories about multiple languages and multimodal design. For data analysis, written explanations of the cartoon drawings were inductively analyzed to generate primary categories (e.g., literacy identity, cultural identity, attitudes and emotions towards language, struggles and success, cognitive process, language and culture, language evolution and dialects, translingual relationships, grammar, semantics, syntactic structure, and ideology). I then coded the cartoon drawings for themes and design, with a particular focus on the use of visual elements (Which shapes, colors, and cultural symbols are used and how are they organized spatially?) and narrative (What is the story/point being told/made?). I then grouped them into theory-informed, secondary analytical constructs (e.g., multimodal design, transcultural identity, translingual relationships, translingual practices), all of them pointing towards translingual relationships and transcultural experiences. Emergent categories and constructs were further triangulated with written reflections and discourse-based interview to uncover further details about student thinking.

Researcher Positioning
As the course instructor and researcher, my own linguistic, cultural, and institutional identities have informed and shaped my research interests. I, like many of these students, came to the United States from China in my early twenties in pursuit of graduate degrees. I, too, attended a public university in my early years of immigration and experienced similar struggles with language and literacy. Yet, I also recognize experiential differences that impose limits on my understanding of these students' translanguaging experiences. For example, I often struggle to understand the Chinese language students use, which is filled with internet phrases and cultural references I am not familiar with. I also came from a different generation of immigrants—a time prior to China's economic boom, when students could only afford to study in the United States with merit scholarships offered by a US university. Even though English is not my first language, I was an English major in college and scored well on my GRE test. Nonetheless, I felt, and responded to, the pressure to add academic English to my linguistic repertoire to maximize my social and academic success in the United States; such a position provides me with unique insights into the translanguaging practices of ELLs.

The Assignment
The writing-theory-cartoon assignment asks students to generate informal theories of languages, literacy identities, and translingual relationships through a mixed use of multiple languages and modes. Students are encouraged to consider their communicative repertoires as a whole and to critically examine how such repertoires are acquired and used in the context of the assignment. Students are prompted to consider the differences and similarities between the languages at their disposal and to develop a set of writing-theory cartoons to capture such insights.

Paul Prior and Jody Shipka's study (2003) of college students' distributed writing process informs the design of this assignment. In their study, the authors used writing-theory cartoons to prompt students' theorization and representation of the contours, spaces, and trajectories of their writing. As "visual metaphors of thought processes and emotions" (182), these drawings captured the material, cognitive, and affective dimensions of the participants' writing processes. I adapted the exercise into a staged process that scaffolded students' understanding of multimodal design and translingual stance in explicit ways.

The assignment involves a sequence of activities that typically unfold across six regular class meetings. Drawing on student-selected multilingual texts, students develop informal theories of the multiple languages at their disposal. Through invention activities, such as a metaphor exercise that invites students to generate two metaphors that most capture their feelings towards, experiences with, and practices with English/home language, this assignment invites conceptual juxtaposition of multiple languages and explicit analysis of language and semiotic differences. The assignment then asks students to invent visual representations of such informal theories in the form of writing-theory cartoons. Through recursive, guided drafting and peer review, students explore multiple pathways for developing and representing meaning, thereby learning to negotiate language and semiotic differences as opportunities for delivering important personal insights.

This assignment is often coupled with a major writing assignment, such as the translation narrative assignment mentioned above, to encourage regular reflection on translingual practices. When used as such, insights gained here can give rise to more systematic examination of one's experiences with multiple languages. Questions students explore in such writing assignments may include but are not limited to these: What has been my relationship with multiple languages? What social and schooling experiences have shaped my perceptions of and attitudes towards different languages? How are different languages organized differently and how does that affect my uses of them? In these written reflections, students often draw on insights developed in the writing-theory cartoons to guide their inquiry. It is through such pedagogical scaffolding that the assignment supports explicit consideration of translingual relationships and multimodal design.

The course, taught weekly through two regular classroom meetings and one lab meeting in a computer classroom, creates opportunities to construct and revisit meaning across print and multiple modes. Across four academic semesters, I repurposed the assignment in alignment with other assignments implemented in the course. Across such iterations, I have come to identify the core procedure of the assignment as constituted by the six stages presented in table 9.1. Stages 1 and 2 involve a series of inventive activities that direct students' attention to and analysis of multilingual artifacts. Students often select familiar artifacts, such as a childhood poem, idiom, or a song written in their home language. Collective exposure to and analysis of a range of genres across languages lends to the development of informal theories about multiple languages. In response to prompts that invite metaphors, students often draw on personally relevant cultural symbols and tropes to capture language differences. One student might describe communication in

Table 9.1. Writing-theory cartoon stages

1.	*Artifact sharing* Students share and analyze short, multilingual texts (e.g., idioms, poems, children's literature) Students develop conceptual understanding of languages (e.g., semantic, syntactic, and lexical)
2.	*Freewriting* Students use freewrite prompt to develop individual keywords and elaborate PROMPT 1: When I think of English/home language, I feel . . . because . . . PROMPT 2: English/home language is like a . . . because . . . PROMPT 3: Living with multiple languages is like . . . , I am a . . . because Instructor uses wordle.net to generate visual representations of class themes Class generates informal theories of languages
3.	*Drafting* Students further develop individual freewrite and personal theories Students use flockdraw.com to complete a first draft of writing-theory cartoon Students upload first drafts for public viewing and peer review
4.	*Multimodal design workshop* Students provide peer review for each other's drawings Instructor leads workshop on multimodal design principles using student work
5.	*Revision* Students revise and finalize writing-theory cartoons Students provide bilingual explanation on theory and multimodal design
6.	*Reflection* Students develop a written reflection Students reflect on multimodal composing process Students develop metalinguistic and metacognitive awareness

English as a football field where the football (the message) is directed at an immediate audience (another player); the same student might describe communication in one's home language as a riddle, for which interpretations of meanings require much guessing. These metaphors are shared and discussed during class.

Stages 3 and 4 engage students to further develop their ideas about language difference across modes. Each student uses a free online drawing tool (flockdraw.com) to compose a set of visual images that embody a key theme of personal relevance and resonance. For example, one student might draw a picture of themselves lying on a sandy beach to illustrate their feeling of ease when using English; they might use a picture of themselves walking under a scorching sun to describe their feeling of anxiety when communicating in English. Another student might draw a flight of stairs to showcase the hierarchical structure of their home language (with different registers for individuals of different genders and seniorities); this student might use an image of a circle to show what they perceive to be the democratic nature of English. The composition of such first drafts is reserved for weekly, two-hour lab meetings, when each student has access to a desktop computer and the time to experiment. These first drafts are uploaded to a class repository, which then becomes a resource for discussion and peer review. Drawing on exemplary student-generated images that illustrate different approaches to multimodal composition, I lead a multimodal design workshop to engage students in focused analysis of the affordances and organizational logics of textual and visual modes. Students consider the choices they make when representing ideas visually and reflect upon their choices. I work to channel the discussion towards important issues of visual design, specifically the orchestration of colors, shapes, spatial relationships, and visual and textual symbols, all in light of the abstract idea being represented. For example, we might question someone's use of the moon in a picture and learn that the moon is a cultural symbol of family reunion; we might discover the surprising cultural narratives that inform students' choice of colors by having students discuss such choices. This is a productive venue through which students bring to the surface a range of experiences, insights, and thought processes that could further replenish their thinking about semiotic differences.

The last two stages invite students to revise and reflect on their informal theories and visual representations. In so doing, they incorporate all previous steps, encouraging students to create a final set of cartoons that represent their thinking about the different (and similar) affordances, functions, and forms of languages. It is often the case that students abandon their first drafts after learning about each other's insights and design. Such changes also become opportunities for reflection. To move further towards a translingual stance, I often ask students to create a bilingual explanation for each of their images, in which they further articulate the underlying theory of language differences and their design processes. For example, a student might draw a cup of tea to represent the affective functions of their home language while using the visual symbol of coffee to represent the affective functions of English. In their written explanation, they might engage the reader in discussing the cultural practice of tea drinking as a form of healing and self-discovery, which reading literature in their home language provides. Similarly, they might use the example of coffee to describe English as a language that involves many "exotic elements" directly or indirectly imported from other cultures, therefore adding to its expressive potential and flavor.

For this chapter, I provide specific examples that illustrate four types of translingual and transcultural work this assignment affords, including performing identities in a transcultural context, analyzing language as linguistics systems, reflecting on language and culture as connected

Table 9.2. Translingual negotiation analytical categories

Category	Student Example
Transcultural identity	Student examines translingual experiences as limiting or affording: –expressions of self –social relationships –experiences with literacies and educational systems
Language as objects of analysis	Student recognizes languages as rule-governed linguistic systems with: –semantic meanings (e.g., words, phrases, idioms) –lexical and morphological features (e.g., word formation, inflections) –syntactic structures (e.g., sentence structures, transitions)
Language and culture	Student makes sense of language as informed by and informing culture: –people's ways of thinking and behaving –cultural practices –rhetorical traditions –value systems
Translingual approach to writing	Student describes approaches to writing across languages: –writing processes as involving multiple languages and modes –strategies developed across languages –translanguaging practices (e.g., translation, marshaling multilingual resources)

dimensions, and thinking about writing as negotiating translingual relationships. While such categories are presented as discrete from each other in table 9.1, it is important to recognize that these analytical categories are not discrete or mutually exclusive. As my discussion shows, there is a great deal of overlap across these categories. In the following, I present each theme with illustrative details from the data.

FINDINGS

Translingual Identities

The recursive process of the assignment creates multiple opportunities to explore the different forms, functions, and contexts of language use. In particular, invention activities that prompt students to consider languages in juxtaposition to each other often lead to reflections on their experiences moving within and across languages. Some students reflect on their experiences with multiple languages in a transnational learning context. When reflecting on their experiences with English in academic and everyday environments, students often describe their encounters as dominated by feelings of frustration, confusion, and anxiety. As Yu illustrates in the following cartoon, speaking English makes him feel he has lost control in the moment of writing and beyond.

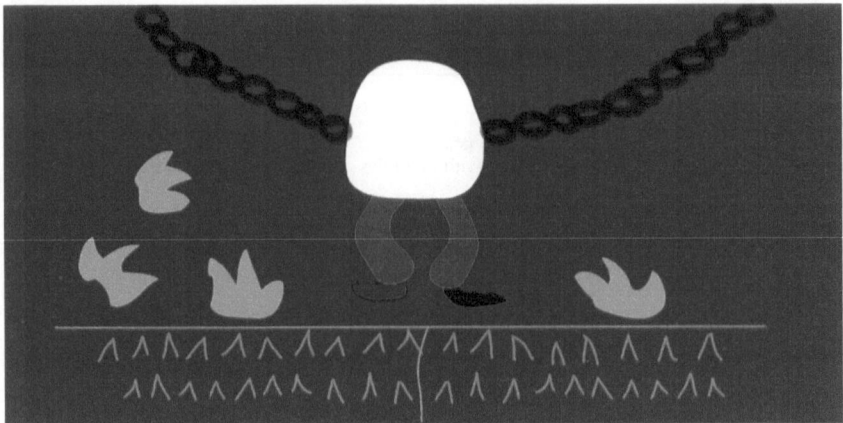

ENGLISH: This is the feeling of saying English. In this picture, this man tries to make his effort to struggle with the cocoon, but he doesn't even know the most dangerous is waiting for him, the heated needles, which is under his legs. Just like the feeling of speaking English, when I was expressing my opinion, I cannot make 100% sure if the audiences understand my original meaning. Even though the audience might get what I am [what I am trying to say], the process is grilling—the feeling of sitting on pins and needles.

CHINESE: 此图大概描绘了一个被茧困住的人想要尽力挣脱，但是他并不知道他的下面还有无数被火焰加热后的针，真是一副危机四伏的画面！有的时候我讲英语并不能百分之百表达出我想表达的意思，听者或许能理解，但对我来说整个过程是一种煎熬——那种如坐针毡的感觉。 (Researcher translation: This picture roughly depicts a person trying to break free of a cocoon, but he is not aware of the numerous heated needles lying underneath. What a moment with dangers lurking all around! When I speak English, sometimes I can't express myself to a hundred percent. My audience might understand [me], the process is grilling for me—the feeling of sitting on pins and needles.)

Figure 9.1. Yu's writing-theory cartoon on English.

I was surprised when I first saw Yu's images. He struck me as a quiet and disengaged student who had missed several important due dates and evaded my attempt to engage him during class discussions. This image, so rich with visual symbols and imagination, fascinated me. I chose it as an exemplary image for the design workshop. Responding to peers' inquiries, Yu brought forth insights revealing his rich experiences with multiple literacies. Responding to a fellow student's comment that the image *had* come from a gamer, Yu confessed that he had been struggling with a challenge in *League of Legends* (a video game) and his visual design was informed by the aesthetic style of the game. When I asked the class to share what they saw in the image, several Chinese students shouted out two Chinese idioms, 作茧自缚 (the caterpillar creating a cocoon to trap itself) and 如坐针毡 (sitting on a carpet of pins and needles). When I asked them to translate/explain the idioms, several students came back from a short online search with English equivalents—"you reap what you sow" and "sit on pins and needles." However, the conversation did not stop there. Other students argued that in translating 作茧自缚 as "you reap what you sow," we missed a very important cultural trope—the use of cocoons to mock those who are encumbered by their own decisions. Students suggested we attend to the symbolic meaning of the idiom, which comments on the irony and struggle experienced by the caterpillar. When asked if his use of the idiom was intentional, Yu blushed and said he often regretted his decision to come abroad. To him, the decision was an act of creating a cocoon that he had ever since tried to break free of.

Aside from what I misconstrued as Yu's reticence, institutional and cultural forces are at work to constrain students' sharing of emotions. Cynthia Lewis calls this the regulation of emotions in schools—the fact that certain dispositions and emotions, such as enthusiasm and passion, are often promoted over anger and depression (Boldt, Lewis, and Leander 2015). According to these authors, the overregulation of emotion might lead to limited opportunities for learning. In this view, the cartoon drawings embody and convey emotions, while the ensuing activities enable the circulation of such emotions in and beyond the classroom, facilitating the cultivation of empathy and understanding.

Language as Object of Analysis

In addition to describing their experiences with multiple languages, students also approach languages as objects of analysis. Many students reflect on various dimensions of language differences as points of discussion. Some reflect on how inflection principles create certain usage problems (e.g., the absence of tense and plural forms in certain languages might lead to errors in writing in English); others reflect on the difficulties of finding the semantic equivalent of a word in English. Ru, for one, used her cartoon to reflect on her observation of the different lexical features of Chinese and English.

Ru's cartoons capture a common observation among students that points to different rules of operation across linguistic systems. As Ru suggests, one of the major distinctions between English and Chinese is that

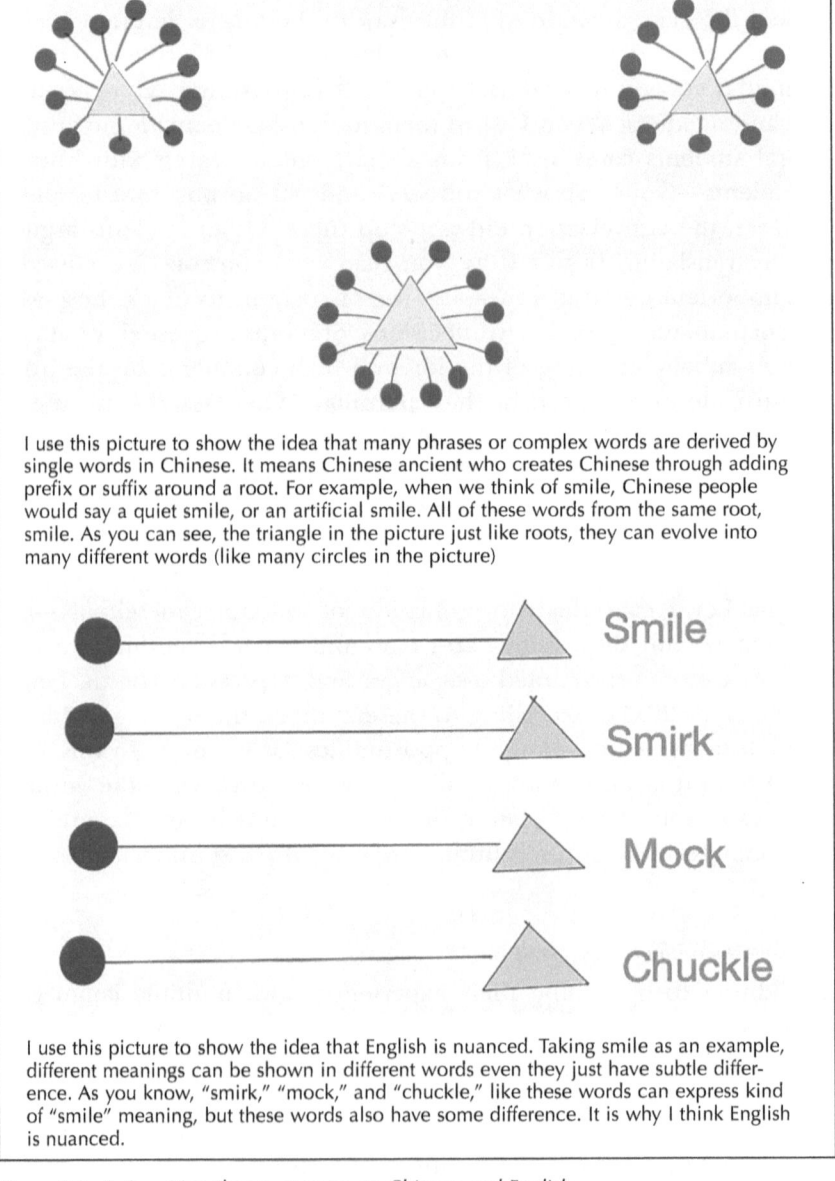

Figure 9.2. Ru's writing-theory cartoon on Chinese and English.

"English words perform functions individually, while Chinese characters act in group and combination." In Ru's reflection, Chinese root words, such as 笑 (smile/laugh), can be used in combination with different characters to convey different types of laughter, such as 偷 (secret) 笑

(laugh), or 假 (fake) 笑 (laugh); on the other hand, English words that denote close meanings of laugh are spelt differently (e.g., *smirk, chuckle, mock*). In this instance, Ru developed a deeper understanding of languages as rule-governed systems. As documented elsewhere (Jimenez et al. 2015), activities that promote translation provide students with opportunities to consider the nature of vocabulary, specifically in terms of how the range of lexical meanings could be constructed differently across languages. This was an important metalinguistic activity because it required Ru to compare, reflect on, and manipulate the two languages in ways conducive to developing a robust and holistic theory of languages.

In many similar instances of reflection, students forge such theories (e.g., English is more specific and accurate, Spanish is more affective, Chinese is more reader dependent). More important, however, the value of the exercise lies in how it gives rise to metacognitive development by encouraging connections between emergent language theories and language learning. For example, Ru attributed much of her struggle with English learning to the presence of a large number of "miscellaneous words" (words with close meaning but spelt differently), which demands she spend much time and energy learning to appreciate the nuanced meanings of words. Rote memorization, as she was taught to do in high school, became inadequate in the face of this daunting task; therefore, Ru set her immediate goal to acquire vocabulary through extensive reading and revising her dictionary-using strategies (e.g., focus on nuanced meanings by studying example sentences in the dictionary).

Language and Culture

In addition to managing languages as objects of analysis and performance, students often engage with broader translanguaging concerns, most tellingly illustrated through the negotiation of a dual set of cultural sensitivities. In particular, students focus on unpacking and articulating culturally specific aesthetics, rhetorical styles, and ideological features of languages as operative within community, disciplinary, and national contexts.

Fan's reflection reveals a recurrent theme—students theorize language as indexical of cultural ways of thinking and behaving. In particular, Fan focuses on a particular rhetorical feature of the Chinese way of thinking—its tendency to be indirect with requests and feelings, as well as its reliance on reader knowledge to interpret meaning. When I asked him about his idea of "politicians [sharing secrets] with entrepreneurs,"

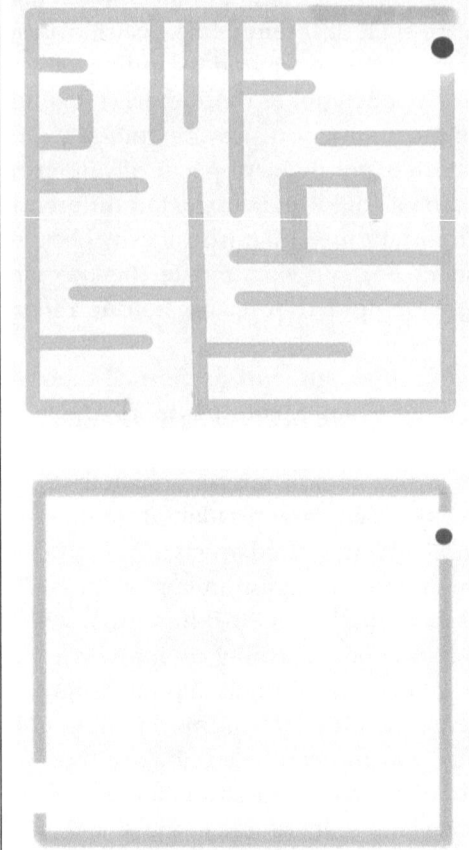

Figure 9.3. Fan's writing-theory cartoon on English and Chinese.

he hesitated for a moment and replied that this observation came from his experience accompanying his father to attend important business dinners with government officials. From Fan's description, his father used these business dinners as an induction ceremony, where Fan was introduced to important business relations he was to inherit. During these encounters, entrepreneurs courted favors from government officials, who might give riddled hints on important government decisions in exchange for bribery.

The cartoon exercise brings to the surface rich, translocally distributed experiences and discourses. For example, Fan's reflection points to a sharpened critique of corruption, which turned into an area of inquiry for a later assignment. When brought into juxtaposition with his experiences in the United States, Fan drew the conclusion of English as mirroring US values as "straightforward and simple." Echoing Paul Kei Matsuda and Tony Silva's cross-cultural composition course (1999), this assignment leverages the rich cultural and linguistic knowledge unique to transnational experiences. It surfaces assumptions students make about culture, values, and ideology that may otherwise remain invisible. Fan's critique of his home culture is grounded in richly textured experiential knowledge, whereas his rather essentialized view of US culture is informed by a comparatively brief encounters with faculty, classmates, and roommates during his first three months in the United States. The assignment therefore creates a space for Fan to formulate a "baseline" understanding of familiar and unfamiliar aspects of both cultures, which he can later interrogate as his experiences with transnational living deepen.

Negotiating Translingual Writing

As mentioned above, the cartoon exercise allows students to forge theories of language as linguistic, cultural, and ideological structures. In addition to managing languages as objects of analysis and performance, students often use these insights to reconsider their own practices as writers. In particular, many students focus on unpacking and analyzing their own processes and struggles in writing across languages.

Xiaoqi's second cartoon captured the overwhelming sense of crisis when one faces challenges at every stage of the writing process. For her, the black zigzags represent her development of ideas—the paucity of writing techniques and lack of knowledge with rhetorical devices specific to Western rhetorical traditions impoverishes her writing. Similarly, the lack of a line that could drive the zigzag forward represents her difficulties in identifying a good thesis. By contrast, her writing in Chinese benefits from a clear focus and a variety of colorful rhetorical devices that make her writing compelling and engaging. In her reflection, she provides an extensive discussion of a major concern with plagiarism: "Americans emphasize on ideas as individual properties. You need to cite the author and source for anything you use. Otherwise, you commit plagiarism, which is considered a major offense. People not only see that as an academic problem, but also a problem with your character. You will get a warning the first time, and then expulsion if you do it again. In China, people pay little heed to this issue. People just 'take' or change others' ideas for themselves. I need to pay particular attention to this bad habit" (pers. comm., November 11, 2013). In these accounts, Xiaoqi performs metacognitive thinking (thinking about one's learning) and

English: I used lines with different colors to stimulate the structure of the paper which I can use my home language. The thickest and vertical line not only represents the theme, but also means construction of the paper. the reason why I used many different colors cross the vertical line because they seem like diverse writing skills, vocabulary and grammar in my home language.

Chinese: 图中黑色的竖线代表一篇文章的"主心骨"和逻辑顺序,循序渐进并且串连起文章其他元素。彩色的线代表多种多样的文章修饰,写作手法等等用于文章润色的方法。(Researcher translation: The black vertical line represents the "backbone" or and the logical order of an essay, which strings together all the elements in a progressive way. Colorful lines represent a wide range of rhetorical devices and writing techniques, which can embellish the essay.)

English: I think this visual design can totally express the structure of my English paper, which is weak, incomplete and insipid. Comparing to the first one, when I use my home language, there are "theme" and consecutive "strung" the paper. However, this one doesn't have the "backbone" same as my English paper often dim the theme of it. The Black zigzag design means I wish I can use diverse writing skills, vocabularies and grammars when i writing and English paper, but it's unpractical till now.

Chinese: 这幅图片和中文设计的最大不同就是图中缺少一条主线,就像英语写作的时候,感觉怎么写都写不到点上去,经常会模糊焦点找不到中心。同样的z字型设计但是使用黑色表达是有种心有余而力不足的感觉,英语学了那么多年学了很多语法和用法,但是真正拼在一起的时候会使用不当没有什么给文章添彩的效果。(Researcher translation: The main difference between this image and the one on Chinese is the lack of a main thesis. It is like when I write an essay in English, the focus is often blurry and I can't find the main idea. The "z" design remains the same, but I use black to represent a feeling of frustration. I have spent years studying English grammar and usage, but I often misuse them when attempting to piece them together in my essay, which works against the purpose of adding to the appeal of my essay).

Figure 9.4. Xiaoqi's writing-theory cartoon on English and Chinese.

identifies her "problems": her struggle to find a focus, inadequacy of English instruction in China, her lack of confidence in using literary strategies and other rhetorical devices, and her concern for plagiarism. In so doing, Xiaoqi articulates what Min-Zhan Lu (2006) describes as "peculiar lived experiences" (609) as she seeks to make meaningful connections across experiences and circumstances of her literacy learning. Her reflection, as framed within transnational contexts, allows her to not only recognize but also interrogate disciplinary conventions and rules such as plagiarism as cultural constructions that embody ideological values and are embedded in power structures.

CONCLUSION

In this chapter, I draw on my data analysis and experience to describe the pedagogical affordance of the writing-theory-cartoon assignment in a bridge writing course. It places value on translingual and transcultural competencies, which mirror a disciplinary shift toward asset-based, culturally sustaining pedagogy (Paris 2009). From a pedagogical point of view, the writing-process cartoon is a generative tool to encourage students' reflection on important feelings, meanings, and stories they otherwise find hard to share because of linguistic, institutional, and cultural reasons. More importantly, it provides creative occasions that lend themselves to meaningful intellectual and identity work. This assignment helps students develop a repertoire of skills towards productive negotiation with languages, semiotic codes, identities, and cultures, enhancing the development of metalinguistic awareness central to their success. Critical to such an effort is the assignment's intention to position students as experts and its emphasis on multimodal experimentation.

Students as Experts

This assignment treats students as experts and intellectuals in their own languages and cultures. In generating metaphors and visual representations, students draw on everyday experiences and disciplinary expertise to forge and test informal theories about languages and cultures. Seeking meaningful connections is especially important for students who claim to have no expertise in language arts. As they compare writing to coding a program, creating an artwork, cooking a meal, or learning a dance move, students engage in serious theory building in accessible and compelling ways. Additionally, this assignment allows students to name translingual practices they already perform in everyday experiences and to strategize their learning accordingly. For many, the difficulty in identifying the accurate and precise meaning of a word mirrors the frustration they encounter in trying to communicate and negotiate small mundane details, including ordering food from the cafeteria or conversing with a roommate. Facing the need to articulate and rationalize the choices they make, students often venture informal theories of languages that can be tested in academic and social situations. The validity of such theories aside, the intellectual work itself pivots around important issues of negotiating translingual relationships.

Also, placing the multiple languages they do use in juxtaposition to each other, students challenge binaries that separate languages as sealed and isolated entities. For many, thinking about English compels them to examine their home language, which often leads to surprising connections. For example, in her process of theorizing English as hybrid and ever changing, a student from Uganda discovered that her home language, Kinyawanda, has also undergone major changes to its spelling rules, leaving her "hanging in a cloud of languages with none [she is] stable at." Others begin to examine the different literacy practices within their language, noticing they "may be fast writers in Chinese, but being a sophisticated Chinese writer is as hard as being an elegant English writer." In so doing, students begin to see all languages as "language in translation" while attending to social, cultural, and historical meanings as conveyed by the linguistic choices and decisions they make (Pennycook 2007).

Using Multimodality

Evidenced in these images are complex ways multimodality enables students to derive meaning from personal experiences, engage in creative semiotic work, and forge agentive identities. First, multimodality gives shape to experiences and emotions hard to describe in linguistic terms. For most students, meaning emerges concurrently across modes. It is not a matter of formulating a theory in words and then translating it into visual symbols or vice versa. Oftentimes, it begins with playful encounters with colors, symbols, and shapes, which leads to discovery of meanings. Second, students demonstrate sophisticated understandings of the affordances, logics, and principles of multiple modes to allow meaning to flow freely across modes. Meaning arises from the emergent process in which ideas are tested, translated, and stabilized in the process of transmedia articulation. In Yu's case, the linguistic mode and visual mode inform each other, as the idioms give shape to the visual symbols and the visual narrative that serve as the basis of Yu's written exposition. In Ru's example, the visual symbols (flower petals and one-to-one match) and textual explanations work in concert to deliver a complex theory on language structures. Thirdly, students' semiotic designs are informed by multiple literacies they acquire from other contexts, such as Yu's gaming experiences, Xiaoqi's fascination with stop-motion animation, or Fan's emulation of East meets West infographics (Liu 2015), a popular meme circulating in students' social networks. In pushing towards a translingual stance on languages, students bring into convergence a range of literacy practices to formulate an integrated multimodal, multilingual repertoire of resources. Building on these insights, I offer several pedagogical recommendations for implementation.

Adoption and Adaptation

The inherent flexibility of the assignment allows multiple pedagogical uses across various teaching contexts. While I have focused on the different approaches students took to the assignment, I would like to stress that teachers can repurpose and reconfigure the assignment for different purposes. For instance, I have used the cartoon exercise within a transnational learning memory assignment in which students use cartoon images to depict the typical settings, procedures, and social-material features of typical classrooms; when coupled with a translation narrative assignment, the assignment could facilitate students' exploration of the cultural and ideological meanings of language structures; the assignment could also help ELL students invent ideas for a traditional literacy-narrative assignment.

Because the assignment is multilingual and multimodal in nature, I recommend teachers create multiple opportunities for discussing issues of linguistic and modal affordances. It is also important to give students opportunities to practice language (and mode) meshing, which can be accomplished by inviting students to incorporate and explain elements of home language and visual symbols into their written products. The process of articulating one's ideas through multiple languages and modes encourages thoughtful and analytical thinking about rhetoric and writing.

Because the assignment creates an exigency for students to invite interrogation and analysis of a broad range of transnational experiences that inform their identities as translingual individuals, I recommend teachers provide opportunities that allow students to comment on the affective and emotional dimensions of their experiences with transnational migration, which is filled with contestation and reconciliation. Such reflections compel students to revise old assumptions, develop new strategies, and grow expertise as efficient and critical readers and writers. In "venting" about how hard it is, celebrating small "aha" moments, and experiencing confusion and resolution, students revisit a wide array of emotional experiences with multilingualism.

To close, this assignment serves as a bridge that connects students' formal and informal literacy learning, as well as cultures/languages of their homes and the US university. It moves students toward using writing (broadly defined) as a way to inquire into their transnationalism as a site of learning. In learning to juggle multiple dialects, cultures, and languages, students not only develop strategies to name unfamiliar aspects of culture but also learn to suspend established understandings of familiar aspects of their lived experiences and thus open up a space for reflection. Such pedagogically scaffolded negotiation is especially important to help transnational students resolve a wide range of personal, academic, social, and cultural struggles that mark their transition into the university. It provides ELLs with opportunities to name and strategize their translingual and multimodal practices, which helps sharpen their understanding of how learning often unfolds through recursive examination of personal, academic, and disciplinary conventions, genres, and practices through preflection and reflection.

APPENDIX 9.A

WRITING-THEORY-CARTOON ASSIGNMENT DESCRIPTION

PURPOSE

For this assignment, you will reflect on your experiences moving across language(s) and modes. Writing and drawing your experiences provides an opportunity to (a) examine your personal beliefs about language(s), (b) develop personal theories of language(s) and cultures, and (c) explore the different ways of representing meanings across modes and cultures.

ASSIGNMENT

Drawing on your personal experiences working with and across multiple languages and cultures, you will develop metaphors that capture language differences. In juxtaposing your multiple languages next to each other, you will identify important differences in how you use different languages (e.g., express yourself, communicate insights, develop literacy and professional identities). Using flockdraw.com, you will design a set of writing-theory cartoons that capture a unique insight you develop. You will write a bilingual explanation for your cartoons, where you discuss language differences and aspects of your visual design (shapes, spaces, colors, and fonts) that capture such differences.

LEARNING OBJECTIVES

This project encourages you to articulate your own theories of what language is. It also encourages you to consider how your language choice is informed by various factors, including familiar and strange cultures, your audience, and language structures.

AUDIENCE

Because you are unpacking the forms and functions of multiple languages for people from outside your culture, it is important that you consider their needs and expectations. Ask yourself, What does my audience know or not know about the culture and history behind phrases, tropes, and symbols I use to construct the cartoons? How will someone from another culture understand a concept or idea differently? In important ways, your drawings and written explanations should be imagined in light of these needs and expectations.

FORMAT

Your writing-theory cartoons should be saved as a jpeg file; they should help deliver a personal theory on languages and language differences. Bilingual illustrations should adequately unpack the meaning and design of your images. It is important that your cartoons and writing work in concert to make explicit your claims about languages.

REFERENCES

Black, Rebecca W. 2006. "Language, Culture, and Identity in Online Fanfiction." *E-Learning* 3 (2): 170–85.

Black, Rebecca W. 2007. "Digital Design: English Language Learners and Reader Reviews in Online Fiction." In *The New Literacies Sampler*, edited by Michele Knobel and Colin Lankshear, 115–37. New York: Peter Lang.

Boldt, Gail, Cynthia Lewis, and Kevin M. Leander. 2015. "Moving, Feeling, Desiring, Teaching." *Research in the Teaching of English* 49 (4): 430–42.

Canagarajah, A. Suresh. 2006. "Toward a Writing Pedagogy of Shuttling between Languages: Learning from Multilingual Writers." *College English* 68 (6): 589–604.

Canagarajah, Suresh. 2007. "Lingua Franca English, Multilingual Communities, and Language Acquisition." *Modern Language Journal* 91 (1): 923–39.

Canagarajah, A. Suresh. 2013. "Negotiating Translingual Literacy: An Enactment." *Research in the Teaching of English* 48 (1): 40–67.

Cummins, Jim. 2006. "Identity Texts: The Imaginative Construction of Self Through Multiliteracies Pedagogy." In *Imagining Multilingual Schools: Languages in Education and Glocalization*, edited by Ofelia García, Tove Skutnabb-Kangas, and Maria E. Torres-Guzmán, 51–68. Clevedon: Multilingual Matters.

Gilje, Øystein. 2011. "Working in Tandem with Editing Tools: Iterative Meaning-Making in Filmmaking Practices." *Visual Communication* 10 (1): 45–62.

Gonzales, Laura. 2018. *Sites of Translation: What Multilinguals Can Teach Us About Digital Writing and Rhetoric*. Ann Arbor: University of Michigan Press.

Halbritter, Bump. 2006. "Musical Rhetoric in Integrated-Media Composition." *Computers and Composition* 23 (3): 317–34.

Hornberger, Nancy H., and Holly Link. "Translanguaging in Today's Classrooms: A Biliteracy Lens." *Theory into Practice* 51 (4): 239–47.

Horner, Bruce, Min-Zhan Lu, Jacqueline Jones Royster, and John Trimbur. 2011. "Opinion: Language Difference in Writing: Toward a Translingual Approach." *College English* 73 (3): 303–21.

Horner, Bruce, Cynthia Selfe, and Tim Lockridge. 2015. "Translinguality, Transmodality, and Difference: Exploring Dispositions and Change in Language and Learning." Enculturation/Intermezzo.

Hull, Glynda A., and Mira-Lisa Katz. 2006. "Crafting an Agentive Self: Case Studies of Digital Storytelling." *Research in the Teaching of English* 41 (1): 43–81.

Hull, Glynda A., and Mark Evan Nelson. 2005. "Locating the Semiotic Power of Multimodality." *Written Communication* 22 (2): 224–61.

Jacobs, Dale. 2007. "Marveling at The Man Called Nova: Comics as Sponsors of Multimodal Literacy." *College Composition and Communication* 59 (2): 180–205.

Jiménez, Robert T., Sam David, Keenan Fagan, Victoria J. Risko, Mark Pacheco, Lisa Pray, and Mark Gonzales. 2015. "Using Translation to Drive Conceptual Development for Students Becoming Literate in English as an Additional Language." *Research in the Teaching of English* 49 (3): 248–71.

Kiernan, Julia, Joyce Meier, and Xiqiao Wang. 2016. "Negotiating Languages and Cultures: Enacting Translingualism through a Translation Assignment." *Composition Studies* 44 (1): 89–107.

Kress, Gunther R., and Theo van Leeuwen. 2006. *Reading Images: The Grammar of Visual Design*. New York: Routledge.

Lankshear, Colin, and Michele Knobel. 2007. "Sampling 'the New' in New Literacies." In *The New Literacies Sampler*, edited by Michele Knobel and Colin Lankshear, 1–25. New York: Peter Lang.

Leander, Kevin M., Nathan C. Phillips, and Katherine Headrick Taylor. 2010. "The Changing Social Spaces of Learning: Mapping New Mobilities." *Review of Research in Education* 34 (1): 329–94.

Lee, Carmen. 2007. "Text-Making Practices beyond the Classroom Context: Private Instant Messaging in Hong Kong." *Computers and Composition* 24 (3): 285–301.

Lewin, Kurt. 1946. "Action Research and Minority Problems." *Journal of Social Issues* 2 (4): 34–46.

Lewis, Cynthia, and Bettina Fabos. 2005. "Instant Messaging, Literacies, and Social Identities." *Reading Research Quarterly* 40 (4): 470–501.

Liu, Yang. 2015. *East Meets West*. Cologne, Germany: Taschen.
Lu, Min-Zhan. 2006. "Living-English Work." *College English* 68 (6): 601–18.
Lu, Min-Zhan, and Bruce Horner. 2013. "Translingual Literacy, Language Difference, and Matters of Agency." *College English* 75 (6): 582–607.
Matsuda, Paul Kei, and Tony Silva. 1999. "Cross-Cultural Composition: Mediated Integration of U. S. and International Students." *Composition Studies* 27 (1): 15–30.
McLaren, Peter. 2007. *Life in Schools: An Introduction to Critical Pedagogy in the Foundations of Education*. 5th ed. Boston: Pearson Allyn & Bacon.
Opendoors. 2016. "Fast Facts." 2016. https://www.iie.org/Research-and-Insights/Open-Doors/Data/International-Students/Enrollment-Trends.
Paris, Django. 2009. " 'They're in My Culture, They Speak the Same Way': African American Language in Multiethnic High Schools." *Harvard Educational Review* 79 (3): 428–539.
Pennycook, Alastair. 2007. "Language, Localization, and the Real: Hip-Hop and the Global Spread of Authenticity." *Journal of Language, Identity, and Education* 6 (2): 101–15.
Pennycook, Alastair. 2008. "English as a Language Always in Translation." *European Journal of English Studies* 12 (1): 33–47.
Prior, Paul, Julie Hengst, Kevin Roozen, and Jody Shipka. 2006. " 'I'll Be the Sun': From Reported Speech to Semiotic Remediation Practices." *Text & Talk* 26 (6): 733–66.
Prior, Paul, and Jody Shipka. 2003. "Chronotopic Lamination: Tracing the Contours of Literate Activity." In *Writing Selves, Writing Societies: Research from Activity Perspectives*, edited by Charles Bazerman and David R. Russell, 180–238. Fort Collins, CO: WAC Clearing House.
Selfe, Cynthia. 2009. "Aurality and Multimodal Composing." *College Composition and Communication* 60 (4): 616–63.
Shipka, Jody. 2016. "Transmodality in/and Processes of Making: Changing Dispositions and Practice." *College English* 78 (3): 250–67.
Vasudevan, Lalitha, Katherine Schultz, and Jennifer Bateman. 2010. "Rethinking Composing in a Digital Age: Authoring Literate Identities through Multimodal Storytelling." *Written Communication* 27 (4): 442–68.
Velasco, Patricia, and Ofelia García. 2014. "Translanguaging and the Writing of Bilingual Learners." *Bilingual Research Journal* 37 (6): 6–23.
Yi, Youngjoo. 2008. "Relay Writing in an Adolescent Online Community." *Journal of Adolescent and Adult Literacy* 51 (8): 670–80.

10
TRANSLINGUALISM AS PEDAGOGICAL METHODOLOGY FOR PRESERVICE TEACHERS AND PEER WRITING CONSULTANTS IN TRAINING

Naomi Silver

INTRODUCTION

This chapter offers a descriptive analysis of the initial introduction and subsequent revision of a unit on translingualism within a semester-long training course for undergraduate peer writing consultants at the University of Michigan (UM), a large midwestern public research university. The curriculum I discuss was offered in the winter semesters of 2015 and 2016. At that time, little published literature on translingual composition pedagogy was available, and even less on writing center pedagogy—a situation that has since begun to be remedied by the appearance of such texts as "Negotiating Languages and Cultures: Enacting Translingualism through a Translation Assignment" (Kiernan, Meier, and Wang 2016), "Translingualism in the Writing Center: Where Can We Meet?" (Hauer 2016), "How Student Writing Works: Celebrating Translingual Innovation and Rhetorical Agency" (*The Writing Center Journal* blog 2016), and *Crossing Divides: Exploring Translingual Writing Pedagogies and Programs* (Horner and Tetreault 2017), as well as the present volume.

In this chapter, I overview the course context and curriculum and introduce the reading and writing assignments I employed. The bulk of the chapter, however, presents and discusses a range of excerpts from my students' low-stakes and more formal writing as a way of gaining insight into how the ideas and practices incorporated into a unit on translingual pedagogy might be taken up (or not) by tutors in training. As I outline, my students experienced both insights and frustrations with these concepts and practices. On the one hand, they needed examples of translingual writing—composed both by other students and by published authors—and of translingual pedagogy in action in order to begin

DOI: 10.7330/9781646421121.c010

to envision such a profound shift in their approach to language norms. On the other hand, the requirement to engage with the translingual approach provoked some very deep reflection among these students, such that even those most resistant to the idea of questioning Standard Written English became newly aware of the effects and power dynamics of language ideology. Those who most opened themselves to these questions and this approach appeared to experience genuinely transformative thinking around linguistic oppression and its connections to social justice pedagogy. My takeaways from these teaching experiences are both practical and aspirational: first, introducing a translingual methodology into a writing center training course requires a careful balance of theoretical and hands-on texts and writing assignments to be effective, as well as patience with the necessarily slow and uneven process of student uptake; second, this methodology and this curriculum, in contributing to the training of antiracist, social justice educators, can begin to play an important role in reshaping the landscape of learning—both for our own students and for the students they in turn encounter in the writing center and other tutoring situations.

CONTEXT

Writing 300: Seminar in Peer Writing Consultation is a semester-long, three-credit course that fulfills UM's upper-level writing requirement (ULWR) in addition to comprising the first step in the undergraduate peer-consultant training program. Students in the program also complete a one-semester peer-consulting practicum the following semester as they work in the peer writing center and participate in various other mentoring and professional-development activities. Students who wish to be peer writing consultants apply to the program, and a new cohort is accepted each semester into Writing 300; these students work together all term to find ways to empower student voices, focus on higher-order concerns in writing, and help students develop requisite skills and mindsets for deepening their thinking about writing through discussion.

Since 2013, the Sweetland Center for Writing—which offers Writing 300—has been charged with the primary responsibility of providing writing and communication resources and curriculum to support international and multilingual undergraduate students within the university's College of Literature, Science, and the Arts. To this end, the center offers elective courses and conversation groups to address these students' needs at various stages of their college experience and supports faculty in other departments to work effectively and empathetically with students from a range of language backgrounds. That exigence goes hand in hand with the center's strong commitment to social justice principles, which includes seeing students' language differences not as obstacles or deficits but as resources to be mobilized in pursuit of their own communicative purposes—a central tenet of the translingual approach. The center has further sought to put its philosophical and pedagogical priorities forward through such activities as creating videos that offer multilingual students' perspectives and advice for incoming multilingual students and for faculty in all disciplines and also investing in opportunities for faculty professional development, such as offering a grant-funded faculty learning community focused on working with multilingual students in first-year writing classes.

COURSE OVERVIEW

Writing 300 instruction in translingual tutoring seeks to support these broader aims, alongside ongoing work to diversify our corps of undergraduate student consultants in regard to language background, as well as other social and personal identity categories (e.g., major). As a seminar-style course, capped at twenty-two students, Writing 300 seeks to provide multiple opportunities for student engagement, both in face-to-face conversations and activities and through online platforms that extend the classroom space, such as a class blog or threaded discussion on our course learning–management system. Designed to offer a comprehensive overview of writing center and peer-consultation pedagogy, Writing 300 is both theory and practice based, working to link concepts in writing center ethos to hands-on best practices by incorporating observations and practice sessions in Sweetland's Peer Writing Center alongside in-class activities with sample student papers, videotaped tutoring sessions, and more conceptual in-class and online discussions. These connected aims emerge in the course's primary learning goals: to familiarize students with theory about peer consulting in writing; to introduce students to the practice of consulting through observation and experience; to teach consultants strategies to empower writers; and to involve students in a recursive and reflective writing process that addresses the goals of the UM upper-level writing requirement. Shaped by these learning goals, the two to four sections of the course taught annually share a general structure and set of topics. That said, this chapter describes only my own experiences teaching translingual theory and practice in the context of the topics outlined in appendix 10.A, drawn from my 2016 syllabus.

Student and Instructor Language Backgrounds
A large majority of the students in the peer-consultant training program are monolingual English-language speakers and writers, though several of them have learned one or more other languages and some have studied abroad. Additionally, each semester we admit to the program a handful of international students, domestic multilingual students, and/or students who speak various dialects of English (primarily African American Vernacular English). In my experience, students from all these language backgrounds often bring with them assumptions about the importance of Standard Written English that influence their approaches to working with multilingual and international students. The students who attend our center (and who receive services from our tutors in training) are quite diverse, with many of them being international students (primarily Mandarin and Korean speakers), as well as domestic multilingual and multidialectal students. In support of the Writing 300 learning objective "to teach consultants strategies to empower writers," the incorporation of training in translingual pedagogy makes up an important component of the curriculum for these populations of students.

As a domestic, monolingual English-language speaker myself, albeit with some undergraduate and graduate experience studying abroad and writing in languages other than English, my own language background is similar to that of a majority of my students. As noted elsewhere in this volume, this circumstance allows me to model how monolingual speakers may nonetheless enact linguistic flexibility and successfully implement a translingual practice.

TRANSLINGUAL CURRICULUM

The pedagogy of Writing 300 aims to engage undergraduate writing tutors in the translingual conversation by offering strategies that will help them approach student writing as an opportunity to negotiate meaning in pursuit of their clients' own communicative purposes rather than as an occasion to prescribe a "correct" approach to a given rhetorical problem. Consequently, a writer's ability to mobilize languages and dialects that address their rhetorical situation imaginatively and resourcefully becomes a valuable resource to identify and nurture. To further this aim, I revised long-standing units on Consulting at the Sentence Level and Consulting with Multilingual Writers (see appendix 10.A) to shift from a more typical ESL approach to tutoring (as in Shanti Bruce and Ben Rafoth's important *ESL Writers: A Guide for Writing Center Tutors* [2009]) to one that introduced the Writing 300 students to theoretical and practice-based texts that furthered this objective for translingual writing and pedagogy.

We read Bruce Horner, Min-Zhan Lu, Jacqueline Jones Royster, and John Trimbur's (2011) opinion piece arguing for the necessity of a translingual paradigm shift, "Language Difference in Writing: Toward a Translingual Approach," as a way of introducing the terms of the conversation and exposing the students to a bold proposal for an idea they likely had not previously encountered. Alongside that text, we read linguist Anne Curzan's (2009) article on language privilege and prescriptive grammars, "Says Who? Teaching and Questioning the Rules of Grammar," which employs a history of language approach to debunk many unexamined assumptions and stereotypes about the varieties of English used in the United States. Our more hands-on examples of translingual writing included the well-known essay "How to Tame a Wild Tongue" from Gloria Anzaldúa's (1987) translingual study *Borderlands / La frontera: The New Mestiza*, which performs her own bilingual and multidialectal experiences of Spanish and English in the context of the US-Mexico border region, as well as her reflections on power and language ideology. We also incorporated some more informal practitioner reflections, such as the posts for the "Beyond a 'Single Language / Single Modality' Approach to Writing" (2014) collection on the *Sweetland Digital Rhetoric Collaborative* blog. (For a complete list of readings for the units on Consulting at the Sentence Level and Consulting with Multilingual Writers, see appendix 10.B.)

Affordances of a Translingual Curriculum

By the time my Writing 300 students encountered these readings on translingualism, both in 2015 and 2016, we were a little over a third of the way through the semester, and we had worked with the topics of identity and diversity in the writing center and power and authority in the writing center, as indicated in appendix 10.A. As a result, students were in a good position to engage with the social justice implications of translingual pedagogy represented in the readings, and indeed, in principle, they fully embraced the idea of writers' rights to their own language and the inclusivity this approach promises.

Further, they were deeply interested in the possibility of questioning what had been represented to them as beyond question, namely, the primacy of Standard Written English. This perspective was voiced by a female bilingual Korean American consultant in training: "The discussions and readings we had on consulting with multilingual writers and consulting at the sentence level were very exciting to me. In particular, the Curzan and Horner et al. articles interested me because I had never before read articles where the authors disagreed so strongly (and openly) with the 'conformities' associated with the English language. It was eye opening to see scholars critiquing and questioning society's definition of 'standard English,' and I found myself agreeing with a lot of their arguments." This student finds it refreshing, but also disturbing to have her eyes opened in this way, as she describes it coming both with a sense of responsibility and of complicity: "I felt as though I have been unknowingly contributing to the reinforcement of these ideas [of the primacy of Standard Written English] all this time simply because I was never taught otherwise." She goes on to make a comparison to a prior learning experience that reinforced the importance of introducing a translingual approach to our undergraduate students. She writes, "Reading Horner et al.'s explanations of the conformist ideologies of monolingualism reminded me of the time I took my first women's studies class only to be shocked throughout the entire semester by the hidden gender norms, microaggressions, and injustices that permeate our society. It's shocking to realize that in language too, there are ways by which injustices permeate our English writing, reading, and teaching." This student's reflection fronts the need for direct instruction about and exposure to systems of oppression that otherwise may pass unremarked—normalized, and therefore invisible—but that may be available for challenge, or at least awareness, once the curtain has been lifted, so to speak.

For students who have found themselves on the receiving end of linguistic bias, discussion of linguistic oppression comes as no surprise. A male international student from Afghanistan acknowledged his early education in the global dominance of English, writing, in relation to Anzaldúa's (1987) essay,

> There are many things I could relate to in her writing. In the beginning she talks about her mother telling her to learn English so she can have a bright future. My mother would say, "joon-am Inglese gab beezan because khoobthar ast." Essentially, what she meant was speak English so that you can have a better command of the language. The reason my parents wanted me to learn English at a young age is because it was considered as the "language of currency." To get a well paying job you must know English. . . . In Afghanistan, just by knowing and speaking English, you are automatically considered a learned individual. Sadly, this societal view of language in the country has pushed aside the country's native languages: Persian, Tajik, Pashtu, Turkmen and Uzbek. Like many Afghans, I am multilingual. So far, I know English, Persian and Tajik.

For this student, the inclusion of Anzaldúa's (1987) bilingual, multidialectal text in connection to Horner et al.'s (2011) argument for the necessity of a translingual approach to language difference becomes an occasion to reflect on his parents' acceptance of the linguistic status quo, even at the expense of a rich linguistic heritage. At the same time, he can draw on this heritage to engage with the concept of translingualism.

> Even within one language, there are many variations and this is mentioned in the [Horner et al. (2011)] article. . . . Also, Gloria Anzaldúa brings up the many variations of Spanish and English she uses in different settings. . . . I too use variations of English and Persian. At home I speak Perso-English, which is like Spanglish, where English and Persian words are used together to communicate. When talking to my grandfather and grandmother, I speak "standard" Persian. During interviews or when speaking with a professor, I use "standard" English, but with my friends I use slang English. In different environments, I use a certain variation of a language that is appropriate for that particular setting.

This student found different lessons in our translingual texts than did his Korean American classmate quoted above—they offered him an opportunity to articulate and practice his own translingual reality, even choosing to write in the hybrid "Perso-English" of the home language his mother speaks with him. Both connections are valuable for these tutors in training as they begin to engage and question linguistic ideology and bias—as a way of beginning to unravel years of unwitting compliance with the "norm" and of becoming empowered in the resources of one's own linguistic variability.

Challenges of Translingual Tutoring and Teaching
I—Power Dynamics and Assimilation

Not all Writing 300 students shared these positive moments of recognition, however. For many, a difficulty with translingual pedagogy arose in regard to imagining how these principles could be enacted in practice within the institutional setting of the university (and, for some education majors in the class, also the K–12 educational system). We can see some of these tensions emerge in students' discussion-board posts (see appendix 10.C for the prompt) responding to Horner et al.'s (2011) "Language Difference in Writing." In particular, students worried about the language expectations of professors who would be grading the papers they tutored, as in this example from a white female monolingual student: "I really liked the Horner, Lu, Royster, and Trimbur piece. . . . I thought it was interesting that the writers suggested tutors 'be more humble about what constitutes a mistake.' But if the professor is strict about grammatical errors, are we doing a disservice to these students by not correcting these errors? I wonder how we can enact social justice in a writing center while still helping students make their papers as 'correct' as possible, especially when they come in with the specific request of sentence-level revision." Other students worried they would not be preparing writers for contexts beyond the university, as in this example from an African American male bidialectal student majoring in education:

> I'm really interested in "Toward a Translingual Approach" because it talks about being more empathetic and, for lack of better words, easy on ESL writers. On one hand I do agree with this, but on the other, I do not. I always was the person who said when I become a teacher, code switching and BEV would be a main component in my classroom. Therefore, I wouldn't negatively impact a grade because a student is using different grammar or syntax, but only on certain writing assignments. So, for ESL writers, I will be soft on grading journals, blogs, etc., but on academic essays, I can't. This world is dominated by the English language and you have to know how to write in Standard English just as well as talk without being ostracized.

For both these students, engaging too fully with translingual methodology seems dangerous, as if they could be facilitating potentially negative outcomes for their clients—though we might imagine this concern to stem from quite different experiences with language norms and linguistic oppression. Both students appeal to a higher authority—professors, "the world"—to justify both their discomfort and their apparent decisions to set aside social justice matters when the stakes appear high, and when "correct," "Standard" English may be called for (in "academic essays," for example).

These students' remarks exemplify a difficulty that seems to arise for many Writing 300 students and that can perhaps be understood to manifest when their commitments to diversity and social justice bump up against their own institutional privilege and the hoops they jumped through to achieve it. The very success these students have achieved in attending the University of Michigan may paradoxically render it difficult for them to imagine a success that would not require assimilation to the majority cultural standard. The consequence of this perspective, however, is that enforcement of the norm (except in what the first monolingual student elsewhere calls "non-formal settings") becomes made over as well-meaning "help" for those students perceived as needing to be rescued.

Challenges of Translingual Tutoring and Teaching II—
Navigating Theory and Practice

Many of my Writing 300 students further struggled with what they considered to be the highly "theoretical" dimension of the Horner et al. (2011) and Curzan (2009) readings, feeling both texts engaged important considerations but offered little in the way of application to help these students know how to proceed with their own clients. As one student writes of Horner et al. (2011), it "reads very much as a call to action, though there is very little that is directly actionable in it," while another student, writing about Curzan (2009), and after posing questions about the kinds of choices a tutor may face, concludes, "Anne Curzan never really gives an answer." Having encountered this perspective in my first iteration of the unit in 2015, in 2016 I took care to pair these readings with others that did depict translingual tutoring in action and offered a more practical, hands-on approach to translingual pedagogy.

In particular, I paired the Horner et al. (2011) piece with Anne DiPardo's (2011) seminal article in the peer-tutoring literature, "'Whispers of Coming and Going': Lessons from Fannie," which describes her study of the difficulties encountered in the consulting relationship of a middle-class African American tutor working with a first-generation Native American writer. This article fronts deep connections between language and identity and the importance of tutor attention to these connections if language oppression is not to be unwittingly reinforced. Additionally, because students in 2015 had been unable to imagine what successful translingual writing might look like, in the 2016 iteration, I incorporated well-known published examples, such as Anzaldúa's (1987) "How to Tame a Wild Tongue," described above, and also, for my education majors, an online slideshow, "Translingual Education as a Phenomenon, a Methodology and an Ideology to Promote Social Justice and Educational Renewal" (Schwarzer, Fuchs, and Hermosilla 2011). Additionally, I added one more day to this unit, after we had completed all of the reading, to workshop two sample translingual essays from an undergraduate college composition class (courtesy of Julia Kiernan, an editor of this volume).

Though students in this iteration of the class still worried over what one referred to as the "knotty" problem of negotiating translingual empowerment and the primacy of Standard Written English, the concrete examples and hands-on activities contributed significantly to their thinking beyond an either-or response and making broader connections among the readings and their own experiences.

Making Connections among Readings

As they thought through the relationships among these new readings and activities, students in the second iteration of the course in 2016 made connections to their own potential practices. A white male education major, who had studied abroad and conducted research in Mexico, becoming a proficient Spanish-language communicator in the process, focused on the interactions depicted in the DiPardo (2011) essay as a way of connecting translingual pedagogy to social justice pedagogy.

> I really enjoyed the DiPardo reading "Whispers of Coming and Going." One of the quotes I found particularly interesting was about the way education may serve to strip minority communities of their non-mainstream identities. Fannie (the student) says, "I mean like, sometimes if you get really educated, we don't really want that. Because then, it like ruins your mind, and you use it, to like betray your people, too." . . . This idea, I thought, was very closely related to the concept of cultural appropriation, how education teaches to the norms and benefit of primarily one culture to the exclusion of others. . . . This topic also recalled to me the reading [from the unit on Identity and Diversity in the Writing Center] by Barron and Grimm [2011]: "Students who bring differences of color, Class, and culture are expected to make themselves over to match the institutionalized image of the typical student."

This student's analysis suggests he has a clear sense of the ways educational institutions unreflectively enforce cultural and linguistic assimilation both as what is *normal* and as what is *best*, though his quotation from Fannie demonstrates the harm this perspective entails for many students.

One way Writing 300 students both grappled with and deflected this problem was by worrying that they, as tutors, did not or would not possess the authority to enact changes on their own. This concern harkens back to those expressed above, that university professors or "the world," perhaps as embodied in university administration and future employers, act as powerful gatekeepers, effectively shutting down smaller-scale pedagogical initiatives aimed at altering the status quo. These concerns are taken up explicitly by a white female monolingual education major, who writes, "I've been thinking a lot about our class discussion yesterday, and the way that we all seemed to interpret the Horner piece about translingualism. I think this may have partially been a heated topic because so many of us that were considering such an approach are going to be either teaching writing, or tutoring writers—both, regardless of whether we choose to 'step into' a role of authority, are automatically spaces of authority." In offering the perspective that the role of educator, whether in one-to-one tutoring or in a classroom, intrinsically carries authority, this student challenges her peers to take up this power and use it to further social justice educational aims.

She continues her analysis by turning to the issue of how theoretical ideals may bump up against available practices and by bringing the concrete example of Anzaldúa's (1987) writing into dialogue with Horner et al.'s (2011) translingual principles as a way of moving this discussion forward. In doing so, she alters the terms of the discussion to create a practical way in for herself.

> As a group of people who are preparing throughout this semester to consult with people on their writing, [the translingual] approach may have initially appeared to be so problematic because it seemed to be asking us to ignore the technical correctness of writing. . . . However, while Horner says that language [difference] is not "a problem to manage," we might instead take this to mean discourse, rather than grammar and structure. In this sense, Horner's translingual approach aligns much better with the Anzaldúa piece, which does take advantage of two completely separate styles of discourse. However, although she takes this approach to her writing, she does not avoid the problems of technicality or structure in her writing.

In shifting the terms of this discussion from "language" to "discourse," this student finds a way to imagine and engage a translingual pedagogy, which, as she goes on to say, she might be able to enact to "undermine traditional approaches to writing."

> I'm not sure if this type of discourse-flexible approach is different from the one that Horner argues for, but this is a writing style that I feel I, and most peer tutors or teachers, would be happy to accept from a student—especially if writing in a more familiar style helps to allow for more motivated engagement. . . . A discourse-flexible form of writing would serve to undermine traditional approaches to writing in a powerful way, but in order to help the writer work on the skills that are necessary for writing, this work would still be [subject] to the same kind of consultation approach as more standard academic forms of writing.

As translingual educators of consultants in training, we might want to push this student harder in regard to her understanding and definitions of "grammar" and "structure," as the former of these often functions as a code word for Standard Written English and the latter can be an important dimension of a writer's linguistic resources. Anzaldúa (1987) employs the grammars and structures of the varied forms of Spanish and English she speaks and writes, and in so doing, displays for us the power dynamics at work in these discursive situations. What her essay demonstrates, and this student implicitly seems to understand, is that translingual writing uses linguistic resources in powerful ways to make arguments about discursive practices. On a more mundane level, what this student's observations also show us is that without such concrete examples of translingual writing, tutors in training may imagine a translingual methodology promotes a kind of formless expressivism that dispenses with rhetorical strategy and discursive structure. With this concern allayed, uptake of the methodology may become possible.

Student Research on Translingual Teaching and Tutoring

Of course, it is naïve to think exposure to translingual pedagogy in a single course will suddenly transform the beliefs and practices of these students. However, the opportunity to engage with this methodology and delve into its difficulties can make some inroads and provide a basis for further inquiry that can ultimately enhance tutors' repertoire of available strategies for working with multilingual writers. By way of example, Alessandra (2016),[1] a white female monolingual English major, was an education major and preservice English language arts (ELA) teacher when she took my Writing 300 class in 2016 and was one of the most vocal critics of translingual methodology—in the class discussions referred to in previous student quotations and in her discussion-board posts on the topic. Nonetheless, her engagement in these conversations and with the course readings and examples led her to want to understand more about the challenges and opportunities she would face with multilingual and multidialectal students in her future teaching career. Consequently, she chose this focus for her research project—our major course assignment in which students choose a topic in teaching or tutoring they wish to learn more about and conduct original research of their own design (see appendix 10.D).

Her paper, "Language in the Classroom: Examining Tensions, Benefits, and Next Steps with Translingualism," is a thoughtfully direct approach to her discomfort with the idea of translingualism and her concern that she might in fact disadvantage her students if she were to introduce the concept and practice to them. To explore this concern, she interviewed three experienced local ELA middle- and secondary-school teachers, and her paper offers fairly extensive quotations from them, as well as her own reflections on how these teachers' perspectives helped shift her own view. Alessandra's paper offers a good example of how grappling with the "knotty" practice of translingualism can broaden the work educators at all levels do with students, perhaps helping them avoid simply reproducing language ideologies in their own teaching and tutoring.

Alessandra's concern with translingualism, as she describes it in her paper, arises from this statement in the Horner et al. (2011) article:

"Against the common argument that students must learn 'the standards' to meet demands by the dominant, a translingual approach recognizes that, to survive and thrive as active writers, students must understand how such demands are contingent and negotiable" (305). Beginning to consider Standard Written English, a form of language and an associated set of values with which she has been so deeply imbued, as "contingent and negotiable" creates anxiety in this nascent teacher. She writes, "I . . . acknowledge that it is difficult to disagree with the elements that define a translingual approach, as they seem positive and constructive to the ELA learning environment. The last sentence, and, more specifically, the word 'against,' is what I take issue with. I find it hard to envision my future job as a middle or high school English teacher if it did not include the teaching of Standard English, but rather encouraging students to work against the expectations of everything I have been taught and accepted for so many years." Alessandra recognizes she may need to revise her approach to teaching English language arts in light of changing perspectives on diversity and inclusivity in K–12 classrooms and a deeper recognition of global interconnectedness. She takes up this possibility by turning to the professional advice of senior practitioners: "I hoped to gain a better understanding of what current teachers think about the translingual approach and definition. I also strived to learn about what types of language difference are most common in secondary ELA classrooms, how teachers view these differences as valuable and/or harmful, and to what extent these teachers believed the demands of Standard English to be 'negotiable.'"

Alessandra presented her findings under the headings "Currently Nonnegotiable Circumstances," "Differences and Goals with Writing," and "Actionable Steps." In her analysis of the first set of interview responses, she begins by noting that "all three teachers agree that there are a few arenas of our society in which the use of Standard Written English, unfortunately, is not up for debate." Interestingly, this stance seems to be aligned with a recognition by these teachers of the biases and power dynamics embedded in Standard Written English ideology. One teacher, for instance, replies that "if the goal is for students to 'thrive as [writers]' then, yes, I agree completely. . . . However, I have not found in my professional life that the demands of standard language are negotiable. Just the opposite, in fact. Negotiation is a feature of power, and most students with minority vernaculars don't have that power." Another teacher adds that she wants her "students to be able to write in Standard Written English so that they are prepared for what academia and much of the workforce expects," a perspective that acknowledges "the assumption that academia and the workforce have strong notions of intelligence and competence associated with Standard English." These experienced teachers offer a version of the desire to inure their own students to the expectations of "the world" that was voiced above by Writing 300 tutors in training, and, like them, the experienced teachers are not yet asking how they might use their accrued institutional power to begin to try to alter these expectations rather than simply assimilating students to them.

Alessandra's next area of analysis with these teachers, "Differences and Goals with Writing," does round out this picture somewhat by introducing the framework of rhetorical situation, and particularly audience and purpose, to the decision of whether to adopt an assimilative stance or something closer to what Paul Kei Matsuda and Michelle Cox (2004) call an "accommodationist stance" that might aim "to help the writer learn new discourse patterns without completely losing the old, so that the writer can maintain both . . . linguistic and cultural identities" (42). At the same time, accommodationist practitioners still alert their student writers to the idea that "some differences may be seen as deficiencies by some readers," with the aim of allowing the student to make a rhetorical choice (42). Alessandra notes, for instance, that "teachers generally agreed that the goals of the writing define whether or not difference can be beneficial or harmful." For one of Alessandra's interviewees, for instance, "In terms of writing as a craft, . . . diversity [of dialect or vernacular] only tends to help a classroom and broaden students' ability to make sense of disparate aspects of their world." When nonstandard writing is deployed out in the world, however, this teacher worries that "the value of difference depends on the openness of the writer's audience. That's where it can get divisive." These statements outline the difficulties of well-meaning educators to truly accommodate language difference by aiding student writers to act more effectively, more powerfully, within the varied rhetorical situations they will encounter rather than defaulting to an assimilative stance in more "divisive" situations.

In turning to "Actionable Steps" for furthering the goals of translingual pedagogy, only one of the teachers Alessandra consulted mentioned specific lessons or assignments designed to help students think beyond Standard Written English. This teacher offered instruction on language history and language difference: "I usually do some type of unit on language change over time and dialects to get students to question some of their notions of 'right' and 'wrong' ways to speak and write." She also reported using journal entries to offer choice and self-expression: "I do not grade for things like grammar, spelling, or even clarity of ideas.

By lifting off the restraints that Standard Written English places onto students' perceptions of writing, I like to think that students are able to focus on their voice and not stop themselves because they may think they are 'not good' at writing." Drawing conclusions from this teacher's example, and from what she has learned in all her interviews, Alessandra writes, "Overall, I feel as though my pedagogy is much more informed in terms of how I will approach language difference and instruction in my classroom. I am not as adamantly opposed to the translingual approach as I once was, as I have come to understand that there are spaces in which questioning and discussing Standard English is not just acceptable, but actually beneficial." While Alessandra has grappled with her reflexive discomfort with and dismissal of translingual pedagogical practices, this work has clearly not unseated the primacy of Standard Written English in her view of writing instruction in high-stakes contexts. In my most recent exchange with her in summer 2017, following her graduation from UM and as she prepared to begin a teaching job at a school in New York City with a largely Dominican student body, she conveyed to me that our Writing 300 readings and discussions regarding language were in the forefront of her mind as she prepared to work with these students—an opportunity to practice the more open-minded approach she claims to have achieved in her research paper. While Alessandra's goals in my class and her ultimate use of these pedagogies was directed outside the writing center, the process of discovery in which she engaged (which was aided by the writing center research project, a common feature of tutor training [see, e.g., Ervin 2016]), as well as the duration of this process stretching beyond her graduation and into her working life, is in keeping with what we know about the long-term effects of peer writing training and consultation on our tutors' experiences (Hughes, Gillespie, and Kail 2010). I find this to be a further argument for the incorporation of translingual pedagogy into tutor training insofar as we wish to send our students into their postuniversity lives with a translingual perspective on the varieties of encounters and interactions they will engage.

In addition to the awareness she has developed regarding language ideology, another benefit Alessandra may experience from her research on and engagement with translingual pedagogy is the possession of a broader repertoire of instructional strategies for working with linguistically diverse writers and a concurrent diminished level of stress in approaching this work. This latter benefit is suggested by the research of one of Alessandra's Writing 300 classmates. Pei Lei (2016),[2] a female Mandarin- and English-speaking Chinese international student, was majoring in political science and training to be a peer writing consultant in my 2016 section of Writing 300. Her research paper for the class, titled "'Grammar SOS': How Tutors' Knowledge of Translingualism Affects Their Sentence-Level Tutoring with Chinese ESL Students," studied how translingual knowledge is put into practice by new peer consultants in the Sweetland Peer Writing Center.

Pei Lei was interested in how a translingual tutoring practice might help consultants navigate the sometimes stressful balance between higher- and later-order concerns when they work with multilingual students who have limited experience writing in English. Might tutors who have adopted a translingual practice be more successful than those who have been trained in more traditional ESL tutoring methods alone? In order to identify tutors with a greater or more limited apparent knowledge of translingual concepts, Pei Lei analyzed the center's client report forms, which she describes as "quick online surveys that tutors fill out after each session." As she goes on to explain, "Client report forms are a reliable resource for me . . . because most tutors are generally honest when reflecting on challenges they face, students' weaknesses and strengths, the effective strategies they use, etc." Pei Lei sorted all the 252 reports completed by peer writing consultants between January and March of 2016 in order to define a sample of 50 reports focused on consultations with "Chinese ESL students," which she defines as those who have indicated in a Sweetland Peer Writing Center intake questionnaire that they "speak Chinese (Mandarin or Cantonese) to their parents." Based on the tutors' reported strategies and sense of confidence in working with these students, Pei Lei further sorted them into those who exhibited a greater "knowledge of translingualism" and a more limited knowledge as determined by the areas the tutors named as their focus in the sessions and their apparent level of stress in working with Chinese-language students. She then followed up with four of these tutors—two with greater translingual knowledge and two with more limited knowledge (which she refers to as "G-tutors" and "L-tutors," respectively)—by observing them in consultation with Chinese ESL students and conducting interviews with them after the observations.

Pei Lei offers the following methodological explanation of her decision to assess peer consultants' knowledge of translingualism using these means: "Tutors rarely explicitly express whether or not they 'see difference in language as resources or not' [following the framework provided by Horner et al. (2011)]. Therefore, based off the existing understanding of translingualism [from that same article], this project proposes a more observable criterion to examine tutors' translingual approaches: Whether or not a tutor's consultation or the general tutoring philosophy is overwhelmed by difference in language, when tutoring at the sentence level with a Chinese ESL student." She found that knowledge of translingual pedagogy is beneficial to tutors in giving them a wider array of strategies to use and lessening their sense of stress during the consultation.

In explaining her choice of a research problem, Pei Lei explicitly addresses the kinds of biases around Standard Written English acknowledged by the teachers Alessandra interviewed. She writes, "It is important to apply a translingual approach to tutor ESL students' writing, because their lack of Standard American English has nothing to do with their intellectual side. The difference in language should not be treated as a barrier for intellectual communications, but ought to be viewed as resources to explore their unrecognized potential. This is why this project is interested in examining the influence of tutors' knowledge of translingualism, and how this difference affects their sentence-level tutoring choices with ESL students." By analyzing the ways writing tutors may enact linguistic bias because they lack strategies for overcoming their own discomfort and bewilderment with linguistic difference, Pei Lei opens a valuable window onto the importance of translingual pedagogy for this population of tutors in training.

Though she is quite clear about the limitations of her research findings because of the small sample size of tutors she observed and interviewed, her project nonetheless suggests that tutors who are comfortable "negotiating priorities" with Chinese ESL students in order to "work through difference in language . . . to meet the needs of each writer," as one G-tutor wrote in her client report form, are also able to focus on these students' higher-order writing interests and to help them successfully pursue their own communicative ends. L-tutors, on the other hand, Pei Lei observed, became bogged down in sentence-level confusion, such that they were unable to progress to the student's higher-order concerns or even establish an effective working rapport, as one L-tutor expressed in an interview: "This session was really difficult because the writer was very concerned with overall structure and arguments, and I wanted to discuss this as well but there were so many language issues that at times I couldn't make out the argument, and the writer struggled with vocal English as well, so it was very difficult to communicate." While Pei Lei's research does not explicitly address these tutors' perspectives on the power dynamics other tutors and teachers identified as a concern—namely, the perceived responsibility to equip multilingual student writers with Standard Written English knowledge sufficient to satisfy potentially biased professors or employers—her descriptions of the attitudes and interactions demonstrated by the more translingually aware tutors suggest this assimilative reflex, if it exists, is subordinated to the tutor's interest in prioritizing the goals of the student writer. Indeed, such an outcome may further suggest that the introduction of translingual pedagogy into peer tutor-training courses could auspiciously affect the uptake and application of core tutoring principles, such as flexibility, creativity, openness, and an ethical sense of peerness. Tutors who feel more comfortable both in their identities as tutors and in considering how writers' varied identities come into play within tutoring sessions (see, e.g., Fitzgerald and Ianetta's "Tutor and Writer Identities" [2016]) may more readily enact these principles as called for by translingual interactions.

CONCLUSION

Based on the lively engagement of our class discussions of translingual methodology in 2016 and the thoughtful written reflections afterward, I was left with the impression that this course unit was important for my students' development as mindful, responsive peer writing tutors. What I further learned from the more deliberate work of analyzing my students' low-stakes and formal written responses to this curriculum is that, as educators, we would be irresponsible not to introduce the future tutors in our classrooms to concrete strategies for combating Standard Written English ideology and that translingual pedagogical principles should play a significant role in writing center pedagogy. As I note throughout my commentary in this chapter, such a brief introduction to a translingual approach can never be sufficient experience to deeply change a student's mind about their responsibilities to existing power structures or to fully equip this student to enact change. Indeed, there is no one-size-fits-all approach to this pedagogy and no guarantee that even far more extensive curricula could ensure a straight line from initial understanding to flexible, responsive, and principled application. But the introduction is necessary if we hope to make progress in chipping away at the structures of linguistic oppression.

One further note I would emphasize is that a part of any effect achieved by this translingual curriculum is likely due also to the fact that it followed by a few weeks an explicit engagement with units on power and social justice in the writing center (see appendix 10.A). In those units, among other questions, students were asked to reflect on their own social identities and how these positionalities might come into play in their roles as tutors. As some of the excerpted student writing in this chapter suggests, students were making connections between these earlier units and the present one (as well as making connections to previous UM classes that raised similar questions regarding bias and social justice). To me these connections suggest that it is likely not enough to teach about translingual methodology alone but that this curriculum must be part of a strategy for making antiracist, social justice pedagogy part of all our curricula. This work has been taken up explicitly for writing center pedagogy by such researchers as Nancy Grimm (2011) and Rasha Diab, Beth Godbee, Thomas Ferrel, and Neil Simpkins (2012, 2013), who call for the transformation of certain canons of writing center philosophy that uphold structures of white supremacy; many in the broader field of writing studies have forcefully engaged this work as well (see Poe, Inoue, and Eliot 2018, and Condon and Young 2016, for only two of the most recent book-length examples). I close this chapter by joining this call and by noticing the small steps in this direction taken by several of the students represented in this chapter—all of them tutors in training in 2015 and 2016 and some of them now teachers in their own classrooms or pursuing other pathways in which they encounter linguistic diversity. In this light, translingual pedagogies in writing center courses can be seen to constitute a crucial aspect of this work of dismantling racist linguistic ideologies and practices in our writing centers.

APPENDIX 10.A

WRITING 300 OUTLINE OF COURSE TOPICS, 2016

- **Writing and the writing center**—What is it that we do here?
- **The consulting process**—Who am I and what do I do when I consult on writing?
- **Identity and diversity in the writing center**—What is the role of social justice here? How can we create a space for it in the writing center despite constraints of time, etc.?
- **Observing in the writing center**—What are some strategies for being careful observers, and making the most of our observations? What are some of the things we might notice?
- **Power and authority in the writing center**—Who has it? How can we best use it? Can we share it?
- **Working with student writing**—What sorts of writing and writing questions do we encounter here?
- **Peer-consultant research**—What can it look like? How can you find a good topic and question?
- **Consulting on academic papers**—How can we help writers go to the next step?

Consulting at the sentence level—What perspectives and strategies are available to us to work with writers on later-order concerns (LOCs)?

Consulting with multilingual writers, part 1—How can we enact translingualism in the writing center?

Consulting with multilingual writers, part 2—What research-based strategies are available in our consultations with multilingual writers?

Consulting on research papers—How can we set priorities with a long paper? What can we learn from them for our own research?

Consulting on scientific writing—What are some of the principles for helping writers in STEM disciplines?

Brainstorming sessions—What do we do when the writer just wants to talk it through (consulting when there's no paper)?

Disability and access in the writing center—How can we make the writing center accessible to all writers? What strategies will help us adapt our practices to work with writers' different needs?

Developing a consulting philosophy—How can we conceptualize and concretize our practice as consultants? How can this work assist our consultations on personal statements and other professional documents?

Writing centers and multiliteracy centers—What is a multiliteracy center? What does it mean to be a multiliterate consultant? What do we need to do the job well?

Consulting in online writing labs (OWLS)—What's different? What's the same?

APPENDIX 10.B

WRITING 300 READINGS AND ACTIVITIES FOR CONSULTING WITH MULTILINGUAL WRITERS, 2015 AND 2016 SYLLABI

WINTER 2015

Week 6			
Th 2/12	Consulting at the Sentence Level	Curzan, "Says Who? Teaching and Questioning the Rules of Grammar" (CTools)	Forum Post 6 due by Saturday, 2/14; replies due by 2/17 (Consulting at the Sentence Level)
		Gottschalk and Hjortshoj, "Teaching Writing at the Sentence Level" (CTools)	
		Young, "Can You Proofread This?" (CTools)	

Week 7

T 2/17	*Consulting with Multilingual Writers, part 1*—How can we enact translingualism in the writing center?	Gillespie and Lerner, "Chapter 9: Working with ESL Writers" (LG)	One discussion question about today's topics (on CTools Forum)
	Activity: Making it personal (in-class writing)	Horner et al., "Language Difference in Writing: Toward a Translingual Approach" (CTools)	
	Activity: In-class peer consulting on our writing	Myers, "Reassessing the 'Proofreading Trap': ESL Tutoring and Writing Instruction" (SMS)	
Th 2/19	*Consulting with Multilingual Writers, part 2*—What research-based strategies are available in our consultations with multilingual writers?	Tseng, "Theoretical Perspectives on Learning a Second Language" (CTools)	Forum Post 7 due by Sunday, 2/22; replies due by 2/24 (Consulting with Multilingual Writers)
	Activity: Working with sample multilingual student paper	Staben and Nordhaus, "Looking at the Whole Text" (CTools)	
		Linville, "Editing Line by Line" (CTools)	

WINTER 2016

Week 7

T 2/16	*Consulting at the Sentence Level*—What perspectives and strategies are available to us to work with writers on "later order concerns (LOCs)"?	Curzan, "Says Who? Teaching and Questioning the Rules of Grammar" (in Canvas Files)	
	Activity: Making decisions about what to do, when	Gottschalk and Hjortshoj, "Teaching Writing at the Sentence Level" (in Canvas Files)	
		Young, "Can You Proofread This?" (in Canvas Files)	
Th 2/18	*Consulting with Multilingual Writers, part 1*—How can we enact translingualism in the writing center?	Horner et al., "Language Difference in Writing: Toward a Translingual Approach" (in Canvas Files)	01. Canvas Discussion Post 6: "Consulting with Multilingual Writers and/or not Consulting at the Sentence Level" → due by Saturday, 2/20; replies due by Monday, 2/22

Th 2/18 (cont.)	Activity: Making it personal (in-class writing)	DiPardo, "'Whispers of Coming and Going': Lessons from Fannie" (in Canvas Files)	
	Activity: Consulting with Fannie	Review *Oxford Guide*, ch. 5, "Tutor and Writer Identities" (pp. 118–127)	
		In-class readings: Gloria Anzaldúa, "How to Tame a Wild Tongue" (in Canvas Files) Blog Carnival on "Beyond a 'Single Language/Single Modality' Approach to Writing" Slideshow on translingual activities in an 8th-grade ELA classroom	
Week 8			
T 2/23	Consulting with Multilingual Writers, part 2—What research-based strategies are available in our consultations with multilingual writers?	Tseng, "Theoretical Perspectives on Learning a Second Language" (in Canvas Files)	
	Special guest: Lori Randall, multilingual specialist, Sweetland Center for Writing	Staben and Nordhaus, "Looking at the Whole Text" (in Canvas Files)	
	Activity 1: Language exercise + in-class writing	Minett, "'Earth Aches by Midnight': Helping ESL Writers Clarify Their Intended Meaning" (in Canvas Files)	
	Activity 2: Consulting a sample essay	Linville, "Editing Line by Line" (in Canvas Files)	
		In class resource: Sweetland Resources for Multilingual Students	
Th 2/25	Translingualism, continued + sharing your research interests		
	Activity: Consulting two sample essays		

APPENDIX 10.C

WRITING 300 ONLINE DISCUSSION FORUM PROMPT, 2016
WRITING 300.002, WINTER 2016

Consulting with Multilingual Writers and/or/not Consulting at the Sentence Level (Week 7)

Prompt

We have a lot of complex and (dare I say) exciting material on the table this week and early next around the variety of strategies we might employ in working with multilingual writers and the ethos we want to embody in this work, as well as how we want to approach working with any writer on style, grammar, or the like. This week, please dig into the readings, engaging an idea you find knotty, a potential contradiction you see, a statement you want to run with—How are you currently understanding our work with multilingual writers (and/or/not at the sentence level)? (No need to be synthetic in your approach if you don't want—you're welcome to focus on something as small as a paragraph if that helps you get at some ideas you're wanting to work through.)

Details

Please write approximately 500–600 words (though you're welcome to write more). Please quote from and/or cite the readings, when you refer to them directly. Due by midnight, Saturday, 2/20. Please reply to at least two members of your **new Discussion Group #2** by midnight on Monday, 2/22. (You can find your new group members' names here, on the Canvas People page.)

These will be graded on a credit/no credit basis ("Complete" or "Incomplete"). To receive credit, these posts should be exploratory, thought provoking, well developed, detailed, specific, clear, and well edited. They do not need to be traditionally academic, though—I encourage you to use your own voice and style, including multimedia elements where relevant and appropriate.

APPENDIX 10.D

WRITING 300 RESEARCHED ACADEMIC PAPER PROMPT, 2016
WRITING 300.002, WINTER 2016
Essay 2—Researched Academic Paper

> A research topic is an interest stated specifically enough for you to imagine becoming a local expert on it. . . . If you can work on any topic, we offer only a cliché: start with what most interests you. Nothing contributes to the quality of your work more than your commitment to it.
> —Booth, Colomb, and Williams,
>   *The Craft of Research*

Objective

The purpose of this essay is to give you the opportunity to deepen your knowledge and develop some expertise about a specific topic in writing center or educational theory and/or practice that is of particular interest to you. To that end, you will conduct in-depth, original research using primary materials (via your experiences observing and conducting consultations and/or in your classroom placements), as well as a number of secondary sources (maybe 7–10), including academic books and journal articles. You are writing for an academic audience of fellow writing center or educational researchers.

An additional aim of this essay is to give you experience working within the genre of the academic research report, and to reflect on its forms and conventions, in order to assist you in your consultations with peer writers. To this end, we will consider genre variations based on discipline (e.g., the differences between an APA-style research report in the social sciences and a research essay in a humanities field such as literary studies or history) and research methods appropriate to discipline-based research questions (e.g., quantitative, qualitative, mixed methods, theoretical, historical).

You will present your research at the in-class Writing 300 Conference at the end of the semester, and you will prepare some form of presentation aid to complement your verbal delivery (e.g., PowerPoint slides, Prezi, poster, handouts, charts, brief video or audio clips, etc.).

Structure and Argument

There is no fixed structure for this research paper, though you may choose to follow a traditional IMRaD format if you're familiar with it.

However you end up structuring it, though, your paper should make the six standard "moves" in academic writing that Teresa Thonney's research (2011) analyzes. It should

- respond to what others have said about your topic;
- state the value of your work and announce the plan for your paper;
- acknowledge that others might disagree with the position you've taken;
- adopt a voice of authority;
- use academic and discipline-specific vocabulary; and
- emphasize evidence, perhaps in tables, graphs, or images, if they are appropriate to the argument.

Your argument needs to be meaty, specific, and . . . arguable. You'll want to follow Wayne Booth, Gregory Colomb, and Joseph Williams's (2003) progression from a *topic* to a *problem* to a *question* whose answer will ultimately be of interest and use to your audience of fellow writing center researchers. You'll also want to ensure that your research *methods* are appropriate to your research question and will result in data gathering that is *reliable*, *valid*, and *ethical* (the *Oxford Guide* research brainstorming and planning templates will be quite useful here [pp. 205–205]).

Format

Your essay should be roughly 7–8 pages (2,100–2,400 words), plus References and any appendices, though it can run longer, if warranted. It should employ an appropriate standard citation style (e.g., APA, MLA, Chicago, etc).

Please give your essay a descriptive title and page numbers. In general, I encourage you to double space it and use 1" margins and a standard font unless the visual/aesthetic considerations of format are explicitly part of your purpose and argument.

The research paper is your chance to explore your interests in tutoring/teaching methodologies and in communicative presentation media. While this essay typically takes the form of a conventional academic paper, I am open to discussing multimodal or multimedia options that may better serve your purpose and argument, though such a project must perform equivalent work of argumentation and evidence analysis.

Your research will be conducted (and due) in stages, as indicated below. I will give you separate prompts for the individual pieces as we go through the process.

Due Dates

Thursday, 2/25	Research Statement of Interest due and on Canvas Assignments
Monday, 3/14	Full Research Proposal + Initial Annotated Bibliography due on Canvas Assignments
Tuesday, 3/29	Full draft due in class (1 hard copy) for peer consulting, and on Canvas Assignments
Week of 3/28–4/1	Conferences with me about your draft
Friday, 4/8	Full Annotated Bibliography due on Canvas Assignments
By Friday, 4/15	"Final" draft (with reflective component) due on Canvas Assignments; specific due date to be determined individually during our conferences

NOTES

1. A pseudonym.
2. A pseudonym.

REFERENCES

Alessandra. 2016. "Language in the Classroom: Examining Tensions, Benefits, and Next Steps with Translingualism." Unpublished manuscript, University of Michigan, Ann Arbor.

Anzaldúa, Gloria. 1987. "How to Tame a Wild Tongue." In *Borderlands / La frontera: The New Mestiza*, edited by Gloria Anzaldúa, 53–64. San Francisco: Spinsters Ink / Aunt Lute Books.

Barron, Nancy, and Nancy Grimm. 2011. "Addressing Racial Diversity in a Writing Center: Stories and Lessons from Two Beginners." In *The St. Martin's Sourcebook for Writing Tutors*, edited by Christina Murphy and Steve Sherwood, 302–35. Boston: Bedford/ St. Martin's.

Booth, Wayne C., Gregory G. Colomb, and Joseph M. Williams. 2003. *The Craft of Research.* 2nd ed. Chicago: University of Chicago Press.

Bruce, Shanti, and Ben Rafoth, eds. 2009. *ESL Writers: A Guide for Writing Center Tutors.* 2nd ed. Portsmouth, NH: Boynton/Cook.

Condon, Frankie, and Vershawn Ashanti Young, eds. 2016. *Performing Antiracist Pedagogy in Rhetoric, Writing, and Communication.* Fort Collins, CO: WAC Clearinghouse.

Curzan, Anne. 2009. "Says Who? Teaching and Questioning the Rules of Grammar." *PMLA* 124 (3): 870–79.

Diab, Rasha, Beth Godbee, Thomas Ferrel, and Neil Simpkins. 2012. "A Multidimensional Pedagogy for Racial Justice in Writing Centers." *Praxis* 10 (1). http://www.praxisuwc.com/diab-godbee-ferrell-simpkins-101.

Diab, Rasha, Beth Godbee, Thomas Ferrel, and Neil Simpkins. 2013. "Making Commitments to Racial Justice Actionable." *Across the Disciplines* 10 (3). https://wac.colostate.edu/atd/race/diabetal.cfm.

DiPardo, Anne. 2011. "'Whispers of Coming and Going': Lessons from Fannie." In *The St. Martin's Sourcebook for Writing Tutors*, edited by Christina Murphy and Steve Sherwood, 233–48. Boston: Bedford/St. Martin's.

Ervin, Christopher. 2016. "What Tutor Researchers and Their Mentors Tell Us about Undergraduate Research in the Writing Center: An Exploratory Study." *Writing Center Journal* 35 (3): 39–75.

Fitzgerald, Lauren, and Melissa Ianetta. 2016. *The Oxford Guide for Writing Tutors: Practice and Research.* Oxford: Oxford University Press.

Grimm, Nancy. 2011. "Retheorizing Writing Center Work to Transform a System of Advantage Based on Race." In *Writing Centers and the New Racism*, edited by Laura Greenfield and Karen Rowan, 75–100. Logan: Utah State University Press.

Hauer, Lara M. 2016. "Translingualism in the Writing Center: Where Can We Meet?" *Working Papers in Composition and TESOL* (Spring). ResearchGate. https://www.researchgate.net/publication/322530220_Translingualism_in_the_writing_center_Where_can_we_meet.

Horner, Bruce, Min-Zhan Lu, Jacqueline Jones Royster, and John Trimbur. 2011. "Opinion: Language Difference in Writing: Toward a Translingual Approach." *College English* 73 (3): 303–21.

Horner, Bruce, and Laura Tetreault, eds. 2017. *Crossing Divides: Exploring Translingual Writing Pedagogies and Programs.* Logan: Utah State University Press.

Hughes, Bradley, Paula Gillespie, and Harvey Kail. 2010. "What They Take with Them: Findings from the Peer Writing Tutor Alumni Research Project." *Writing Center Journal* 30 (2): 12–46.

Kiernan, Julia, Joyce Meier, and Xiqiao Wang. 2016. "Negotiating Languages and Cultures: Enacting Translingualism through a Translation Assignment." *Composition Studies* 44 (1): 89–107.

Matsuda, Paul Kei, and Michelle Cox. 2004. "Reading an ESL Writer's Text." In *ESL Writers: A Guide for Writing Center Tutors*, edited by Shanti Bruce and Ben Rafoth, 39–47. Portsmouth, NH: Heinemann.

Pei Lei. 2016. "'Grammar SOS': How Tutors' Knowledge of Translingualism Affects Their Sentence-Level Tutoring with Chinese ESL students." Unpublished manuscript, University of Michigan.

Poe, Mya, Asao B. Inoue, and Norbert Elliot, eds. 2018. *Writing Assessment, Social Justice, and the Advancement of Opportunity.* Fort Collins, CO: WAC Clearinghouse.

Schwarzer, David, Mary Fuchs, and Chris Hermosilla. 2011. "Translingual Education as a Phenomenon, a Methodology and an Ideology to Promote Social Justice and Educational Renewal." Presented at the National Network for Educational Renewal 2011 Annual Conference [PowerPoint slides]. https://www.slideshare.net/schwarzerd/translingualism.

Thonney, Teresa. 2011. "Teaching the Conventions of Academic Discourse." *Teaching English in the Two-Year College* 38 (4): 347–62.

11
A FRAMEWORK FOR LINGUISTICALLY INCLUSIVE COURSE DESIGN

Julia Kiernan

This semester, we did lots of assignments, all of which are very meaningful, and they all share a common topic, which is transnational. As an international student, I have quite deep feelings for it. This topic not only lets me write essays in English, but also more visually allows me to understand English and learn to use English.
—Chinese student

Before I have attended this class, the only reason that I want to be an expert in English is because I think it could be a beneficial for me to get a good GPA and it could help to get my degree . . . after I have attended this class, I have realized that I can get so much benefit from learning different language and other cultures. When I learn about other cultures, I learn about other people and how they see life, what they have to cope with, what they think is important. It gives me a better perspective on my own life.
—Thai student

INTRODUCTION

Despite the fact that my dissertation was steeped in multilingual theory, and that my data drew upon a variety of multilingual student experiences and expectations of university writing, I entered my career with few practical experiences teaching multilingual learners. In this chapter, I examine the barriers I encountered as a monolingual instructor of multilingual students in order to make visible the practical moves I made in classroom discussions, assignment scaffolding, and curricular design. A primary goal of this chapter is to provide a framework for monolingual teachers who are interested in (or required to engage with) multilingual inquiry in Standard Written English (SWE) writing courses. What I offer is threefold: reflections on my pedagogical experiences with diverse learners, examples of a semester-long framework of assignments, and student reactions to these assignments.

Much current translingual work focuses on one or two assignments that can be adopted into a writing class, but this chapter's focus is different in that the very theme of the course being discussed is transnationalism and every aspect of the course and course assignments works to engage some aspect of the trans approach (Horner et al. 2011), or in my students' terms, the trans experience. When we think of a translingual assignment, there is often the recognition of code mixing—or movement between languages—or code meshing—the integration of two languages—and while this is certainly one way to interpret translingual composition, I work to broaden the scope of how we take up a translingual approach and what this may (or may not) look like in the SWE classroom. Consequently, this chapter acknowledges the text-based production of translingualism on the page (e.g., the incorporation of multiple languages, or code meshing) but also recognizes the importance of allowing for translingual invention, translingual brainstorming, and translingual drafting—to name a few of the often "invisible" methods of translingual composing. And, although I don't necessarily teach these "invisible" practices, I do take them up in the classroom, inviting students to discuss their place within the writing process and also drawing attention to the usefulness of such practices for many multilingual writers. Moreover, in positioning transnationalism as a curricular theme, wherein a translingual disposition (Lee and Jenks 2016) is the nexus of inquiry, this chapter works to both recognize and move beyond a focus on the final, text-based production of translingualism on the page and instead offers new ways for students and teachers to engage with translingualism throughout the writing process. A primary objective is to provide new inroads into how writing teachers can foster multilingual student agency, even when the target language of these texts is SWE.

At the heart of this research project are four major assignments, as well as a final reflective essay, which asks students to consider what assignment worked best for them and why. As students move through the assignment sequence, they compose traditionally, multimodally, and translingually, working both independently and collaboratively. During data collection, I experimented with different assignment sequences, differing modes of authorship, differing moments of collaboration, and differing assignment prompts. What I provide you with in the following pages is what I found to work best for my students; however, I fully acknowledge that how these assignments are taken up and used depends not simply on the students but also on a variety of other factors: the teacher(s), the institution, the course learning outcomes, and so forth.

INSTITUTION CONTEXT, SOCIOPOLITICAL CLIMATE, AND LINGUISTIC MAKEUP OF STUDENTS

This chapter explores research findings from a three-year project at a large public midwestern university in the United States. In this study, a group of teacher-researchers worked independently and collaboratively to reimagine an introductory writing course. Historically, the course was created for first-generation domestic English students who did not meet the first-year writing (FYW) requirements; however, in the year I joined the department, the focus of the course transitioned. In response to a substantial rise in the numbers of international students, the course was being reimagined in terms of this new student demographic; the new curriculum was to be designed as translingual and transcultural in scope.

As many of the chapters in this collection acknowledge, US institutions of higher education are witnessing a rapid and drastic increase in international student enrollment. At my own institution, the rate of growth rose from 5 to 8 percent annually for each of the past five years. In 2015, international students constituted 13 percent of the entire undergraduate student body. Consequently, the majority of students now enrolling in the course being discussed herein (and many other FYW courses across the United States) are no longer domestic but are now often international students (mostly from China but also from South Korea, United Arab Emirates, Thailand, Mexico, and many other countries). Consequently, this introductory course was "redesigned to explicitly frame the students' languages and cultures as assets and sites of inquiry" (Kiernan, Meier, Wang 2016, 92). In this way, the new course initiatives highlight students' ongoing negotiations of languages, cultures, and genres (Canagarajah 2013), placing value on developing transnational competences (for students) and developing culturally sustaining pedagogical practices (for teachers).

One strength of this research project is that the various teacher-researchers, myself included, had diverse linguistic and cultural positionalities, which not only helped us learn from each other but also provided us with unique insights into the translingual composing processes of our students. Of note is the fact that most of my colleagues in this study were domestic and monolingual—myself being an exception only in the fact that I was international and monolingual. Nevertheless, despite my English-only, monolingual capabilities I was able to develop pedagogies based transnationally—translingually, transculturally, translocally, and transmodally. Moreover, while the majority of writing teachers in the United States are monolingual—and while it is most definitely an asset to have a multilingual background when teaching multilingual students—I would like to emphasize that such a linguistic background is *not necessary* in order for translingualism to function as a pedagogical benefit (Hornberger and Link 2012). I point this out because at this moment in US writing studies, two aspects of teacher background continue to hinder the ways translingual pedagogy is taken up: (1) many teachers are monolingual and therefore feel they have limited strategies for supporting translingual learning and (2) many teachers have not been explicitly trained to teach the growing numbers of international multilingual students that are enrolling in their courses.

I use myself, then, as an example of how a monolingual teacher, with little to no practical multilingual experience, can successfully implement a transnational curriculum that encourages students to engage a translingual disposition. I argue that teachers do not need to take up the many languages our students enact on a daily basis but can instead design and foster learning spaces open to the diverse translingual realities of our students. I do this through offering a framing of assignments for a transnational curriculum, as well as a contemplation of the opportunities and challenges of implementing a transnationally themed writing course via self- and student reflection.[1]

During the three years this research took place, I taught twelve sections of the aforementioned course; in each iteration of the course, adaptations were made, with the final curricular outcome being a course themed in transnationalism. At the heart of this course was inquiry into cultural and linguistic choice; four assignments were designed to focus both on student movement (trans) and student identity (nationalism). Namely, the assignment sequence consisted of a transcultural learning memoir, a translation narrative, a translocal artifact essay, and a transmodal project. In the following pages I examine each assignment and elaborate upon the pedagogical moves inherent to these assignments. Full assignments can be found in the appendix of this chapter.

A TRANSNATIONAL ASSIGNMENT SEQUENCE

The first assignment, the transcultural learning memoir is, in essence, a form of literacy narrative that considers learning across cultures. For this short, two-page essay, students are provided with two options: work in groups or work individually to compare, contrast, and question how and why learning situations are dynamic processes that change over place and time. In other words, students are invited to write about two cultures of learning (e.g., high school versus college, math class versus writing class, China versus United States, etc.) and offer their own personal insights into the different learning environments. As this was the first assignment, and all students were either new to the university or new to the country, I provided them with the choice of working individually or in groups. In previous iterations of this assignment, I had found that students' background, cultural and educational, affected their preference working alone or collectively, so as this was their first experience with university writing, and because they all came to the class with various writing experiences—both positive and negative—I chose to empower them through letting them decide whether or not to work in groups. Moreover, because the topics do not have to be transnational but must simply cross cultures (with a small *c*, such as cultures of learning in high school versus the university), the assignment can easily be adapted for monolingual students who may also be enrolled in the class.

As mentioned, central to this assignment is personal narrative. Students are encouraged to consider their own experiences with learning and how these experiences are shaped by their past as well as their present (see appendix for complete assignment). At the heart of this narrative is self-reflection; the assignment asks students to consider personal learning experiences in the context of "different cultures of learning," "present and past relationships," "cultural expectations of learning," and "personal definition(s) of learning." Thus, the central move of this assignment, as well as the overall transnational theme of this course, is to position students as experts in their writing topics. Essentially, this assignment asks students to write about a topic that is familiar but to approach it in a new way. Asking students to provide their own definitions based on their own lived experiences also encourages students to consider how learning is affected by personal experiences not necessarily shared with, or familiar to, their audience.

What you may notice is that there is no explicit mention of translingualism in this assignment; in fact, while the trans theme is central to the class, we did not openly take up and discuss the term *translingual* at this early stage of the course. Nevertheless, we did discuss how the different stages of composing are open to linguistic negotiation. Indeed, drafting, brainstorming, and note taking throughout this assignment happened in multiple languages (depending on student preference). Additionally, peer-review sessions and small-group discussions often engaged languages other than English. Instead of ignoring or condemning such acts, we discussed the benefits of utilizing languages other than English in the classroom, which fostered learning because it established our classroom as a safe place where difference was acknowledged and accepted.

The second assignment, the translation narrative, does engage the term *translingualism* in each stage of the assignment. This essay is also considerably longer than the initial assignment (about six to eight pages) and moves through three stages: translation, reflection, and narrative. At the assignment's core is attention to primary research, peer review, and personal reflection. This assignment, while developing out of library research, continues to engage with personal narrative and invites students to document their own translation processes, as well as consider how their language choices affect their writing processes. Specifically, this assignment requires students to translate an academic text from their home language into classroom English and then write a paper about this process (see appendix for complete assignment). While the assignment was originally designed for multilingual students, it can also be taken up by monolingual students, which is discussed below.

This assignment is lengthy and layered; in fact, at first glance, it may seem somewhat daunting. However, it is broken into multiple stages, each building towards the final narrative. The first stage involves a library information session and asks students to work in groups to find an academic text in their home language—it is best if they choose a topic they are already interested in or are somewhat familiar with. Students are then given several days to work individually and translate the academic text into classroom English. They then submit both the original untranslated text and their student-translated text. I ask monolingual students to work in groups to find an SWE academic article written in highly sophisticated, jargon-heavy prose; while it may seem these students would easily be able to translate these texts into classroom English, I have found this is actually a difficult and cumbersome task for the monolingual students to undertake. The second stage of the assignment asks students to look at each of the translations of their group members and consider (through freewriting and group discussion) why specific linguistic choices were made; in a short written reflection they then explore how words and phrases from their home language are able to (or not able to) be reimagined in SWE and how and why this reimagining is not the same for each member in their group. In these written reflections, students are working translingually in their constant negotiation between languages, particularly in terms of rationalizing meaning making.

While each step of the assignment is important in positioning students to begin inquiry into their own process of translation, I see the final stage of this assignment, where students bring together all their data (e.g., original text, peer translations, reflective paper) and rearrange them in the writing of their translation narrative, as the most important aspect of this assignment. In this cumulative, narrative, six-to-eight-page essay, students make a claim about their own personal composing processes and show elements of this process (e.g., offer multilanguaged, layered stages of translation via code meshing and code mixing), as well as "analyze and interpret" the impacts of moving between languages in terms of their own writing process.

The third assignment, the translocal artifact essay, is an individually authored text in which students consider and write about the adaptations of a cultural artifact across cultures. In this four-page essay, students begin by choosing an artifact familiar to them and consider its purpose in their own lives and (often) home cultures (see appendix for complete assignment). The types of artifacts students choose to write about vary widely; a Japanese student wrote about the futon, a Chinese student wrote about Kung Fu, a Korean student wrote about kimchi, a Thai student wrote about dragon racing, and a monolingual American student wrote about the *Nike* brand. Once students have brainstormed their topic, the next move is to consider another culture the artifact exists in and how the artifact's purpose is the same and different in this second culture. The latter part of the assignment is inquiry based, asking students to work in groups to come up with questions about the changes in the artifact across cultures. Students then compile a list of questions and work to answer these questions using their own lived experiences or those of family, friends, and/or classmates. In this assignment, library research is discouraged so that students look inward to consider why the artifact has adapted to its new cultural habitat.

Central to this assignment, again, is the role of personal narrative and reflection. Students continue practicing inquiry-based writing, which encourages them to consider their own experiences first, with the ultimate pedagogical goal of supporting student agency via emphasizing the usability of their prior knowledges and experiences for an unfamiliar audience. Like the previous two assignments, particularly the translation narrative, audience comprehension is a major pedagogical takeaway of this writing project. Students are regularly encouraged to "discuss the relationships between aspects of different cultures," as well as their "personal history and experiences," in order to create a text that is accessible to an unfamiliar reader. Moreover, students are encouraged to consider the different appeals of their chosen artifact for different audiences, and highlight the trans nature of their artifact, specifically how its purpose may change as it "crosses, or moves between, cultures." Regularly, students incorporate short excerpts of non-English text (e.g., words and phrases); students who have chosen to do this often cite the inability to translate these necessary ideas into English (inclusions like these are also seen in the final transmodal project). Additionally, students usually choose this assignment (as well as the last transmodal assignment) as their favorite in the series. I believe this is because while I choose the broad topic (e.g., translocalism), they have the opportunity to choose an artifact they know they are more knowledgeable about than their teacher is (and often other members of the class as well). Thus, the room for choice provides students with a level of intimacy with the topic, which consequently bolsters their ethos in this assignment.

The final assignment in the series, the transmodal project, is a collaborative, digital revision of the translocal artifact essay (see appendix for complete assignment). Students are put in groups of three to four and consider which of their pool of translocal artifact topics is best suited to revise into a short video project. I ask students to do this assignment in groups primarily because it is the first and only assignment that is multimodal, so there is not a huge amount of time to engage with and practice composing multimodality. Instead, student groups are based on students' self-recognition as experts in one of four areas: technical savvy, writing savvy, musical savvy, and leadership savvy. As I have stated elsewhere, with the inclusion of student work (Kiernan 2015, 315), the group dimension of the digital revision is a central component in the transmodal project's movement toward considerations of linguistic negotiation: translingualism. However, while linguistic and cultural choice is central to how students shape this assignment for audience consumption, another significant goal of this assignment is to engage students in reflecting upon how their own rhetorical choices are collaboratively constructed. Most important, however, is that this assignment "creates spaces for students to author texts that are meaningful to them as well as their classmates and the larger communities that they are members of" (318). As mentioned, this is one of the two assignments students prefer in the sequence. There are a number of reasons students enjoy this assignment: the multimodal dimension, the group dynamic, and the expertise they bring to the topic. Because this assignment requires them to engage a "broader audience" and bring that audience into a "conversation" about their topic, students must consider the "social and cultural implications" of their topic across cultures, specifically how time and place orientations affect the consumption of a digital video. In this way, students must design videos that focus on audience engagement. They then individually write a brief essay that explains their rhetorical choices throughout the composing of the transmodal project; for instance, inquiry into how their "understanding of audience, purpose, and meaning changes" is central throughout the stages of this assignment. In this way, the fourth assignment in this series emphasizes one of the key features of all these assignments: audience engagement and comprehension.

ADOPTION AND ADAPTATION

In the appendix I offer full representations of each assignment, and in the preceding section I offer my own interpretation and analysis of how to engage with these assignments, as well as some examples of student topics. I do this for two reasons: the first is so you can take up these assignments and shape them to fit your own institutional contexts and pedagogical goals; the second is so I can emphasize the framing of these assignments as translingually and rhetorically negotiative. In this section, I focus on the latter of these two points and situate my discussion of these assignments in terms of student feedback and reflection.

As discussed earlier, the final writing assignment of the course is reflective and asks students to consider the course theme and assignments in terms of opportunities and challenges. In these reflections, six primary themes arise: the first three are based explicitly in considerations of three of the four assignments (translation, translocal, and transmodal); the second three consider the class assignments in terms of student agency and discuss the rhetorical concepts of ethos, audience, and situation.

Student Reflections on the Assignments

Of the four transnationally themed assignments, the final two, the translocal and transmodal assignments, were discussed most prominently by students in final course reflections (although there were many implicit discussions of translation throughout many of the reflections). The various excerpts from student writing provided below explain, in the students' own unedited words, why they prefer these assignments; however, my positionality as a teacher-researcher reflecting back on the curriculum offers reasoning beyond simply student preference. I think students focused on the last two assignments for two reasons, the most obvious being that the translocal and transmodal assignments were not only versions of the same assignment but also the most recent projects, which means they were still fresh in the students' minds. The other reason is that these two assignments were more enjoyable for students, as they situated student experience as central to meaning making and knowledge building. As one student explained, the topics were "fun to write." However, I begin in chronological order with the translation narrative.

The translation assignment is the second assignment in the sequence and asks students to perform the familiar task of translation but to do so with a focus on not only their own choices but also those of their peers. Moreover, the reflective written element of this assignment requires students to consider movement between languages in terms of multiplicity of choice,² wherein students consider how previous experiences with English both inside and outside their academic histories shaped their interactions with language in our classroom. For instance, one Chinese student explains, "The accumulation of conversations enlarges my eyes that I have more views on one object. For the translation assignment, my eyes allow me to see why the differences exist in my group. . . . Translation is not as easy as interpreting the text word by word. It has to be understandable to another language speaker, who does not have any culture background. My American culture background helps me to make the American readers understand, and I also try to make the translation interesting by adding in some American humor." What I find most notable in this reflection is the student's nuanced understanding of writing as an "accumulation of conversations" that lends to "more views," and the many "differences [that] exist" between linguistic interpretations is central to this passage. Moreover, what is at the heart of this student reflection is not the translation—"interpreting the text word by word"—it is the realization, by this multilingual writer, that she must tailor her translation to specific audience expectations that are not necessarily her own. Similarly, another student in discussing the translocal assignment explains that in writing this essay, "It's necessary for us to connect both Chinese and American culture together. Oddly enough, that is precisely what opens my mind. Before that time, I never think about combine two countries' culture together. The comparison of these two countries' culture always creates unexpected result. So that both American and Chinese audiences have much more interests in reading my paper." The important takeaway from this reflection is that the fluidity of the transnational theme allowed room for students to consider the benefits of integrating multiple cultural experiences within their own writing in terms of audience "so that both . . . audiences have . . . more interest" in the text. Hence, it was the curricular focus on cultural and linguistic connection that was "precisely what open[ed] [her] mind." As a monolingual outsider looking in, it is quite jarring to me that this student (and many like her) had not previously considered the function of their own culture within their communicative processes; however, I also think this realization is an important one for those of us who teach writing. We cannot make assumptions about our students' prior knowledge and experiences with linguistic negotiation, despite the fact that it is something multilingual students do on a very regular—often daily—basis. Consequently, I see transnationally based writing assignments as especially useful, not simply in allowing students to better realize their own capabilities but also in educating teachers on the variety of ways multilingual students approach and encounter their multiple lived experiences—culturally and linguistically.

Consequently, an essential lesson of engaging with transnationalism in the classroom is that it opens up more possibilities for the writer, which students often noted as a benefit of composing the transmodal project.

> All people from all different nations have or use different language, culture, mind-set. . . . It's undeniable fact. . . . However, there is some[thing] you can feel even if you don't know about their culture and even if you can't speak their language. That is Image . . . we can say the image is trans-modal and also transnational. . . . I want to say having different cultural background and language is as same as using different brush and paint . . . I noticed it when I made trans-modal project. As that project was presented in the US, knowing American culture is also important for presentation. As my target audiences were American, I needed to know about them for their better understanding. . . . Image is multinational but there are preferred or more suitable image based on cultures and nations. As I know about American culture, I can make suitable image (video) for American with my personal brush and paint based on where I made presentation and who will be my audiences. This means knowing more about American culture is helpful tool for successful trans-modal project.

What is especially interesting about this reflection is that while the topic of the transmodal video was specific to Chinese culture, the student works very hard to acknowledge that due to members of the class being American, there was a strong need to "know them" in order for this audience to have a "better understanding" of the unfamiliar topic. Moreover, it is of note that this student (and many others) identifies images, or modality, as a "transnational" strategy when creating a text to be consumed by an international audience. Moreover, this student goes further, identifying that it is not simply the choice of images that enables understanding of unfamiliar material but also the choice of "suitable image[s]" that results in a successful viewing experience.

Student Reflections on Rhetorical Agency

In end-of-semester reflections, I also saw themes emerging in terms of rhetorical awareness. While the latter two of these themes—audience and situation—were most developed by students, I also want to briefly explore the ways ethos surfaced in these final texts. While students were not explicitly tasked with discussing rhetoric (the jargon of rhetoric was never directly discussed in class), they did acknowledge three rhetorical devices at play in their experiences authoring transnational texts.

As alluded to in the chapter epigraphs, students indisputably enjoyed the transnational theme of the course; however, what these examples do not fully illustrate is that students not only enjoyed the transnational theme but also developed agentive ethos with this content, which allowed for better engagement with not simply the course material (e.g., readings, discussions, etc.) but also their writing assignments. One Chinese student explained that the transnational theme was "fun to write": "It speed up my length of time in writing, I started to use English to think outline and main paragraph straight instead of using Chinese to think. Learning and improving are fun just as the same about writing the topic you like." Similarly, another Chinese student explained her new approach to writing as "unbeliveable [*sic*]": "[In the past I] always needed other information with other references or online to complete writing. It was completely different [this] time, the draft I was written by my own ideas, I feel when I write this draft without pause. Perhaps, when doing something about the things they like, people will be full of power and passion to do this." These student reflections are useful in illustrating student agency in the writing of the four assignments; however, I would also like to briefly address the benefits of developing student ethos in terms of readership.

In the process of developing this transnational course, there was much experimentation with what types of activities, readings, and so forth this population of students would find engaging. Consequently, during my tenure teaching this course, assignments were not always exclusively transnational in scope. Early in the process, writing assignments were a combination of status quo assignments (e.g., mainstream, traditional) such as traditional literacy narratives. While iterations of the transnational assignments outlined herein developed slowly, early on I noticed the essays based in transnational themes were much more interesting to read. In reading them, I (as a monolingual outsider) was learning not only about my students as writers but also about their many experiences, cultures, and languages. As a reader, I was also more engaged in these transnational texts because, as the above student quote explains, these essays were "full of power and passion." So, while I hold strong in my position that a transnational curricular framework is beneficial to students because it provides them with agency with which they can showcase their diverse multilingual and multicultural assets and resources, I further argue these assignments are a pleasure to read and are useful for teachers because they bring forth perspectives and voices not always present in the writing prompts we traditionally assign our students.

It is not a coincidence that student agency led to audience engagement; in fact, the majority of the student reflections focused on how they approached their writing with different audiences in mind. Students reflected on the ways considering audience shaped their writing both "generally and globally," as one Chinese student explained: "Talking about using personal language experiences when I write an essay, I would say that using personal language history and background could help me to make my essay more interesting and easy to read. . . . Using personal talking or speaking style can make the essay closer to the real life, thus the reader could read your essay more enjoyable and relaxed. . . . Being multilingual and multicultural help myself to be a critical thinker and think more generally and globally." While this quote begins as primarily introspective (e.g., "when I write," "could help me," etc.), it shifts midstream to also consider how personal choices affect audience experiences with the text. In making the connection that authorship is tied to readership, this student—and many others—is realizing a text must be able to speak to those outside the writer's own experiences, which was a realization new for many students in the class. For instance, a Thai student explained that considering diverse perspectives worked to "develop [their] own personality and broaden [their] perspective on the world. It opens up the idea that there are billions of different kinds of ideas and experiences that the world has to offer." And, a Korean student similarly described the transnational theme as reminding her, "I needed to think what is the difference and similarities among these international students, including myself." Essentially, this shift in audience awareness can also be understood in terms of development of critical-thinking skills.

While much scholarship shows that moving between languages requires attention to nuanced rhetorical choice (e.g., Bawarshi 2016; Canagarajah 2013; Gonzales 2015; Kiernan, Meiers, and Wang 2016), articulations of this cognitive development are not as readily available, particularly in terms of translingual scholarship. Thus, I think it is important to point out that students themselves associate cognitive benefits with writing transnationally themed assignments. Below are excerpts from two Chinese student reflections, which illustrate these developmental moves. The first student explains, "In my opinion, my multicultural background not only brings new way of thinking in my life, it also influence the way of thinking toward my own culture . . . in other words, the two cultures I both have acquired influences and changes one another, which brings me new way of seeing things." As a teacher-researcher I see this student's explicit mentioning of "new way[s] of thinking" and "new way[s] of seeing things" as useful examples of critical inquiry and critical-thinking development. I take this position because the student appears to be encountering both her past and future experiences in new ways; we see similar movement towards shifting perspectives in the second student reflection: "Being a multilingual and multicultural also provide me a different way of thinking and understanding. As we all know language and culture may be the most important factors that affect the thinking mode. Being a multilingual and multicultural means my thinking process is no longer base on one specific thinking mode but I can reflect my thinking in another thinking mode. Being a multilingual and multicultural will made me not only a better writer but also a better critical thinker." Again, the words of this student suggest the transnational theme provides not only "a different way of thinking" but also "understanding." Both these student reflections offer insight on the benefits of engaging multilingual and multicultural students in writing projects that invite students to reconsider how the past experiences they bring to US writing classrooms can function as cognitive assets rather than deficits, which consequently provides them with an ethos that nontransnationally themed courses may not encourage.

CLOSING THOUGHTS

As I finish this essay, I want to impress upon you not only the adaptability of these assignments but also what I see as the fundamental pedagogical core of this project: an opportunity to engage students—often marginalized students—in writing that surfaces their prior experiences as important assets and resources. While these transnational assignments primarily position international students to reconsider their own identities and move beyond the often-ingrained ideology of difference as a deficit, it is also important to note that in the majority of these classes, there were always a handful of domestic, monolingual students. While I have not gone into great detail about the ways these students took up and adapted these assignments to their own backgrounds, I have indicated several ways monolingual students were able to shape the course to their own linguistic backgrounds; moreover, the primary forces driving domestic students' interpretations of these transnational assignments were also their own backgrounds and experiences, which were notably varied. Consequently, it was the students who shaped the context and execution of these assignments, and all students—even monolingual—were able to make connections to these texts because the class worked on realizing not only our own mobility but also our own participation in multiple cultural contexts (where culture is not necessarily tied to place or nation-state).

I believe no one would argue against reassessing, reimagining, and redesigning writing assignments that invite students to pause and consider their own layered processes of cognitive negotiation, and rhetorical choice should be a necessary part of all writing-course development. However, there exists a sort of pedagogical backwater throughout our writing programs when it comes to the creation of writing courses that accept translingual dispositions. To this, I argue that as educators we have an obligation to invite our multilingual students to deeply consider the practical ways their multiple languages come into play throughout all stages of writing because such examinations are key in engaging our ever-growing multilingual student populations in meaningful writing practices.

APPENDIX 11.A

ASSIGNMENT 1: TRANSCULTURAL LEARNING MEMOIR

Purpose . . .

This assignment asks you to consider the different ways that you have been taught "to learn" and, specifically, how you have been taught "to write." I would like you to think about the different cultures of learning you have experienced. It will be useful for you to describe these to your reader and explain how they were useful to you as a learner and how they were not useful to you.

In order to help you (and your readers) learn from your experience(s), you need to carefully consider how your present and past relationships are informed by the various cultural groups you have been (and are) a member of, your cultural expectations of learning, and your personal definition(s) of learning. Thus, you are encouraged to reflect upon your past and present relationships with learning. In other words, it may be useful to think about this paper as a <u>compare and contrast</u> essay, where it is important to emphasize the similarities and differences you have encountered with learning in different cultures.

Invention . . .

It is important to remember that the experiences you choose to write about are significant to you—if not, you wouldn't have chosen them—but you will also need to spend time explaining (a) why you chose these examples and (b) why they are important. In other words, you will be not just be writing a personal story, you will be analyzing and interpreting the story you offer, which will serve to illustrate this moment's significance to your readers.

When considering what cultures are central to your narrative, you need to question (a) what culture(s) are present, (b) why they are present, and (c) how they are present. This line of inquiry will provide you with the opportunity to invent a narrative of yourself in relation to your experiences as a learner and consider your experiences as important and useful as tools of inquiry.

Some questions that might help you include:

- Where have you learned?
- In what types of cultures have you experienced learning?
- What were the similarities in these cultures (or places) of learning?
- What were the differences in these cultures (or places) of learning?
- In what culture (or place) was learning easiest? Why?
- In what culture (or place) was learning hardest? Why?
- How did your past learning experiences prepare you for being an MSU student?
- How did your past learning experiences fail to prepare you for being an MSU student?
- How did your past learning experiences prepare you to be a writer?
- How did your past learning experiences fail to prepare you to be a writer?

Your peer review draft should be two pages.
Your assessment draft should be four pages.

ASSIGNMENT 2: TRANSLATION NARRATIVE
Purpose . . .

In your second assignment, you will be writing a translation narrative (or story). This assignment asks you to think about how you move between and across languages when you write. You will need to consider the choices you make as you translate from your home language to English. You will also need to think about how and why your practices of translation are not always the same as your peers who are working with the same languages. This assignment is broken into three parts:

1. **Translation**
   a. If possible, in a group (of two or three students), go to the library and find an excerpt of <u>academic writing</u> that is between 200 and 250 words long. This piece of text must be written in either (a) a shared language other than English or (b) dense academic English.
   b. On your own (individually) translate this piece of writing into a form of English that we use in our classroom. <u>It is important that you do this step in isolation.</u>
   c. Groups will compare TRANSLATIONS (October 1) and pay special attention to what is the same and what is different.

2. **Reflection** (600–750 words)
   a. You will then write <u>INDIVIDUAL</u> REFLECTIONS about your process of translation. This REFLECTION is similar to the weekly discussion boards in that you will need to analyze and interpret information. You will need to consider why parts of your TRANSLATION differ between group members and why you think these differences exist.
   b. You will also need to think and reflect upon what parts of the TRANSLATION were especially hard and explain why you think this was. I would like you to consider how the meanings may have changed when you translated and how this affected the English text (e.g., What were the benefits and drawbacks?).
   c. I also want you to think about what was gained and what was lost in your TRANSLATION (and all translations) and discuss your conclusions on this topic of gain and loss.

3. **Narrative** (1500–1800 words)
   a. Your final draft will be a combination of your translation and your reflection paper. You will be bringing these two texts together; for example, in order to prove an argument you make in your REFLECTION PAPER, you will use examples from your TRANSLATION. You will not use all the material from your TRANSLATION or all the material from your REFLECTION PAPER; what you will be doing is creating a new paper that brings together the most useful parts of each of your earlier drafts.
   b. This paper will have a clear thesis that may be the same as, or be a revision of, the thesis statement you presented in your REFLECTION PAPER.

ASSIGNMENT 3: TRANSLOCAL ARTIFACT ESSAY

Purpose...

In your third assignment, you will choose a "translocal artifact" to write about. This assignment asks you to consider an artifact that crosses, or moves between, cultures, something that you have encountered in one country or culture but you have also experienced in some way in another country or culture. You will be expected to discuss the relationships between aspects of different cultures when explaining why you chose this artifact.

There are two parts to this assignment, which do not have to appear in the order provided; however, consider arrangement and how the order of information is central to the message your essay will provide. You are expected to include the following: (1) cultural comparison of the ways this artifact is used, seen, exists in at least two cultures and (2) your personal history and experience with this artifact.

Invention...

In order to help you (and your readers) learn from your knowledge, you need to carefully consider the ways that your chosen cultural artifact forms relationships between and across <u>nation</u>, <u>history</u>, <u>culture</u>, and <u>language</u>.

- Why is this artifact important to you? What story does it tell about you?
- Who else do you know that uses this artifact? What does this tell us about the artifact?
- What is the history of this artifact, both in your culture and in other cultures? How long has this artifact existed? Is there a historical story that explains the origination of this artifact?
- What does the message of this story say about your culture? What does this artifact say about your culture?
- Are there any specific words or feelings associated with this artifact? What are they, and if they are not English, are they easy to translate? Why or why not? Or, do you even need to translate them? Why or why not?

Remember: <u>A central goal of this assignment is to describe the cultural impacts of this artifact on your life; you will need to offer your readers moments of in-depth analysis and interpretation</u>. It is important to remember that the artifact you choose to write about is obviously important to you—if not, you wouldn't have picked it—but you will also need to spend time explaining (a) why you picked this artifact and (b) how it is important. In other words, you will be not just writing about what something is, you will be analyzing and interpreting what "it" is, which will serve to illustrate this artifact's significance to your readers.

Don't Forget . . .
- You need a thesis statement that is introduced in your first paragraph and then repeated and returned to in all body paragraphs (and conclusion paragraph).
- Include topic and return sentences in each body paragraph.
- The peer-review draft of your essay should be three pages long.
- The assessment draft of your essay should be five pages long.

ASSIGNMENT 4: TRANSMODAL PROJECT
Purpose . . .

In your third assignment, you will revise one of your TRANSLOCAL ARTIFACT papers using a digital platform. A central goal is to consider how presenting writing using a new medium (video) will allow you to strengthen your original purpose and reach—potentially—a broader audience. Like all your assignments, you will need to consider the social and cultural implications of your chosen topic, particularly in relation to digital media.

Part 1

For this assignment you will be working in groups, which I will assign, to create a digital video (no more than three minutes in length) that revises and re-visions a previous assignment. You will need to discuss, as a group, whose paper would be the most useful to revise (and distribute this paper to every member of the group); who your audience for this video will be; and how video allows you to come into "conversation" with a larger audience.

Part 2

Each member of the group will also have to write (their own!) two-page reflection paper where you address the choices you made and considered when transforming written text into a digital text (see below list of questions), as well as the specific contributions you made to this project. The central purpose of this reflection is to consider how the drafting, editing, and overall composing of the TRANSMODAL assignment differs from the writing of the TRANSLOCAL assignment. It is important to make comparisons and contrasts based on your understanding of audience, purpose, and meaning change between these two assignments.

Invention . . .

In order to help you decide what topic to choose, what direction to take, and what to address in your reflection paper I have provided <u>some</u> questions to consider:

- How does the medium of video provide new opportunities to explain the thesis of this topic?
- How might your audience for this paper have different expectations, due to the medium of video?
- How does the medium of video affect how you communicate the purpose of this project?
- When creating transitions between ideas, what are the similarities and differences when writing a paper and creating a video?
- When creating introductions and conclusions, what are the similarities and differences when writing a paper and creating a video?
- What points are you able to make using video that were not available to you when you used written text?
- When creating a video, how and why are word and language choices important? What types of words and languages best suit the audience?
- Does video change the meaning of your argument? How? Why?
- What is harder, writing a paper or creating a video? Why?
- What is harder, working alone or working in a group? Why?

Don't Forget . . .

For this assignment you will be graded by me (your instructor), as well as your classmates.

- 1/3 of your grade is peer evaluation
- 1/3 of your grade is based on your video
- 1/3 of your grade is based on your reflection paper

NOTES

1. Students' responses were collected over a three-year period. I taught approximately 250 students over the course of this period. The student reflections included in this chapter were collected in years two and three of the project.
2. This may also be a reason students did not choose to reflect on this assignment in the final project—they had already spent a lot of time considering these choices throughout the various stages of the translation narrative.

REFERENCES

Bawarshi, Anis. 2016. "Beyond the Genre Fixation: A Translingual Perspective on Genre." *College English* 78 (3): 243–49.

Canagarajah, A. Suresh. 2013. "Negotiating Translingual Literacy: An Enactment." *Research in the Teaching of English* 48 (1): 40–67.

Gonzales, Laura. 2015. "Multimodality, Translingualism, and Rhetorical Genre Studies." *Composition Forum* 31 (Spring). https://compositionforum.com/issue/31/multimodality.php.

Hornberger, Nancy H., and Holly Link. 2012. "Translanguaging and Transnational Literacies in Multilingual Classrooms: A Biliteracy Lens." *International Journal of Bilingual Education and Bilingualism* 15 (3): 261–78.

Horner, Bruce, Min-Zhan Lu, Jacqueline Jones Royster, and John Trimbur. 2011. "Opinion: Language Difference in Writing: Toward a Translingual Approach." *College English* 73 (3): 303–21.

Kiernan, Julia E. (2015). "Multimodal and Translingual Composing Practices: A Culturally Based Needs Assessment of Second Language Learners." *Journal of Global Literacies, Technologies, and Emerging Pedagogies* 3 (1): 302–32.

Kiernan, Julia, Joyce Meier, and Xiqiao Wang. 2016. "Negotiating Languages and Cultures: Enacting Translingualism through a Translation Assignment." *Composition Studies* 44 (1): 89–107.

Lee, Jerry Won, and Christopher Jenks. 2016. "Doing Translingual Dispositions." *College Composition and Communication* 68 (2): 317–47.

AFTERWORD

Thomas Lavalle

Language does not exist as an entity. Language is not a code, not a means of expression, not a resource. . . . What we call language consists of practices—patterns of behavior that arise out of interactions.
   —Marilyn M. Cooper

The "normal" exercise of hegemony . . . is characterized by the combination of force and consent variously balancing one another, without force exceeding consent too much. Indeed one tries to make it appear that force is supported by the consent of the majority, expressed by the so-called organs of public opinion.
   —Antonio Gramsci

Writing an afterword is a privilege because of the double opportunity it affords the writer. First, there is an early encounter with an exciting body of work, in this case the eleven educational innovations introduced and elaborated upon in this collection. Then comes the opportunity, and attendant responsibility, to engage that body of work as it reaches the academic community at large and perhaps in some small way to affect the work's reception, application, and further development. As far as application is concerned, each of the contributions here is, in some respects, self-sufficient. My own reading of the chapters was interrupted regularly by mental digressions as I planned and imagined ways to incorporate into my own teaching the interventions, assignments, and perspectives described. I am confident, therefore, that other readers will find far-reaching inspiration, just as the editors intended. We can be confident, too, that as these innovations move into different institutional, linguistic, and cultural settings, at least some of them will evolve and stimulate further innovations that speak to the aims that drive translingual theory and practice in composition studies: greater fairness for

DOI: 10.7330/9781646421121.c012

student writers, more accurate representations of language to inform writing instruction, and active resistance to the monolingualist ideology that both expedites unfair instruction and assessment and propagates inaccurate representations throughout the academy and beyond.

However, many of the chapters share a characteristic that tempers that confidence. That characteristic is a reliance upon remarkably inclusive definitions of translingualism, sometimes explicitly inclusive and sometimes not. Practitioners can, of course, choose to work with modified or idiosyncratic versions of translingualism, but such choices make precise and explicit definitions even more important. Moreover, regardless of whether a pedagogy rests upon an established or novel conception of translingualism, there are compelling educational reasons for instructors to be clear and explicit about their own understanding of the nature of language and language differences since that understanding will affect (if not guide) any writing pedagogy. After a brief discussion of definitions, I return to those reasons, which turn on the transformative, threshold-like learning translingualism entails and how students have been shown to respond to that kind of learning.

The editors begin their definition of translingualism with the notion of disposition offered by Bruce Horner, Min-Zhan Lu, Jacqueline Jones Royster, and John Trimbur in 2011, a disposition of "openness and inquiry" toward language difference (311). Important, both the editors here and the authors of the 2011 essay narrow their definitions, the former in light of recent scholarship and the latter by taking clear ideological and linguistic stances (305 and 307 on ideology and especially 307 on language). Nevertheless, there are contexts where a maximally inclusive, broad-church, big-tent approach to emergent theory may be most appropriate. Arguably, that 2011 call to action may have been written in one such context, aiming as it did to engage an extended community of scholars and teachers in the translingual enterprise. The context of this volume may well be another, aiming as it does to offer a range of descriptions of "pedagogies that develop a translingual disposition and are replicable and adaptable" (introduction, this volume). More precision, however, is required in individual contributions if the pedagogies they describe and advocate are to help students understand the troublesome knowledge translingualism represents and to help teachers overcome the kinds of institutional/ideological obstacles to translingual pedagogies cataloged at length by the contributors to Horner and Laura Tetreault's (2017) collection.

The remarkably inclusive definitions in this volume seem to be working in two ways. Some innovations and interventions seem to settle simply for openness and curiosity as an adequate definition of translingualism. While openness and curiosity are certainly desirable, they are an inadequate basis for a translingual pedagogy because a solely dispositional definition leaves unanswered at least two questions, the answers to which are essential to a coherent understanding of translingualism. And, of course, our students need some coherent understanding of translingualism in order to develop a confident translingual disposition and the rhetorical possibilities that may follow from it. The first of these questions is, What distinguishes translingualism from accommodationist approaches to linguistic variation? The second is, Is translingualism relevant to all writing or only to the writing of so-called multilinguals, however they may be defined? While it is not necessary to answer these questions here, any responsible translingual pedagogy will require teachers to have carefully considered answers at hand. Those answers should, among other things, reconcile any gestures toward special status for multilingual writing and every suggestion of special challenges facing monolingual composition teachers or students with the stream of research that identifies translingualism "not as an option writers may choose to pursue or not, nor as a feature marking some writing but not others, but as an inevitable feature of all writing, whatever form that writing may take" (Horner 2016, 88). Such gestures and suggestions occur throughout this volume—for instance in the editors' introduction and in the contributions by Ming Fang and Tania Lopez; Norah Fahim, Bonnie Vidrine-Isbell, and Dan Zhu; Esther Milu and Mathew Gomes; and Julia Kiernan—so instructors inspired to apply the pedagogies described in those chapters will need either to prepare and carry out this reconciliation themselves or leave their students to wrestle with a truncated explanation of translingualism.

Overly inclusive definitions operate differently in chapters that do evoke a more narrow definition of translingualism. One example is the chapter by Daniel Bommarito and Emily Cooney. The core of the authors' innovation is their migration of Bob Broad's criteria mapping out of program-level contexts into course-level contexts. The benefits the authors identify are both laudable and achievable, including the explicit negotiation of the meaning of technical terms and the enhanced sense of participation provided to students. The definitional problem emerges as the authors endeavor to bridge their work with criteria mapping to translingualism. They do this largely by applying their notion of negotiation to the negotiation of rubrics and grading criteria. However, this bridging, which is how they define their pedagogy as translingual, fails for two reasons. First, a translingual perspective, or any performative perspective on language, acknowledges the cocreation of meaning as a general condition of communication, so while the negotiation of criteria in the classrooms certainly "creates meaning [as] an emergent property" (chapter 2), all communication does that. So in this respect, those negotiations have no special status but instead operate just like every other linguistic exchange. Second, not all negotiations are cases of "negotiating linguistic differences" (chapter 2). In fact, as a contested conversation over the forms and interpretations of a document imbued with social and institutional power, the negotiation of assessment rubrics shares many family resemblances with the negotiation of leases, sales contracts, loan agreements, plea bargains, and other transactional documents. Nevertheless, even though these bridging efforts ultimately fail, it is important to acknowledge them as definitional work if only to show that not all definitions of translingual pedagogy are convincing or helpful. Most important though, Bommarito and Cooney's efforts to define their pedagogy as translingual fail because all the teaching and all the policies they describe could be enacted with, for example, an eradicationist approach to language difference. This is not to say the authors employ such an approach. On the contrary, I read their chapter as positive, progressive, and attractive, but I cannot read it as translingual. While there isn't currently an orthodox definition of translingual pedagogy, any credible or coherent one would include a necessary incompatibility with the eradication of language difference and the reification of language(s). Criteria mapping is agnostic on these points.

While my concerns over definitions may come across as theoretical fussiness or even pedantry in a book devoted to pedagogical applications, the source of these concerns is strictly didactic. In educational settings, a translingual approach to language is a *threshold concept*. Threshold concepts were identified by Jan Meyer and Ray Land (2003) in their research into features of high-quality learning environments in tertiary education. In learning processes, such concepts function as portals because they open "a new and previously inaccessible way of thinking about something" and thus transform the students' "way of understanding, or interpreting, or viewing something without which the learner cannot progress" (1). Three of the defining features attributed to threshold concepts are particularly germane to students coming to understand a translingual approach to language, which is in turn a necessary stage in their reaching the intended learning outcome identified throughout this volume: the development of translingual dispositions in order to promote greater rhetorical flexibility.

One feature is that threshold concepts are *transformative*. While many students, teachers, and scholars intuitively recognize their own language practices as translingual, conscious engagement with translingualism's claims about linguistic representations both requires and brings about new and transformed ways of understanding and interpreting those representations. Moreover, as several chapters here and in other books on translingual pedagogy clearly show (cf. Horner and Tetrault 2017; Frost et al. 2020), the transformation is not merely an intellectual one. When threshold concepts bring about a "significant shift in the perception of a subject," that shift can "lead to a transformation of personal identity, a reconstruction of subjectivity" (Meyer and Land 2003, 5). Glynis Cousin (2006) describes this as "an ontological as well as a conceptual shift" (4).

A second feature is that threshold concepts, like a translingual take on language, are *integrative* in the sense that they reveal interconnections among phenomena whose relatedness had previously been hidden from or unnoticed by the learner. Meyer and Land (2005) illustrate this by pointing to the integrative power of the concept *hegemony* for first-year students of cultural studies. In addition to uncovering connections to other disciplinary concepts, these students recognize "the implications of the concept of 'hegemony' for the ways in which their personal choices and behaviour might be culturally constrained, determined or gendered" (375).

A third characteristic follows from these two; threshold concepts are *troublesome*, that is, not only do they prove difficult for many students to learn, retain, and apply, they also bring about anxiety, self-doubt, and frustration (Meyer and Land 2006, i). Initially, Meyer and Land follow David Perkins (1999) and account for the troublesome nature of these concepts largely through features inherent in the concepts themselves: they strike learners as counterintuitive, alien, or incoherent (Meyer and Land 2003, 7). These are reactions we may well see in students on their first hearing that language is performance not system, that the borders between languages are soft and permeable, and that so-called standard English is illusory or at least provisional or contingent. Important, Meyer and Land (2005) also foreground more clearly that what is troublesome about these thresholds goes beyond conceptual change and follows from "the inter-relatedness of the learner's identity with language and thinking" (375). There they enter terrain very familiar to the composition community and underscore the magnitude of the task students face in trying to understand their reading and writing differently.

Specifically, encounters with translingual pedagogy lead students not only "to transformed thought but [also] to a transfiguration of identity"

(Meyer and Land 2005, 375). It goes without saying that transfiguration of a student's identity is a complex and difficult process, and that difficulty and complexity may help explain some of the resistance by students occasionally mentioned in the contributions in this collection. For instance, the English-only student Ghanashyam Sharma describes (chapter 1) successfully seals off any troublesome need to change by declining Sharma's invitation to translingualism and hangs onto both an identity as a pragmatic user of English and a conception of language that supports that identity.

It is, however, another dimension of threshold concepts and their acquisition that is particularly pertinent to translingual pedagogy and that therefore motivates my concern with careful and explicit definitions. Simply put, simplifying threshold concepts proves to be counterproductive. Drawing upon three empirical studies, Meyer and Land (2005) report that when teachers introduce, or scaffold, a version of a threshold concept that is "a deliberately simplified and limited delineation[,] it seems to act to a certain extent as a proxy for the threshold concept" (382). Naturally, this scaffolding is intended to support students' understanding of troublesome material, but "this was often not the case"; instead the simplification became a false proxy, "a false proxy leading students to settle for the naïve version and enter into a form of ritualized learning or mimicry. The concept offered appeared to have an enchanting, beguiling or ensnaring effect, simultaneously promising understanding but curtailing it at the same time by seeming to close down further avenues of enquiry or complexity" (382).

I argue that an introduction to translingualism is a "simplified and limited delineation" if it doesn't answer definitional questions like those I raise earlier. There is, of course, no way short of an empirical study to know whether or to what extent the mimicry Meyer and Land warn of actually takes place in classrooms where pedagogical innovations appeal to or rest upon overly simplified definitions of translingualism. What we can do, however, is acknowledge a risk for superficial learning of that kind. That risk alone justifies providing students with more help, more answers, more support for a coherent understanding, not less.

In some cases, however, it is possible to appraise a classroom setting to identify learners who are engaged with the troublesome consequences of learning about translingualism. A translingual approach to language is not merely difficult; because it runs counter to other approaches our students have met and because it explicitly conflicts with the "common sense" of schoolish conceptions of language and dominant language ideology, translingualism is also "alien knowledge" (Meyer and Land

2003, 9). As such, it is troublesome, and we should expect to see signs of that trouble among the students coming to terms with it. Among students mimicking a simple, proxy translingualism, we would not see those signs. Tellingly perhaps, the chapters operating with open or imprecise definitions of translingualism report few signs of translingualism being troublesome for the students involved.

Although we cannot draw any conclusions from an absence of evidence, we can, however, reason with confidence in the other direction. Examples of students responding to translingualism as though it were troublesome suggest those students are engaging with an approach to language that is transformative, integrative, and threateningly alien. Naomi Silver's chapter is rich in such examples; the students she describes and quotes seem to experience translingualism as a threshold concept, which is at times troublesome. Silver herself identifies the "transformative thinking" among some of her students (chapter 10). Integrative thinking characterizes another student's understanding of translingualism as she uncovers first her own complicity in reproducing standard-English ideology and then recognizes the similarities between the "conformist ideologies of monolingualism" and "the hidden gender norms, microaggressions, and injustices that permeate our society." However, along with the personally transformative and integrative features of threshold concepts comes trouble. One of Silver's students expresses the self-doubt that Meyer and Land anticipate: "How can we enact social justice in a writing center while still helping students make their paper as 'correct' as possible" (243). Another, the student Silver identifies as Alessandra, provides an extended study in the troublesome effects of translingualism. Silver points out Alessandra's "anxiety" when a "contingent and negotiable" framing of standard English threatens to transform (or undermine) her protoprofessional identity. Alessandra finds it "hard to envision [her] future job as a middle or high school English teacher if it did not include the teaching of Standard English, but rather encouraged students to work against the expectation of everything [she has] been taught and accepted for so many years" (248).

Silver identifies features of her course that may help to explain why her students respond to translingualism as troublesome knowledge (which in my reading suggests their genuine engagement with its disruptive insights). First, they encounter the concept after working with another theme that makes ideology visible, power and social justice in the writing center (chapter 10). Second, they work directly and actively with the Horner et al. (2011) essay and therefore encounter not just a dispositional definition of translingualism but also strong linguistic and ideological stances. Finally, these students are preparing for professional engagement as writing center tutors, language teachers, or both. While all three features are probably equally significant, I want to foreground briefly the implications of their prospective working lives. For these students, the challenges of translingualism are not limited to a course, an assignment, or a grade; much more is at stake. They cannot afford to mimic a proxy version of translingualism, so they work through all the trouble translingualism, as a threshold concept entangled in ideological conflict, entails for them. Silver, then, documents some of this working through and in doing so opens an additional avenue for both thinking about and executing translingual pedagogies.

When students are motivated to engage with them, threshold concepts often bring trouble. When students and teachers work with ideologies in conflict with dominant ideologies, they typically run into trouble. When students, teachers, or scholars speak and write about language as performance in an inherited vocabulary that frames language as form or system, they are inevitably awash in troubles. This, of course, is why translingualism is difficult—difficult to grasp, to explain, to teach. In various ways and in varying degrees, the contributions to this volume acknowledge and demonstrate this difficulty. Yet they also acknowledge, each in their own way, something that outweighs that difficulty, the commitment of composition teachers and scholars to continue working toward greater fairness, more accurate representations, and more effective resistance.

REFERENCES

Cousin, Glynis. 2006. "An Introduction to Threshold Concepts." *Planet* (17): 4–5.

Frost, Alanna, Julia Kiernan, and Suzanne Blum Malley, eds. 2020. *Translingual Dispositions: Globalized Approaches to the Teaching of Writing*. Fort Collins, CO: WAC Clearinghouse.

Horner, Bruce. 2016. *Rewriting Composition: Terms of Exchange*. Carbondale: Southern Illinois University Press.

Horner, Bruce, Min-Zhan Lu, Jacqueline Jones Royster, and John Trimbur. 2011. "Opinion: Language Difference in Writing: Toward a Translingual Approach." *College English* 73 (3): 303–21.

Horner, Bruce, and Laura Tetreault, eds. 2017. *Crossing Divides: Exploring Translingual Writing Pedagogies and Programs*. Logan: Utah State University Press.

Meyer, Jan, and Ray Land. 2003. "Threshold Concepts and Troublesome Knowledge 1: Linkages to Ways of Thinking and Practising." In *Improving Student Learning and Practice—Ten Years On: Proceedings of the 10th International Symposium Improving Student Learning*, edited by Chris Rust, 53–64. Oxford: Oxford Center for Staff and Learning Development.

Meyer, Jan, and Ray Land. 2005. "Threshold Concepts and Troublesome Knowledge 2: Epistemological Considerations and a Conceptual Framework for Teaching and Learning." *Higher Education* 49 (3): 373–88.

Meyer, Jan, and Ray Land. 2006. Preface to *Overcoming Barriers to Student Understanding: Threshold Concepts and Troublesome Knowledge*, edited by Jan Meyer and Ray Land, xiv–xxiii. Abington: Routledge.

Perkins, David. 1999. "The Many Faces of Constructivism." *Educational Leadership* 57 (3): 6–11.

INDEX

action-research project, 212
Advanced Placement English Literature and Composition, 194–95
advertisements, visual rhetorical strategies in, 86–87
affect socialization, 102, 116
affirmation, pedagogy of, 126, 142
After-School Tutor for Chinese & Vietnamese English Language Learner Students, 97–98
agency, 33, 37; language use and, 21, 26; rhetorical, 166, 274–76; student writers, 41–42
Alessandra, "Language in the Classroom," 247–50
American "Multilingualism": A National Tragedy (Raff), 69
analysis paper/analytical essay, on cultural sayings/expressions, 143–44, 145–46
Anderson, Gary, 173
Anzaldúa, Gloria, 92, 158, 241, 242, 246; "How to Tame a Wild Tongue," 240, 244; on language and identity, 129–30
Arizona State University (ASU), first-year writing courses, 43–44
artifacts: translocal, 269, 270; in writing-theory cartoon exercises, 216, 219(table)
assessment tools, 57(n1); student negotiation in, 41–42, 44–47, 49–50, 51–52
assignment procedures, student negotiation, 51–52
assimilation, to majority cultural standard, 243
audience, 46, 80, 233, 270; for cultural-critique essay, 55–56; for literacy-autobiography, 156–57, 168; for visual rhetorical essay, 86–87
auditory codes, 214
authenticity/authentic, essay exercise, 47–48, 51, 53–57
autobiography, 9. *See also* literacy-autobiography assignment
(auto)ethnography, 201

Backhaus, Peter, 178
Bangkok: linguistic landscapes in, 178, 180, 181–82

Bawarshi, Anis, 163
Ben-Rafael, Eliezer, gestalt theory, 178, 179
"Beyond a 'Single Language/Single Modality' Approach to Writing," 240
bilingualism, 104–5, 122(n2), 176, 200
Blackledge, Adrian, 127
Bohannan, Laura, "Shakespeare in the Bush," 157
Bloom, Melanie, 31
Bloom's taxonomy, 138
Blumenfeld, Warren J., *"English Only" Laws Divide and Demean*, 69
Borderlands/La frontera: The New Mestiza (Anzaldúa), 240
Bourdieu, Pierre, 178
Bourhis, Richard, 177
brainstorming, linguocultural, 136
Brandt, Deborah, 184
Bratta, Phil, 164
bridge writing programs, 10, 11; for English language learners, 215–16
Broad, Bob, 43, 286; dynamic criteria mapping, 7–8, 50; *What We Really Value*, 40–41
Bruce, Shanti, *ESL Writers*, 239
Bunn, Mike, 80
Burbules, Nicholas, "A Theory of Power in Education," 33

Canagarajah, A. Suresh, 7, 43, 50, 65, 68, 74, 93, 99, 153, 154, 155, 192; *Literacy as Translingual Practice*, 39; on translingual literacy, 18, 61
Candel-Mora, Miguel, 32
Carlson Leadership and Public Service Center (CLPSC), 97–98; service-learning course, 112–20
cartoons: language and culture in, 225–27; language as linguistic system in, 223–25; negotiation in, 227–29; writing-theory, 10, 216–23, 232–33
Chinese Information and Service Center (CISC), 98; service-learning course at, 112, 115
chronotopic lamination, 200–201
class, as community, 30, 37
class activities: body and textual movements, 194–95; translingual, 35–37

classrooms: diversity of, 75–76; mapping mobilities in, 194–96; multilingual pedagogies, 40
CLPSC. *See* Carlson Leadership and Public Service Center
code meshing, 29, 150, 166, 182, 264; in literacy-autobiography, 155, 159, 160, 161
code mixing, 264
codes, visual, 214, 222–23
code switching, 92, 150; in digital space, 198–99
cognitive development, 275–76
cognitive dissonance, 161
collaboration, 268; English as a Second Language Program, 196–98; Preparation for College Writing, 215–16; service-learning program, 97–98
collaborative action-research projects, 215–16
collective-identity principle, 178
collective participation, English as a Second Language Program, 196–97
color terms activity, 142–43; linguocultural lexicons, 134–37
Common Core Standards, mapping, 203–4
common learning goals, in first-year writing classes, 154–55
communication, 212; in digital space, 198–99; and language, 68–70; and translingual practice, 151–52
community, communities, 30, 37; discourse, 67, 175; rhetorical strategies, 162–64; university as, 27–28
competence, 43, 100; translingual and transcultural, 67, 229
context, words and, 49
"Contrastive Rhetoric: An American Writing Teacher in China" (Matalene), 17
Coulmas, Florian, 177
Cousin, Glynis, 288
Cox, Michelle, 249
creative writing, curriculum prompts for, 121
Creese, Angela, 127
criteria mapping, 7–8, 40, 42; classroom use of, 50–51, 57(n2); first-year writing, 43–44
critical analysis, of cultural sayings, 145–46
critical geography, 201
critical language awareness, multilingualism and, 70
critical literacy, 173, 176, 186
critical thinking, 22, 175, 275; in composition classrooms, 71, 72
crossing, 29

cross-language writing: poetic, 105–9, 120–21; self-reflection in, 103–5; service-learning course, 116–20
cultural-critique essay, on restaurant authenticity, 54–57
cultures: cross-learning, 36; language and, 220–21, 225–27; national, 186; reflective essays, 272–73; symbols, 218–19
Cummins, Jim, multimodal learning, 214–15
Curzan, Anne, 244; "Says Who? Teaching and Questioning the Rules of Grammar," 240

Diab, Rasha, 254
digital literacies, 214
digital space: code switching in, 198–99; translingual exchange in, 205–7
DiPardo, Anne, "'Whispers of Coming and Going': Lessons from Fannie," 244, 245
discourse: over curriculum rubric, 44–47
discourse communities, 67, 175
Discourses in Place: Language in the Material World (Scollon and Scollon), 183
distributed writing process, 217
diversity, 66, 161; of classrooms, 75–76; linguistic, 73, 74, 96, 127, 149, 150
"Don't Insist on English" (Ryan), 157
drafting, in writing-theory cartoon exercise, 219–20

Ebonics, 158
educational resources, 125–26
"Effective Practices and Theories of G1.5 and L.2 Writing consultants on a Diverse Campus," 66
elementary-school students, translanguaging practices, 214
"Elements of Literacy" (Lindquist), 157
ELLs. *See* English Language Learners
emojis, translanguaging, 162–63
emotions, and language acquisition, 109, 111
empowerment, of language differences, 77
English, 34, 268; in Bangkok, 178; diversity of, 29, 161; global dominance of, 241–42; grammar and structure in, 246–47; monolingualism, 32, 152; in Singapore, 176; student success and, 100–101, 242–43. *See also* Standard Written English
English as a Second Language (ESL) tutoring, 239–40
English as a Second Language (ESL) Program (Jefferson County Public

Schools), 193; classroom mobilities, 195–96; collaboration and collective participation in, 196–98
English-language development, 164–65
English Language Learners (ELLs), 98, 193, 213, 215
English Only, 59, 63
"English Only" Laws Divide and Demean (Blumenfeld), 69
Engrish.com, 35
ESL Writers: A Guide for Writing Center Tutors (Bruce and Rafoth), 239–40
Espaillat, Rhina, 105
ethnography, multisited, 193
EthOS (ethosapp.com), 202, 208
evaluation, 41–42; student participation in, 44–47
EWP. *See* expository writing program
expectations, student participation in, 44–47
experiences, 72, 110; and linguistic knowledge, 140–41; multilingual, 126–27
expertise, student, 229–30
exploratory writing, 87–89
expository writing program (EWP), 93–94, 95, 122(n1)
expressions: personal identity with, 138–39; social definition and use, 139–40; translanguaging, 165–66; writing project, 143–46

Facebook, group chats, 198–99
faculty, 60, 64; at Florida International University, 62–63; monolingual, 59, 265–66
family, language links, 138–39
fanfiction writing, 214
Ferrel, Thomas, 254
Ferris, Dana, 59, 62
first-year writing (FYW)/composition, 7–8, 60–61, 75, 127, 150, 175, 213; assessment and agenda setting, 44–47; authenticity, 47–48; criteria-mapping, 43–44; curricula, 59–60, 77–87; exploratory writing, 87–89; expository writing, 93–94, 95; at Florida International University, 64–66; grading criteria, 83–85; language and communication issues, 68–69; at Michigan State University, 151–52, 154–56; service-learning, 96–97
Fisher-Martins, Sandra, *The Right to Understand*, 69
flockdraw.com, 219–20
Florida International University (FIU): exploratory writing class, 87–89; first-year writing course curriculum, 59–61, 64–66; multilingual faculty at, 62–63; visual rhetorical analysis assignment, 86–87; writing and rhetoric assignment, 77–86
Fox, Tom, 202
Fraiberg, Steven, 153–54
Franklin High School, English Language Learners at, 98
freewriting, in writing-theory cartoon exercise, 219(table)
Friere, Paulo, on sociocultural oppression, 71–73
FYW. *See* first-year writing/composition

Garcia, Ofelia, 214
genre analysis, 138; cultural-critique essays, 55–57; narrative writing assignment, 117–18
gestalt theory, 178, 179
gestural codes, 214
Gillespie, Paula, 65, 66
global citizenship, 30, 32–33
Global Citizenship class, 21–22
Godbee, Beth, 254
Goffman, Irving, presentation of self principle, 178
Gonzales, Laura, 153, 163
good reasons principle, 178
Google MyMaps, 202
Gorter, Durk, linguistic landscape research, 177, 179
grading criteria, for cultural-critique essay, 56–57
grading rubric, for multilingual classroom, 52–53
"'Grammar SOS': How Tutors' Knowledge of Translingualism Affects Their Sentence-Level Tutoring with Chinese ESL Students" (Pei Lei), 251–52
Grimm, Nancy, 254
Guerra, Juan, 69, 92, 154, 155
Gutiérrez, Kris, on "Third Space," 101

Harrison, Kimberly, *Linguistically Diverse Immigrant and Resident Writers*, 64
hawker centers, in Singapore, 181, 182–83, 186
high school: classroom mobilities, 194–96; collective participation and collaboration in, 196–98; Common Core Standards, 203–4; digital space in, 198–200, 205–7; student literacies and identities, 193–94, 202–3
Hispanics, at Florida International University, 63, 75

Hispanic-serving institutions (HSI), 63
history of ideas module, 175
home languages, 230; use of, 25–27
Horner, Bruce, 5, 63, 94, 100, 152, 156, 160, 191, 285; "Language Difference in Writing," 240, 242–43
How Language Transformed Humanity (Pagel), 69
"How to Tame a Wild Tongue" (Anzaldúa), 240, 244
Huebner, Thom, Bangkok sign study, 178, 180, 181–82
Hughes High School Advanced Placement English Literature and Composition: classroom mobilities, 195–96; collective participation in, 196–97; student literacies and identities, 193–94
Hull, Glynda, 214

identity, identities, 128; bilingual, 104–5; cross-lingual poetic writing, 105–9; language and, 21, 129–30; multilingual, 61–62, 95, 100–101, 110; national, 175–76, 186; self-reflection about, 103–4; social, 253–54; student, 193–94; translingual, 74, 221–23, 288–89
identity performance, transcultural, 220–21
idioms, 23; visual, 214, 222–23
instructors, 8; monolingual, 265–66; of translingual orientation, 64–66
interculturalism, 19
interlingualism, 30
international students, 212, 265
internet searches, of universal terms, 25
interrogation, 159
intralingual practice, 29
intrapersonal skills, 102
Introduction to Academic Writing for Multilingual Writers (ASU), 44; authenticity in, 47–48
Irving, Patricia, 173

Jefferson County Public Schools (Kentucky), English as a Second Language Program, 193
Jenks, Christopher, 4, 154
Jerskey, Maria, 65
journals, journaling, 157–58, 202

Kellman, Steve, 31
Kenya, translingualism in, 150
Kirkland, David, "Skin We Ink," 157
knowledge, 36; alien, 289–90; cultural, 22; decompartmentalizing, 127–29;
linguistic, 126, 140–41; troublesome, 288, 290–91
Korenea, Elena, 102
Krall-Lanoue, Aimee, 99
Kramsch, Claire, 204; "Trans-Spatial Utopias," 3

Land, Ray, 287, 289
Landry, Roderigue, 177
language(s), 9, 35, 36, 63, 76, 92, 93, 104, 111, 158, 159, 174, 218; acquisition of, 109–10; and communication, 68–70; components of, 129–30; and culture, 220–21, 225–27; diversity of, 59, 73, 77, 96; expectations of, 242–44; fluidity of, 8, 213; and global citizenship, 30–31; as linguistics systems, 220, 223–25; literacy autobiography assignment, 167–69; national, 175–76; negotiating, 43–44; personal narrative essays, 144–45; use of different, 26–27, 99–100
language acquisition, 109
language-attachment-theory (LAT), 102
language communities, rhetorical practices, 162–66
"Language Difference in Writing: Toward a Translingual Approach" (Horner et al.), 240, 242–43
"Language in the Classroom: Examining Tensions, Benefits, and Next Steps with Translingualism" (Alessandra), 247–50
language practices, 72, 179, 212; body and textual movements, 194–95; student, 201–2
language resources, 128; in classroom setting, 134–36
language transfer, negative, 128
languaging, 3, 9, 76
LAT. *See* language-attachment theory, 102
Lavalle, Thomas, 5
learning, 232; multimodal, 214–15
learning across cultures, 266
learning objectives, Preparation for College Writing, 216
Lee, Jerry, 4, 154
Leonard, Rebecca, "rhetorical attunement," 29
Lewis, Cynthia, 223
Lindquist, Julie, "Elements of Literacy," 157
Linguistically Diverse Immigrant and Resident Writers (Harrison), 64
linguistic differences, negotiation of, 287
linguistic fluency, 22
linguistic heterogeneity, negotiation of, 10

linguistic landscapes (LL), 176; assignment, 187–89; in Singapore, 180–85; studies of, 177–80
linguistic repertoire, 129
linguistic resources, 67; Singaporean students, 176; of students, 8–9, 125–26, 129–31
linguistics, 3; diversity, 74, 96; social justice, 72–73
linguistics system, language as, 220, 223–25
linguocultural activities, 133; color exercise, 134–37
literacies, 193–94, 214; diachronic movement of, 179; digital, 214; networking, 208–9; reflections on, 155–56; translingual, 18, 23, 29, 33, 67, 68, 192, 215
Literacy as Translingual Practice: Between Communities and Classrooms (Canagarajah), 39
literacy-autobiography (LA) assignment, 9–10, 149–50, 155; assignment description, 167–69; English-language development, 164–65; language communities, 162–64; outcomes of, 158–59; pedagogy of, 156–58; translanguaging, 158–62
literacy practices, 175, 194; mapping, 202–3; in Singapore, 183–84
Lockridge, Tim, 152, 156
Long Island, multilingualism on, 18–19
Louisville, Kentucky, 209(n1); student literacies and identities, 193–94
low-stake writing tasks, 72
Lu, Min-Zhan, 5, 29, 63, 94, 100, 152, 160, 191, 229, 285; "Language Difference in Writing," 240, 242–43

Malay language, in Singapore, 176
Manguel, Alberto, "Reading Ourselves and World Around Us," 157
Mao, LuMing, 24
mapping, 200–201, 207: classroom mobilities, 194–96; Common Core Standards, 203–4; literacy practices, 202–3, 208–9; translingual, 192–93
Matalene, Carolyn, "Contrastive Rhetoric: An American Writing Teacher in China," 17
MATESOL program, University of Washington, 92, 93
Matsuda, Paul Kei, 59, 62, 134, 173, 227, 249
meaning, 230; logic of, 35–36; negotiating, 39–40; translation of, 204–5
meaning-making, 26

media: digital, 198–99, 205–7, 214; visual, 162–63
memoir, transcultural learning, 266, 277–78
memories, 109; and language use, 138–39
memos, in literacy autobiography assignment, 168
metacognitive practice/skills, 94, 102; cross-language narrative, 119–20
metacognitive thinking, in writing-theory cartoon, 227–29
metanarrative, 126
metaphors, 138–39; writing-theory cartoons and, 218–19
Meyer, Jan, 287, 289
Miami, translingual practices, 67–68
Michigan State University (MSU), 150; first-year writing class at, 151–52, 154–56
microaggression, linguistic, 150
mobile observation apps, 202
mobilities, 202; classroom, 194–96; digital space, 198–99; linguistic, 201, 204, 205
Molina, Claire, 32–33
monolingualism, 20–21, 32, 100, 111, 152, 241, 290; and translanguaging, 156–57
monomodality, 157
multiculturalism, 175, 275, 276
multilingualism, 18–20, 21, 28, 29, 31, 37, 59, 68–70, 74, 100, 178, 263, 275, 276; empowerment of, 73, 76; and first-year writing programs, 93–94, 122(n1); service-learning courses, 112–20; in Singapore, 182–83; and teaching practices, 61–62, 63; and translingualism, 8, 92, 132–33; tutor training course, 254–61
multilingual writing classroom, 40, 64; grading rubric for, 52–53; restaurant authenticity exercise in, 53–57
multimodality, 230–31; design workshop, 219(table), 220; learning, 214–15, 270

Nakamura, Koji, 27
narratives, translation, 218
National Council of Teachers of English (NCTE), Second Language Writing instruction policy, 63
National University of Singapore: linguistic landscapes study, 180–84; University Scholars Programme, 174–75
negotiation, 10; of language practices, 42–43, 72, 77, 213; of linguistic resources, 67, 176; of meaning, 39–40; student-driven, 51–52; translingual, 49, 94, 95, 106–7, 108, 110, 214, 227–29, 286–87

Nelson, Mark, 214
Neo-Sapir Whorf hypothesis, 110
Nepal, education system in, 34
Networking Literacies (Syracuse University), 202; course description, 208–9
new literacy, 176
nonnative English speakers, 20
non-Standard Written English (SWE), 132

Office for International Students and Scholars (OISS), 151
online resources, 44, 219
Otsuji, Emi, 179

Pagel, Mark, *How Language Transformed Humanity*, 69
parablas, translanguaging, 165–66
Pavlenko, Aneta, 102
PCW. *See* Preparation for College Writing
Pedagogy of the Oppressed (Friere), 72
peer review, 27, 36, 205, 207, 219(table), 267
peer writing consultants, 11, 236, 238
Pei Lei: "'Grammar SOS,'" 250–52; on translingual tutoring, 250–53
Pennycook, Alastair, 152, 179
personal argument essay, 119
personal narratives, 144, 267, 269
Piaget, Jean, self-to-social trajectory, 138
poetic writing, cross-language, 105–9, 120–21
Politics of Language and Literacy in Singapore module, 176
polyglot dialog, 29
pop-up museum of language, 140, 146
Powell, Malea, 164
power dynamics, 33, 34, 93, 134, 174
power-relations principle, 178
Preparation for College Writing (PCW), as collaborative action-research project, 215–16
presentation of self principle, 178
Prior, Paul, 191, 201, 217
privilege, of Standard English, 76
process genres, for cultural-critique essay, 55
professional development, of writing faculty, 60
proverbs, 23; writing project, 138–39, 143–46
public reading, for cross-language poetic writing class, 121
Purdue Online Writing Lab, 44

quantitative reasoning (QR) module, 175
Quiocho, Alice, 128

race, language and, 93
Raff, Franklin, *American "Multilingualism": A National Tragedy*, 69
Rafoth, Ben, *ESL Writers*, 239
reading: collaborative, 216; and rhetorical writing, 78–81
"Reading Ourselves and World Around Us" (Manguel), 157
recontextualization, 192, 200, 207
reflection, 113, 158, 212, 269; on linguocultural repertoire, 134–35; rhetorical agency, 274–76; in writing-theory cartoon exercise, 219(table), 225–27
reflection papers, 79–80
reflective encounters, 24, 36
reflective essays, 216, 264, 266, 271, 272–73; service-learning course, 98–99
research papers/reports, 24–25; in first-year writing courses, 81–82; home language use, 25–26; peer review, 27
restaurants, in authenticity exercise, 47–48, 53–57
rhetoric, 3–4, 24, 88, 92; agency, 274–76; translingual, 66, 94, 95, 105, 110, 287; textual analysis, 69–70; and writing curriculum, 78–81
"Rhetorical Activities of Global Citizens" (Wible), 157
rhetorical strategies/practices: of language communities, 162–166; visual, 86–87
Right to Understand, The (Fisher-Martins), 69
Rogerian practices, 141
Royster, Jacqueline Jones, 5, 63, 100, 152, 285; "Language Difference in Writing," 240, 242–43
RSA Summer Institute workshop, 65
rubrics, 41; discourse over curriculum, 49–50; grading, 44–47, 52–53
rules of operation, across linguistic systems, 223–25
Ryan, Patricia, "Don't Insist on English," 157

sameness-of-difference, 111
sayings: identification with, 138–39; social definition and use, 139–40; translanguaging, 165–66; writing project, 143–46
"Says Who? Teaching and Questioning the Rules of Grammar" (Curzan), 240
scaffolding, cognitive, 138
Schwarzer, David, 31, 128
Scollon, Ron and Suzie, *Discourses in Place*, 183
second language learning/learners (SLL), 65–66, 153–54

Second Language Writing policy (NCTE), 63
sedimented white/Western English (SWE), 125
self-analysis, 94
Selfe, Cynthia, 152, 156
self-identity, multilingual, 101, 110
self-reflection narrative, 103–4, 121, 146, 168, 266
self-to-social trajectory, 138
semiodiversity, 159
semiotic systems, 10, 158, 166, 214, 218
sentence-inventory tasks, 46
service-learning courses, 94, 95, 96, 111; collaboration in, 97–98; cross-language narrative writing, 116–20; curriculum, 112–16; student experiences in, 99–100
"Shakespeare in the Bush" (Bohannan), 157
"Shifting the Paradigm: Towards at Translingual Rhetoric of Writing" (RSA workshop), 65
Shipka, Jody, 201, 217
Shomo, Sarah, 31
signs: in linguistic landscapes, 180–82, 185; Tokyo study of, 178
Silva, Tony, 134, 227
Simpkins, Neil, 254
Singapore, 177; linguistic landscapes in, 180–85; national identity and languages, 175–76, 186
"Skin We Ink" (Kirkland), 157
Sloboda, Marian, "State Ideology and Linguistic Landscapes," 184
small-group discussion/work, 121, 267, 269, 270
smartphone apps, 202
Smitherman, Geneva, 158
social action, and comparative research, 215–16
social engagement, language and, 110
social justice, 245, 253, 290; curriculum in, 240, 254; focus on, 71–72; linguistic, 72–73
socially constructed divisions, 125
social meaning, stratified pattern of, 184
sociocultural oppression, as research framework, 71–73
sociopolitics, 71
Spanish: Anzaldúa's use of, 158; *parablas*, 165
spatial codes, 214
spatial repertoires, 192
Spolsky, Bernard, 179
Standard American English (SAE), 150

Standard English, 62, 76, 196; teaching, 63–64
Standard Written English (SWE), 7, 158, 237, 238, 239, 252, 263; expectations of, 248–49; primacy of, 240–42, 244; thinking beyond, 249–50; and translingual practices, 246–47. *See also* non-Standard Written English
"State Ideology and Linguistic Landscapes" (Sloboda), 184
Stony Brook University (SUNY), internationalization, 19–20
storytelling, multimodal, 214
structuration principles, 179
students: agency of, 41–42; assessment of, 44–47; on authenticity, 47–48; as experts, 229–30; grading rubrics for, 52–53; language diversity of, 59, 127; as language experts, 133; linguistic resources of, 8–9; literacy experiences, 23–24; multilingual, 19–20, 263; as second language writers, 63; in service-learning courses, 98–99; success of, 100–101
"Students' Right to Their Own Language" (CCCC), 4
student-teacher relations, 41–42
SWE. *See* sedimented white/Western English; Standard Written English
Sweetland Center for Writing (UM), 237–38
Sweetland Digital Rhetoric Collaborative blog, 240
Sydney, linguistic landscapes in, 179
symbolic interactions, 162–63
symbols, cultural, 218–19
Syracuse University, *Networking Literacies*, 202

Tardy, Christine, 33
teacher-researchers, positionality of, 271
teachers, 33; program assessment, 41–42; and translingual practices, 247–50
teaching, translingual writing, 64–66
teaching assistants, 60
Tetreault, Laura, 285
"Theory of Power in Education, A" (Burbules), 33
texting, 200, 206–7
textual rhetorical analysis, 69–70
Thai language, English influence on, 178
Third Space, 101
threshold concept, translingualism as, 287–91
Title V grants (US Department of Education), 60

Tokyo, sign study, 178
topos of memory, 184
traffic in meaning, 204, 214
transcultural competencies, 229
transculturalism, 33; learning memoir, 266, 277–78
transformative thinking, 290
translanguaging, 3–4, 5, 6, 30, 129, 156–57, 214, 215; literacy autobiography and, 158–62; sayings and, 165–66; visual media, 162–63
translation, 23, 30, 34, 159, 160, 161, 223, 230; of meaning, 204–5; narrative assignment, 218, 268–69, 272–73, 278–79
translingual competency, 229
"Translingual Education as a Phenomenon, a Methodology and an Ideology to Promote Social Justice and Educational Renewal" (Schwarzer, Fuchs, and Hermosilla), 244
translingualism, translingual practices: classroom use of, 60–61, 132–37; as disadvantage, 247–50; pedagogy of, 94, 102, 125, 126, 128, 129, 131, 141–42, 236, 286; and Standard English, 242–43, 246–47
Translingual Practice (Canagarajah), 29
translingual rhetoric (TR), 94, 95, 102, 105, 110, 150; poetic writing, 106–7
translingual work (TW), 94, 102, 110
translocal artifact essay, 269, 270, 271, 280–81
transmodality, 152, 153, 214, 270, 271; project, 281–82
transnational issues/perspectives, 36, 231, 274
"Trans-Spatial Utopias" (Kramsch), 3
Trimbur, John, 5, 63, 100, 152, 285; "Language Difference in Writing," 240, 242–43
Tung-Chou, Huang, 31
tutors, tutoring, 196, 244; English as a Second Language, 193, 196, 239–40; and "Language Difference in Writing," 242–43; roles of, 245–46; sentence level, 250–53; social identities of, 253–54; and Standard Written English, 247–50; training class, 254–61; translingual practices, 238–39

Ulanoff, Sharon, 128
undergraduate peer writing consultants, training, 11
US Department of Education, Title V grant, 60

university: agency and power in, 33; as community, 27–28
University of Michigan (UM), 236; Sweetland Center for Writing at, 237–38
University of Washington, Seattle, 92; Carlson Leadership and Public Service Center, 97–98; expository writing program, 93–94; multilingual students at, 95–96; service-learning course at, 98–100
University Scholars Programme (USP), 174; linguistic landscapes in, 180–81

Vagnoni, Nick, 65–66; on language and communication, 68–70; visual rhetorical analysis assignment, 86–87
Velasco, Patricia, 214
videos, 144; transmodal project, 270, 273
visual codes/idioms, 214; in writing-theory cartoons, 222–23
visual interactions, 162–63
volunteer work, reflective essays on, 98–99

Walker, Jay, "The World's English Mania," 157
Wang, Xiqiao, 153–54
Warman, Patsy, 66; course redesign, 71–73; exploratory writing assignment, 87–89
Wei, Li, 4
What We Really Value: Beyond Rubrics in Teaching and Assessing Writing (Broad), 40–41
"'Whispers of Coming and Going': Lessons from Fannie" (DiPardo), 244, 245
Wible, Scott, "Rhetorical Activities of Global Citizens," 157
Worden, Dorothy, 65
words: and context, 49; difficult-to-translate, 23
workshops: faculty, 60; multimodal design, 220, 222–23
"World's English Mania, The" (Walker), 157
writing, 40, 41, 42, 200, 269; assignments, 274–75; exploratory, 87–89; translingual, 66, 92–93
writing-across-languages course, 94, 101–3, 111
Writing and Critical Thinking (WCT) module (National University of Singapore), 175
writing centers: training courses, 238–39, 254–61; University of Michigan, 237–38

writing classroom, multilingual, 40, 70
writing-theory cartoons assignment, 10, 216; adaptation in, 231–32; description of, 232–33; language and culture in, 225–27; language as linguistic system, 223–25; process in, 217–21; students as expert in, 229–31; translingual identities, 221–23
Writing 300: Seminar in Peer Writing consultation: context of, 237–38; curriculum of, 254–61; educator's role, 245–46; language expectations and, 242–44; overview, 238–39; primacy of Standard Written English essay, 247–50; translingual research, 250–53

Yang, Yuching, 42
Young, Vershawn, 92

Zheng, Xuan, 74

ABOUT THE AUTHORS

Daniel V. Bommarito is assistant professor and core faculty in the doctoral program in rhetoric and writing at Bowling Green State University. His research theorizes the teaching and learning of writing at undergraduate and graduate levels and has appeared in *Composition Studies*, the *Journal of Writing Research*, the *Journal of Teaching Writing*, *Syllabus*, *E-Learning and Digital Media*, and in various edited collections.

Mark Brantner is a senior lecturer at New York University Shanghai (NYUSH), where he teaches in the writing program. Before joining NYUSH, he was a senior lecturer in the University Scholars Programme at the National University of Singapore. He has also held positions at Binghamton University, Eastern West Virginia Community and Technical College, and Potomac State College of West Virginia University. His research interests include rhetorical theory, multilingual literacies, writing program administration, and, more recently, food rhetorics.

Emily Cooney is a lecturer at Arizona State University. She is a specialist in environmental rhetorics, place-based literacies, and second language writing pedagogy. With a focus on access and representation, she is currently at work with a colleague on a funded project designing and creating an interactive map of digital and technological resources available for students. Other work includes a study of global NGOs' romanticized representation of rural small farmers. Cooney holds a PhD in English (rhetoric, composition, and linguistics) from ASU.

Ellen Cushman is a citizen of the Cherokee Nation, Dean's Professor of Civic Sustainability, and associate dean of Academic Affairs, Diversity, and Inclusion in the College of Social Sciences and Humanities at Northeastern University. Her decolonial scholarship has recently appeared in the *Community Literacy Journal*, *Rhetoric Review*, *College English*, and the *Journal of Writing Assessment*. She has also published two coedited collections: *Landmark Essays: Rhetorics of Difference* with Damián Baca and Jonathan Osborn (Routledge 2018) and *Literacies: A Critical Sourcebook* with Christina Haas and Mike Rose (Macmillan 2020).

Norah Fahim is a lecturer at the program in writing and rhetoric, as well as associate director at the Hume Center for Writing and Speaking at Stanford University. She received her PhD in language and rhetoric from the University of Washington, Seattle, and has taught multilingual students both in the United States and in Egypt for the past fourteen years. Through narrative inquiry, her research focuses on the experiences of non-TESOL-trained TAs working with an increasingly multilingual student population, as well as the experiences and needs of multilingual students within a four-year institution, in order to better help advocate for the needs of multilingual students within the classroom, the writing center, and at a wider institutional level.

Ming Fang is the multilingual writing specialist in the writing and rhetoric program at Florida International University. She teaches both first-year and upper-division writing courses, provides training and support in multilingual writing pedagogy, and collaborates with faculty across disciplines to integrate writing tasks into their courses. Her research interests include second language writing, multilingual writing pedagogy, transnational writing program administration, and writing across the curriculum.

ABOUT THE AUTHORS

Gregg Fields completed his bachelor's and master of arts degrees in literature and writing with an emphasis on writing at California State University at San Marcos, where he also interned briefly in CSU's writing center. Fields is currently pursuing his doctorate at Arizona State University in the writing, rhetorics, and literacies program. During his first year in the doctoral program, he began working at CGC as a tutor in the writing center and has served as adjunct faculty for the last three years, having participated in designing and teaching in learning communities with faculty from chemistry, business, and mathematics.

Alanna Frost is an associate professor in the English Department at the University of Alabama Huntsville. Her work is invested in the intersections of students' communicative realities, English-education practice, and English-language policy. She served as a founding executive-committee member of the Rhetoric, Composition, and Writing Studies (RCWS) Literacy Studies Forum of the Modern Language Association (2015–2020, chair 2019, secretary 2018).

Matt Gomes is an assistant professor of English at Santa Clara University. He is interested in relationships between the teaching of writing and social justice and how student-engaged modes of assessment can contribute to more just cultures of education. His research has been recently published in *Writing Assessment, Social Justice, and the Advancement of Opportunity* and is forthcoming in *Community Action for Social Justice: A Digital Archive*. He has also recently produced podcasts for the annual Conference on College Composition and Communication.

Julia Kiernan is an assistant professor of communications at Kettering University. Her scholarly interests include pedagogical and curricular design across the digital humanities, translingual and transnational writing, science communication, and STEAM education. She currently directs and coordinates the GREEN program, a clustering of interdisciplinary, environment-focused courses at her home institution.

Thomas Lavelle directs the Center for Modern Languages at the Stockholm School of Economics. His current research projects address topics at the interface of language and learning in higher education. Beyond translingualism and the challenges of translingual pedagogy, these topics include lingua francas as media of instruction, materiality in forms of written feedback, and the interplay of speech and writing in undergraduates' academic communication. He currently chairs the CCC Group on Transnational Composition.

Tania Cepero Lopez is a Cuban exile who has made South Florida her adopted home since 1998. She is a senior writing and rhetoric instructor at Florida International University, where she has also participated in programmatic initiatives to support multilingual writing pedagogy. Her research interests include translingual writing instruction, community writing, and writing about the exile experience.

Suzanne Blum Malley is provost and professor of English at Methodist University. Her scholarly interests include multilingual and digital/multimodal literacies and globally networked learning environments. She served as a founding executive-committee member of the Rhetoric, Composition, and Writing Studies (RCWS) Literacy Studies Forum of the Modern Language Association (2015–2019, chair 2018, secretary 2017). Her recent publications include "Ludic Is the New Phatic: Making Connections in Global, Internet-Mediated Learning Environments" in *Thinking Globally, Composing Locally*.

Esther Milu is an assistant professor of writing and rhetoric at the University of Central Florida. She earned her BA and MA degrees in literature from the University of Nairobi and a PhD in rhetoric and writing from Michigan State University. Her research interests revolve around translingual literacies, identities, and pedagogies. Her research on translingualism focuses on first-year writing classrooms, Kenyan hip hop, and African immigrant students and communities.

Brice Nordquist is an assistant professor of writing and rhetoric and the director of the composition and cultural rhetoric graduate program at Syracuse University. His book *Literacy and Mobility: Complexity, Uncertainty and Agency at the Nexus of High School and College* received the 2019 Conference on College Composition and Communication's Advancement of Knowledge Award, presented annually for "the empirical research publication in the previous two years that most advances writing studies."

Ghanashyam Sharma is associate professor and graduate program director in the program in writing and rhetoric at the State University of New York in Stony Brook. His scholarship and teaching focus on writing in the disciplines, cross-cultural rhetoric, international students and education, and issues about language and language policy. His works have appeared in a variety of venues, including *College Composition and Communication, JAC, Across the Disciplines, Composition Studies, CCCC Studies in Writing and Rhetoric Series, Hybrid Pedagogy, Kairos,* and *Professional and Academic English.*

Naomi Silver is associate director of the Sweetland Center for Writing at the University of Michigan, where she is also a faculty lecturer. Her research focuses on reflective pedagogies, multiliteracies, and digital rhetoric. Her work with translingual pedagogy and teaching for social justice grows out of her engagement with Sweetland's antiracist task force and DEI initiatives at UM.

Bonnie Vidrine-Isbell holds the position of assistant professor and English-language program director at Biola University in Southern California. She enjoys multidisciplinary research on second language composition, specializing in bilingual brain studies, social neuroscience in education, and L2 pedagogy. She has taught English as a second and foreign language for thirteen years in California, Washington, Louisiana, Thailand, Spain, and Belize, and she has focused on second language composition for the last eight years. Her most recent publication introduces *language attachment theory,* a multidisciplinary theory linking social bonding to language acquisition and pedagogy.

Xiqiao Wang is assistant professor in the Department of Writing, Rhetoric, and American Cultures at Michigan State University. Her research has explored the pedagogical implications of translingualism and multilingual writers' literacy and spatial practices. Her ethnographic research traces multilingual basic writers' literacy learning across formal, informal, and digital spaces around first-year writing. Her research has appeared in a coauthored book entitled *Inventing the World Grant University: Chinese International Students' Mobilities, Literacies and Identities,* as well as professional journals such as *Research in the Teaching of English, College Composition and Communication, Computers and Composition, the Journal of Basic Writing,* and *Language and Education.*

Dan Zhu is currently working as the assistant director of the Center for International Relations and Cultural Leadership Exchange (CIRCLE) at the University of Washington and is the creator of and oversees the Unite UW program that connects domestic and international students. She received her PhD in composition and rhetoric, specializing in international student writing and writer identity. Born and raised in China, Dan earned her BA in English from Beijing Normal University and her master's in education and TESOL from UW. For the last decade, Dan has taught EFL in China, Chinese in the United Kingdom, and ESL and FYC in the United States.

www.ingramcontent.com/pod-product-compliance
Lightning Source LLC
Chambersburg PA
CBHW031057080526
44587CB00011B/727